Manga from the Heart

grand Guignol orchestra
1
KAORI YUKI
CREATOR OF ANGEL SANCTUARY & GODCHILD
On Sale 10/05/10

Available at
store.viz.com
and wherever books and comics are sold

1
Art by
Kairi Yura
Story by
On Sale 11/02/10

Kamisama Kiss
Story & Art by
Julietta Suzuki
1
On Sale 12/07/10

Visit
ShojoBeat.com
for more great titles!

Shojo Beat
MANGA from the HEART

viz media
www.viz.com

RATED T FOR TEEN ratings.viz.com
RATED T+ FOR OLDER TEEN ratings.viz.com

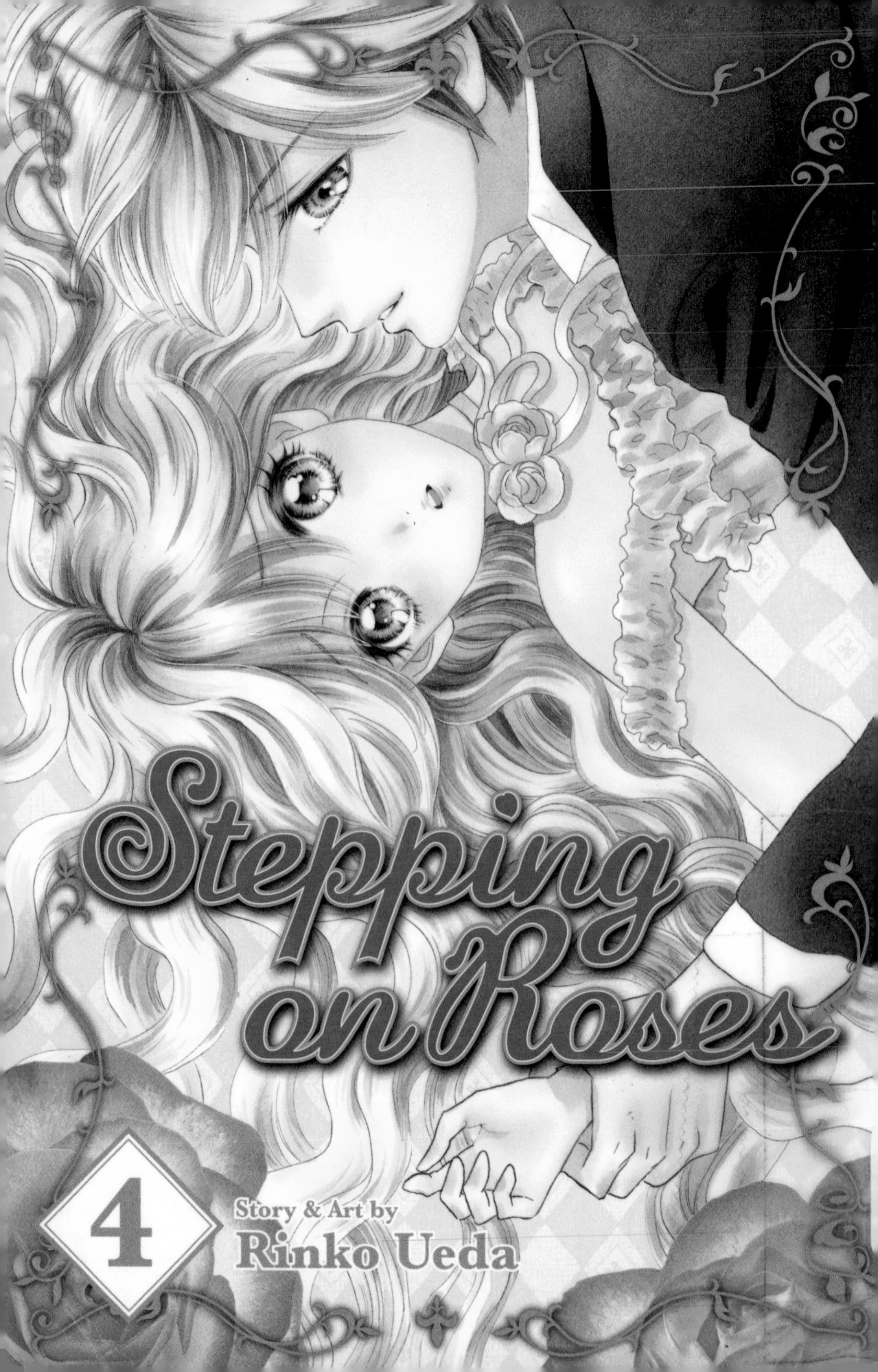
Stepping on Roses
4
Story & Art by
Rinko Ueda

Shojo Beat

Stepping on Roses

Vol. 4

Story & Art by
Rinko Ueda

Stepping on Roses

Volume 4
CONTENTS

Story Thus Far

Sumi Kitamura was living a life of poverty and taking care of young orphans that her elder brother Eisuke would bring home from the streets. Then, in order to pay off Eisuke's debts, she marries Soichiro Ashida, the heir to a wealthy conglomerate. However, Sumi has feelings for Soichiro's friend Nozomu Ijuin, and Nozomu successfully convinces her to run off with him.

Sumi has a change of heart after realizing that she cannot betray Soichiro, but Nozomu won't let her leave. A fire breaks out at the inn they're staying at, but Soichiro arrives in time to save them. Soichiro is badly injured, and Sumi decides to never see Nozomu again.

Nozomu then marries Miu, a woman of aristocratic lineage. The Ashida household regains some peace, but trouble arrives when Soichiro's step-cousin Natsuki Kujo sends a maid to come work for them...

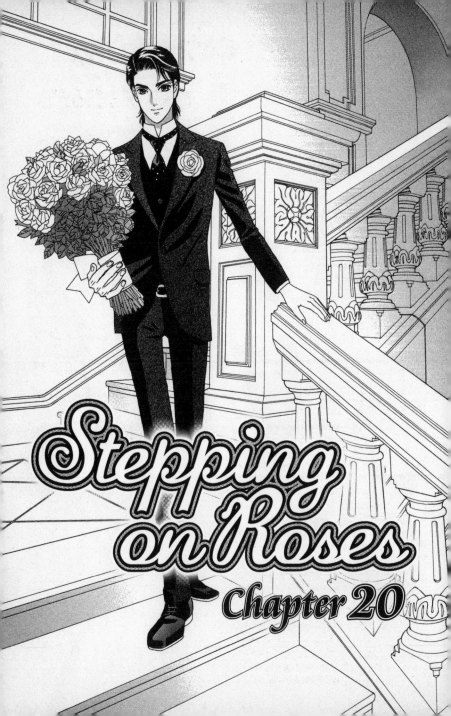

Stepping on Roses

Chapter 20

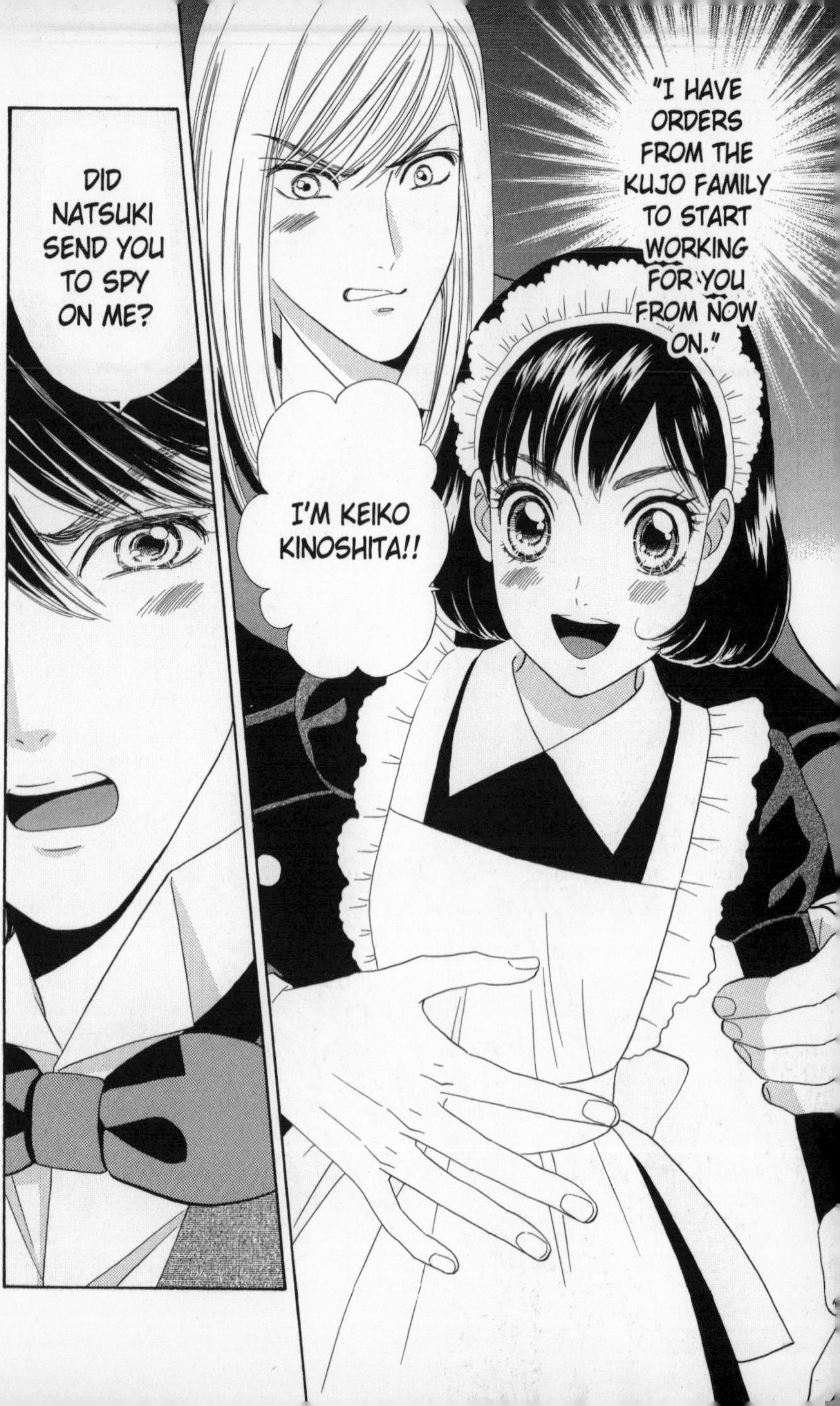
"I HAVE ORDERS FROM THE KUJO FAMILY TO START WORKING FOR YOU FROM NOW ON."
I'M KEIKO KINOSHITA!!
DID NATSUKI SEND YOU TO SPY ON ME?

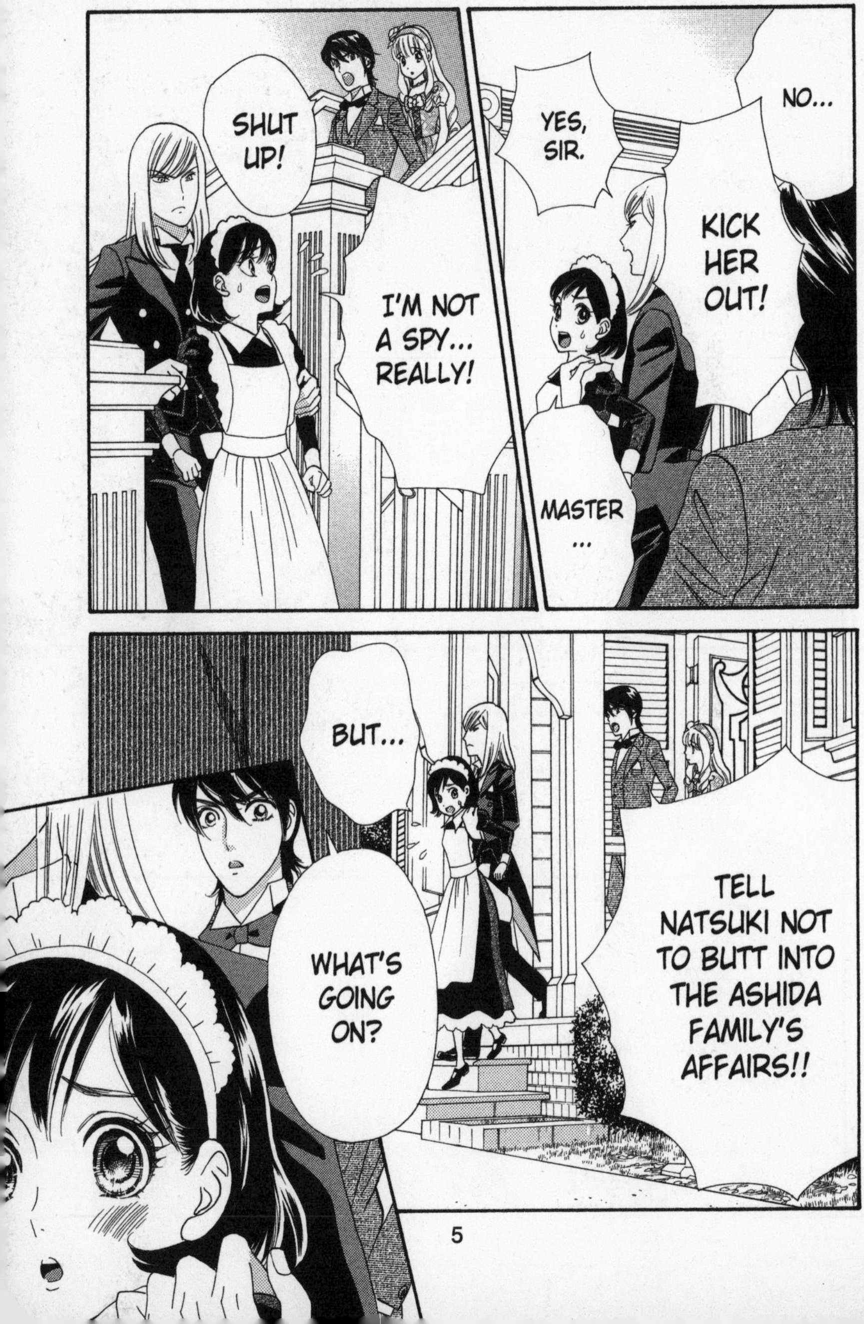
NO...
KICK HER OUT!
YES, SIR.
MASTER ...
I'M NOT A SPY... REALLY!
SHUT UP!
TELL NATSUKI NOT TO BUTT INTO THE ASHIDA FAMILY'S AFFAIRS!!
BUT...
WHAT'S GOING ON?

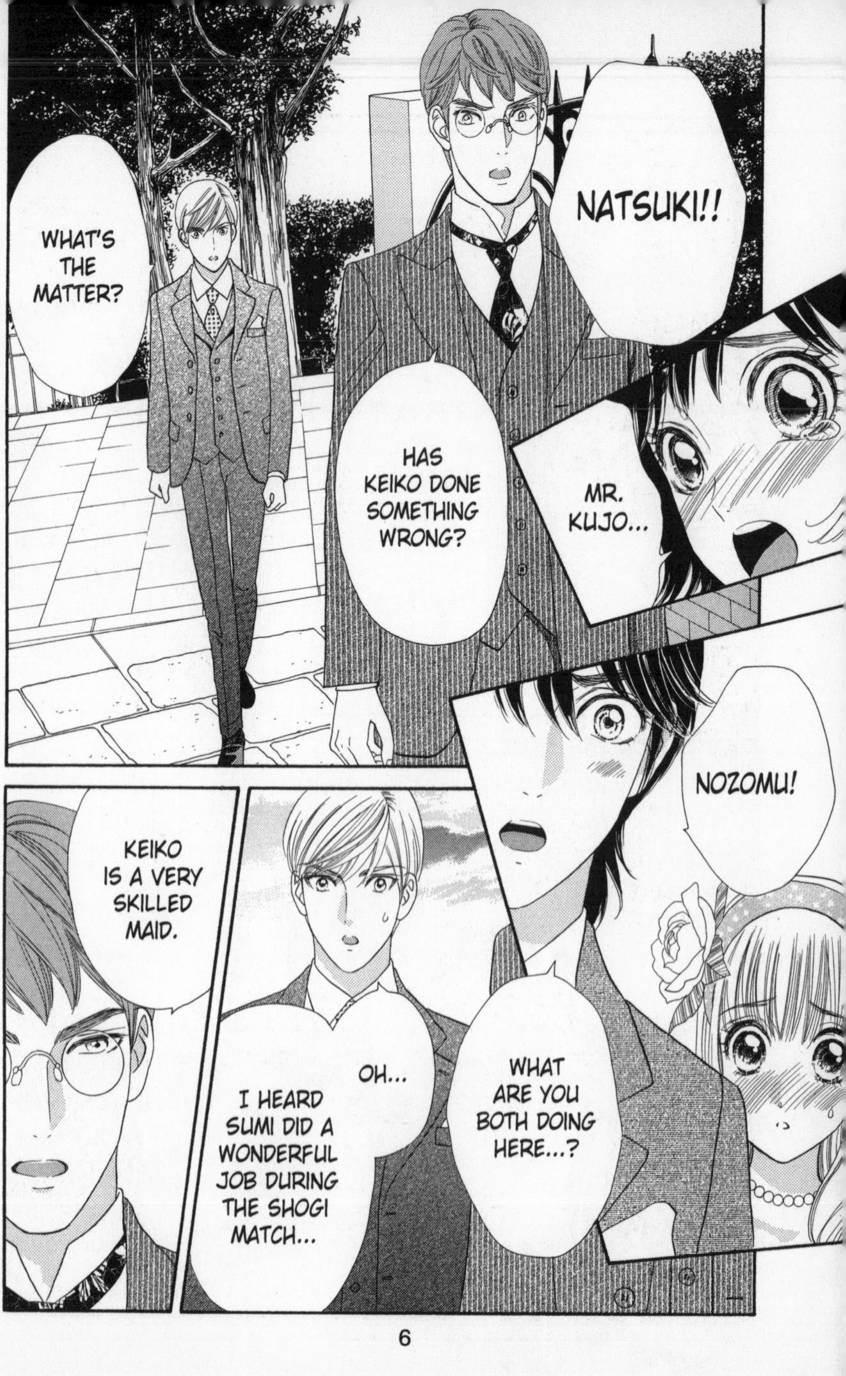
NATSUKI!!
MR. KUJO...
HAS KEIKO DONE SOMETHING WRONG?
WHAT'S THE MATTER?
NOZOMU!
WHAT ARE YOU BOTH DOING HERE...?
OH...
I HEARD SUMI DID A WONDERFUL JOB DURING THE SHOGI MATCH...
KEIKO IS A VERY SKILLED MAID.

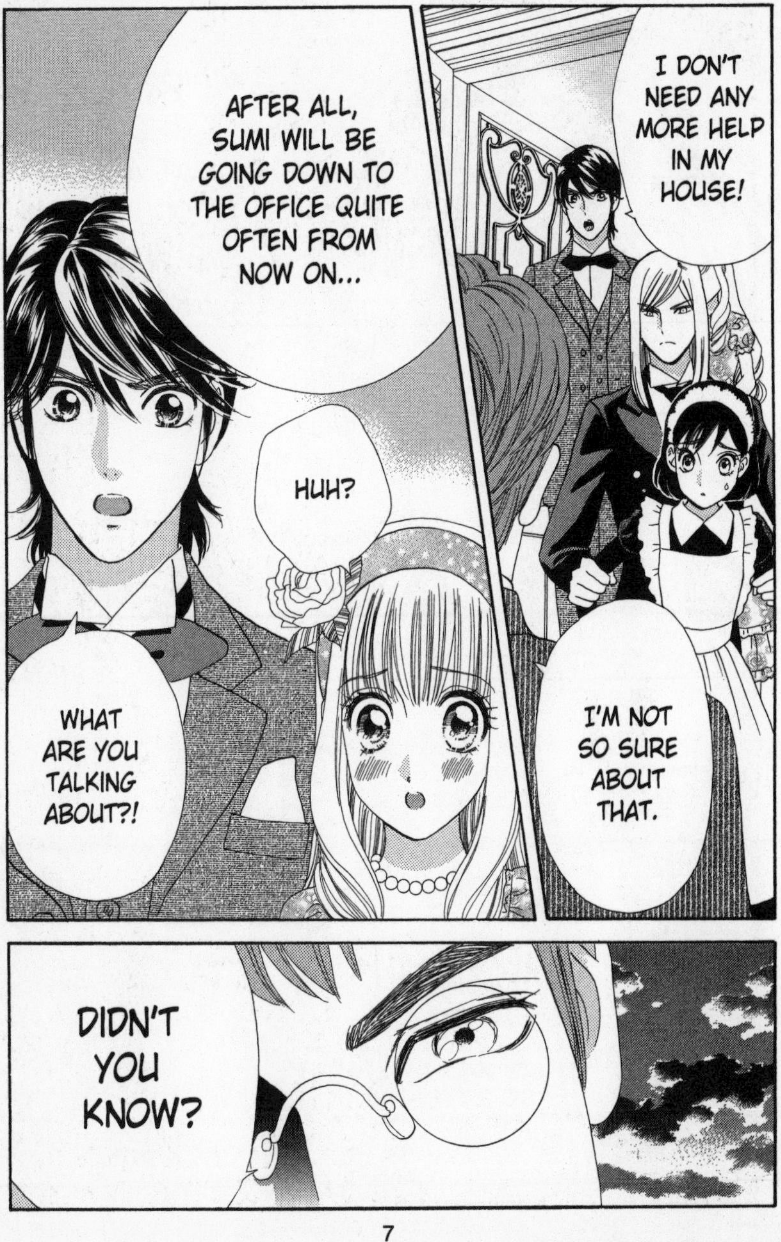
I DON'T NEED ANY MORE HELP IN MY HOUSE!
I'M NOT SO SURE ABOUT THAT.
AFTER ALL, SUMI WILL BE GOING DOWN TO THE OFFICE QUITE OFTEN FROM NOW ON...
HUH?
WHAT ARE YOU TALKING ABOUT?!
DIDN'T YOU KNOW?

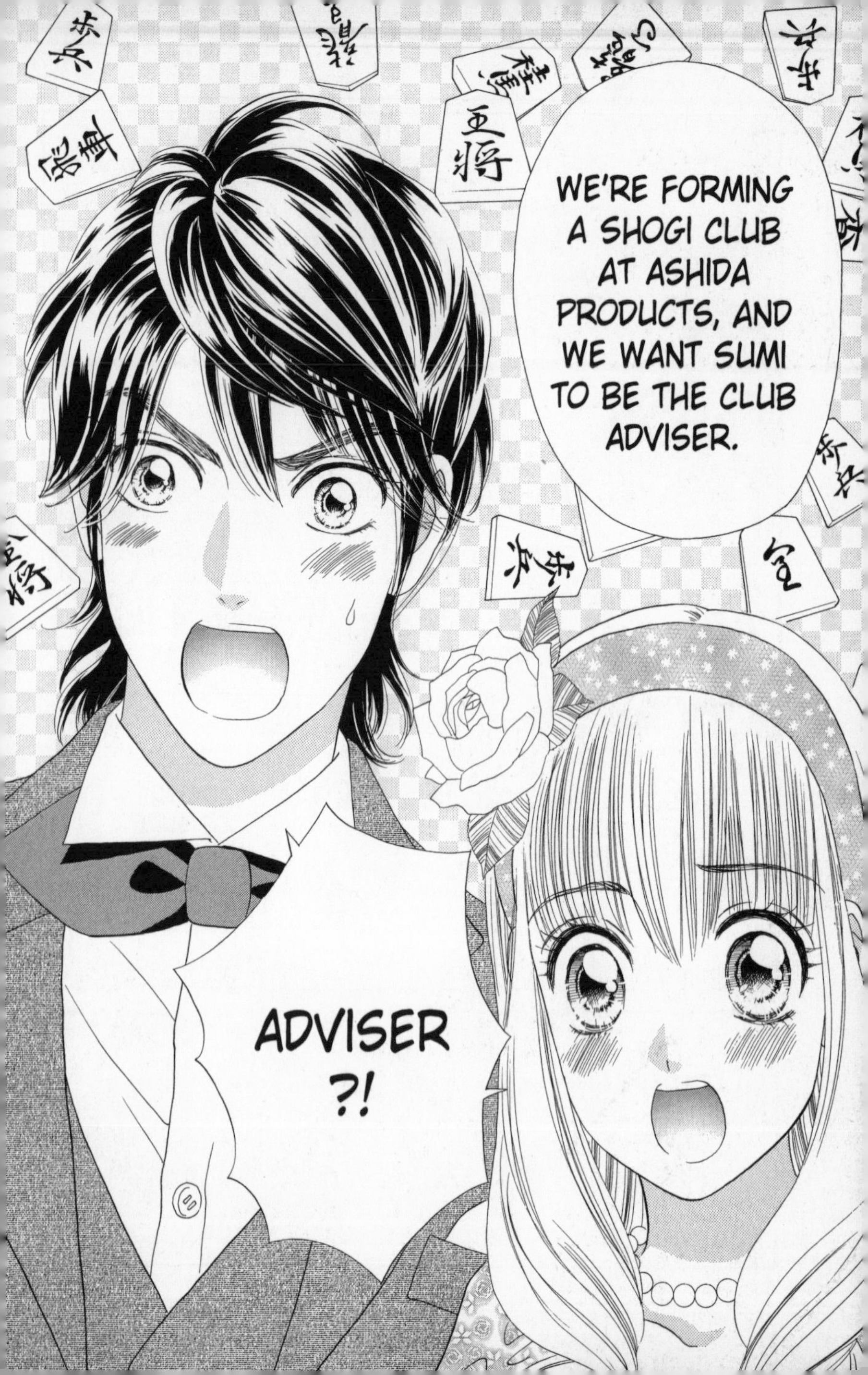
WE'RE FORMING A SHOGI CLUB AT ASHIDA PRODUCTS, AND WE WANT SUMI TO BE THE CLUB ADVISER.
ADVISER ?!

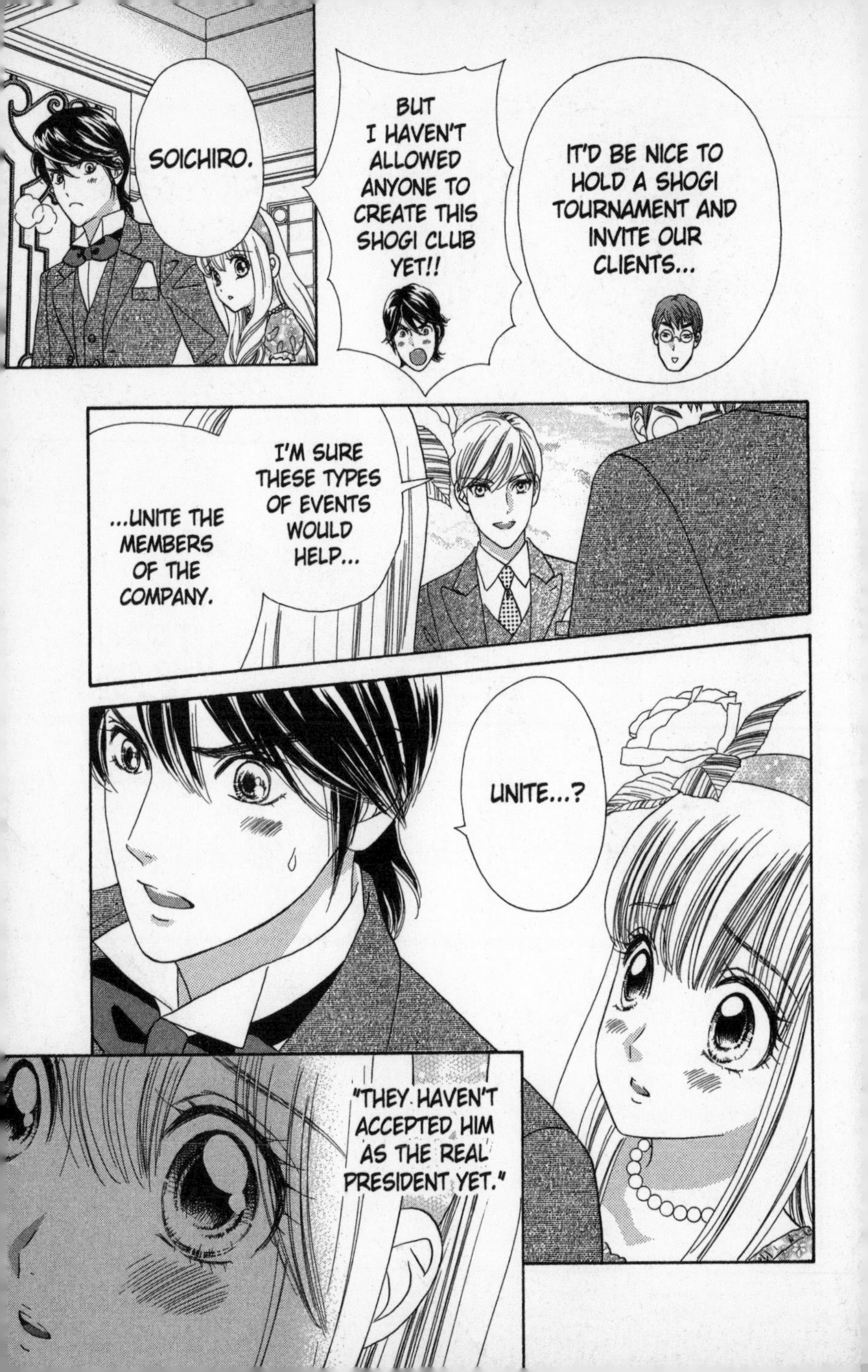
IT'D BE NICE TO HOLD A SHOGI TOURNAMENT AND INVITE OUR CLIENTS...
BUT I HAVEN'T ALLOWED ANYONE TO CREATE THIS SHOGI CLUB YET!!
SOICHIRO.
I'M SURE THESE TYPES OF EVENTS WOULD HELP...
...UNITE THE MEMBERS OF THE COMPANY.
UNITE...?
"THEY HAVEN'T ACCEPTED HIM AS THE REAL PRESIDENT YET."

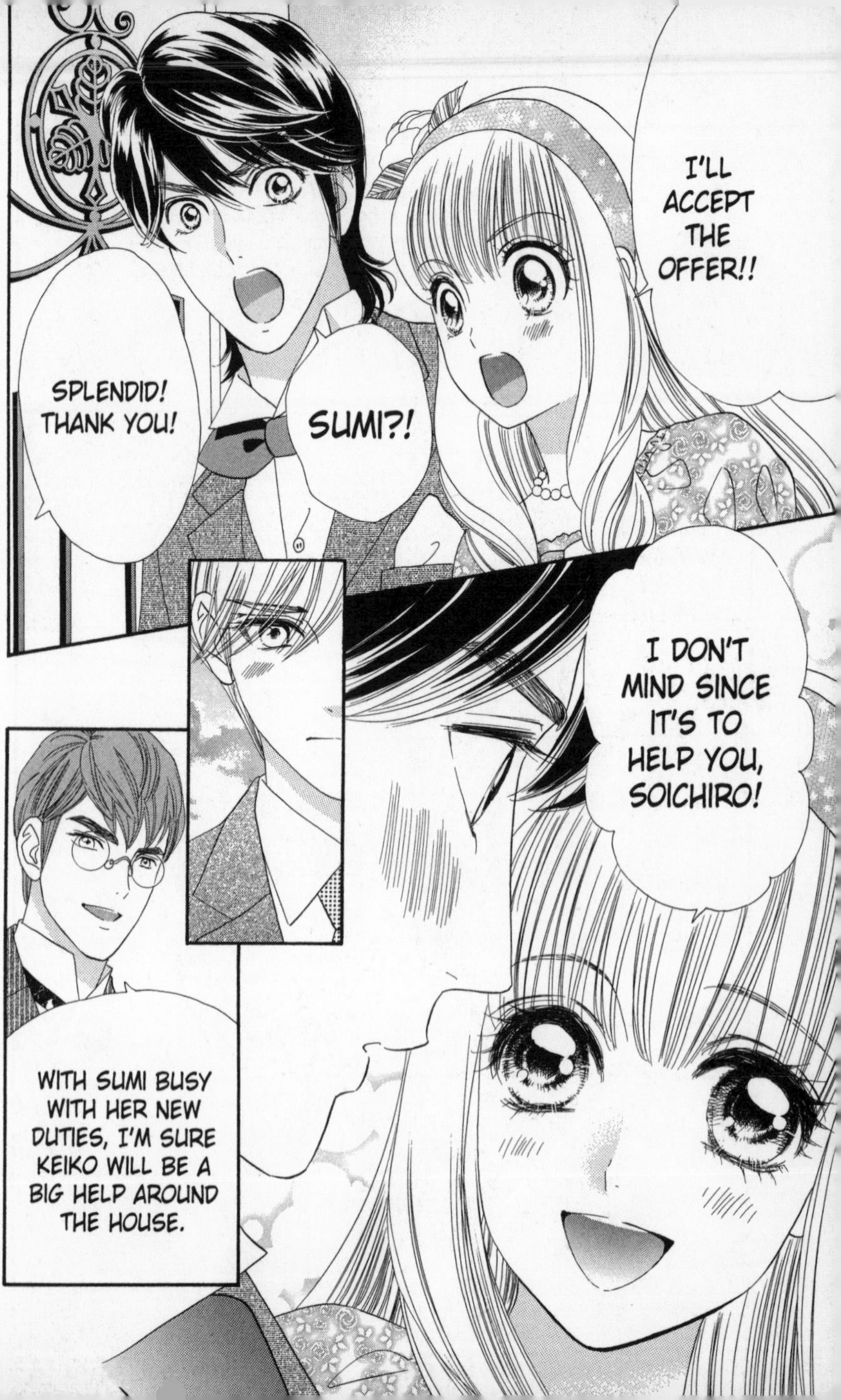
I'LL ACCEPT THE OFFER!!
SUMI?!
SPLENDID! THANK YOU!
I DON'T MIND SINCE IT'S TO HELP YOU, SOICHIRO!
WITH SUMI BUSY WITH HER NEW DUTIES, I'M SURE KEIKO WILL BE A BIG HELP AROUND THE HOUSE.

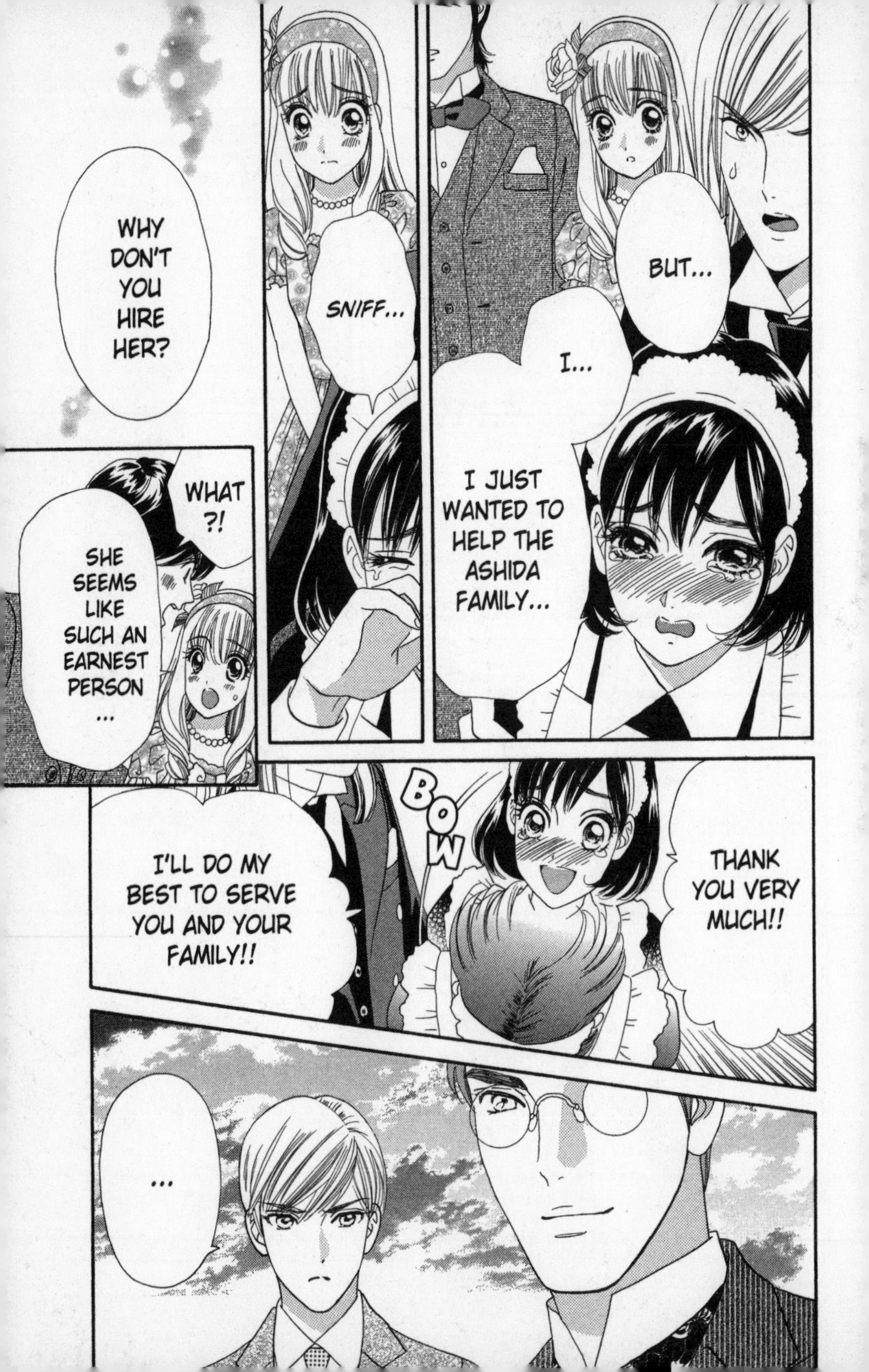
BUT...
I...
I JUST WANTED TO HELP THE ASHIDA FAMILY...
SNIFF...
WHY DON'T YOU HIRE HER?
WHAT?!
SHE SEEMS LIKE SUCH AN EARNEST PERSON...
THANK YOU VERY MUCH!!
BOW
I'LL DO MY BEST TO SERVE YOU AND YOUR FAMILY!!
...

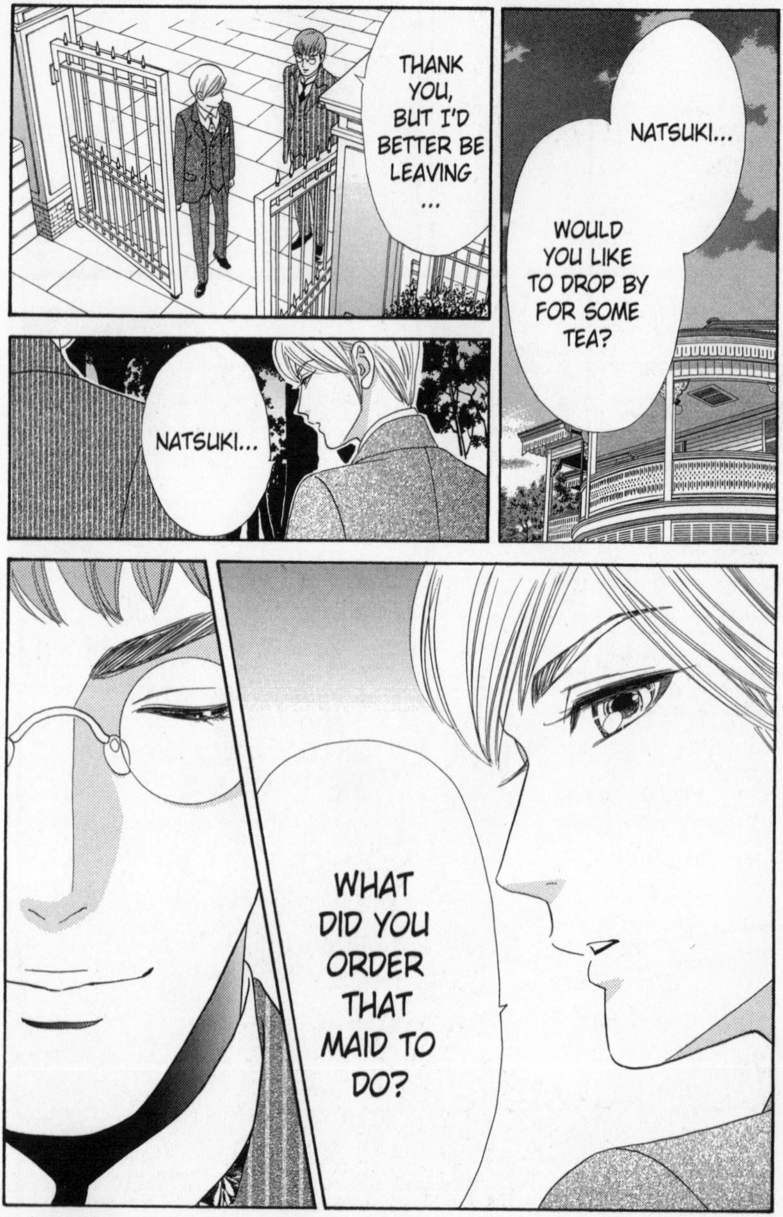
NATSUKI...
WOULD YOU LIKE TO DROP BY FOR SOME TEA?
THANK YOU, BUT I'D BETTER BE LEAVING ...
NATSUKI...
WHAT DID YOU ORDER THAT MAID TO DO?

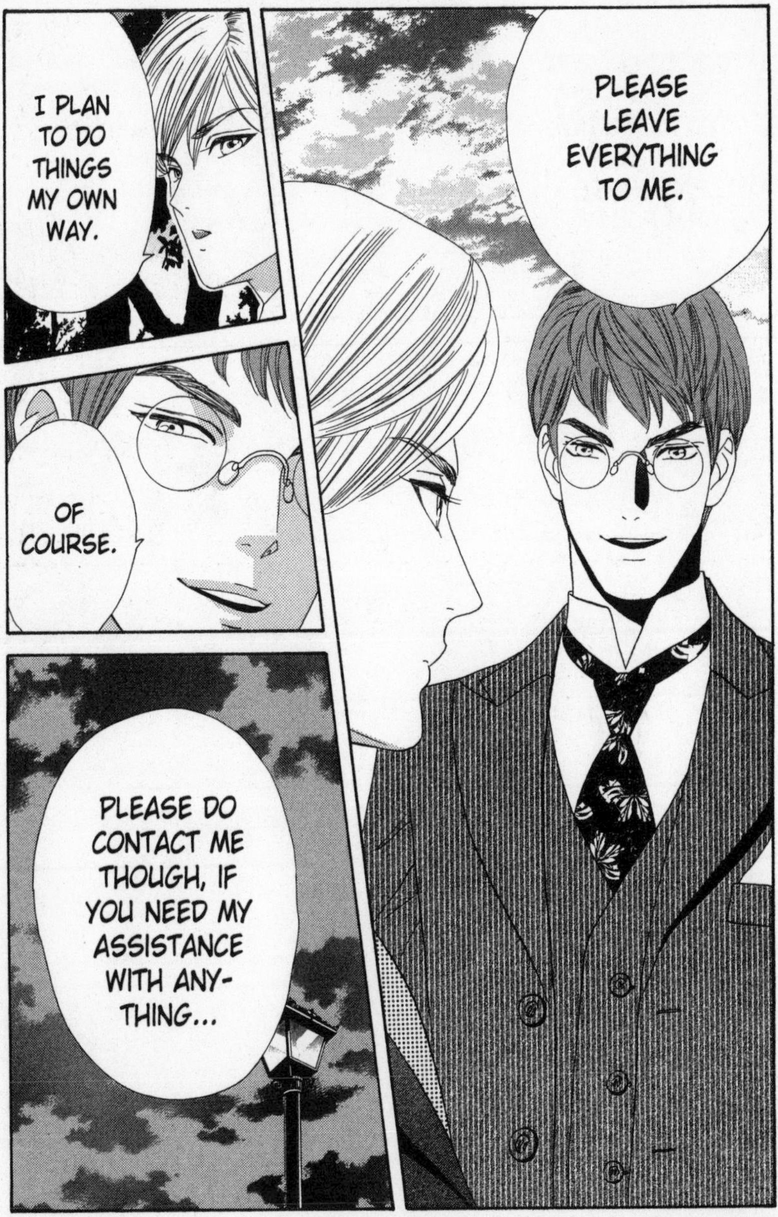
PLEASE LEAVE EVERYTHING TO ME.
I PLAN TO DO THINGS MY OWN WAY.
OF COURSE.
PLEASE DO CONTACT ME THOUGH, IF YOU NEED MY ASSISTANCE WITH ANY-THING...

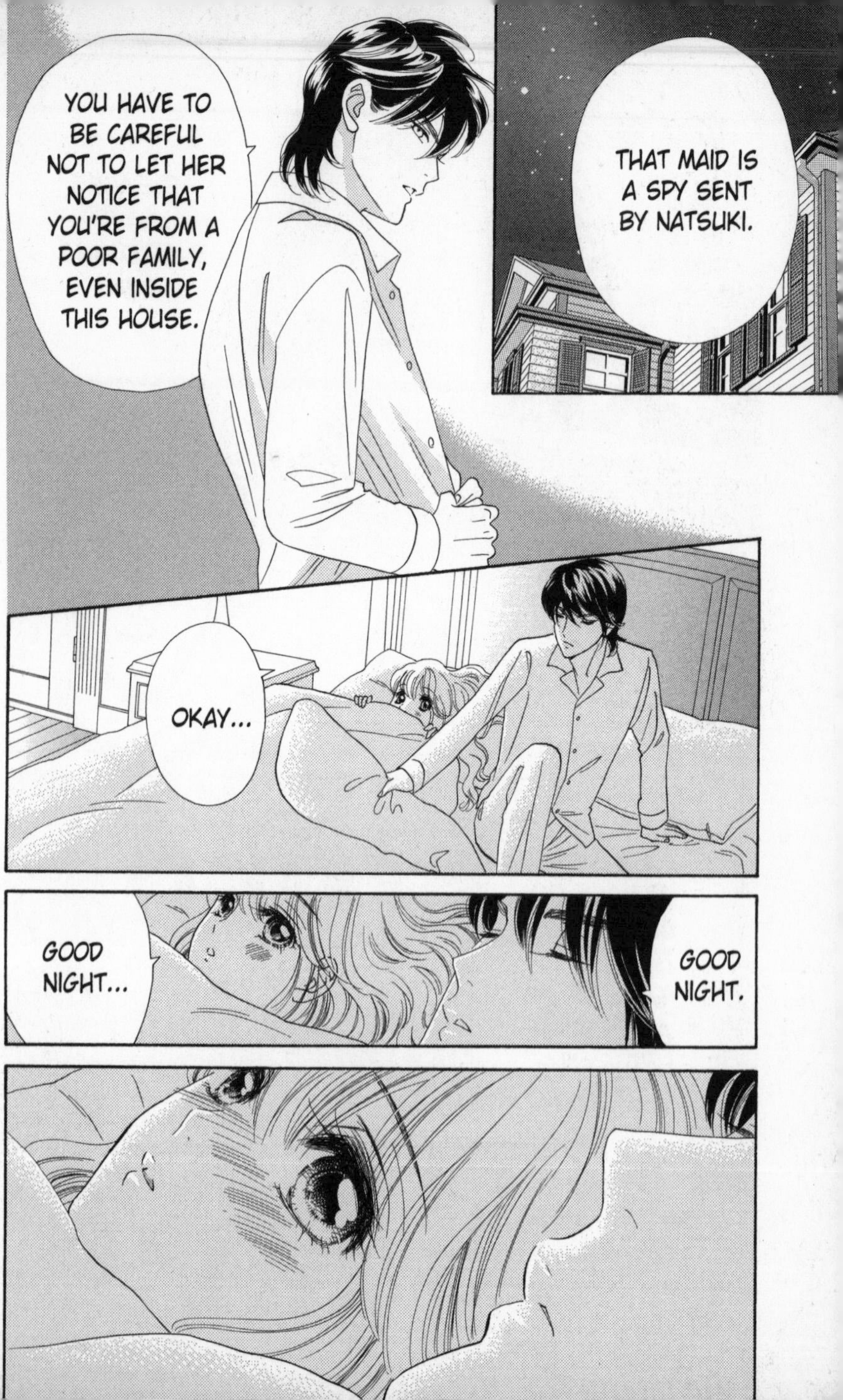
THAT MAID IS A SPY SENT BY NATSUKI.
YOU HAVE TO BE CAREFUL NOT TO LET HER NOTICE THAT YOU'RE FROM A POOR FAMILY, EVEN INSIDE THIS HOUSE.
OKAY...
GOOD NIGHT.
GOOD NIGHT...

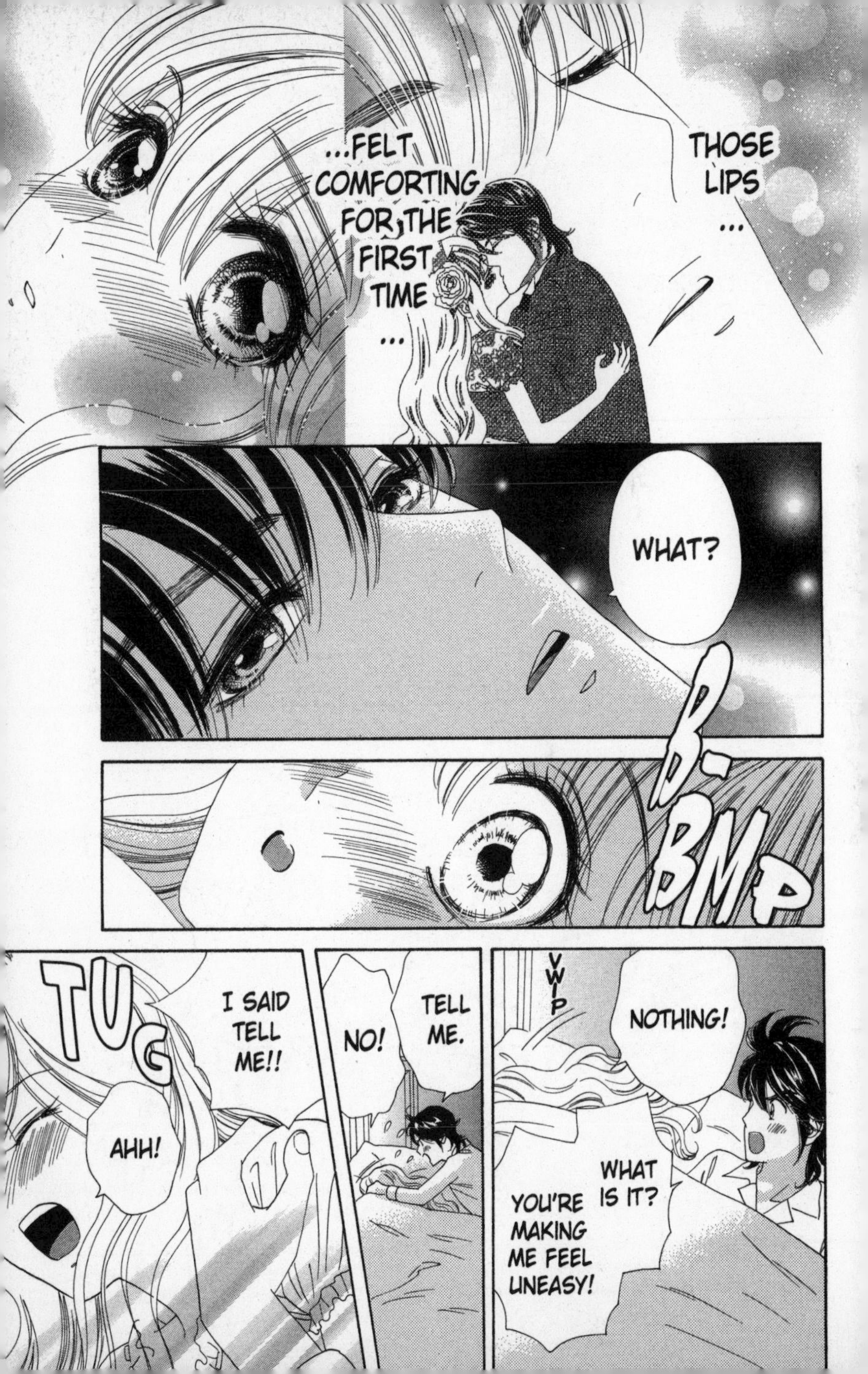
THOSE LIPS ...
...FELT COMFORTING FOR THE FIRST TIME ...
WHAT?
B-BMP
NOTHING!
VWIP
WHAT IS IT?
YOU'RE MAKING ME FEEL UNEASY!
TELL ME.
NO!
I SAID TELL ME!!
TUG
AHH!

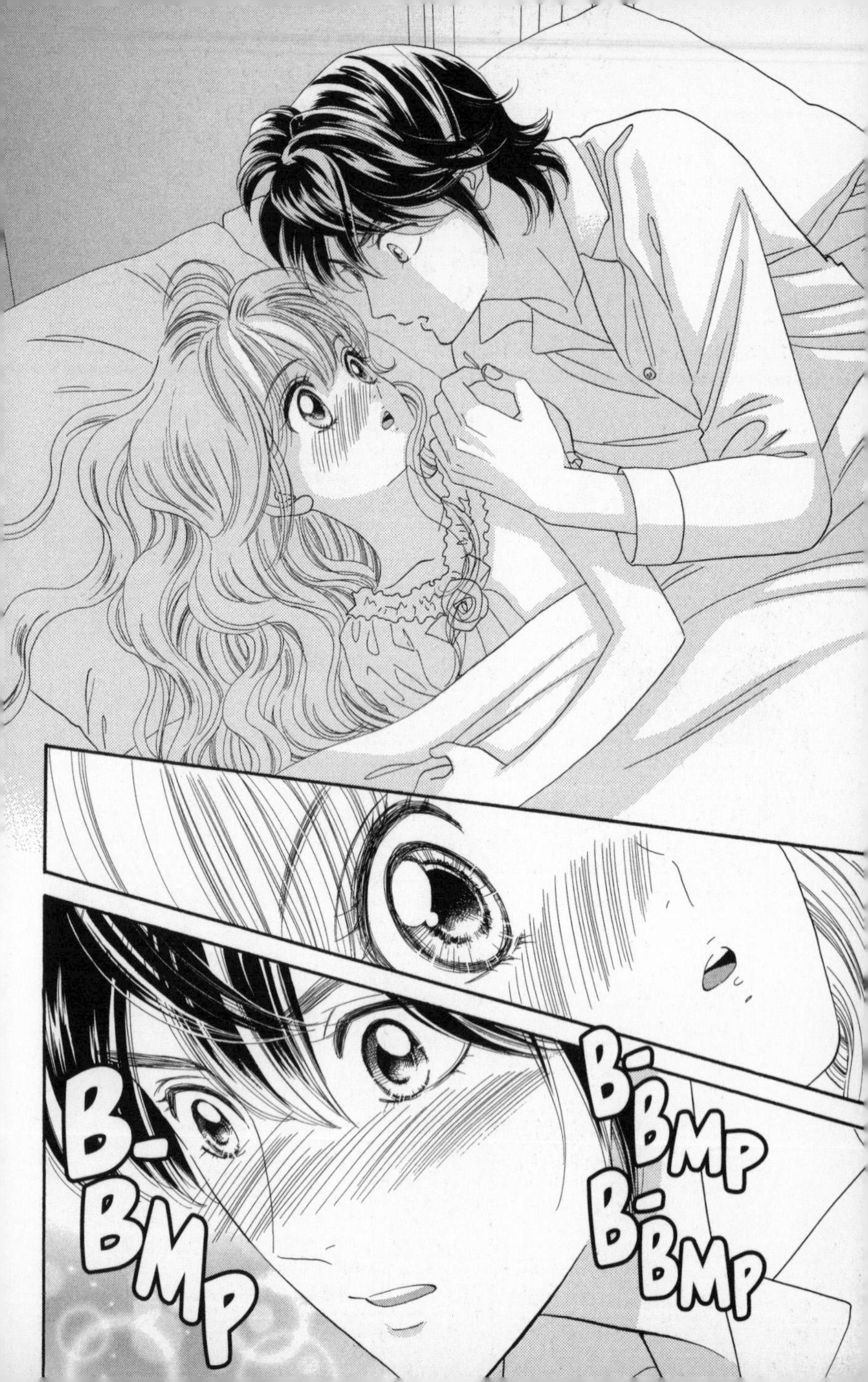
B-BMP
B-BMP
B-BMP

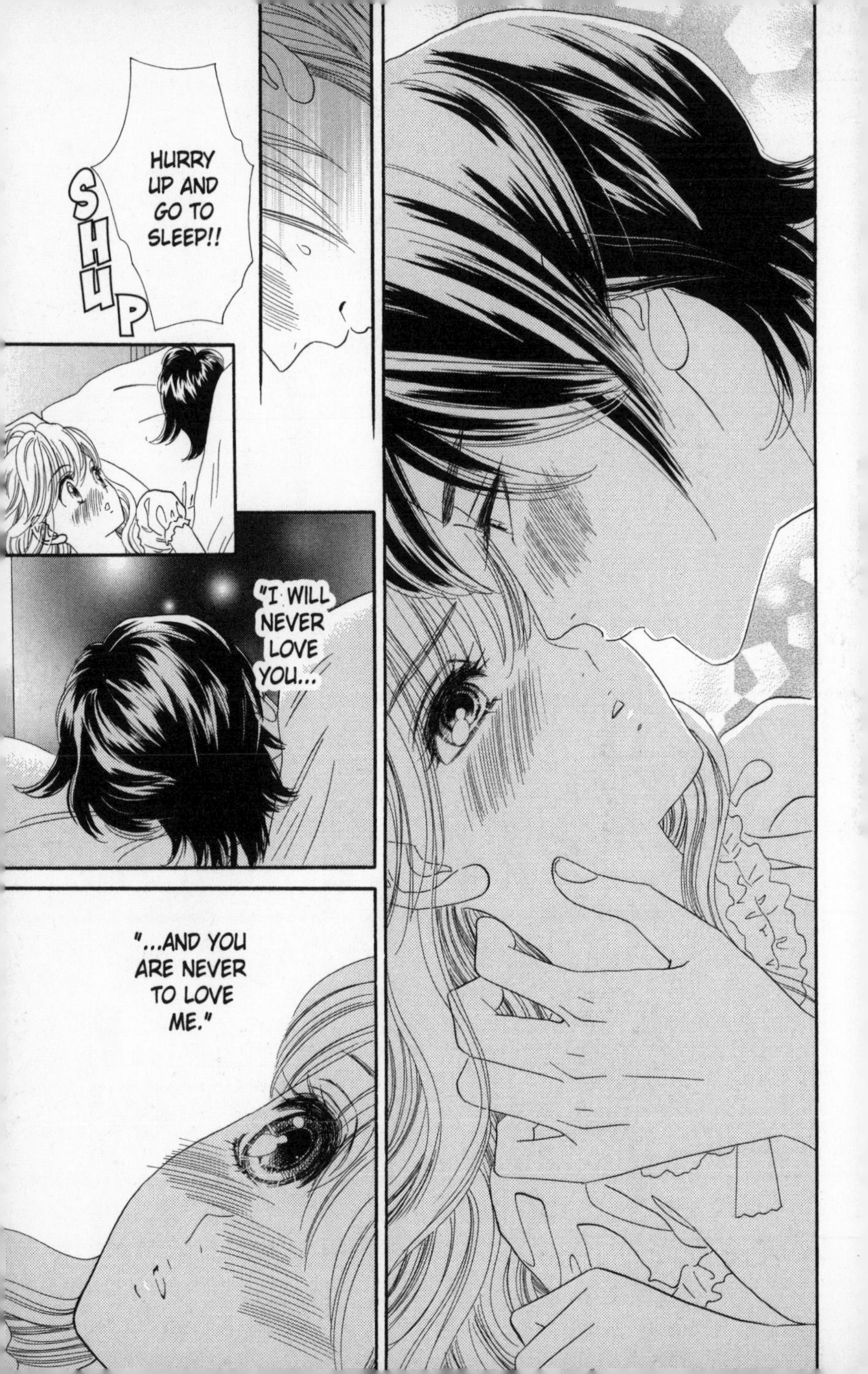
HURRY UP AND GO TO SLEEP!!
SHUP
"I WILL NEVER LOVE YOU...
"...AND YOU ARE NEVER TO LOVE ME."

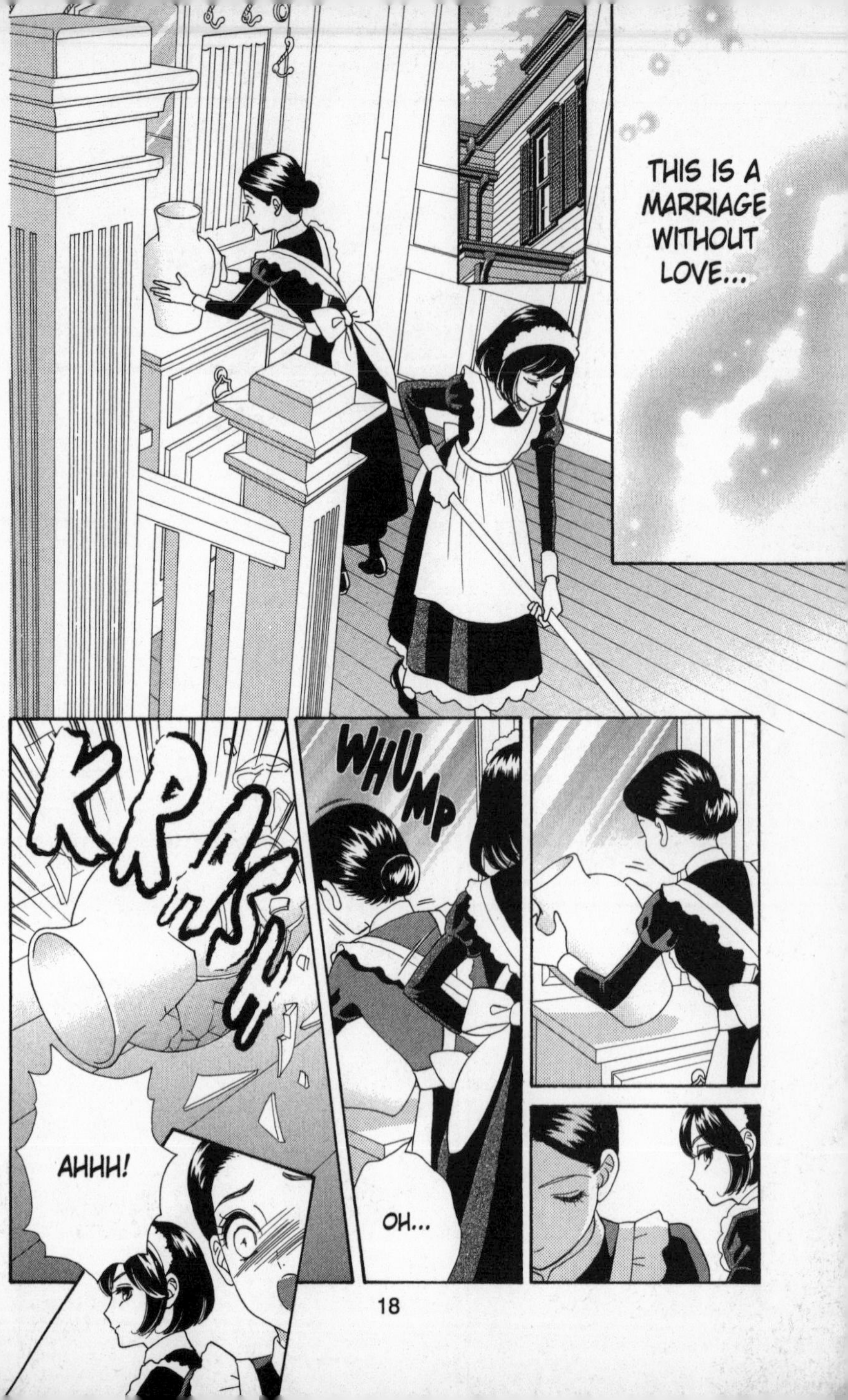
THIS IS A MARRIAGE WITHOUT LOVE...
WHUMP
OH...
KRASH
AHHH!

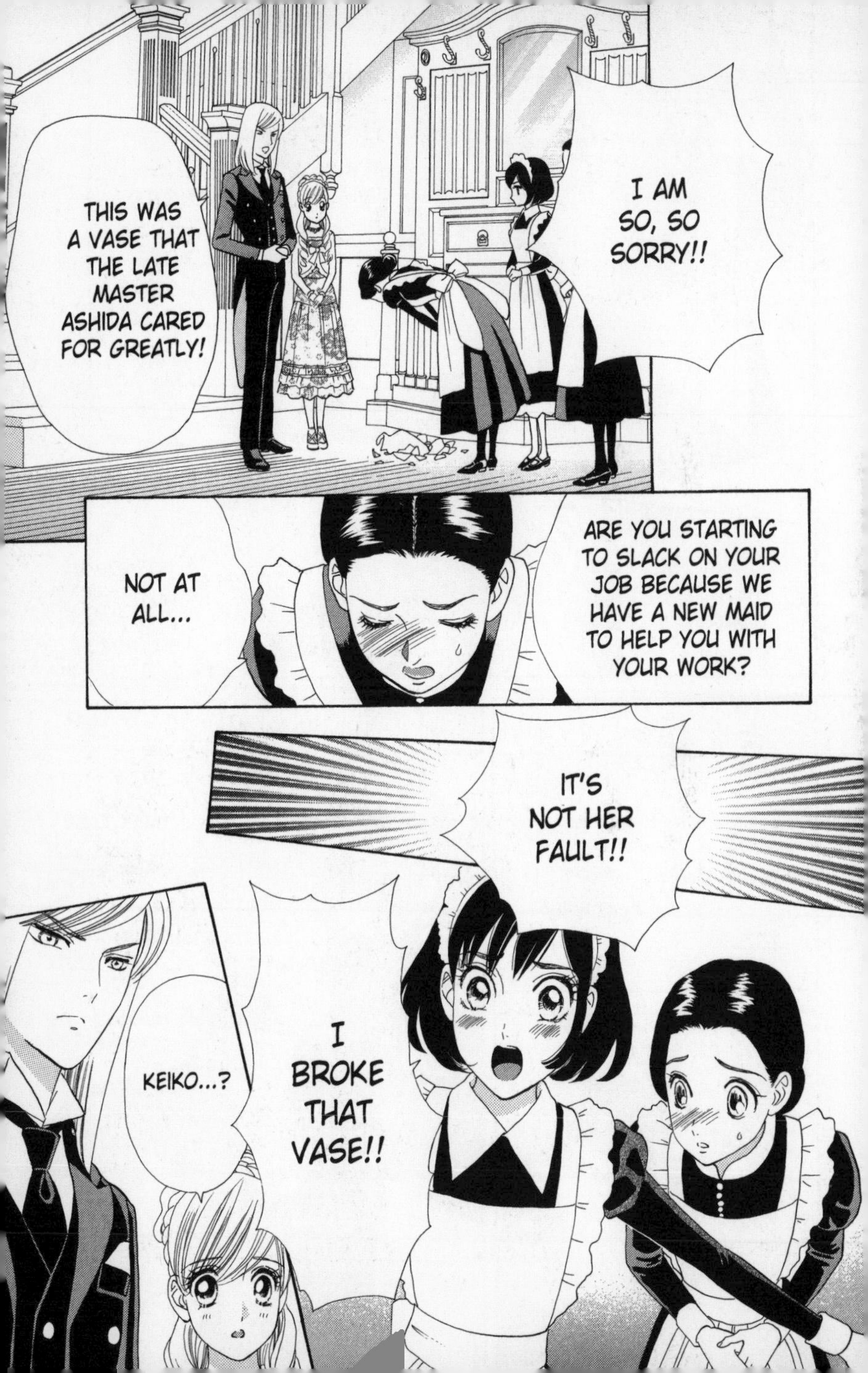
I AM SO, SO SORRY!!
THIS WAS A VASE THAT THE LATE MASTER ASHIDA CARED FOR GREATLY!
ARE YOU STARTING TO SLACK ON YOUR JOB BECAUSE WE HAVE A NEW MAID TO HELP YOU WITH YOUR WORK?
NOT AT ALL...
IT'S NOT HER FAULT!!
I BROKE THAT VASE!!
KEIKO...?

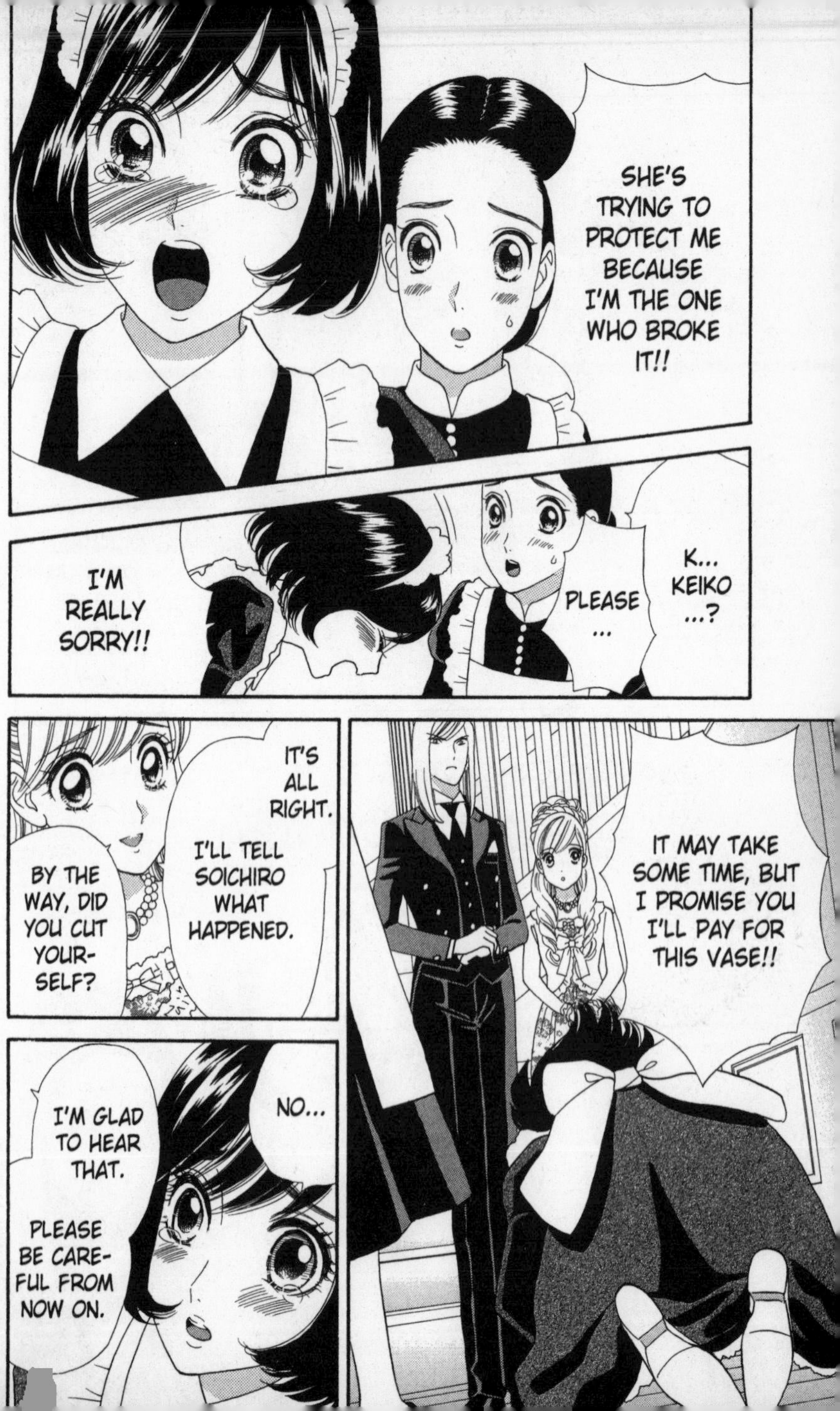
SHE'S TRYING TO PROTECT ME BECAUSE I'M THE ONE WHO BROKE IT!!
K... KEIKO ...?
PLEASE ...
I'M REALLY SORRY!!
IT MAY TAKE SOME TIME, BUT I PROMISE YOU I'LL PAY FOR THIS VASE!!
IT'S ALL RIGHT.
I'LL TELL SOICHIRO WHAT HAPPENED.
BY THE WAY, DID YOU CUT YOUR-SELF?
NO...
I'M GLAD TO HEAR THAT.
PLEASE BE CARE-FUL FROM NOW ON.

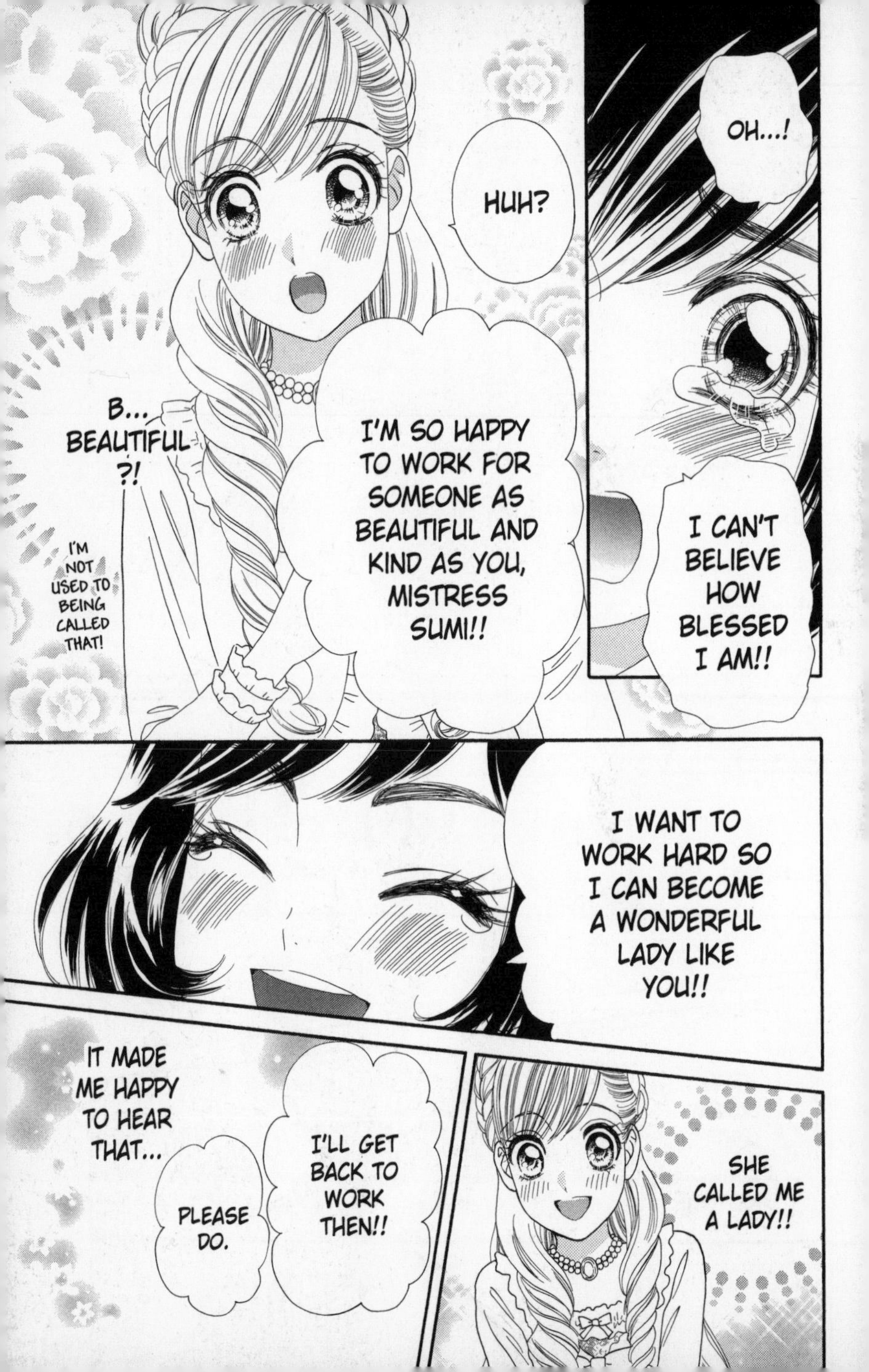
OH...!
I CAN'T BELIEVE HOW BLESSED I AM!!
HUH?
I'M SO HAPPY TO WORK FOR SOMEONE AS BEAUTIFUL AND KIND AS YOU, MISTRESS SUMI!!
B... BEAUTIFUL ?!
I'M NOT USED TO BEING CALLED THAT!
I WANT TO WORK HARD SO I CAN BECOME A WONDERFUL LADY LIKE YOU!!
SHE CALLED ME A LADY!!
I'LL GET BACK TO WORK THEN!!
PLEASE DO.
IT MADE ME HAPPY TO HEAR THAT...

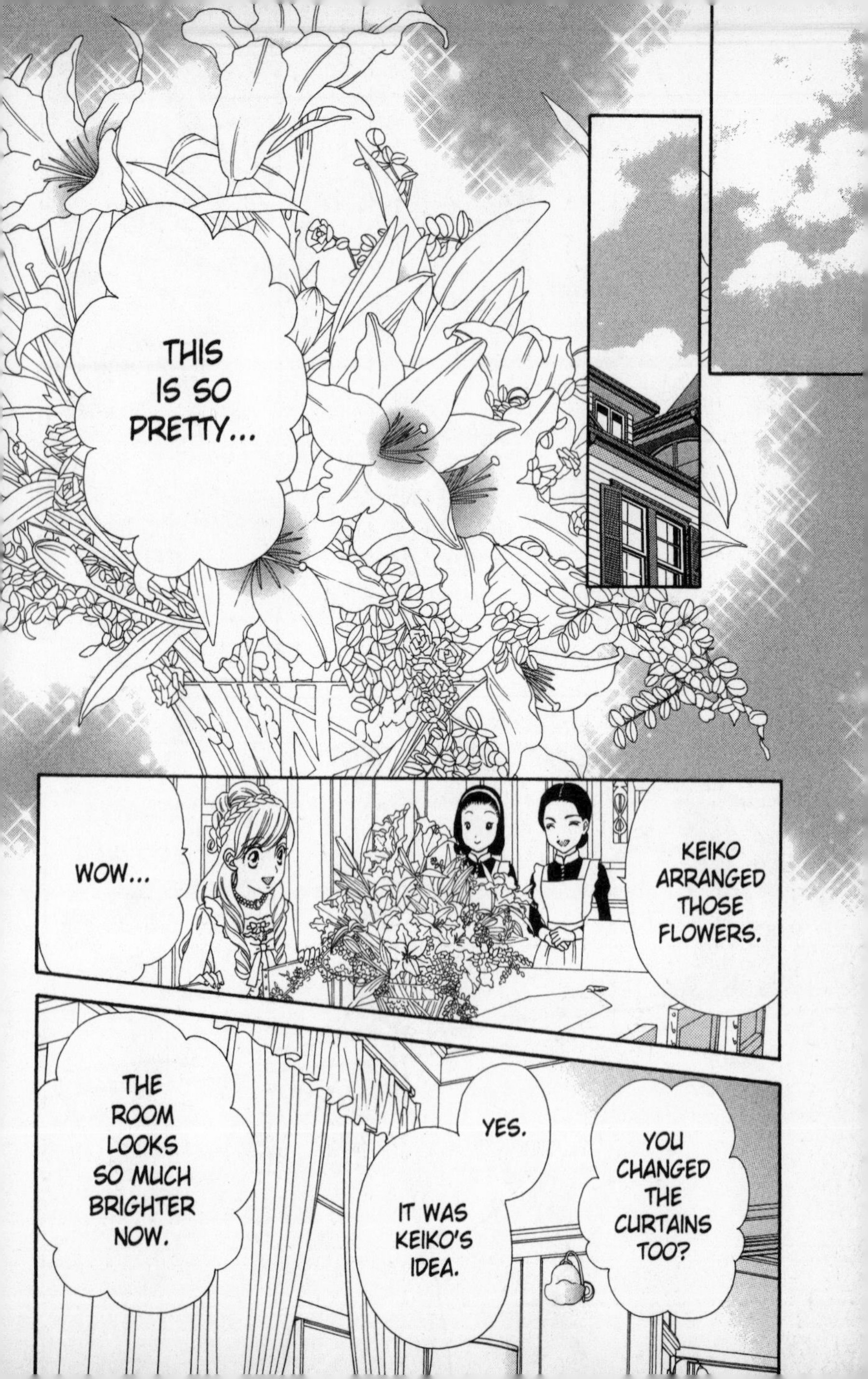
THIS IS SO PRETTY...
KEIKO ARRANGED THOSE FLOWERS.
WOW...
YOU CHANGED THE CURTAINS TOO?
YES.
IT WAS KEIKO'S IDEA.
THE ROOM LOOKS SO MUCH BRIGHTER NOW.

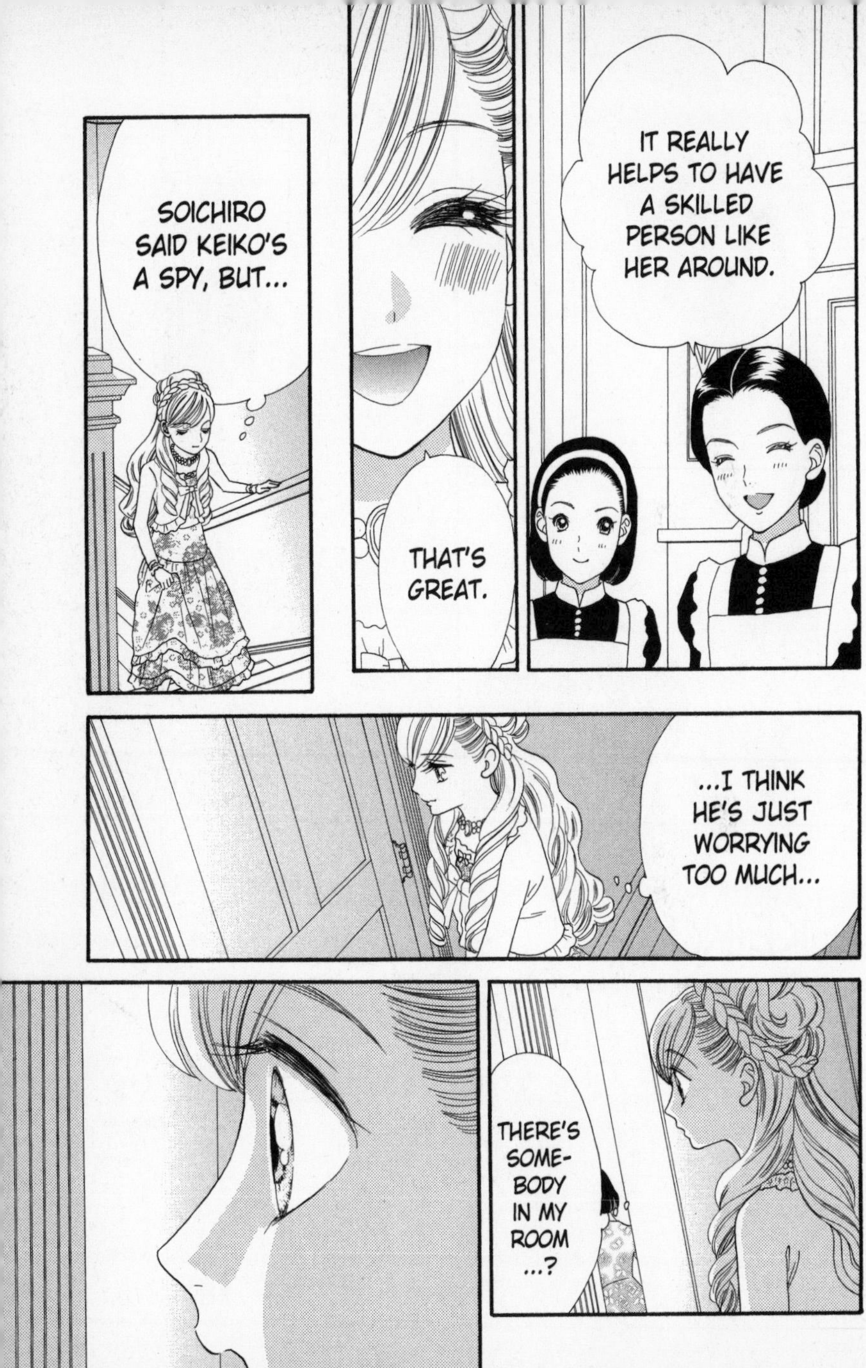
IT REALLY HELPS TO HAVE A SKILLED PERSON LIKE HER AROUND.
THAT'S GREAT.
SOICHIRO SAID KEIKO'S A SPY, BUT...
...I THINK HE'S JUST WORRYING TOO MUCH...
THERE'S SOME-BODY IN MY ROOM ...?

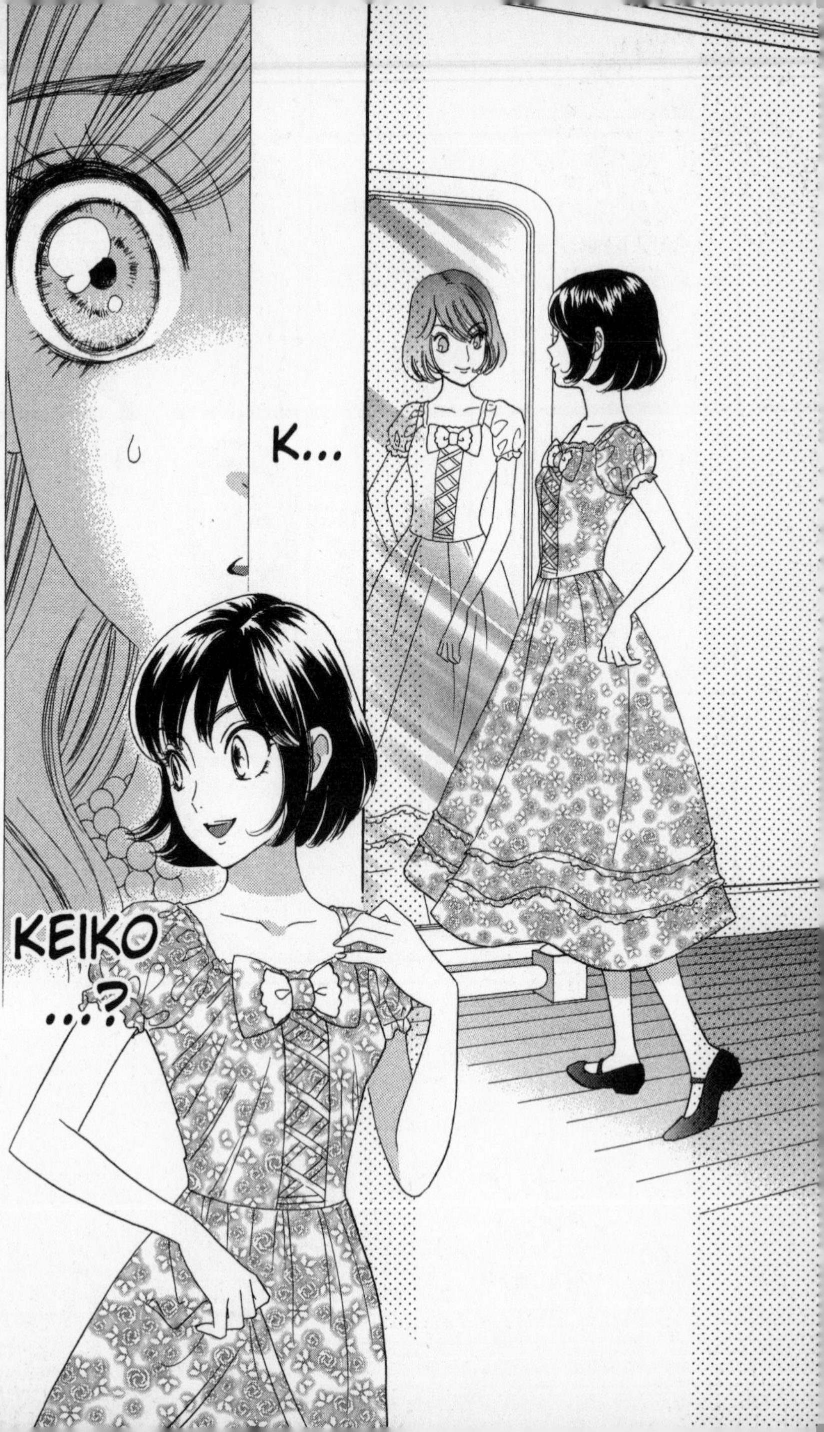
K...
KEIKO ...?

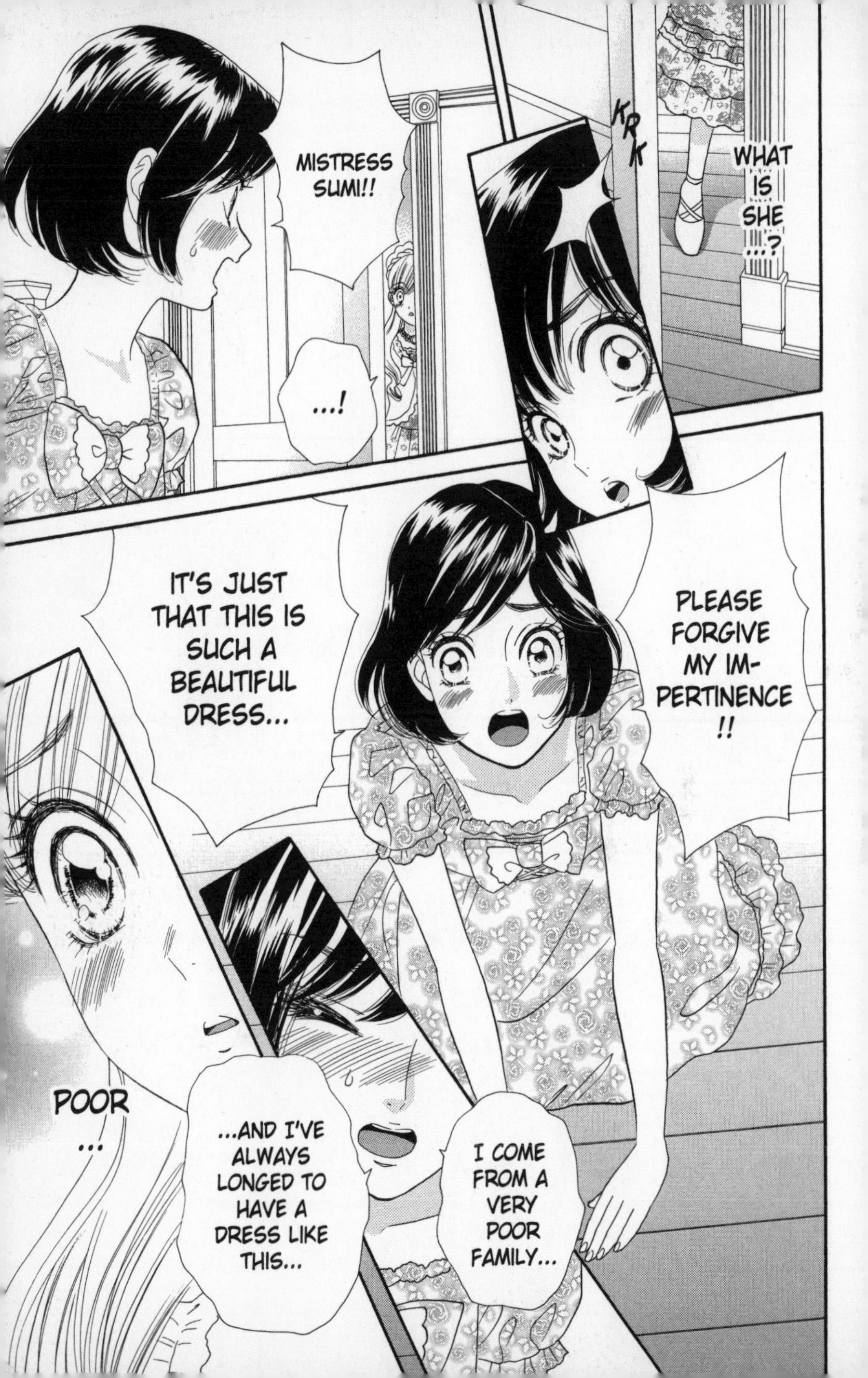
WHAT IS SHE ...?
KRK
MISTRESS SUMI!!
...!
PLEASE FORGIVE MY IM-PERTINENCE!!
IT'S JUST THAT THIS IS SUCH A BEAUTIFUL DRESS...
I COME FROM A VERY POOR FAMILY...
...AND I'VE ALWAYS LONGED TO HAVE A DRESS LIKE THIS...
POOR...

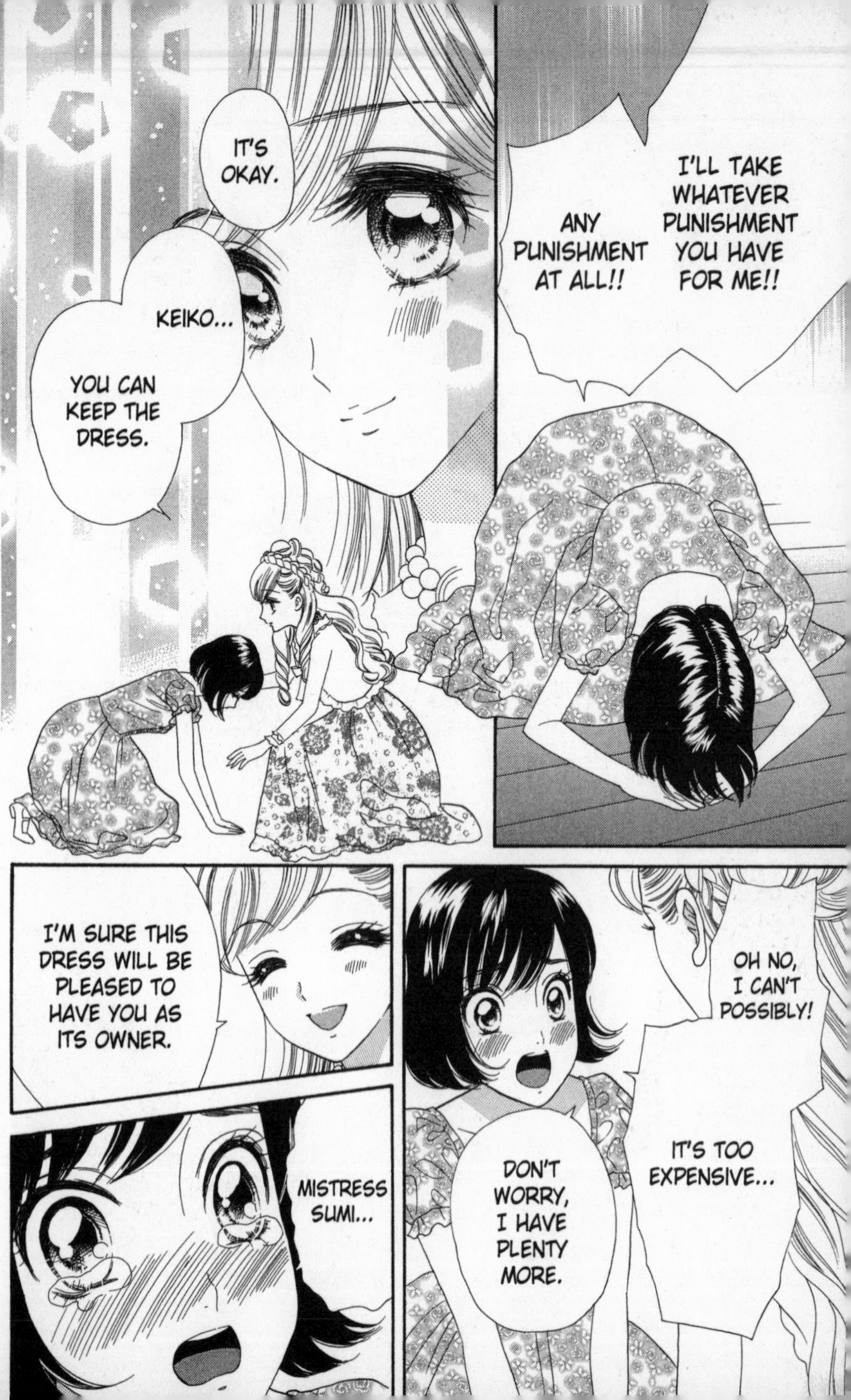
I'LL TAKE WHATEVER PUNISHMENT YOU HAVE FOR ME!!
ANY PUNISHMENT AT ALL!!
IT'S OKAY.
KEIKO...
YOU CAN KEEP THE DRESS.
OH NO, I CAN'T POSSIBLY!
IT'S TOO EXPENSIVE...
DON'T WORRY, I HAVE PLENTY MORE.
I'M SURE THIS DRESS WILL BE PLEASED TO HAVE YOU AS ITS OWNER.
MISTRESS SUMI...

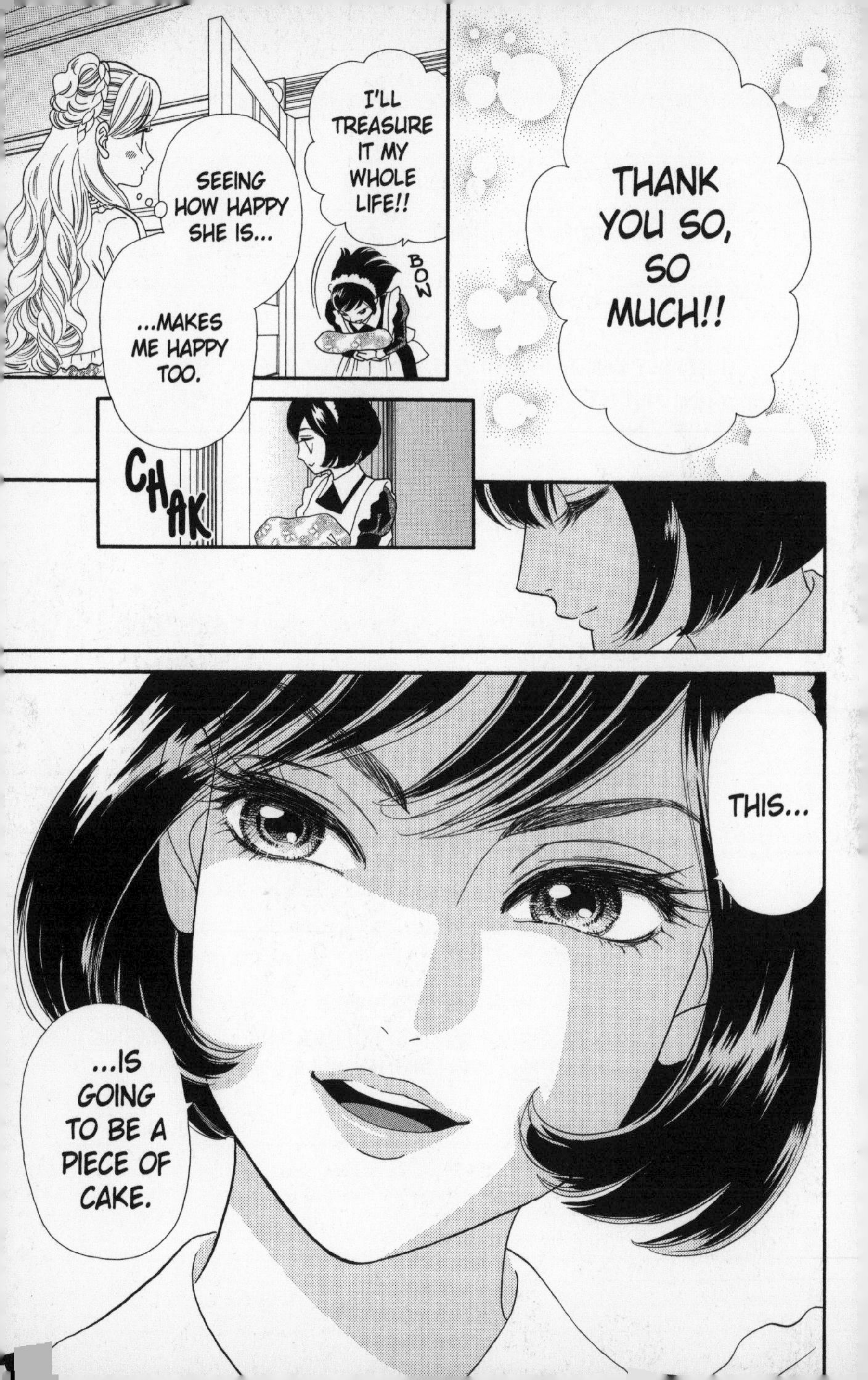
THANK YOU SO, SO MUCH!!
I'LL TREASURE IT MY WHOLE LIFE!!
BOW
SEEING HOW HAPPY SHE IS...
...MAKES ME HAPPY TOO.
CHAK
THIS...
...IS GOING TO BE A PIECE OF CAKE.

No. 1

RANDOM CHITCHAT!

Date . .

❀ HELLO, IT'S UE-RIN!!

I REALLY ENJOY DRAWING *STEPPING ON ROSES* AS IT CONTINUES TO HAVE THIS STEREOTYPICAL, MELODRAMATIC STORYLINE.

IN THE MIDDLE OF ALL MY WORK, I HAD A COUPLE OF NEW ADDITIONS TO MY FAMILY!!

THE ONE WITH THE YELLOW BODY AND ORANGE FACE IS PITCH. ⇨

THE "NORMAL COLOR" ONE WITH AN OLIVE BODY AND PINK FACE IS MAMEZO. ⇨

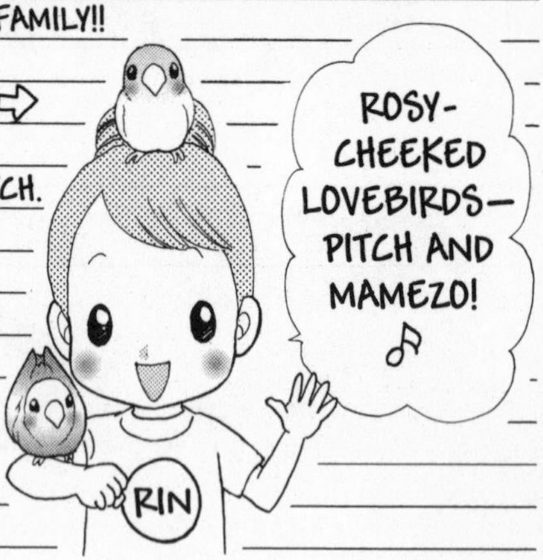
ROSY-CHEEKED LOVEBIRDS—PITCH AND MAMEZO! ♪
RIN

❀ THE LAST TIME I HAD A PET LOVEBIRD WAS BACK IN ELEMENTARY SCHOOL, SO I CURRENTLY HAVE A GUIDEBOOK CLOSE AT HAND AS I'M ENJOYING MY LIFE WITH THEM.♡

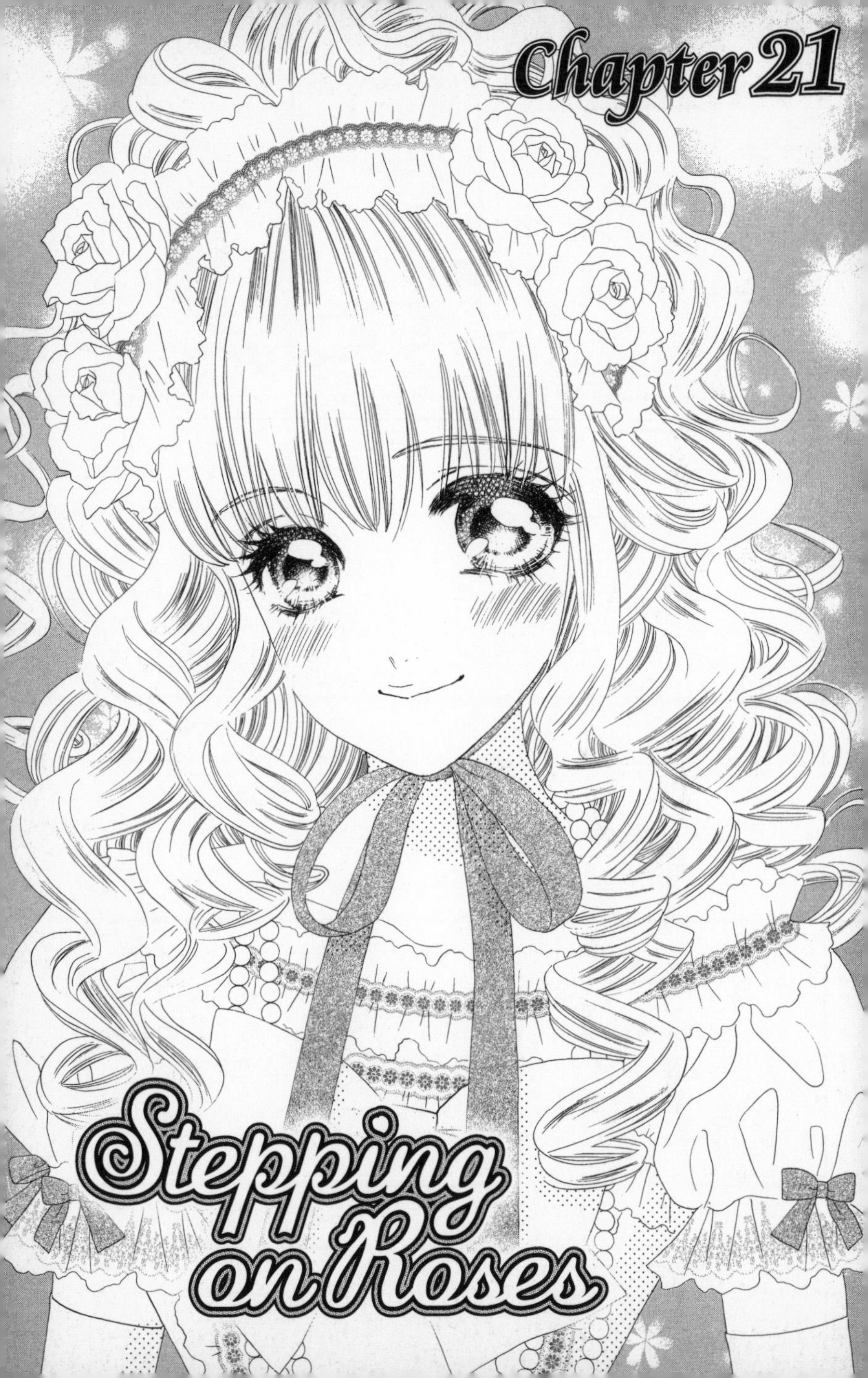
Chapter 21
Stepping on Roses

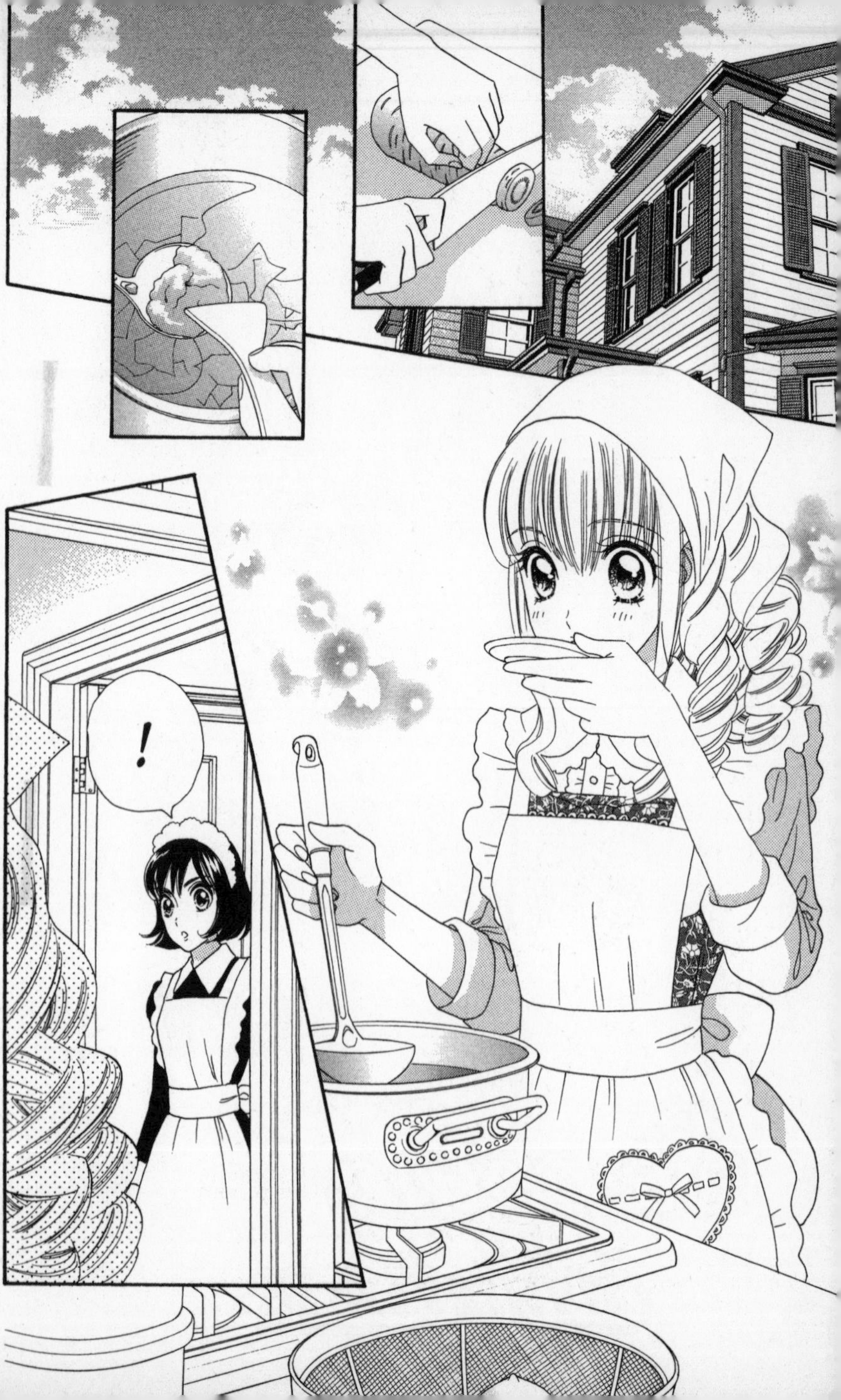
!

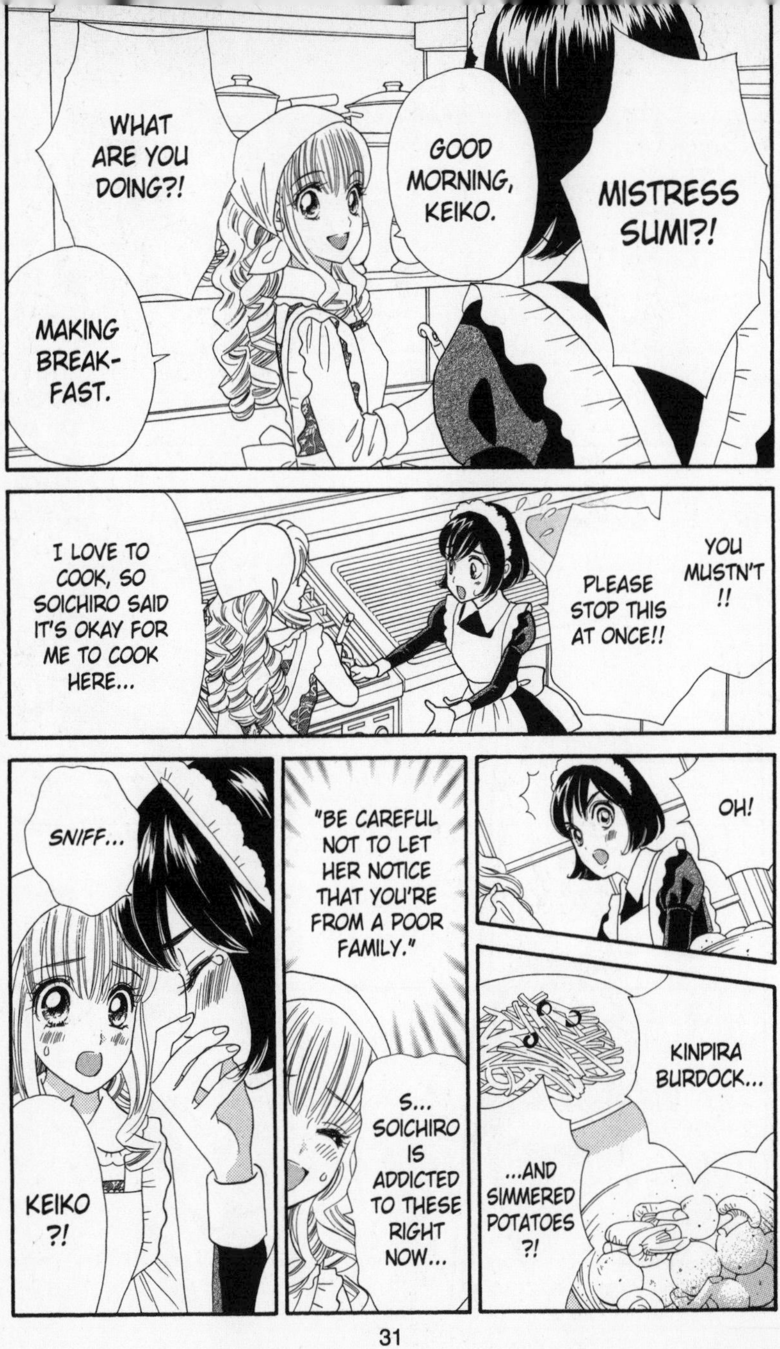
MISTRESS SUMI?!
GOOD MORNING, KEIKO.
WHAT ARE YOU DOING?!
MAKING BREAK-FAST.
YOU MUSTN'T!!
PLEASE STOP THIS AT ONCE!!
I LOVE TO COOK, SO SOICHIRO SAID IT'S OKAY FOR ME TO COOK HERE...
OH!
KINPIRA BURDOCK...
...AND SIMMERED POTATOES?!
"BE CAREFUL NOT TO LET HER NOTICE THAT YOU'RE FROM A POOR FAMILY."
S... SOICHIRO IS ADDICTED TO THESE RIGHT NOW...
SNIFF...
KEIKO?!

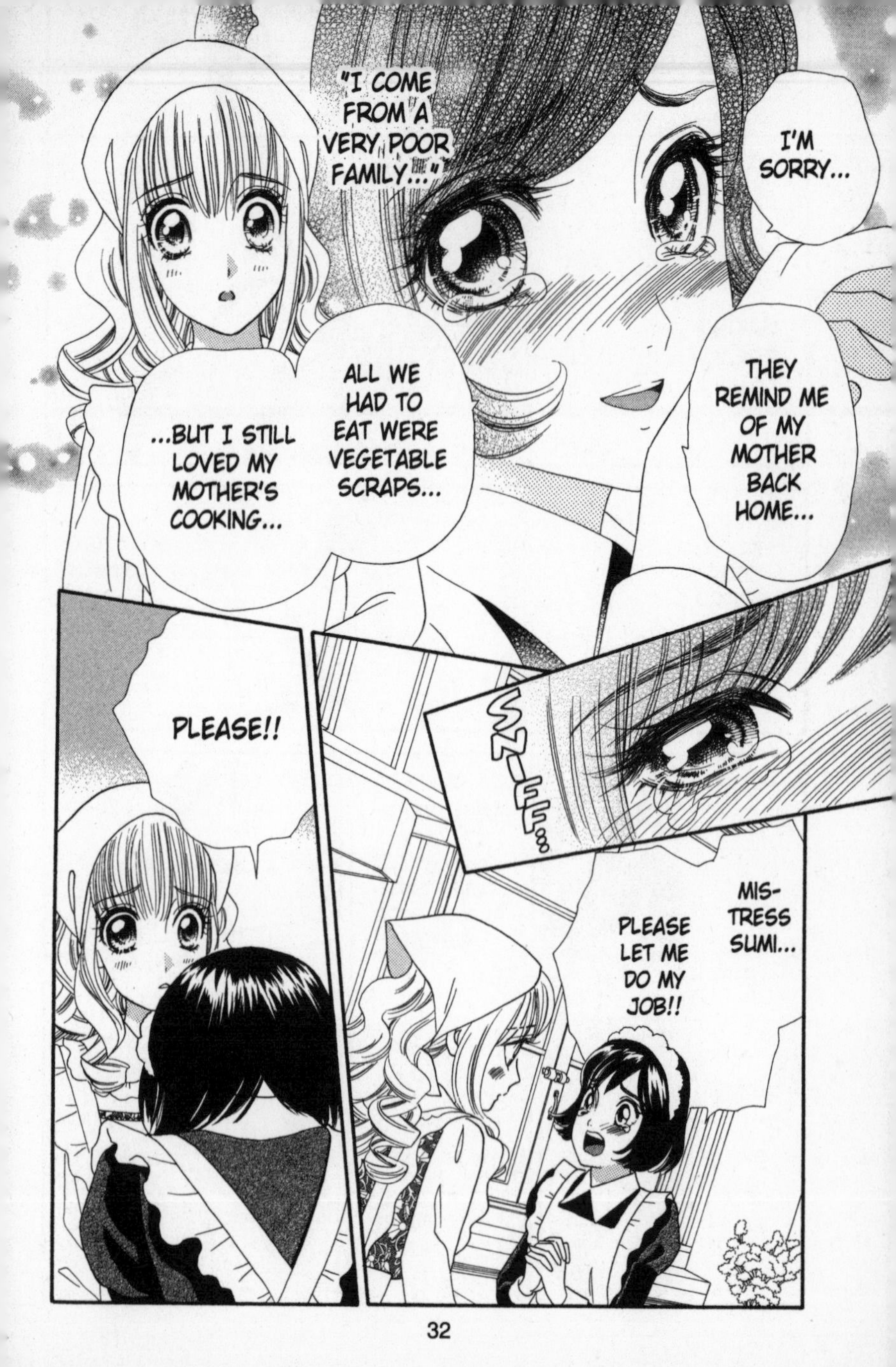
I'M SORRY...
"I COME FROM A VERY POOR FAMILY..."
THEY REMIND ME OF MY MOTHER BACK HOME...
ALL WE HAD TO EAT WERE VEGETABLE SCRAPS...
...BUT I STILL LOVED MY MOTHER'S COOKING...
SNIFF...
MIS-TRESS SUMI...
PLEASE LET ME DO MY JOB!!
PLEASE!!

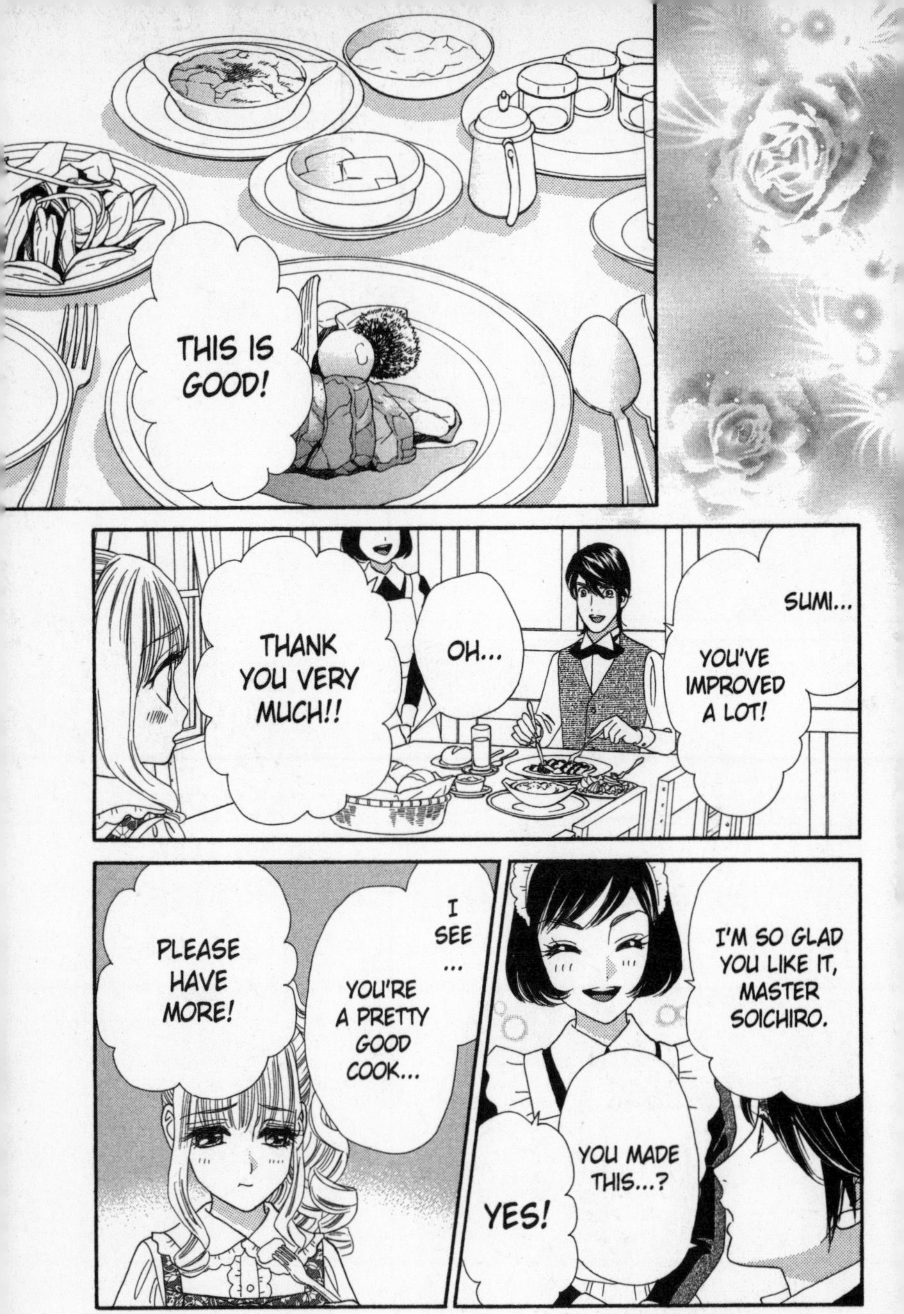
THIS IS GOOD!
SUMI... YOU'VE IMPROVED A LOT!
OH...
THANK YOU VERY MUCH!!
I'M SO GLAD YOU LIKE IT, MASTER SOICHIRO.
YOU MADE THIS...?
YES!
I SEE... YOU'RE A PRETTY GOOD COOK...
PLEASE HAVE MORE!

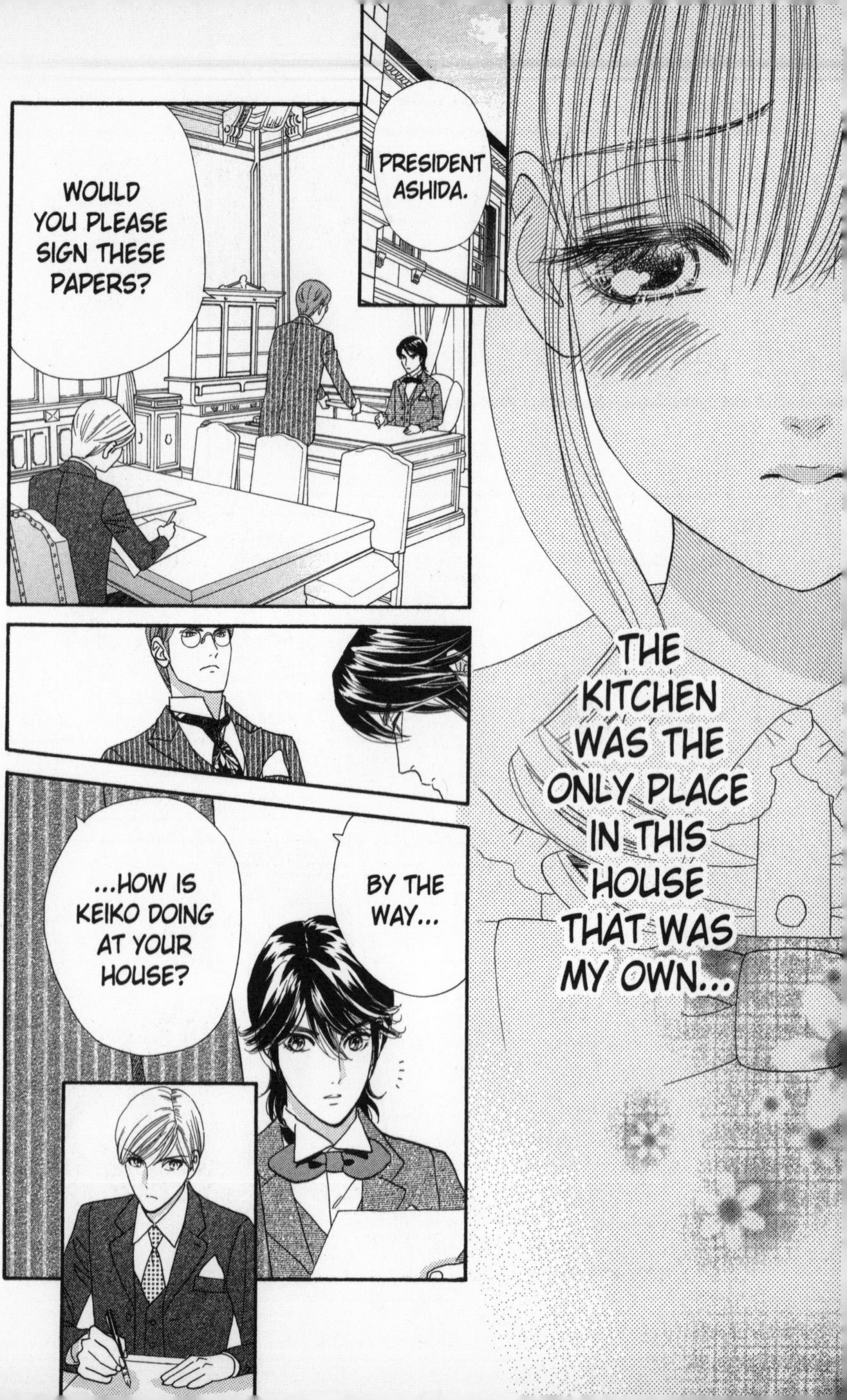
THE KITCHEN WAS THE ONLY PLACE IN THIS HOUSE THAT WAS MY OWN...
PRESIDENT ASHIDA.
WOULD YOU PLEASE SIGN THESE PAPERS?
BY THE WAY...
...HOW IS KEIKO DOING AT YOUR HOUSE?

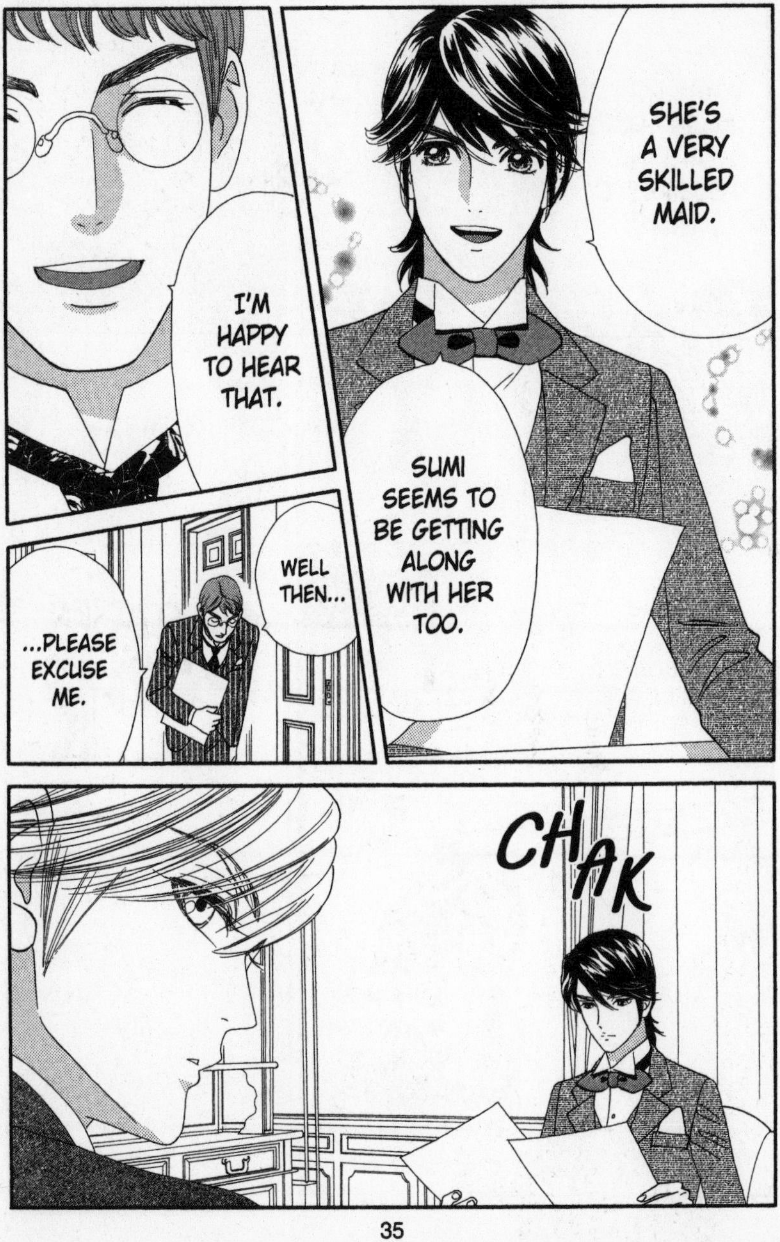
SHE'S A VERY SKILLED MAID.
SUMI SEEMS TO BE GETTING ALONG WITH HER TOO.
I'M HAPPY TO HEAR THAT.
WELL THEN...
...PLEASE EXCUSE ME.
CHAK

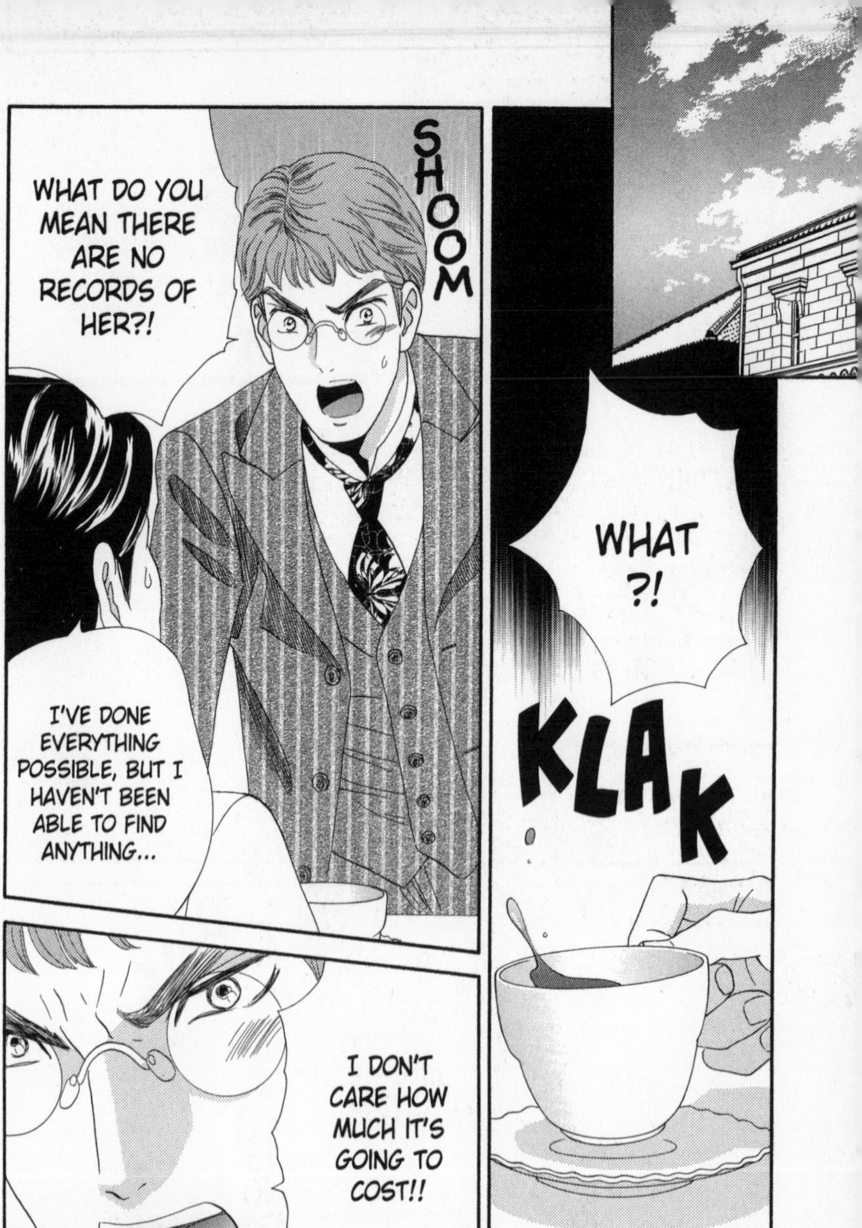
WHAT ?!
KLAK
WHAT DO YOU MEAN THERE ARE NO RECORDS OF HER?!
SHOOM
I'VE DONE EVERYTHING POSSIBLE, BUT I HAVEN'T BEEN ABLE TO FIND ANYTHING...
I DON'T CARE HOW MUCH IT'S GOING TO COST!!

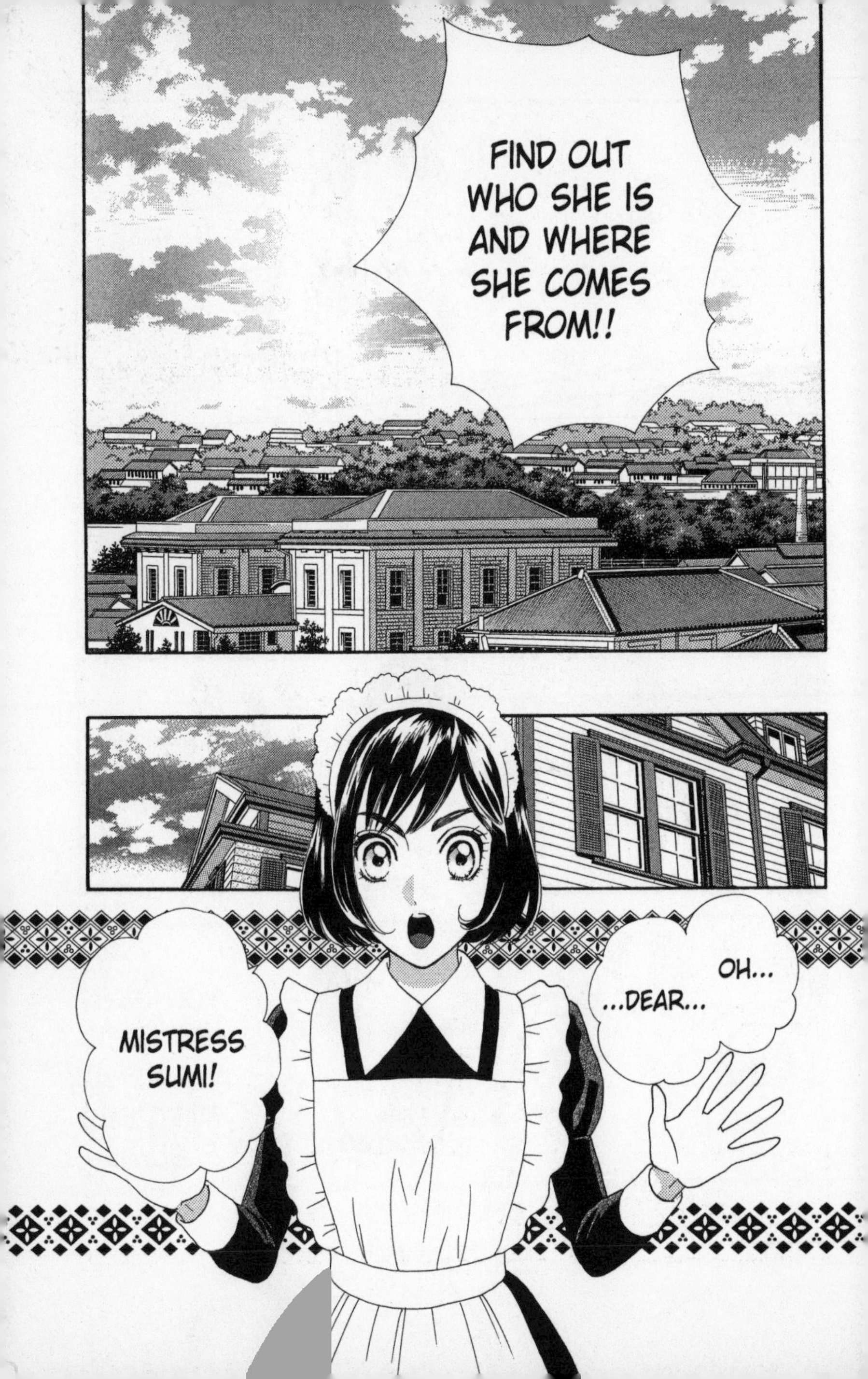
FIND OUT WHO SHE IS AND WHERE SHE COMES FROM!!
OH... ...DEAR...
MISTRESS SUMI!

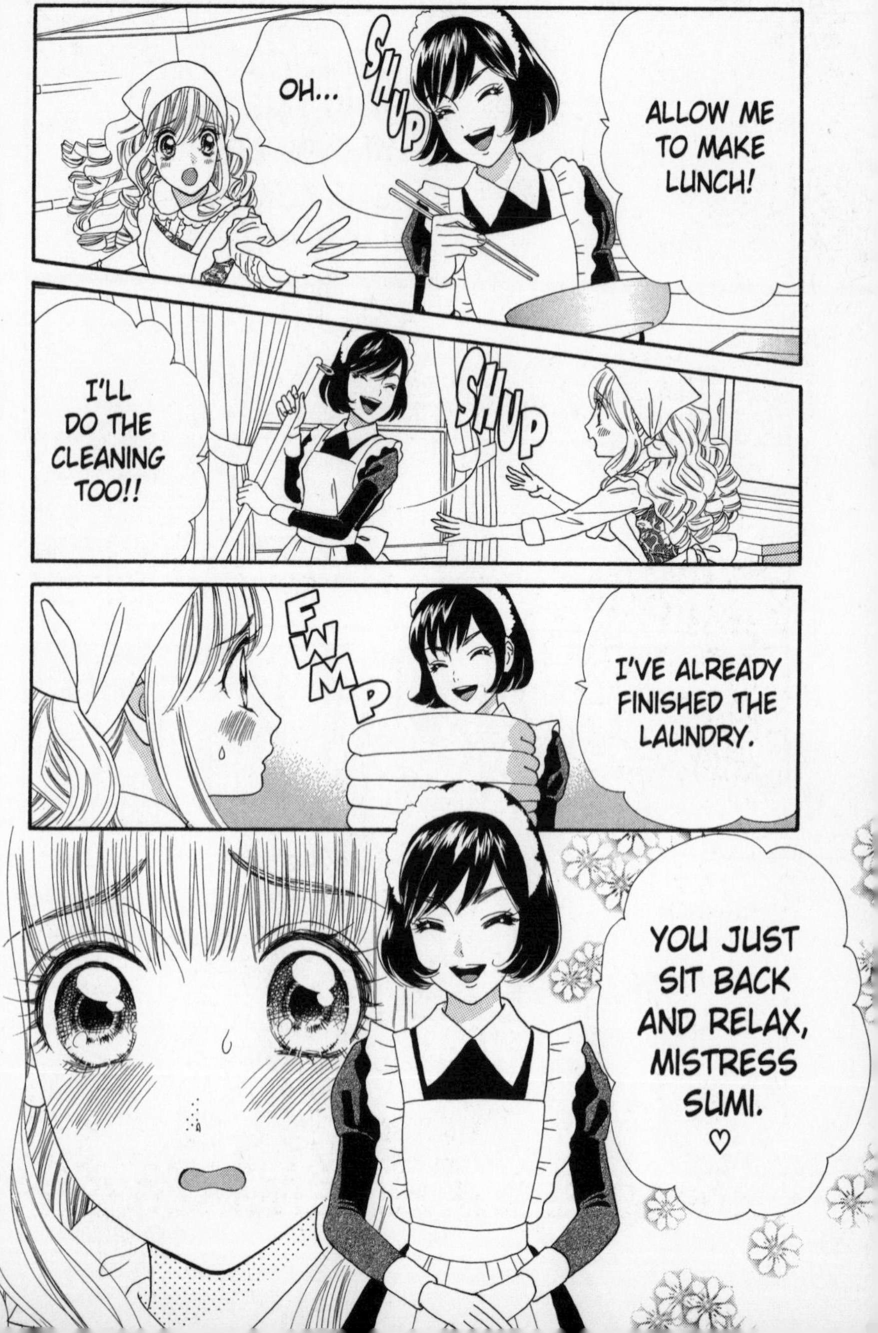
ALLOW ME TO MAKE LUNCH!
SHUP
OH...
SHUP
I'LL DO THE CLEANING TOO!!
I'VE ALREADY FINISHED THE LAUNDRY.
FWMP
YOU JUST SIT BACK AND RELAX, MISTRESS SUMI. ♡

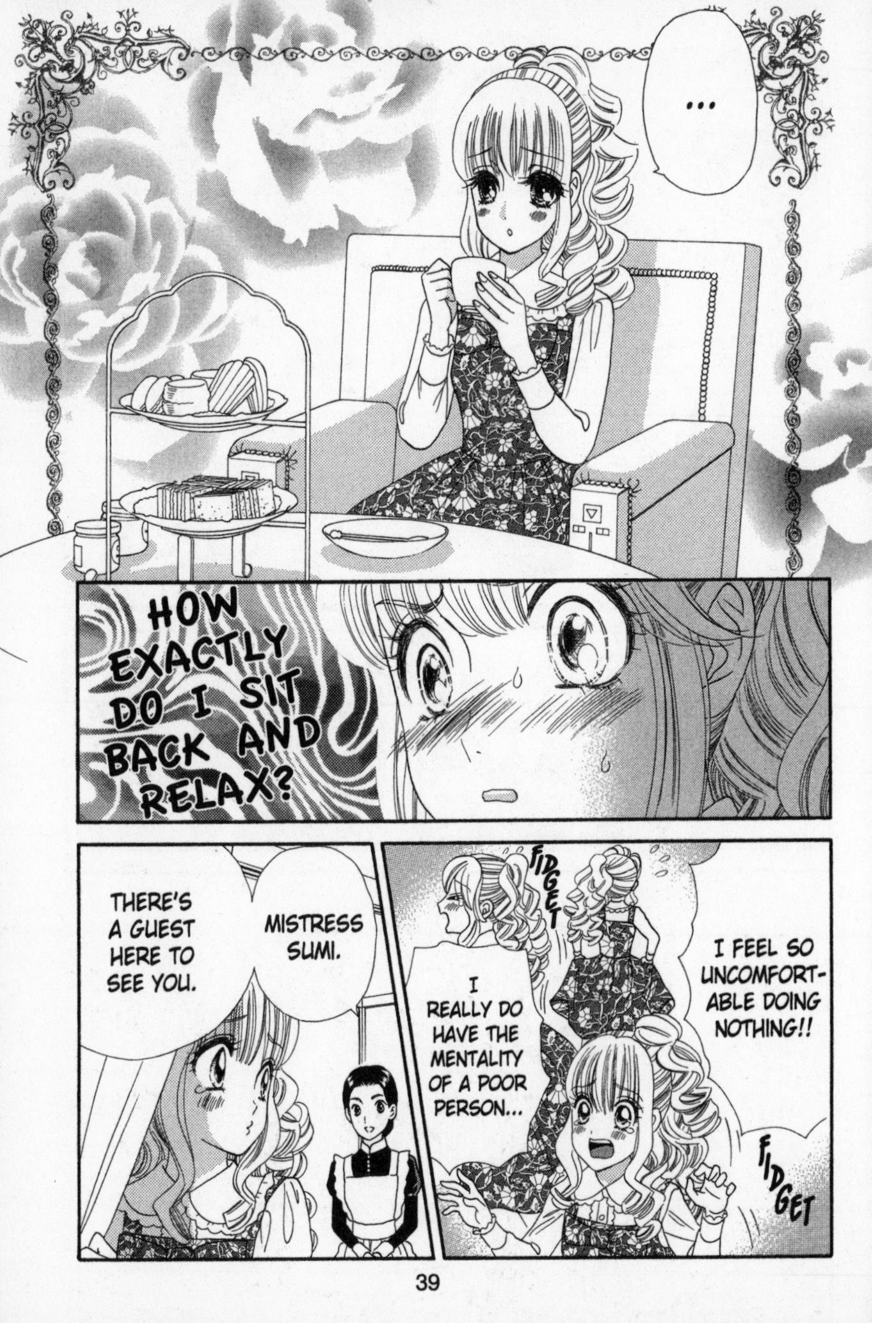
...
HOW EXACTLY DO I SIT BACK AND RELAX?
FIDGET
I FEEL SO UNCOMFORT-ABLE DOING NOTHING!!
I REALLY DO HAVE THE MENTALITY OF A POOR PERSON...
FIDGET
MISTRESS SUMI.
THERE'S A GUEST HERE TO SEE YOU.

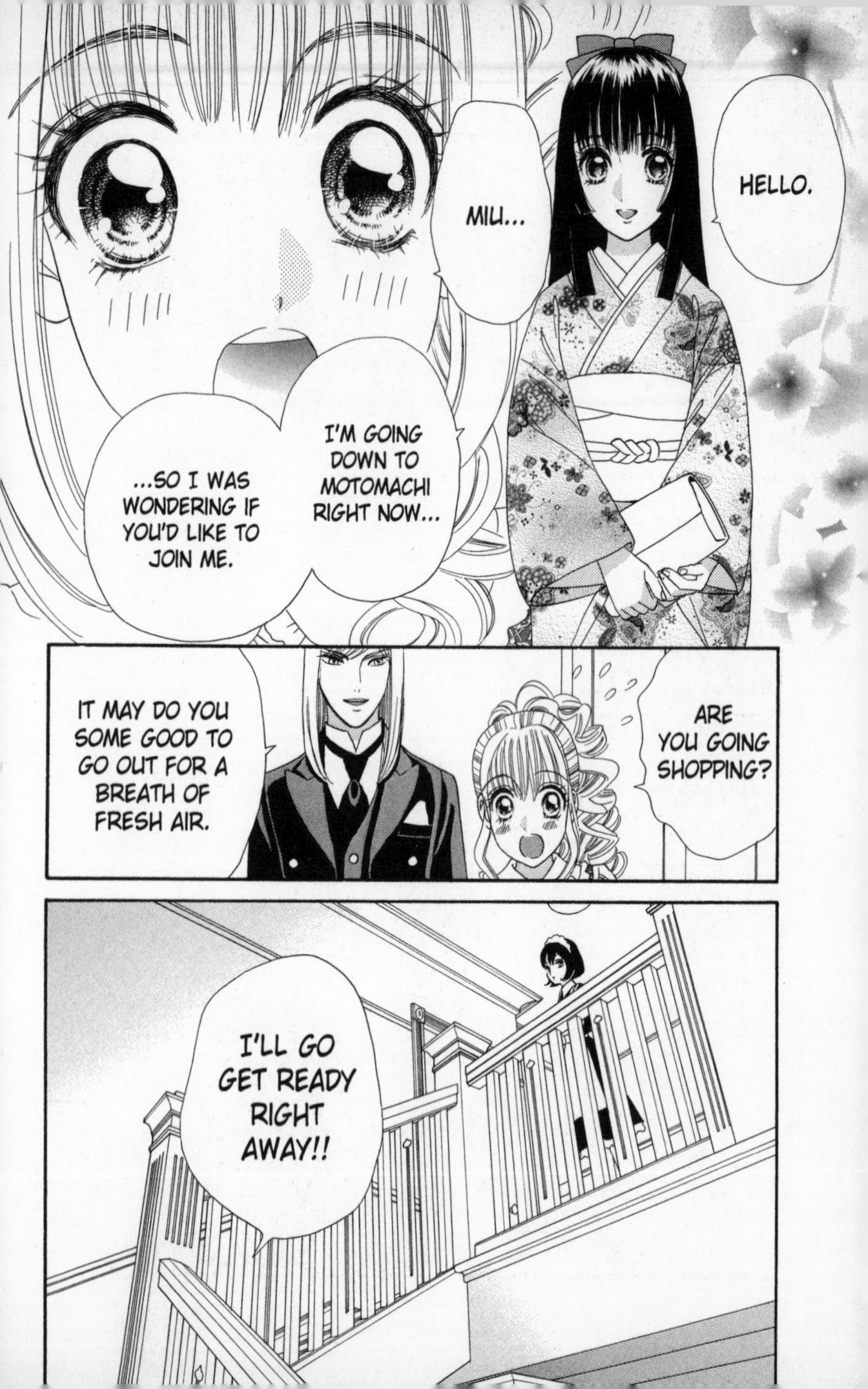
HELLO.
MIU...
I'M GOING DOWN TO MOTOMACHI RIGHT NOW...
...SO I WAS WONDERING IF YOU'D LIKE TO JOIN ME.
ARE YOU GOING SHOPPING?
IT MAY DO YOU SOME GOOD TO GO OUT FOR A BREATH OF FRESH AIR.
I'LL GO GET READY RIGHT AWAY!!

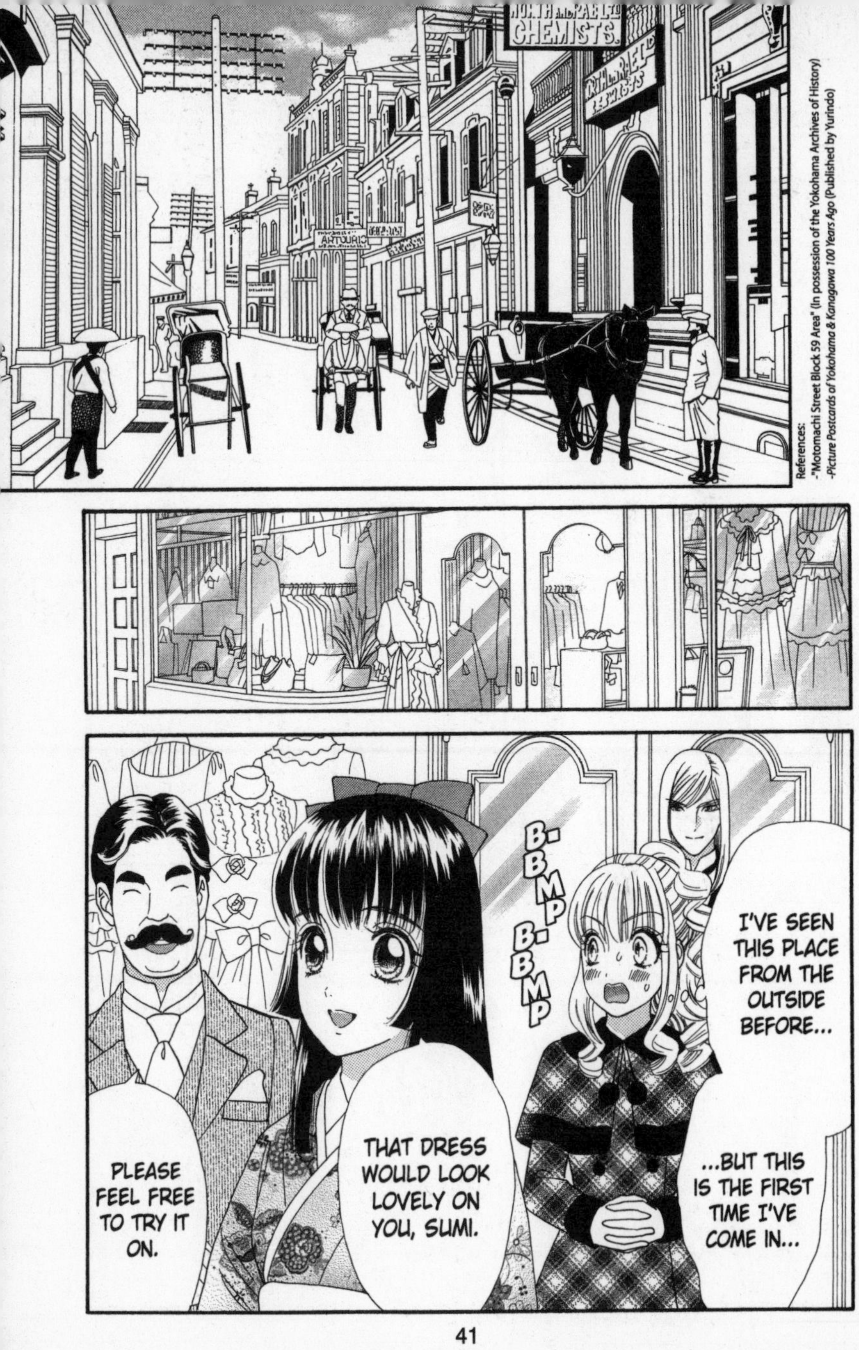
CHEMISTS.
I'VE SEEN THIS PLACE FROM THE OUTSIDE BEFORE...
...BUT THIS IS THE FIRST TIME I'VE COME IN...
B-BMP B-BMP
THAT DRESS WOULD LOOK LOVELY ON YOU, SUMI.
PLEASE FEEL FREE TO TRY IT ON.

References:
-"Motomachi Street Block 59 Area" (In possession of the Yokohama Archives of History)
-*Picture Postcards of Yokohama & Kanagawa 100 Years Ago* (Published by Yurindo)

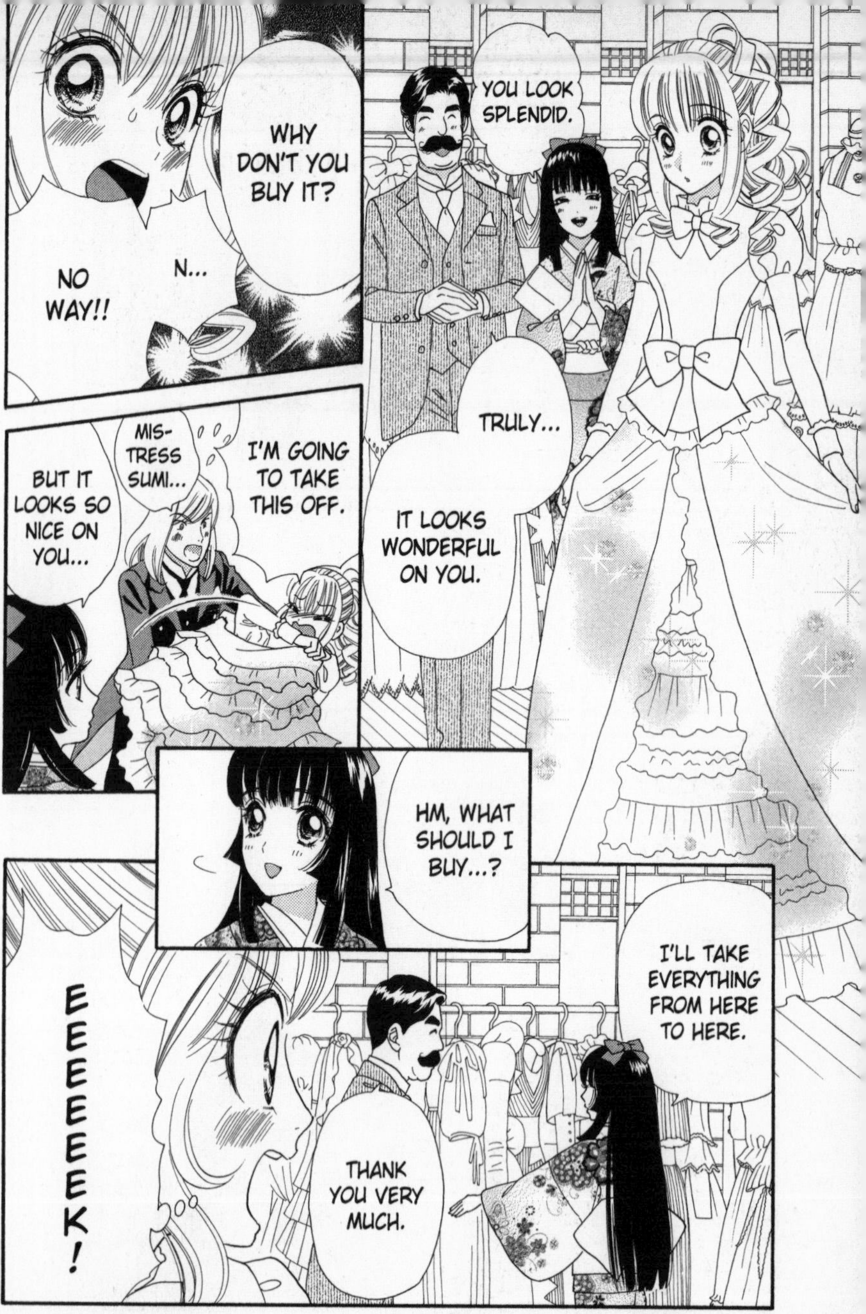
YOU LOOK SPLENDID.
TRULY...
IT LOOKS WONDERFUL ON YOU.
WHY DON'T YOU BUY IT?
N...
NO WAY!!
I'M GOING TO TAKE THIS OFF.
MIS-TRESS SUMI...
BUT IT LOOKS SO NICE ON YOU...
HM, WHAT SHOULD I BUY...?
I'LL TAKE EVERYTHING FROM HERE TO HERE.
THANK YOU VERY MUCH.
EEEEEEEK!

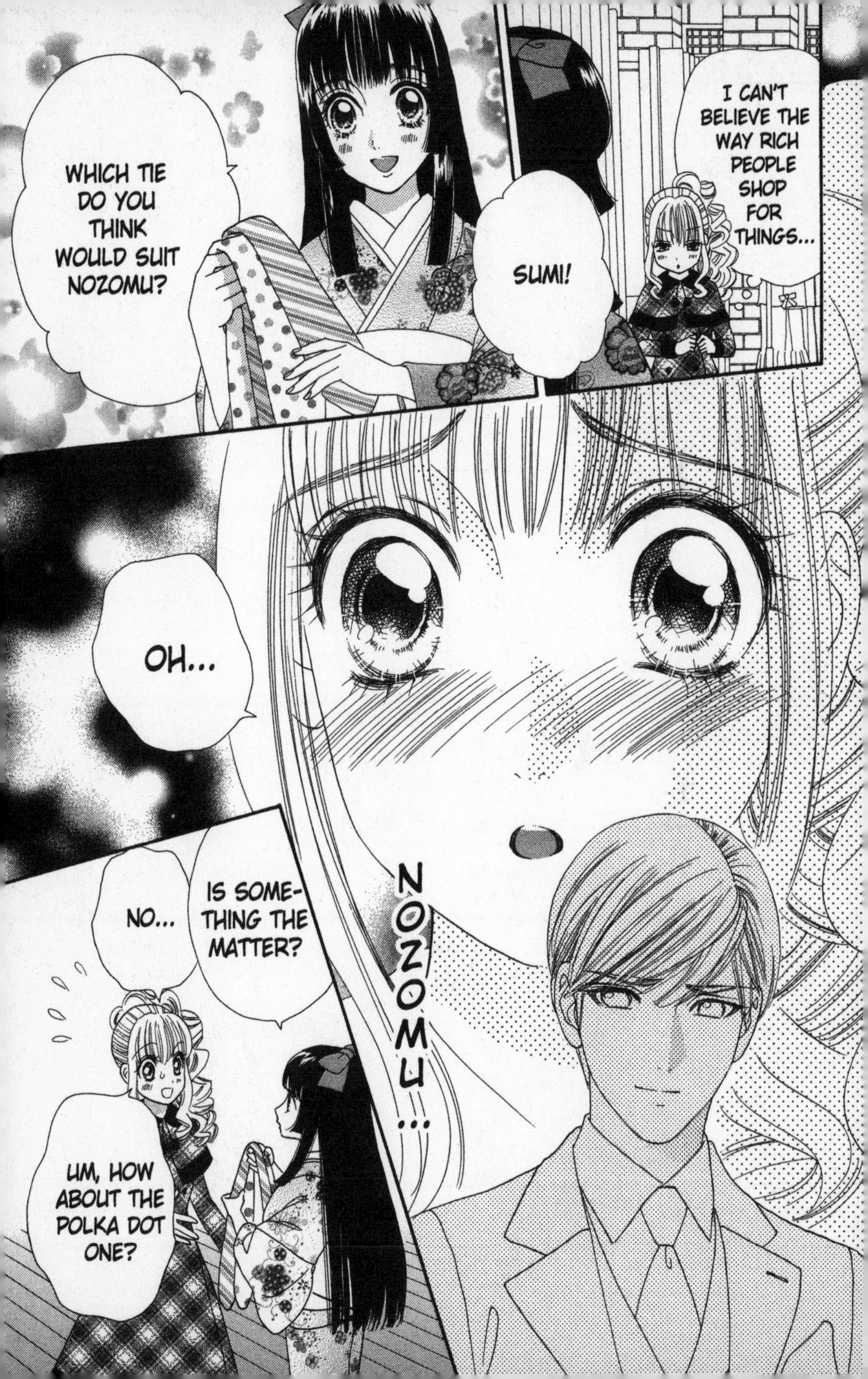
I CAN'T BELIEVE THE WAY RICH PEOPLE SHOP FOR THINGS...
SUMI!
WHICH TIE DO YOU THINK WOULD SUIT NOZOMU?
OH...
NOZOMU...
IS SOME-THING THE MATTER?
NO...
UM, HOW ABOUT THE POLKA DOT ONE?

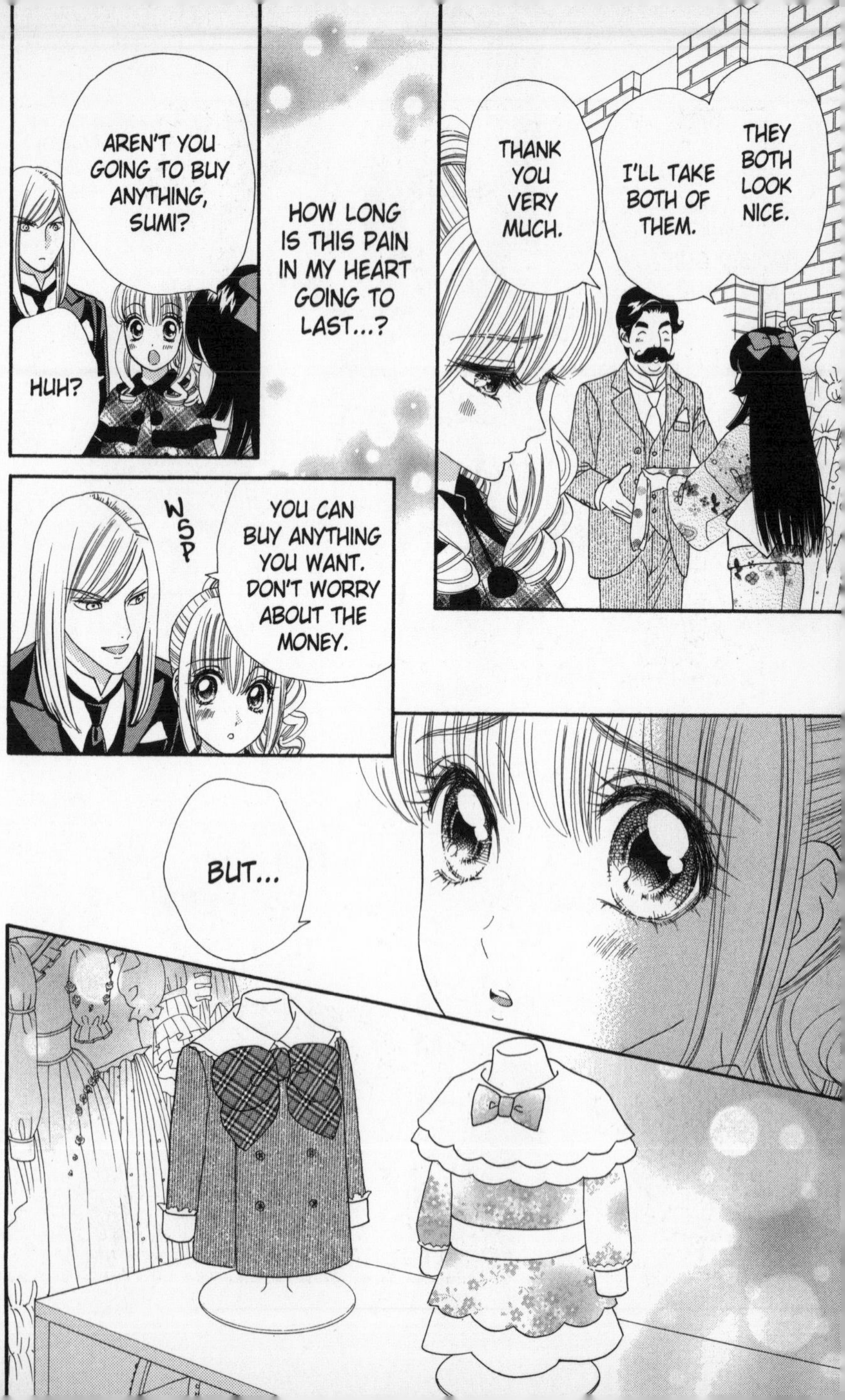
THEY BOTH LOOK NICE.
I'LL TAKE BOTH OF THEM.
THANK YOU VERY MUCH.
HOW LONG IS THIS PAIN IN MY HEART GOING TO LAST...?
AREN'T YOU GOING TO BUY ANYTHING, SUMI?
HUH?
WSP
YOU CAN BUY ANYTHING YOU WANT. DON'T WORRY ABOUT THE MONEY.
BUT...

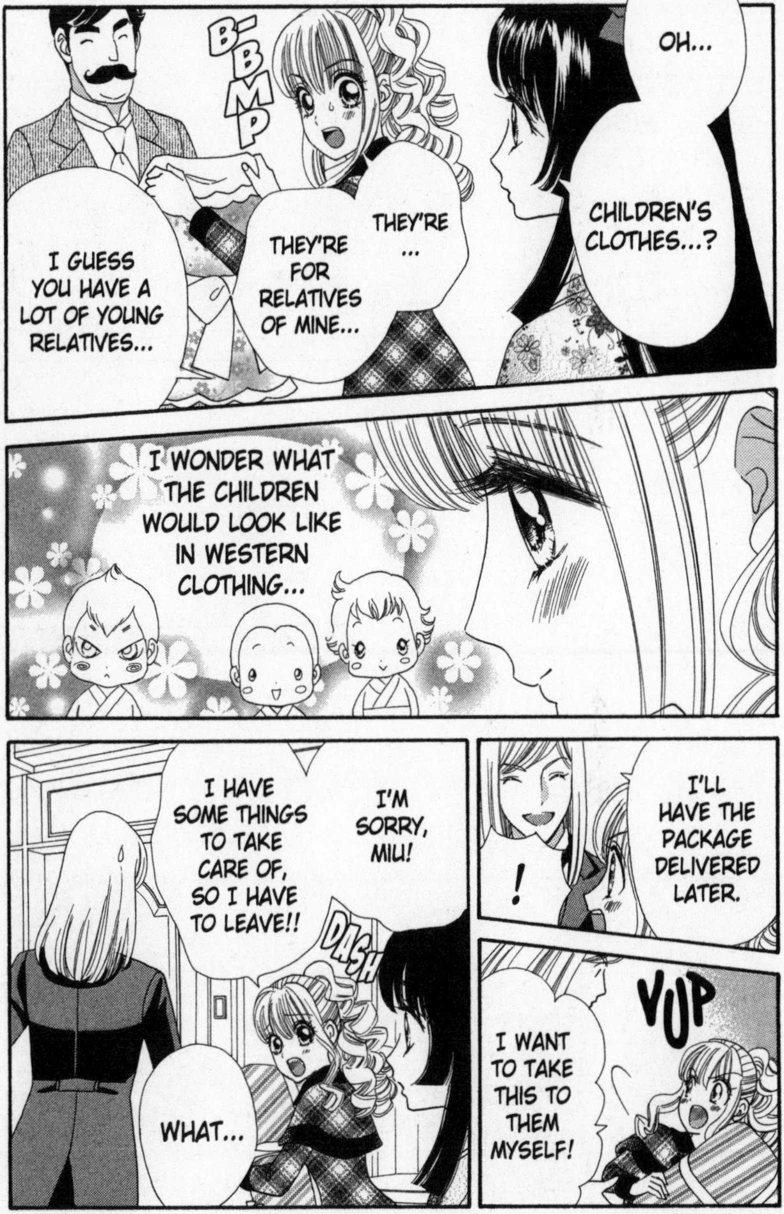
OH...
CHILDREN'S CLOTHES...?
B-BMP
THEY'RE ...
THEY'RE FOR RELATIVES OF MINE...
I GUESS YOU HAVE A LOT OF YOUNG RELATIVES...
I WONDER WHAT THE CHILDREN WOULD LOOK LIKE IN WESTERN CLOTHING...
I'LL HAVE THE PACKAGE DELIVERED LATER.
!
VUP
I WANT TO TAKE THIS TO THEM MYSELF!
I'M SORRY, MIU!
I HAVE SOME THINGS TO TAKE CARE OF, SO I HAVE TO LEAVE!!
DASH
WHAT...

MIS-TRESS SUMI?
I WANT TO GIVE THIS TO THEM RIGHT NOW.
BUT...
I PROMISE IT'LL BE QUICK!
KLANG
KRASH

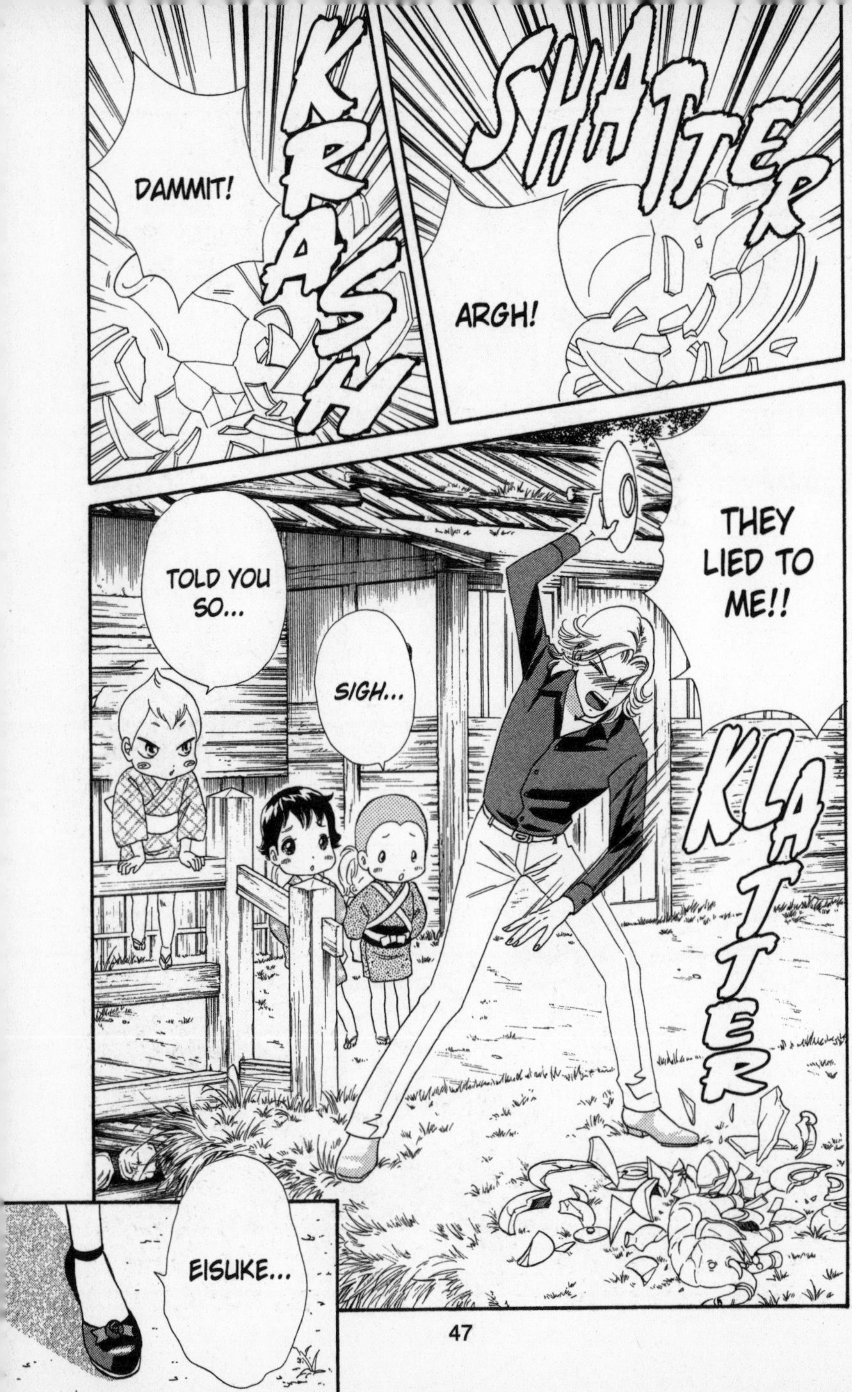
SHATTER
ARGH!
KRASH
DAMMIT!
THEY LIED TO ME!!
KLATTER
SIGH...
TOLD YOU SO...
EISUKE...

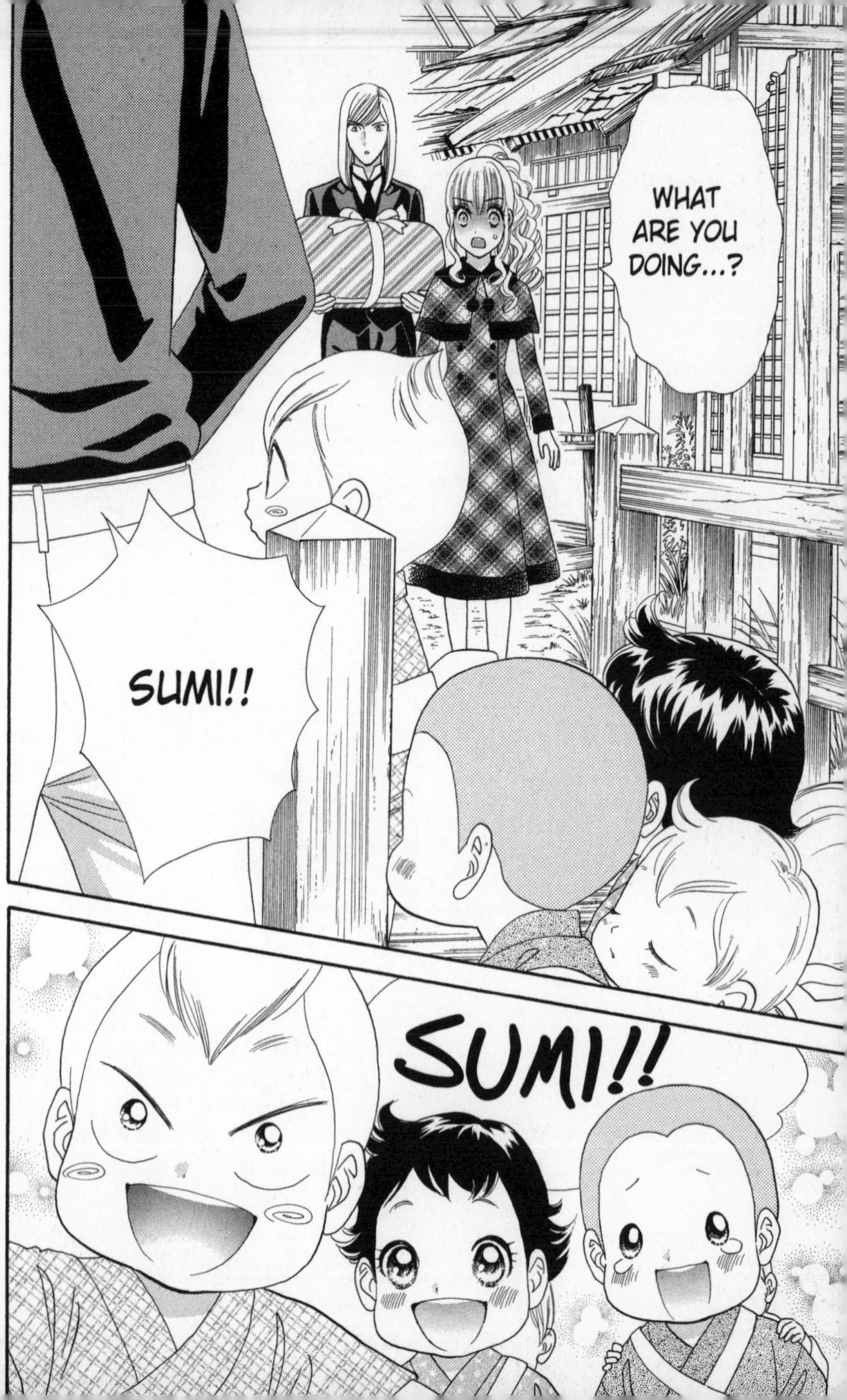
WHAT ARE YOU DOING...?
SUMI!!
SUMI!!

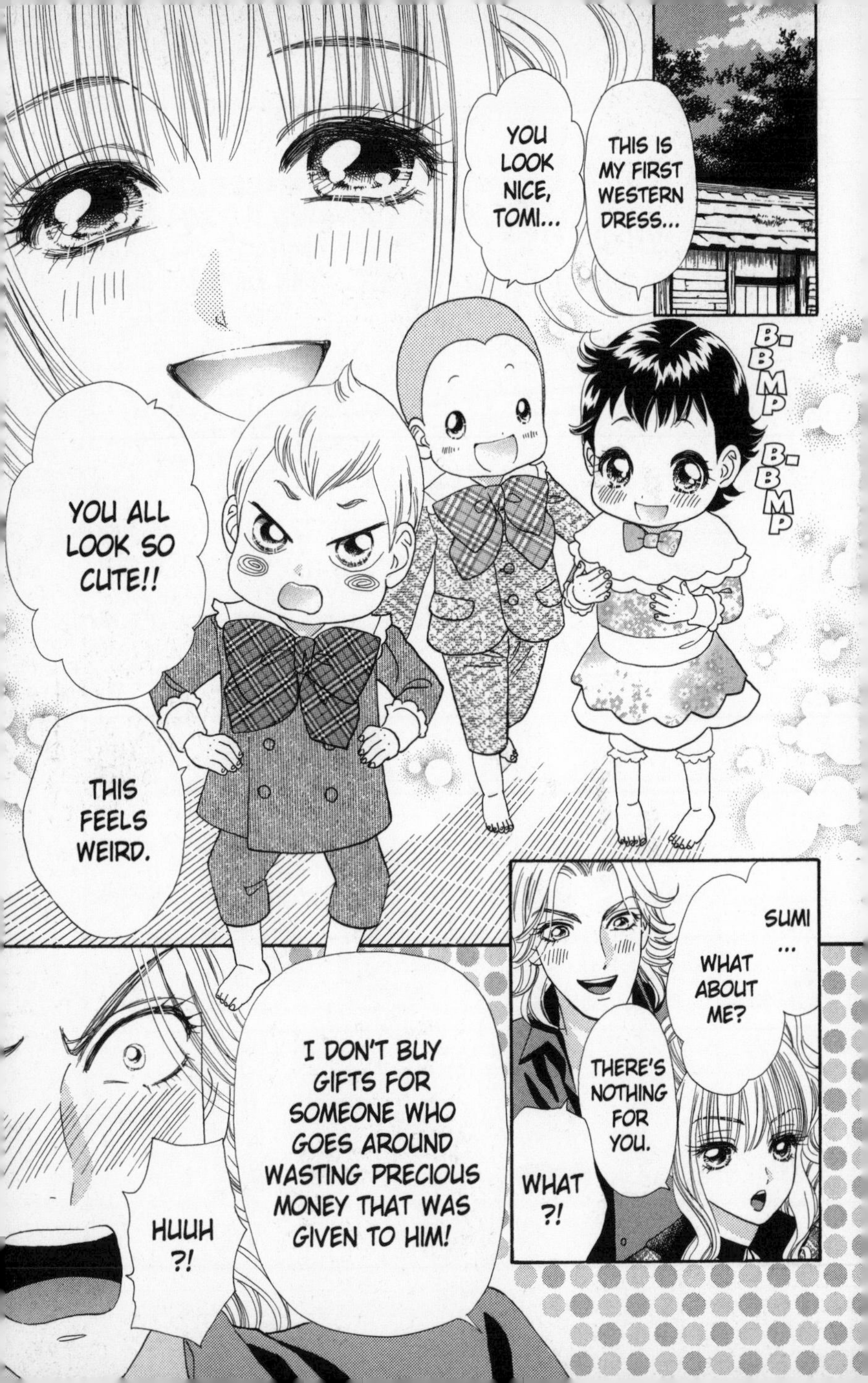
THIS IS MY FIRST WESTERN DRESS...
YOU LOOK NICE, TOMI...
B-BMP
B-BMP
YOU ALL LOOK SO CUTE!!
THIS FEELS WEIRD.
SUMI... WHAT ABOUT ME?
THERE'S NOTHING FOR YOU.
WHAT?!
I DON'T BUY GIFTS FOR SOMEONE WHO GOES AROUND WASTING PRECIOUS MONEY THAT WAS GIVEN TO HIM!
HUUH?!

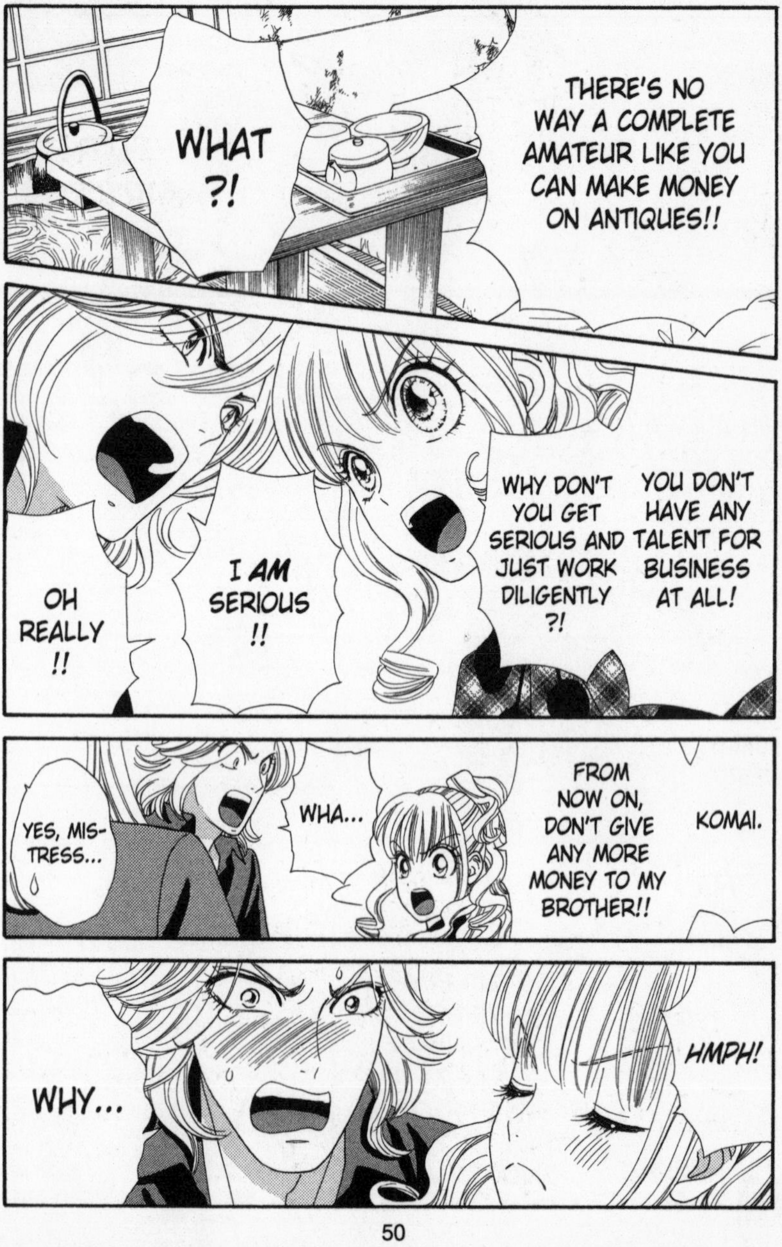
THERE'S NO WAY A COMPLETE AMATEUR LIKE YOU CAN MAKE MONEY ON ANTIQUES!!
WHAT ?!
YOU DON'T HAVE ANY TALENT FOR BUSINESS AT ALL!
WHY DON'T YOU GET SERIOUS AND JUST WORK DILIGENTLY ?!
I *AM* SERIOUS !!
OH REALLY !!
KOMAI.
FROM NOW ON, DON'T GIVE ANY MORE MONEY TO MY BROTHER!!
WHA...
YES, MIS-TRESS...
HMPH!
WHY...

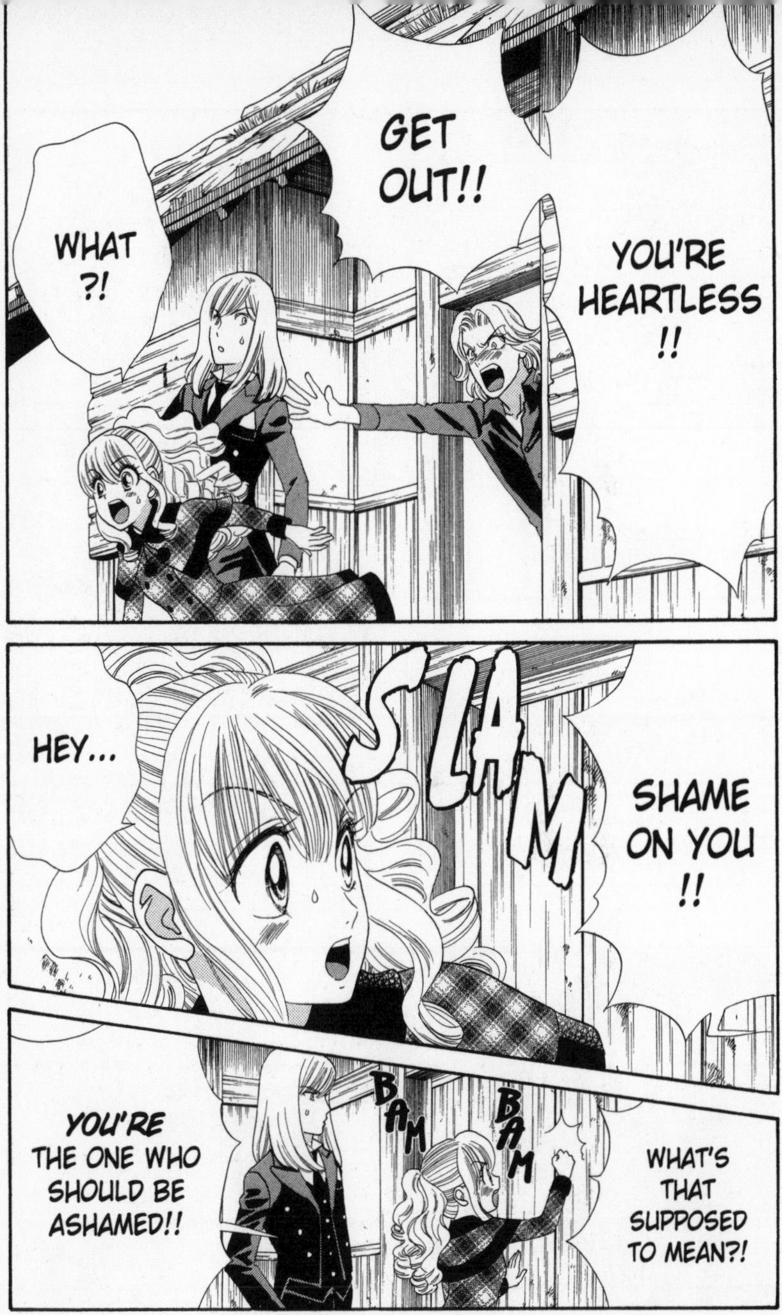
GET OUT!!
YOU'RE HEARTLESS !!
WHAT ?!
SLAM
SHAME ON YOU !!
HEY...
WHAT'S THAT SUPPOSED TO MEAN?!
BAM BAM
YOU'RE THE ONE WHO SHOULD BE ASHAMED!!

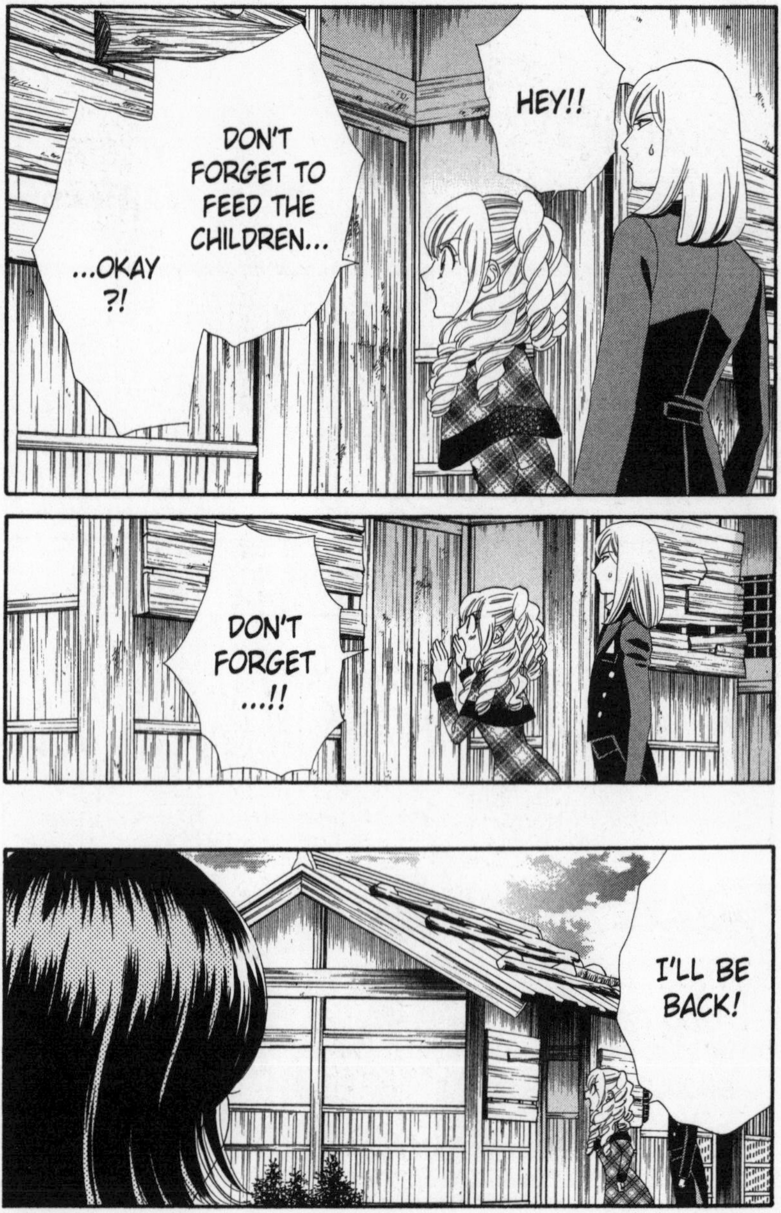
HEY!!
DON'T FORGET TO FEED THE CHILDREN...
...OKAY ?!
DON'T FORGET ...!!
I'LL BE BACK!

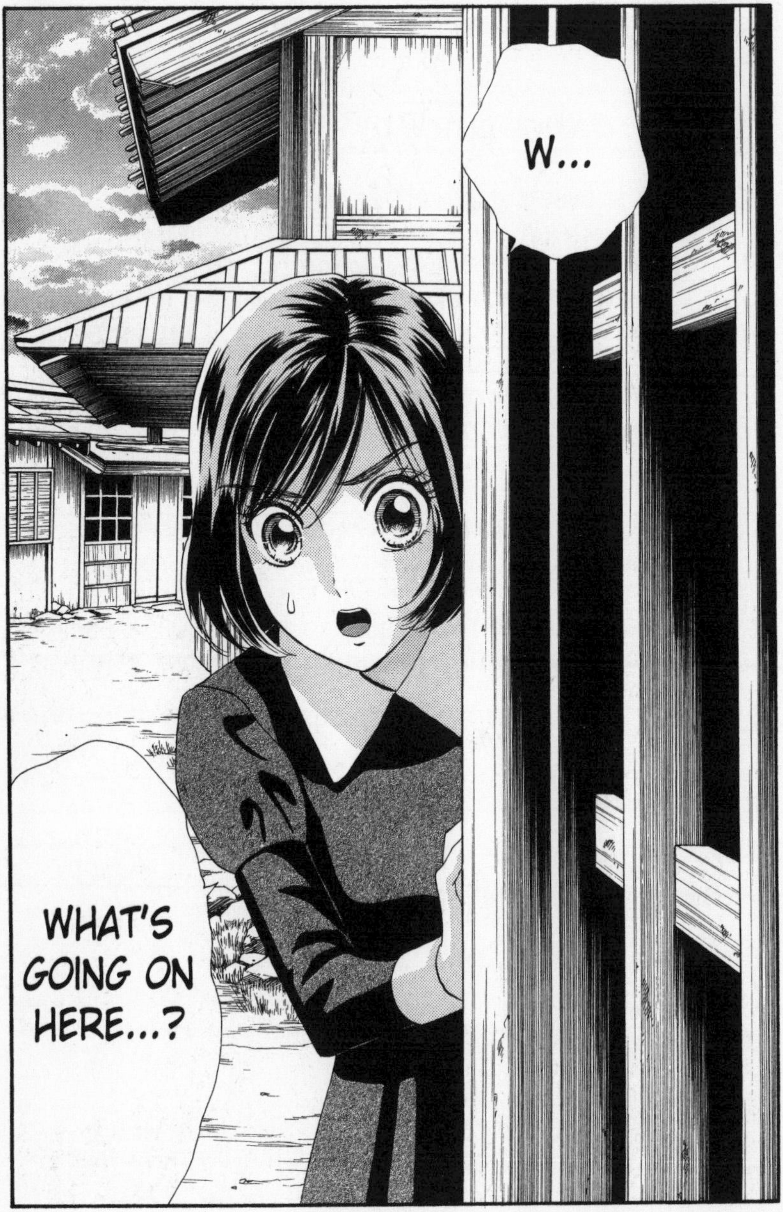
W...
WHAT'S GOING ON HERE...?

No. 2

RANDOM CHITCHAT!

Date . .

❀ I GOT LOVEBIRDS AS PETS BECAUSE I "NEEDED" THEM FOR A MANGA. THE FORMER CHIEF EDITOR OF *MARGARET* (THE PERSON WHO'D ASKED ME TO CREATE SOMETHING "GORGEOUS" WHO I WROTE ABOUT IN VOLUME 1) HAD BEEN TRANSFERRED TO *RIBON* MAGAZINE, AND I WAS ASKED TO DO A ONE-SHOT MANGA IN IT. SINCE A LOVEBIRD APPEARS IN THE STORY, I DECIDED TO GET SOME LOVEBIRDS SO THAT I COULD OBSERVE THEIR BEHAVIOR.

❀ I ALWAYS THOUGHT I WAS A COOL AND COMPOSED PERSON WHEN IT CAME TO PETS, BUT THEY ARE JUST ADORABLE!! AT FIRST I WAS TOO SCARED TO EVEN TOUCH THEM, BUT THEN I STARTED TO GET USED TO THEM. NOW I'VE BECOME CLOSE ENOUGH TO THEM WHERE THEY'LL COME PERCH ON MY HAND.

IF I DRAW THEM REALISTICALLY, THEY LOOK LIKE THIS.

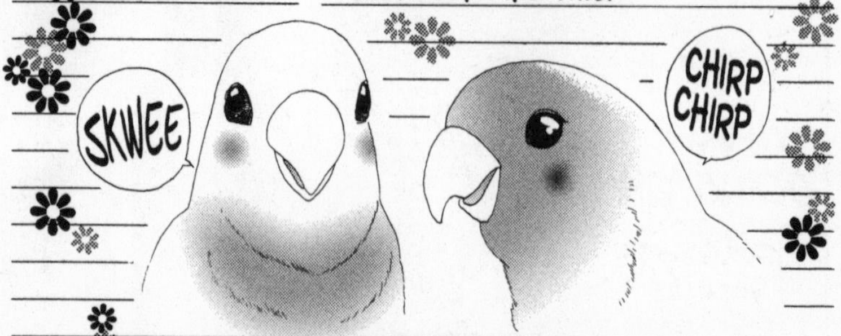
SKWEE
CHIRP CHIRP

PITCH AND MAMEZO'S BEAKS LOOK LIKE THEY ALWAYS HAVE A SLIGHT SMILE ON THEIR FACES...

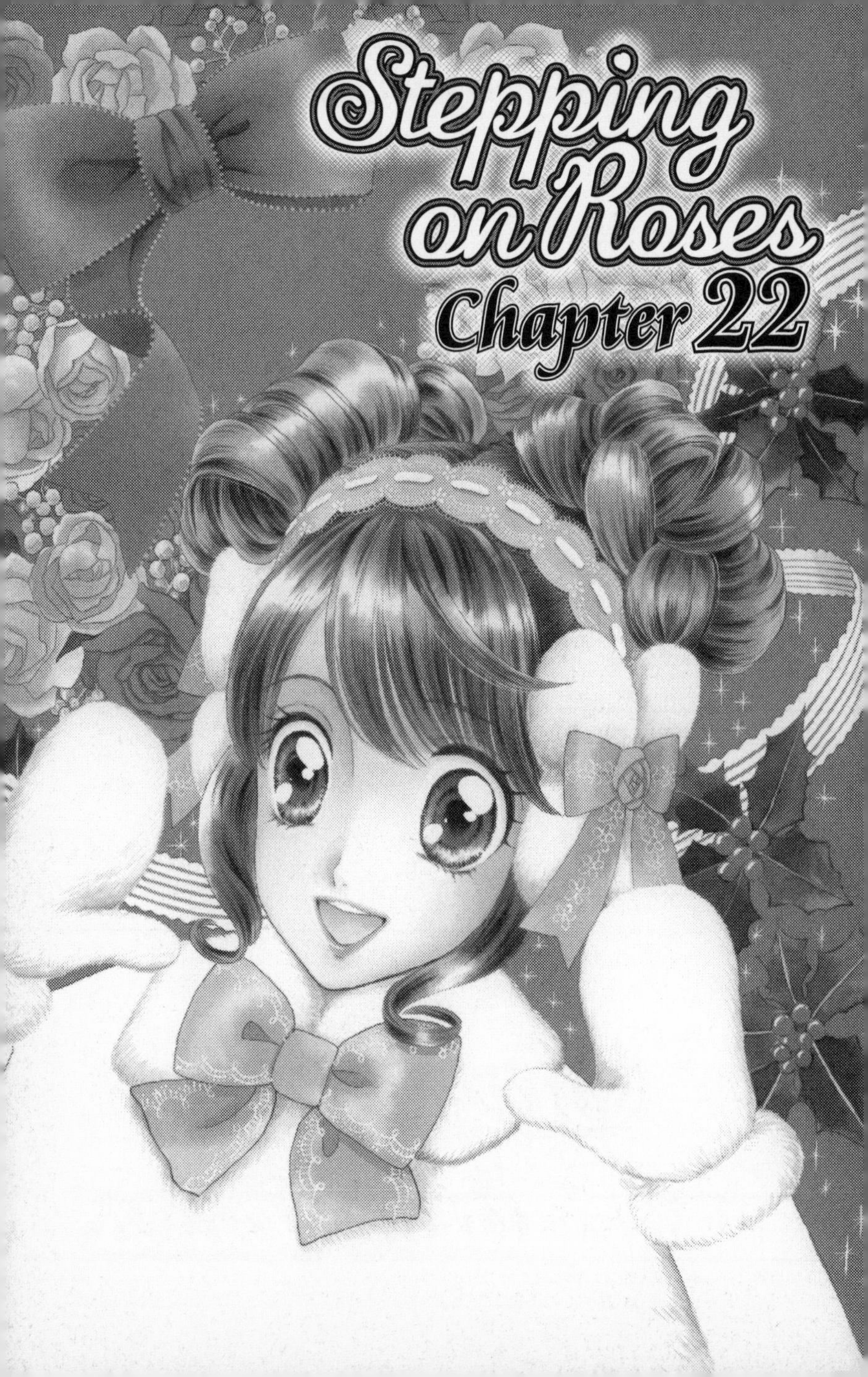
Stepping on Roses
Chapter 22

Stepping on Roses

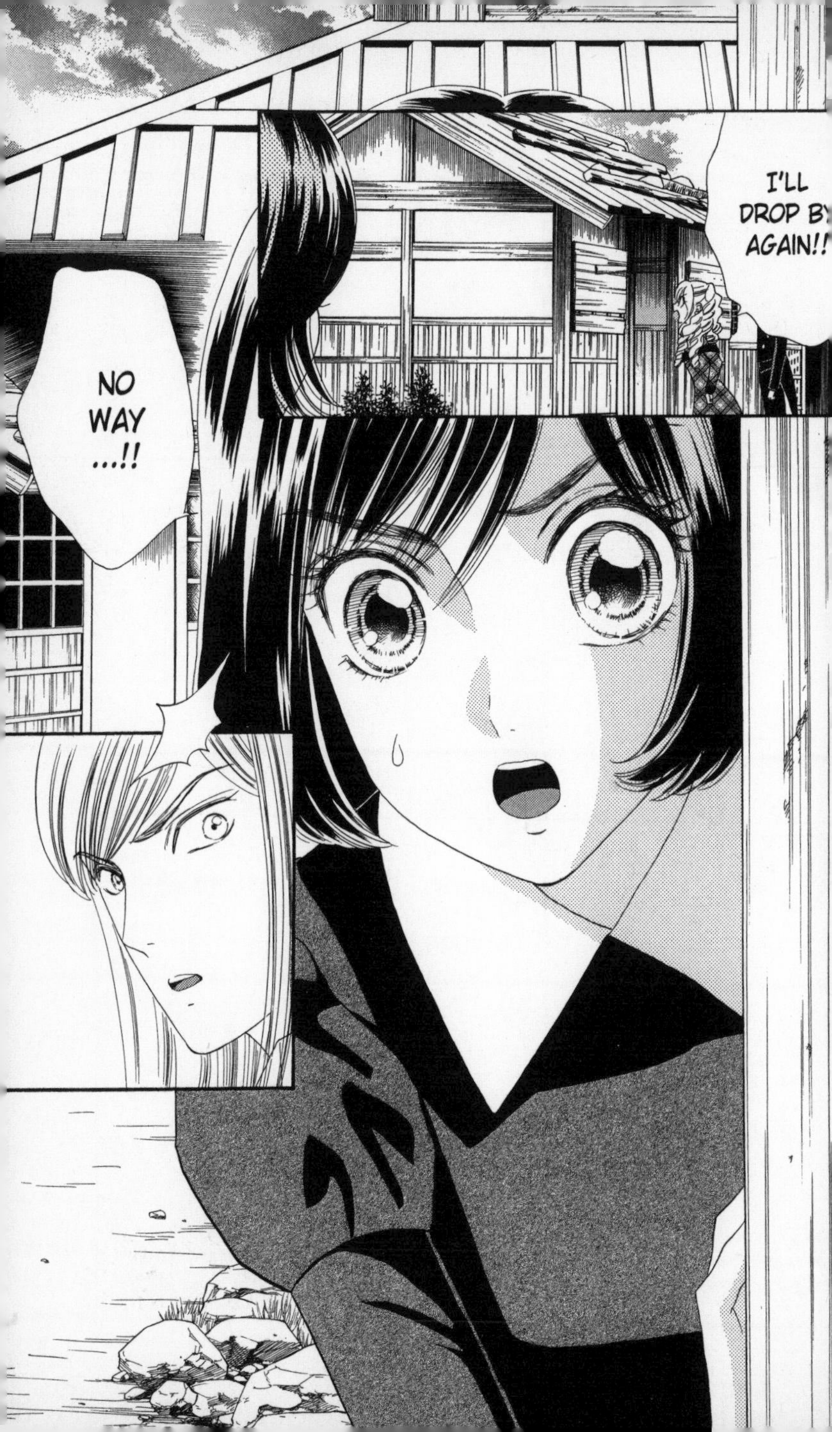
I'LL DROP BY AGAIN!!
NO WAY ...!!

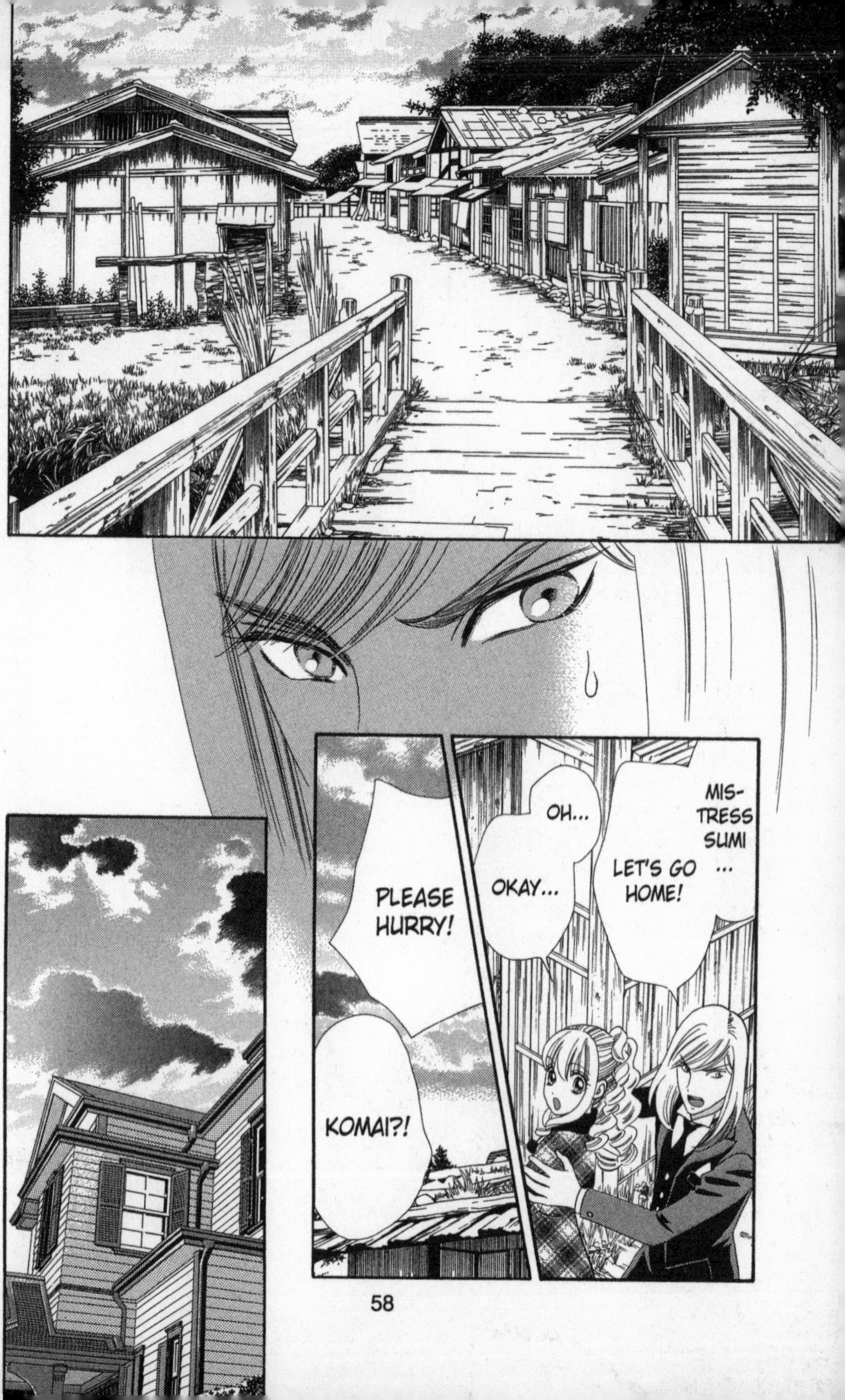
MIS-TRESS SUMI ...
LET'S GO HOME!
OH...
OKAY...
PLEASE HURRY!
KOMAI?!

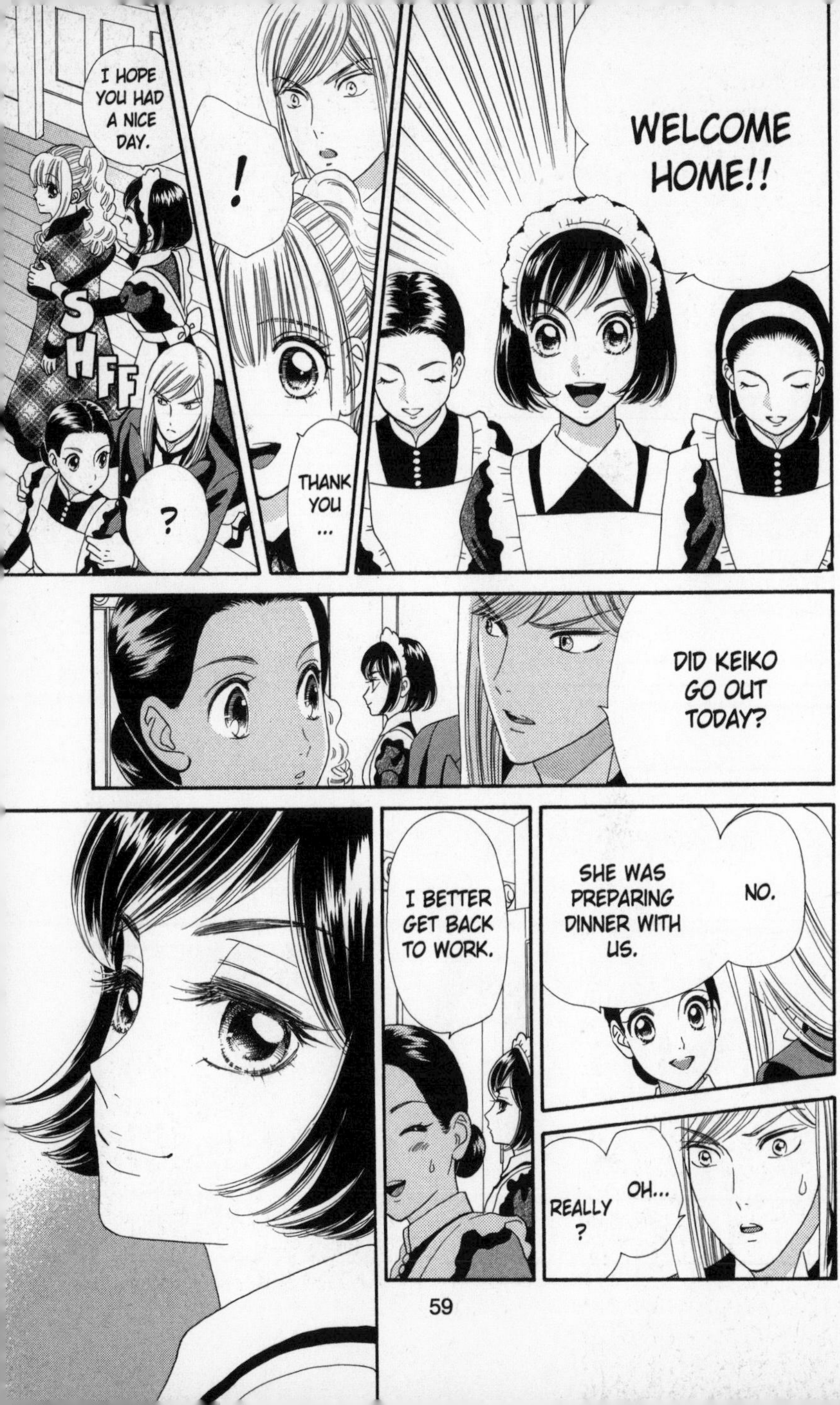
WELCOME HOME!!
!
THANK YOU ...
I HOPE YOU HAD A NICE DAY.
SHFF
?
DID KEIKO GO OUT TODAY?
NO.
SHE WAS PREPARING DINNER WITH US.
OH...
REALLY ?
I BETTER GET BACK TO WORK.

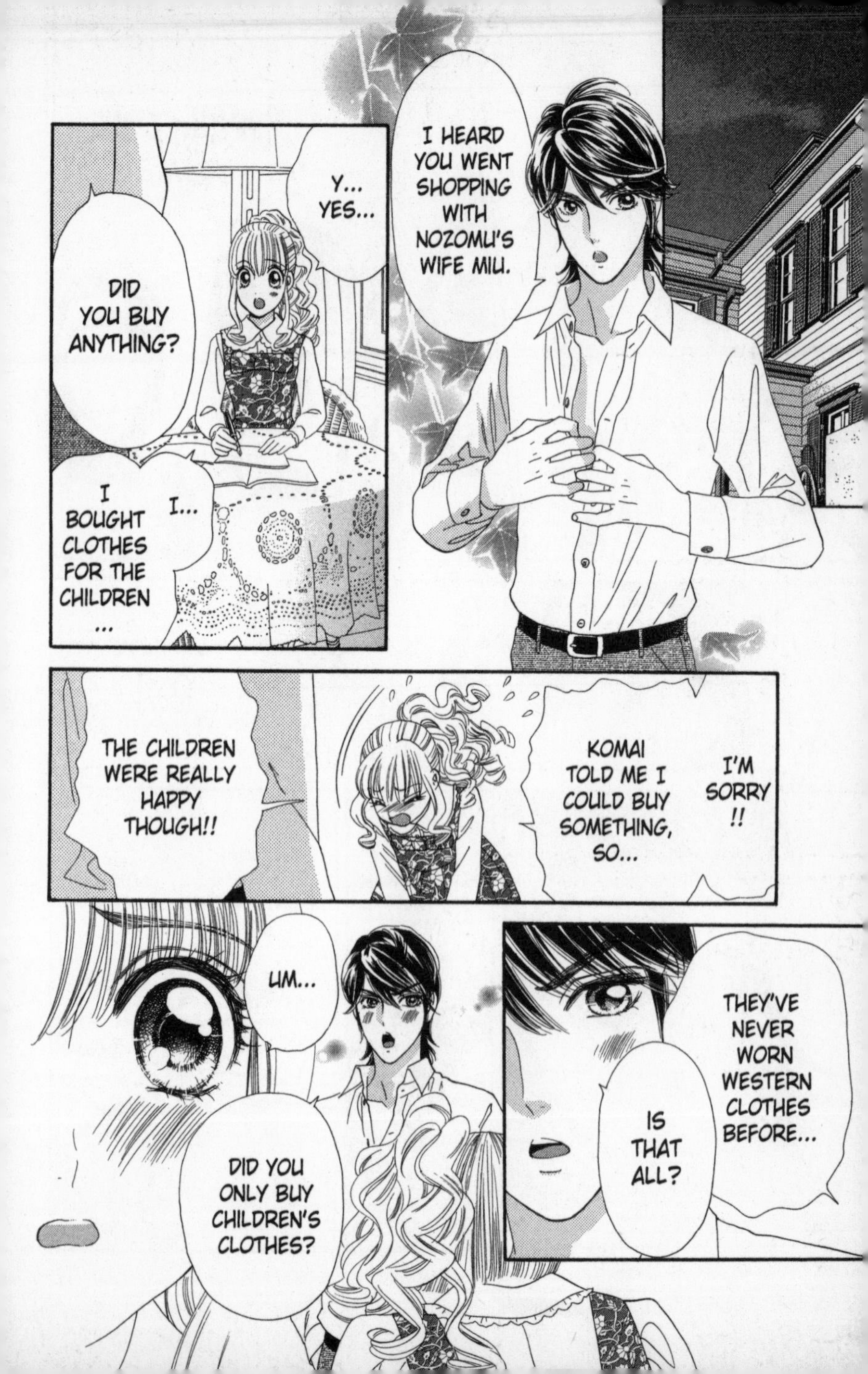
I HEARD YOU WENT SHOPPING WITH NOZOMU'S WIFE MIU.
Y... YES...
DID YOU BUY ANYTHING?
I...
I BOUGHT CLOTHES FOR THE CHILDREN ...
I'M SORRY !!
KOMAI TOLD ME I COULD BUY SOMETHING, SO...
THE CHILDREN WERE REALLY HAPPY THOUGH!!
THEY'VE NEVER WORN WESTERN CLOTHES BEFORE...
IS THAT ALL?
UM...
DID YOU ONLY BUY CHILDREN'S CLOTHES?

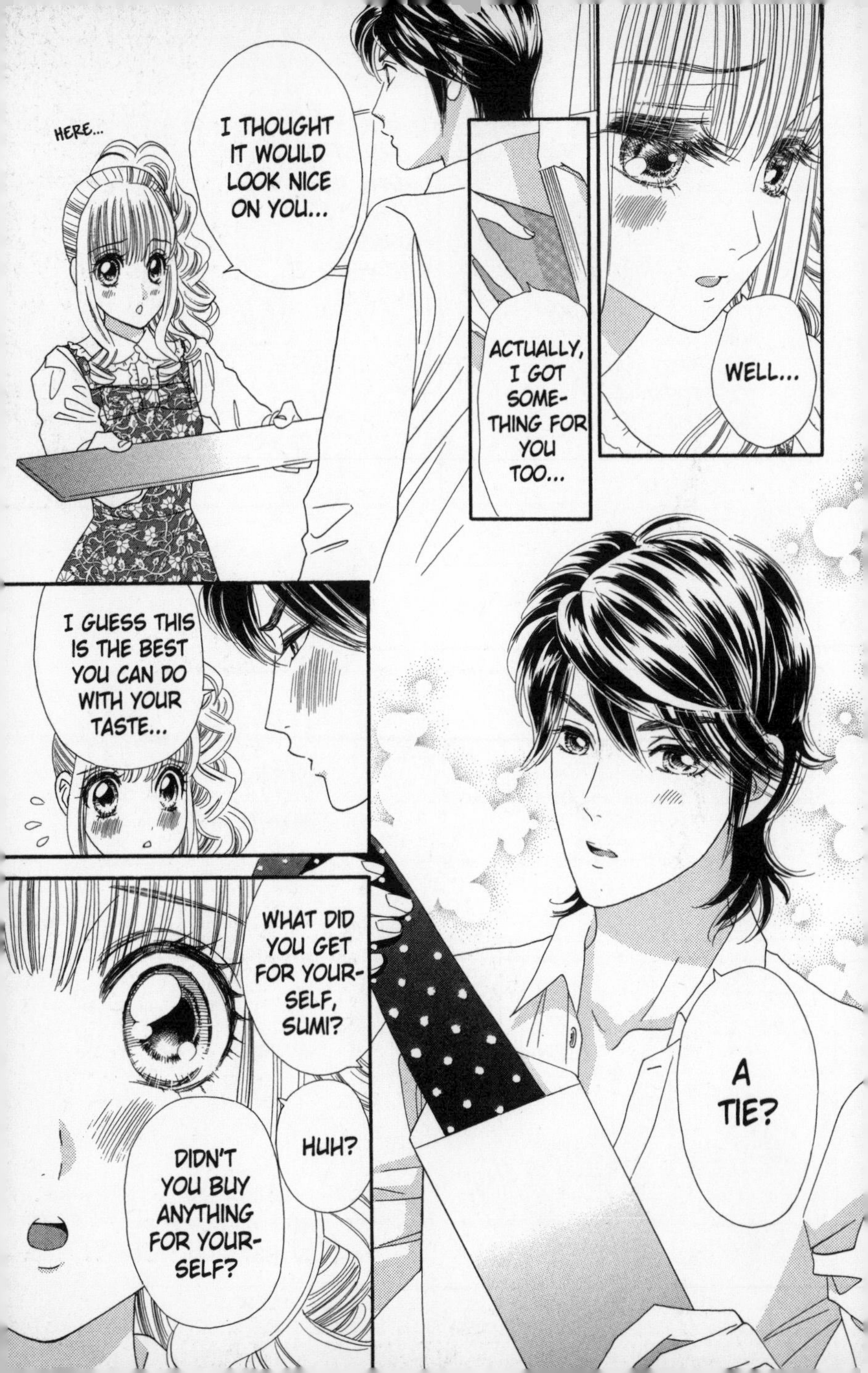
WELL...
ACTUALLY, I GOT SOME-THING FOR YOU TOO...
I THOUGHT IT WOULD LOOK NICE ON YOU...
HERE...
A TIE?
I GUESS THIS IS THE BEST YOU CAN DO WITH YOUR TASTE...
WHAT DID YOU GET FOR YOUR-SELF, SUMI?
HUH?
DIDN'T YOU BUY ANYTHING FOR YOUR-SELF?

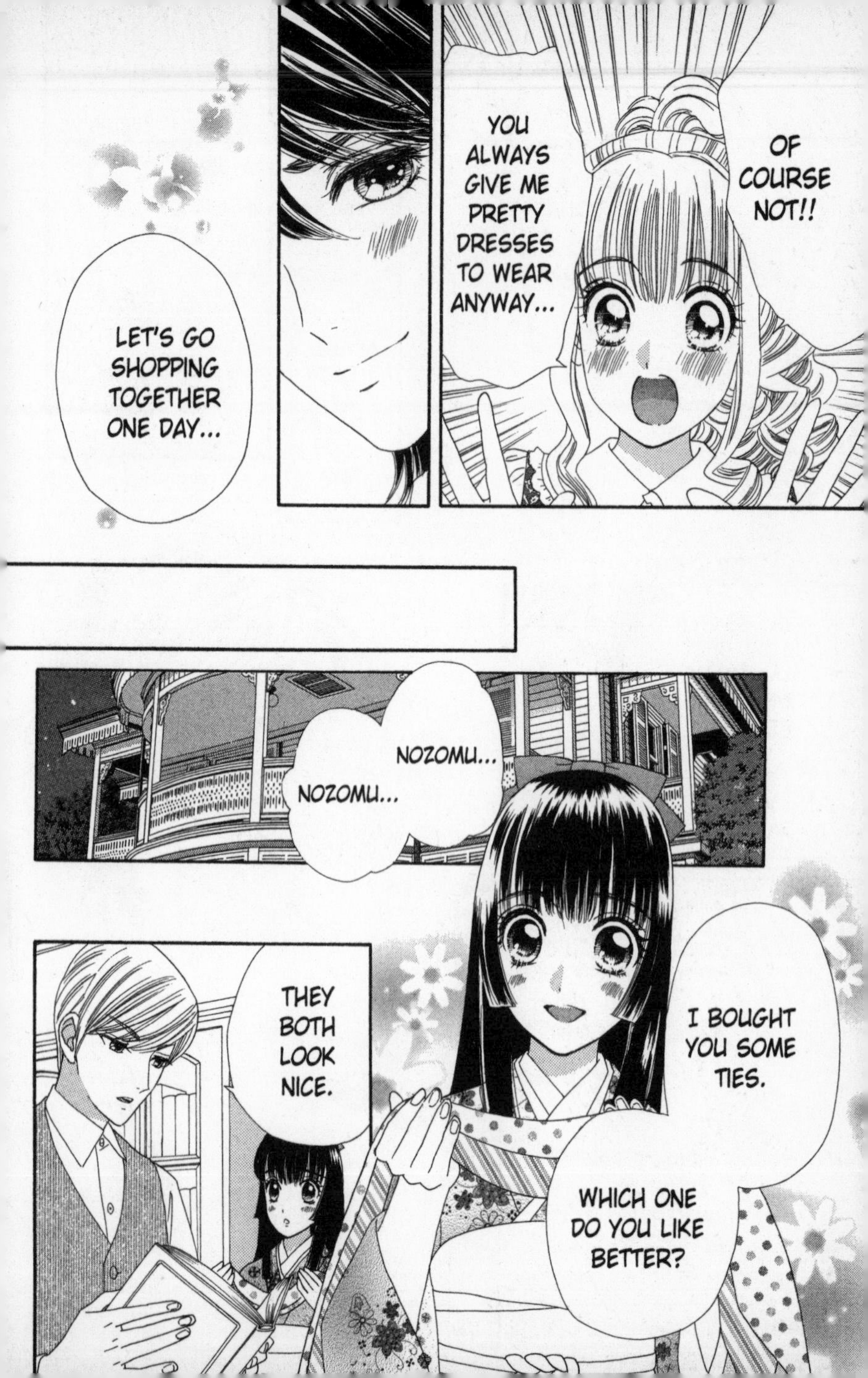
OF COURSE NOT!!
YOU ALWAYS GIVE ME PRETTY DRESSES TO WEAR ANYWAY...
LET'S GO SHOPPING TOGETHER ONE DAY...
NOZOMU...
NOZOMU...
I BOUGHT YOU SOME TIES.
WHICH ONE DO YOU LIKE BETTER?
THEY BOTH LOOK NICE.

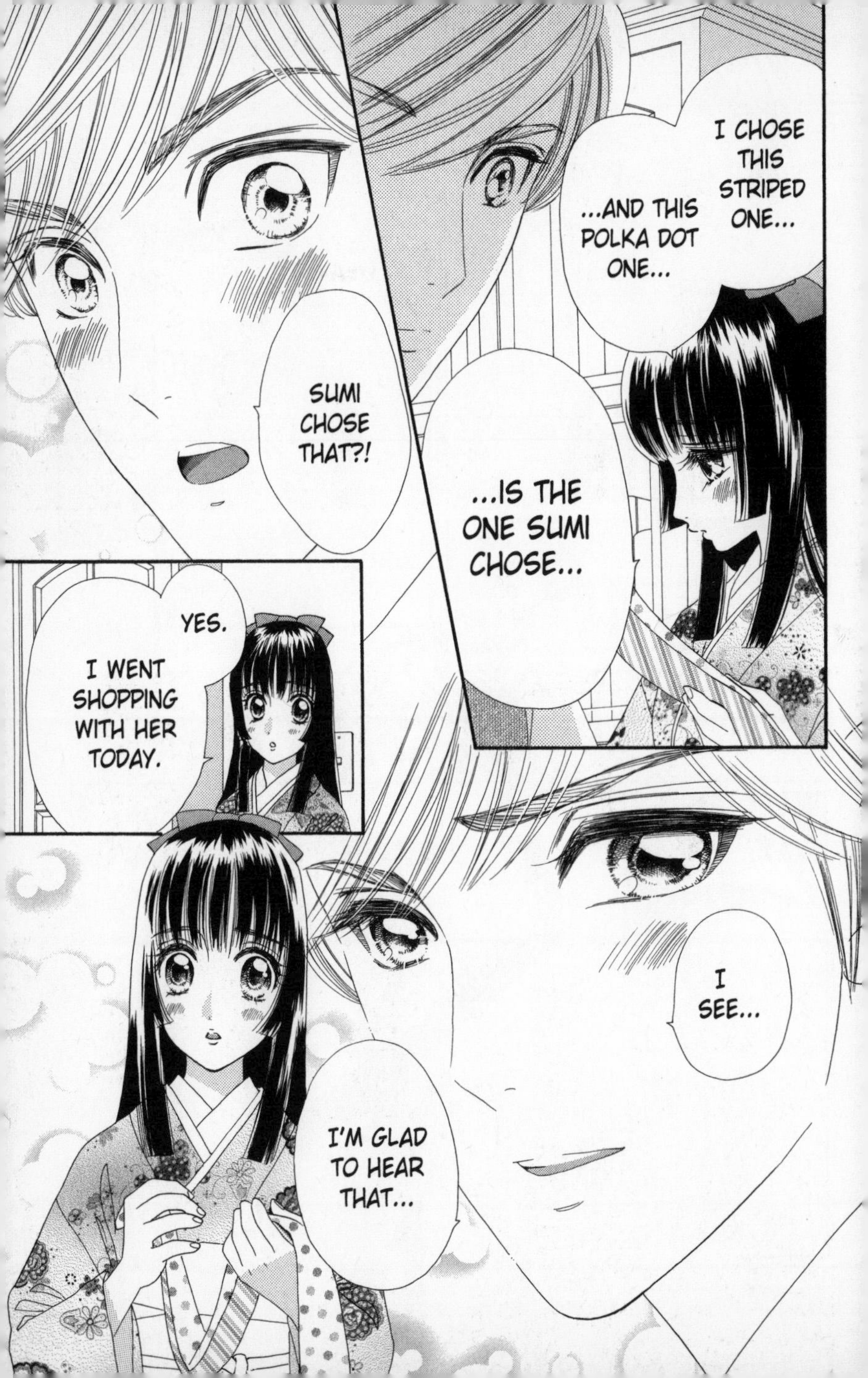
I CHOSE THIS STRIPED ONE...
...AND THIS POLKA DOT ONE...
...IS THE ONE SUMI CHOSE...
SUMI CHOSE THAT?!
YES.
I WENT SHOPPING WITH HER TODAY.
I SEE...
I'M GLAD TO HEAR THAT...

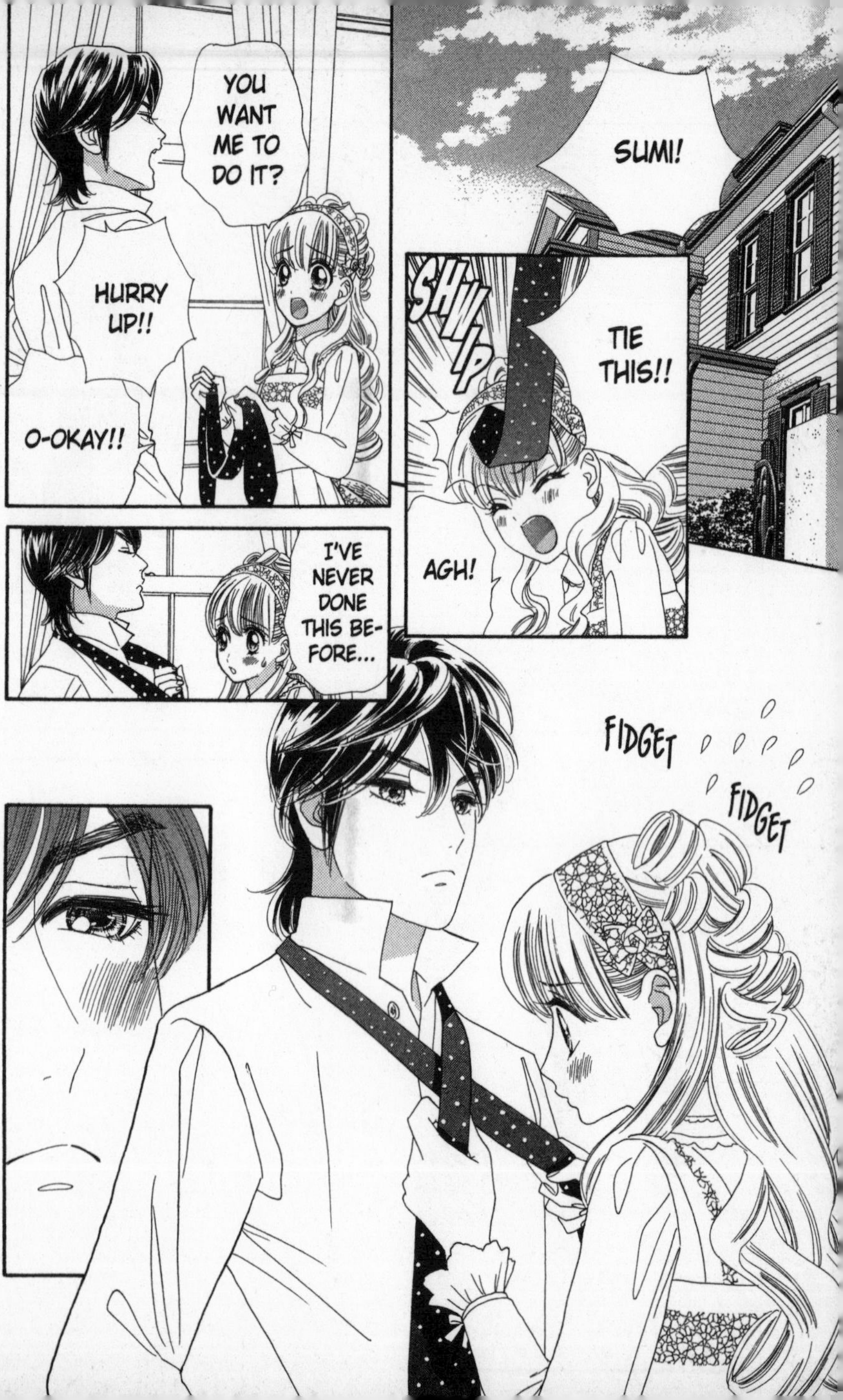
SUMI!
SHWIP
TIE THIS!!
AGH!
YOU WANT ME TO DO IT?
HURRY UP!!
O-OKAY!!
I'VE NEVER DONE THIS BE-FORE...
FIDGET
FIDGET

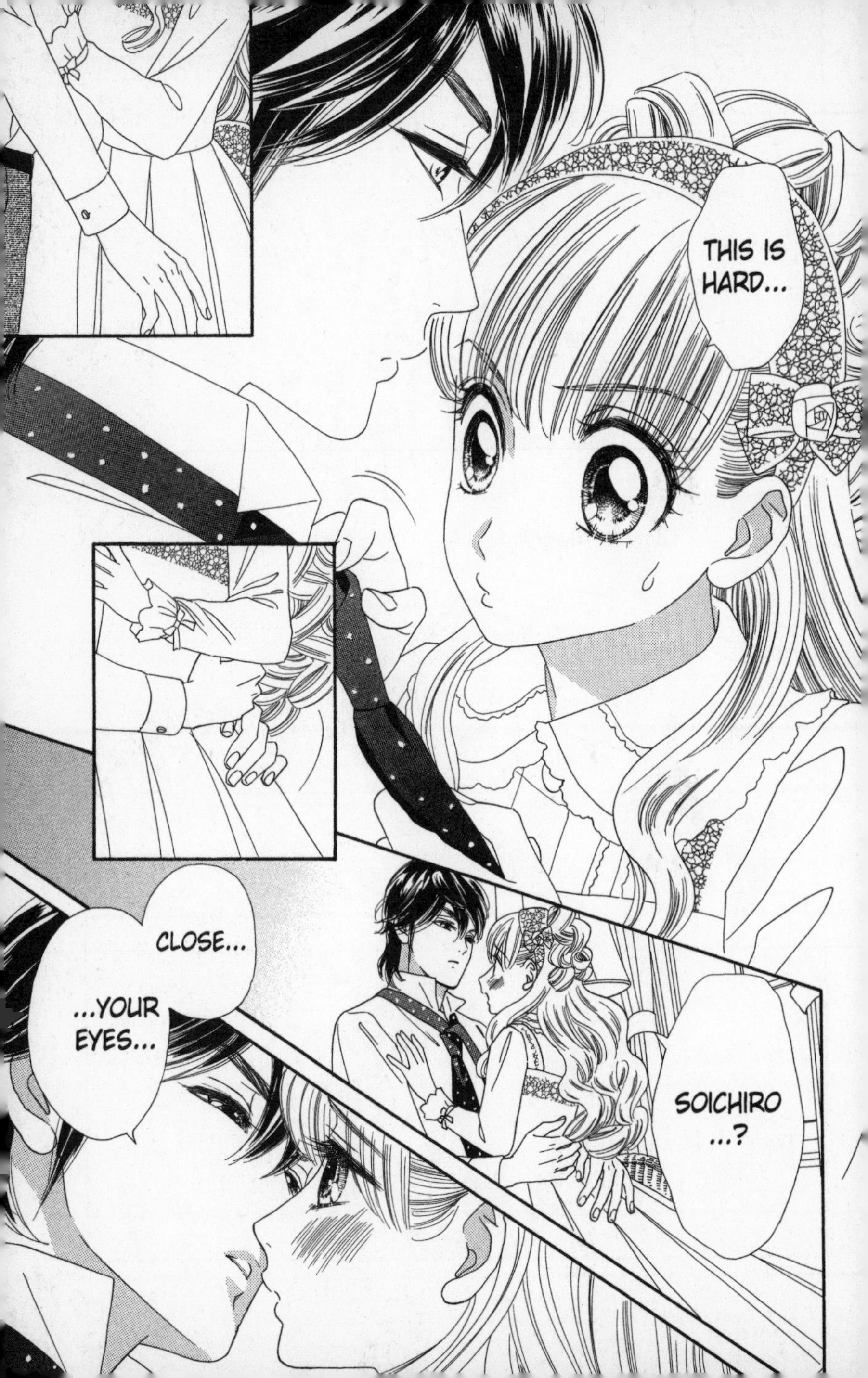
THIS IS HARD...
SOICHIRO ...?
CLOSE...
...YOUR EYES...

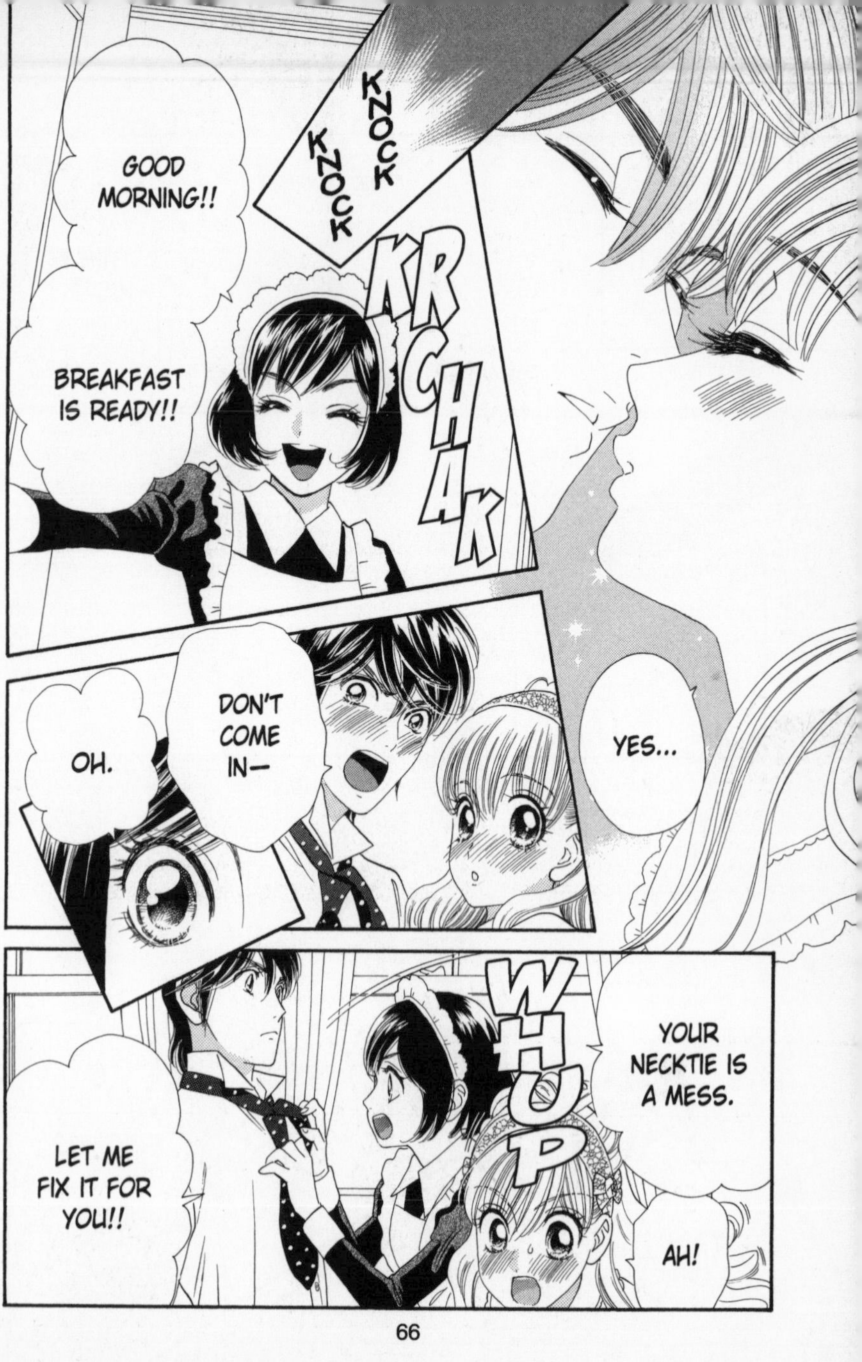
YES...
KNOCK KNOCK
KRCHAK
GOOD MORNING!!
BREAKFAST IS READY!!
DON'T COME IN—
OH.
YOUR NECKTIE IS A MESS.
WHUP
AH!
LET ME FIX IT FOR YOU!!

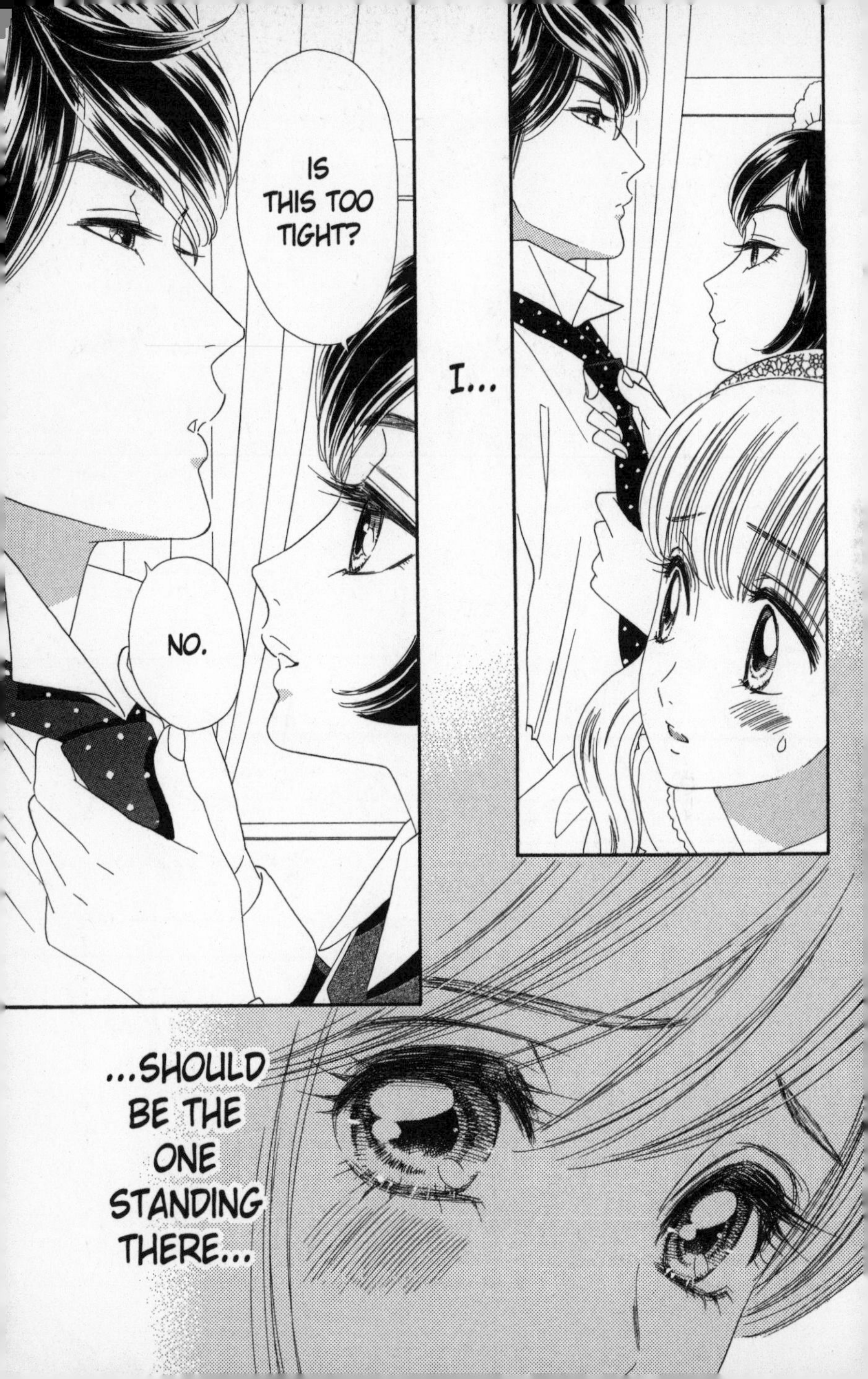
I...
IS THIS TOO TIGHT?
NO.
...SHOULD BE THE ONE STANDING THERE...

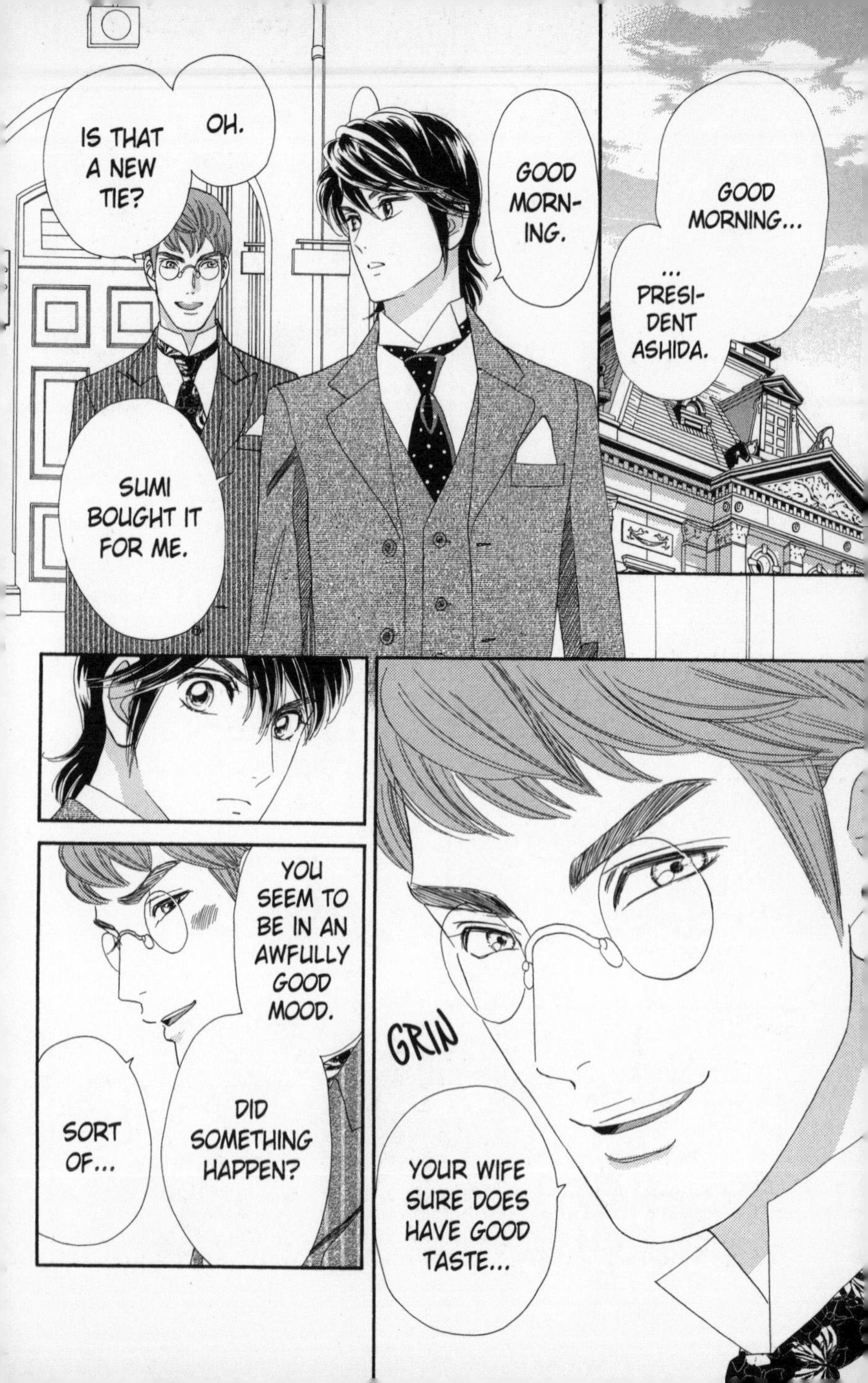
GOOD MORNING...
... PRESIDENT ASHIDA.
GOOD MORNING.
OH.
IS THAT A NEW TIE?
SUMI BOUGHT IT FOR ME.
GRIN
YOUR WIFE SURE DOES HAVE GOOD TASTE...
YOU SEEM TO BE IN AN AWFULLY GOOD MOOD.
DID SOMETHING HAPPEN?
SORT OF...

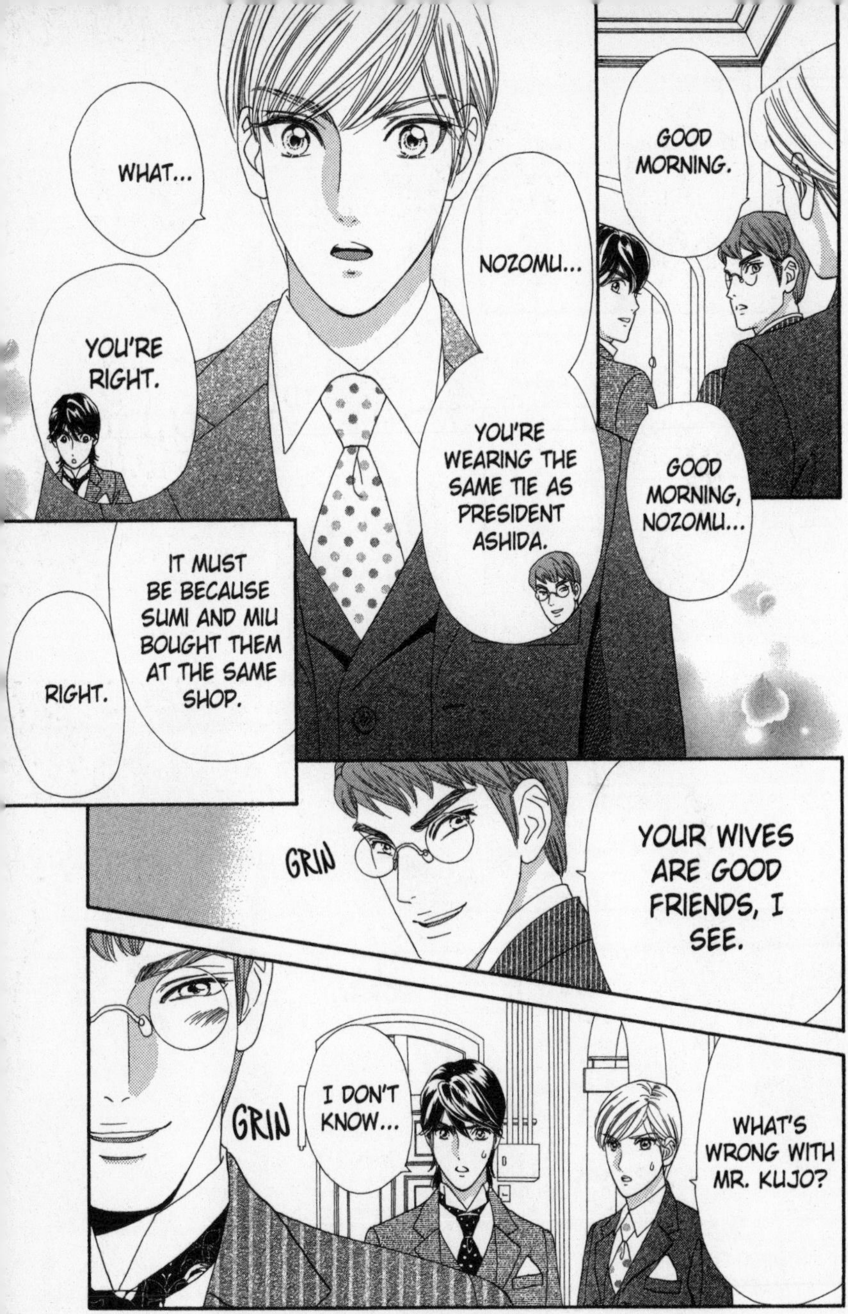
GOOD MORNING.
GOOD MORNING, NOZOMU...
NOZOMU...
YOU'RE WEARING THE SAME TIE AS PRESIDENT ASHIDA.
WHAT...
YOU'RE RIGHT.
IT MUST BE BECAUSE SUMI AND MIU BOUGHT THEM AT THE SAME SHOP.
RIGHT.
YOUR WIVES ARE GOOD FRIENDS, I SEE.
GRIN
WHAT'S WRONG WITH MR. KUJO?
I DON'T KNOW...
GRIN

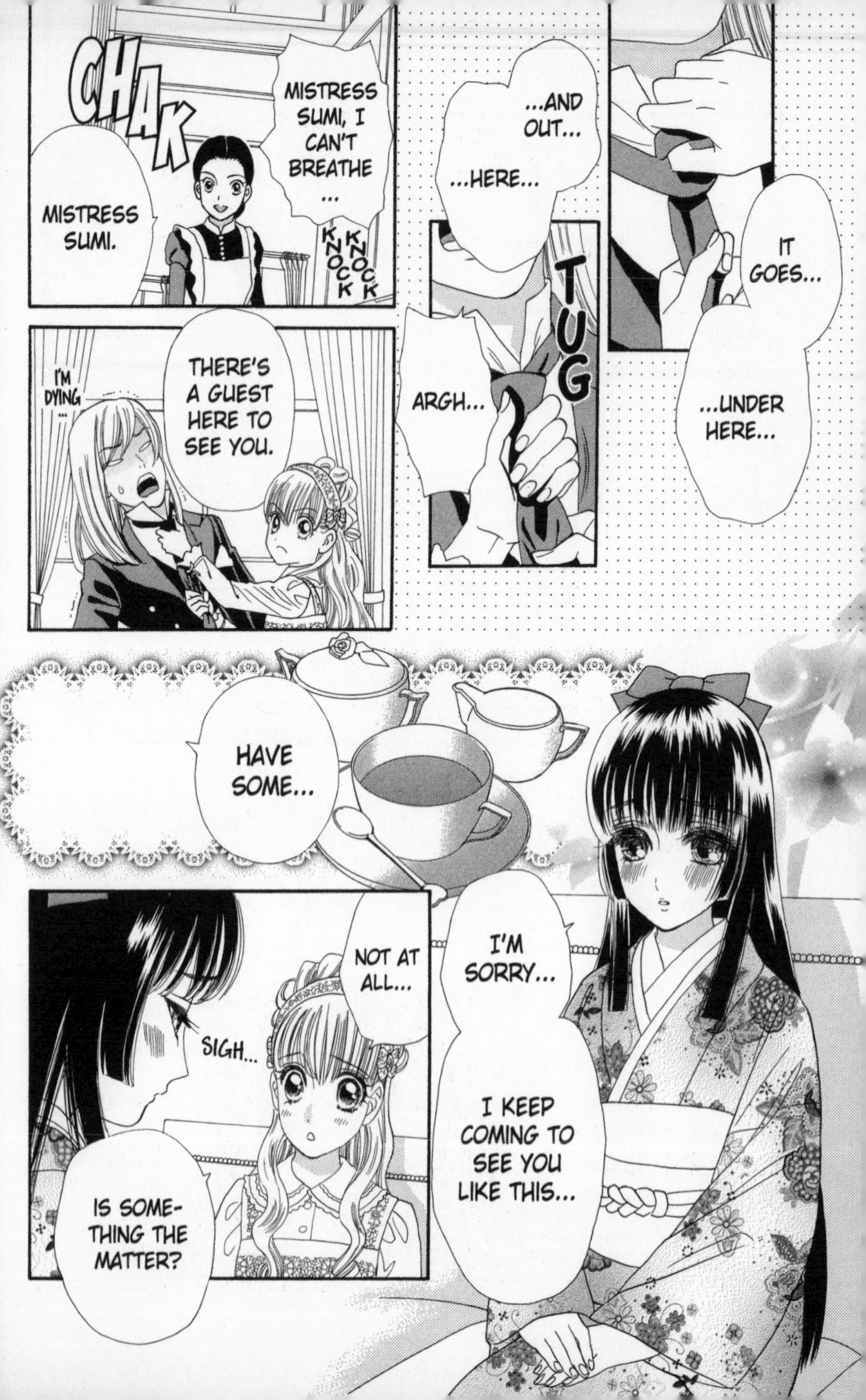
IT GOES...
...UNDER HERE...
...AND OUT...
...HERE...
TUG
ARGH...
MISTRESS SUMI, I CAN'T BREATHE...
KNOCK KNOCK
CHAK
MISTRESS SUMI.
THERE'S A GUEST HERE TO SEE YOU.
I'M DYING...
HAVE SOME...
I'M SORRY...
I KEEP COMING TO SEE YOU LIKE THIS...
NOT AT ALL...
SIGH...
IS SOMETHING THE MATTER?

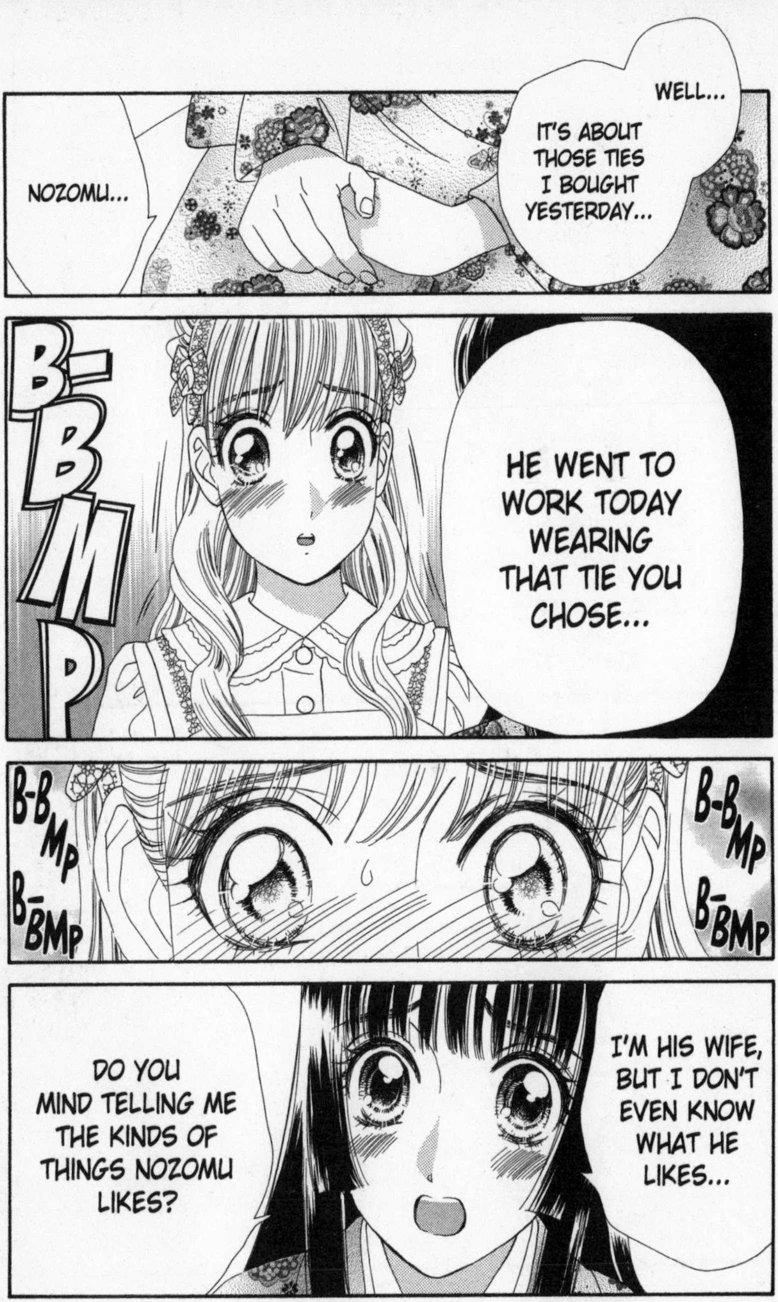
WELL... IT'S ABOUT THOSE TIES I BOUGHT YESTERDAY...
NOZOMU...
HE WENT TO WORK TODAY WEARING THAT TIE YOU CHOSE...
B-B-BMP
B-BMP B-BMP
B-BMP B-BMP
I'M HIS WIFE, BUT I DON'T EVEN KNOW WHAT HE LIKES...
DO YOU MIND TELLING ME THE KINDS OF THINGS NOZOMU LIKES?

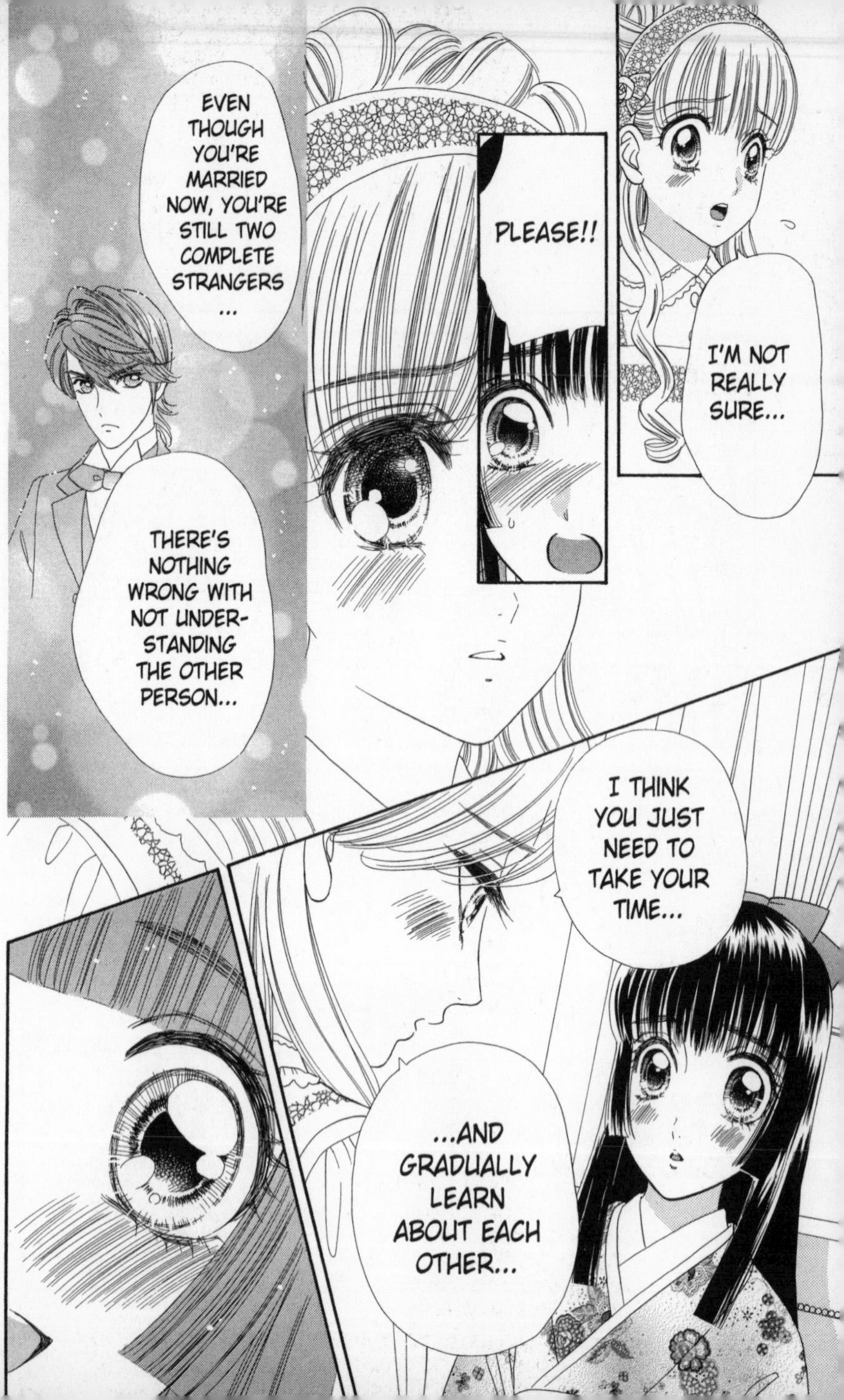
I'M NOT REALLY SURE...
PLEASE!!
EVEN THOUGH YOU'RE MARRIED NOW, YOU'RE STILL TWO COMPLETE STRANGERS...
THERE'S NOTHING WRONG WITH NOT UNDER-STANDING THE OTHER PERSON...
I THINK YOU JUST NEED TO TAKE YOUR TIME...
...AND GRADUALLY LEARN ABOUT EACH OTHER...

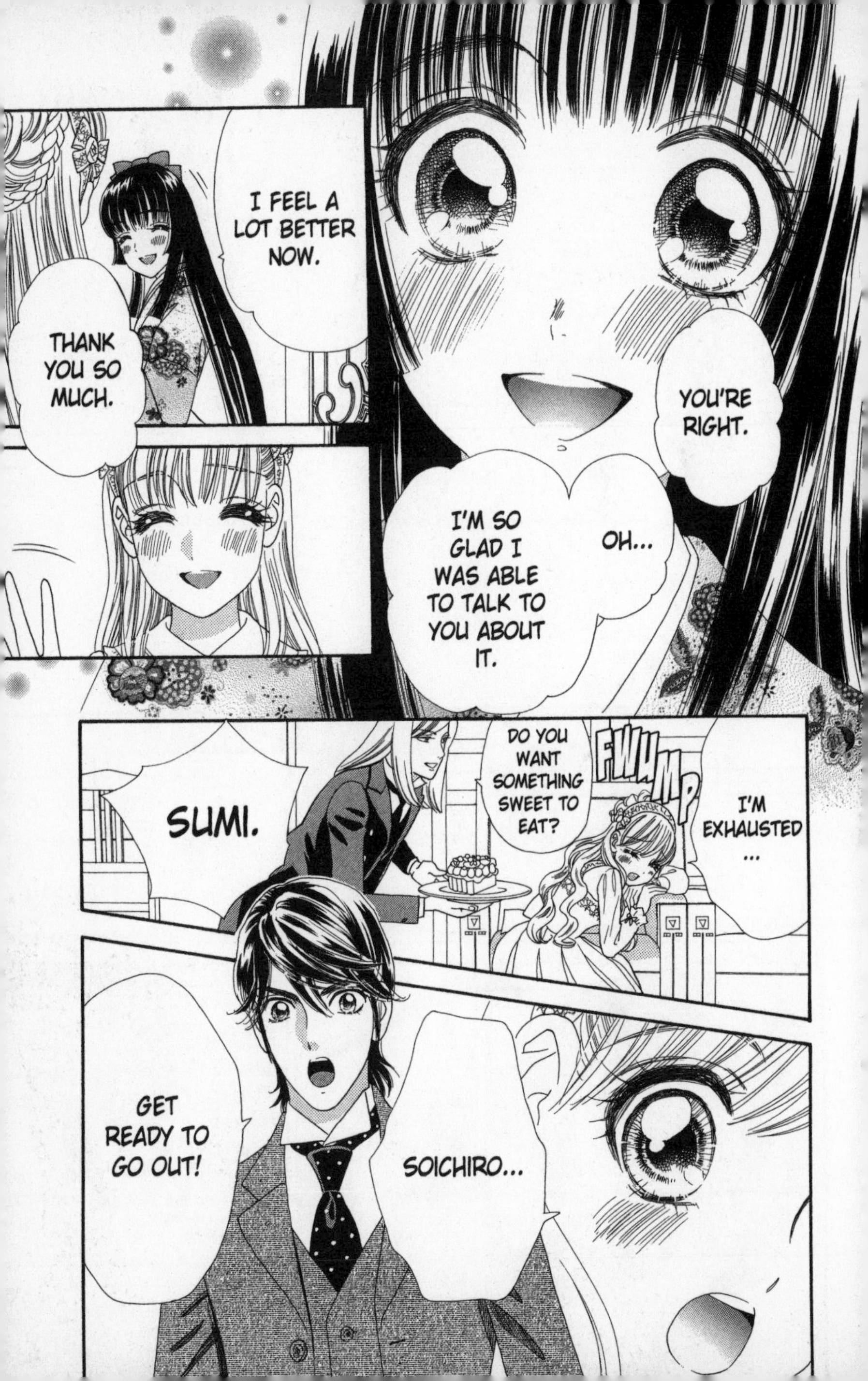
YOU'RE RIGHT.
OH...
I'M SO GLAD I WAS ABLE TO TALK TO YOU ABOUT IT.
I FEEL A LOT BETTER NOW.
THANK YOU SO MUCH.
I'M EXHAUSTED ...
FWUMP
DO YOU WANT SOMETHING SWEET TO EAT?
SUMI.
SOICHIRO...
GET READY TO GO OUT!

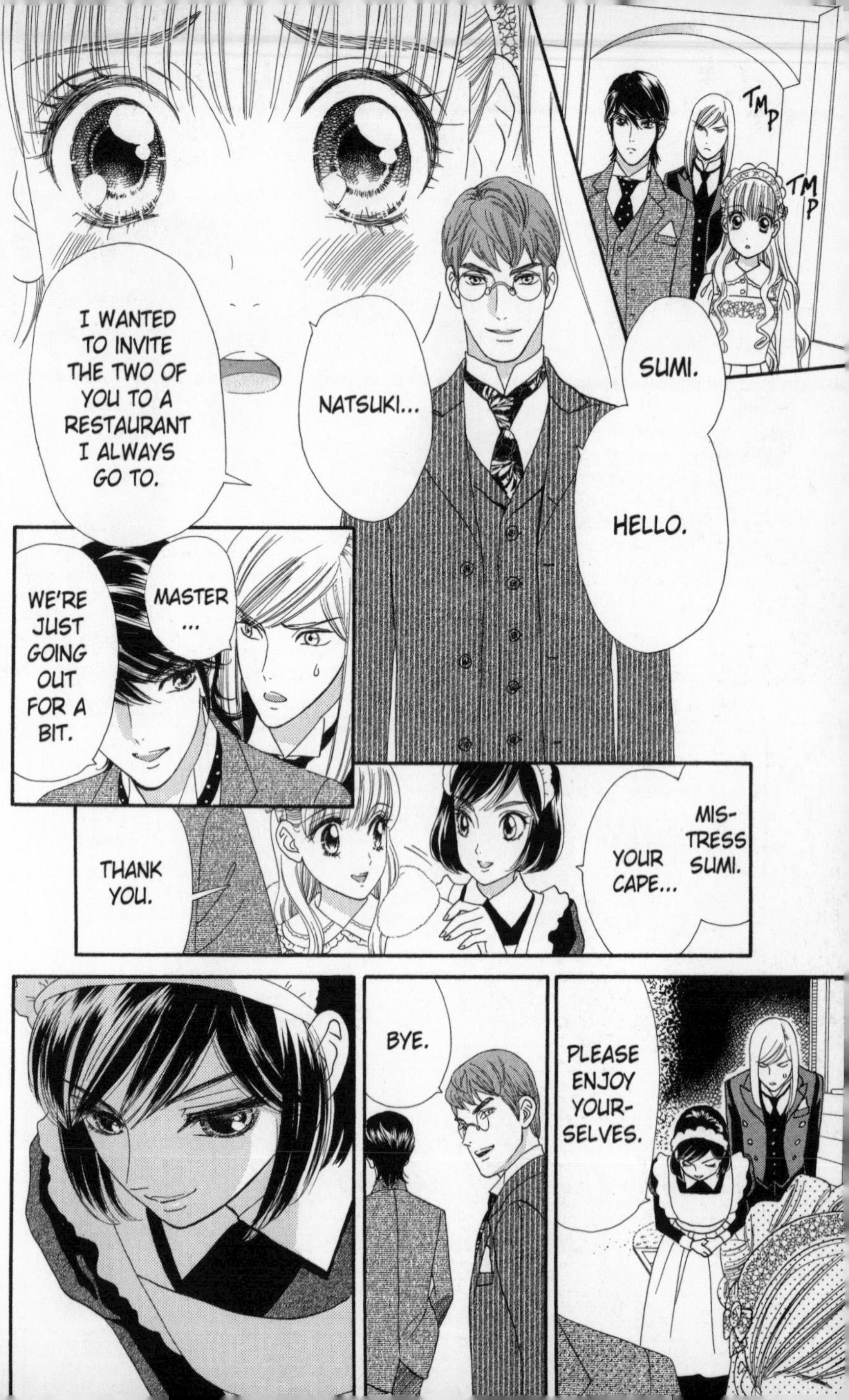
TMP
TMP
SUMI.
HELLO.
NATSUKI...
I WANTED TO INVITE THE TWO OF YOU TO A RESTAURANT I ALWAYS GO TO.
MASTER...
WE'RE JUST GOING OUT FOR A BIT.
MIS-TRESS SUMI.
YOUR CAPE...
THANK YOU.
PLEASE ENJOY YOUR-SELVES.
BYE.

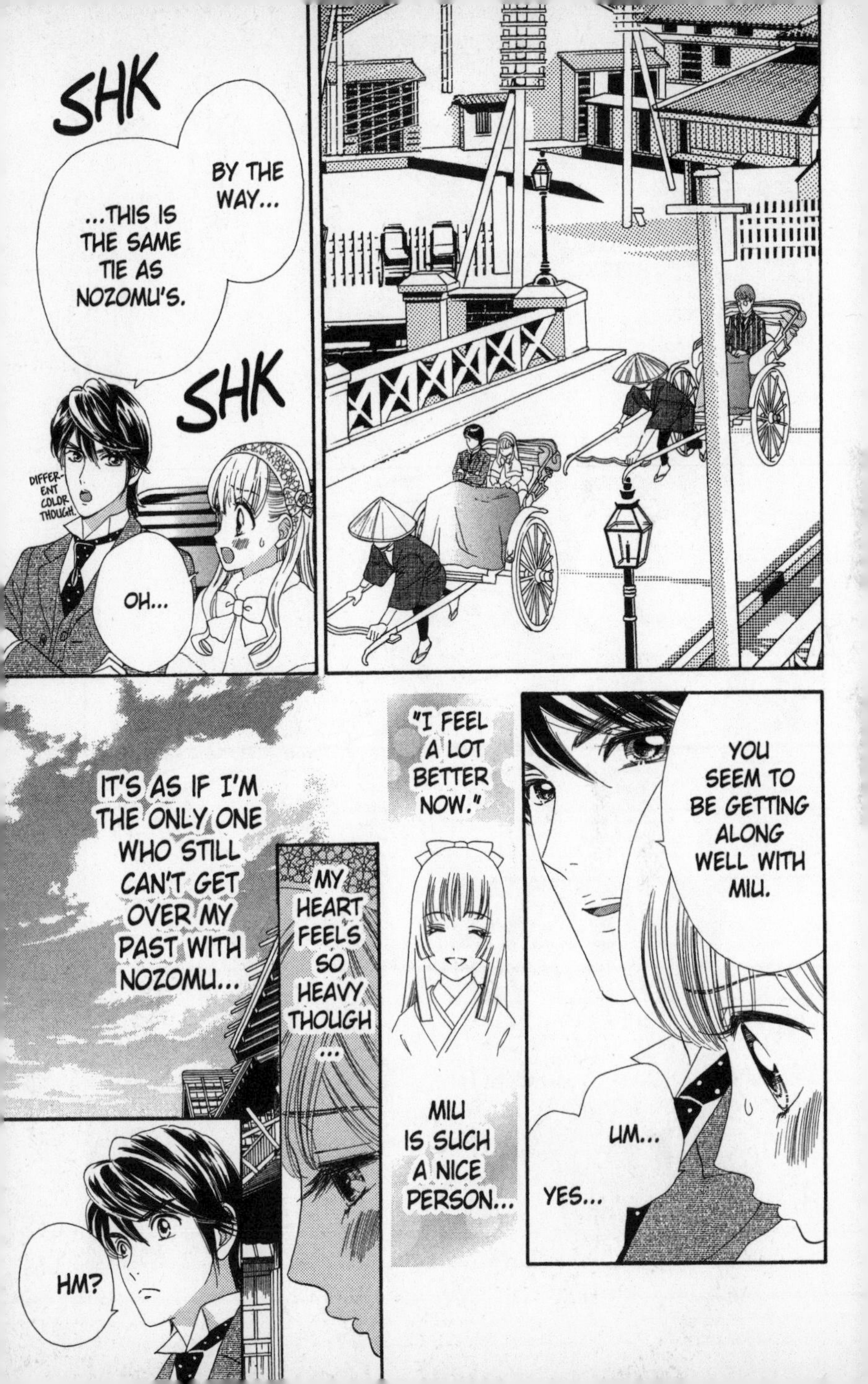
SHK
BY THE WAY...
...THIS IS THE SAME TIE AS NOZOMU'S.
SHK
DIFFERENT COLOR THOUGH.
OH...
YOU SEEM TO BE GETTING ALONG WELL WITH MIU.
UM...
YES...
"I FEEL A LOT BETTER NOW."
MIU IS SUCH A NICE PERSON...
IT'S AS IF I'M THE ONLY ONE WHO STILL CAN'T GET OVER MY PAST WITH NOZOMU...
MY HEART FEELS SO HEAVY THOUGH...
HM?

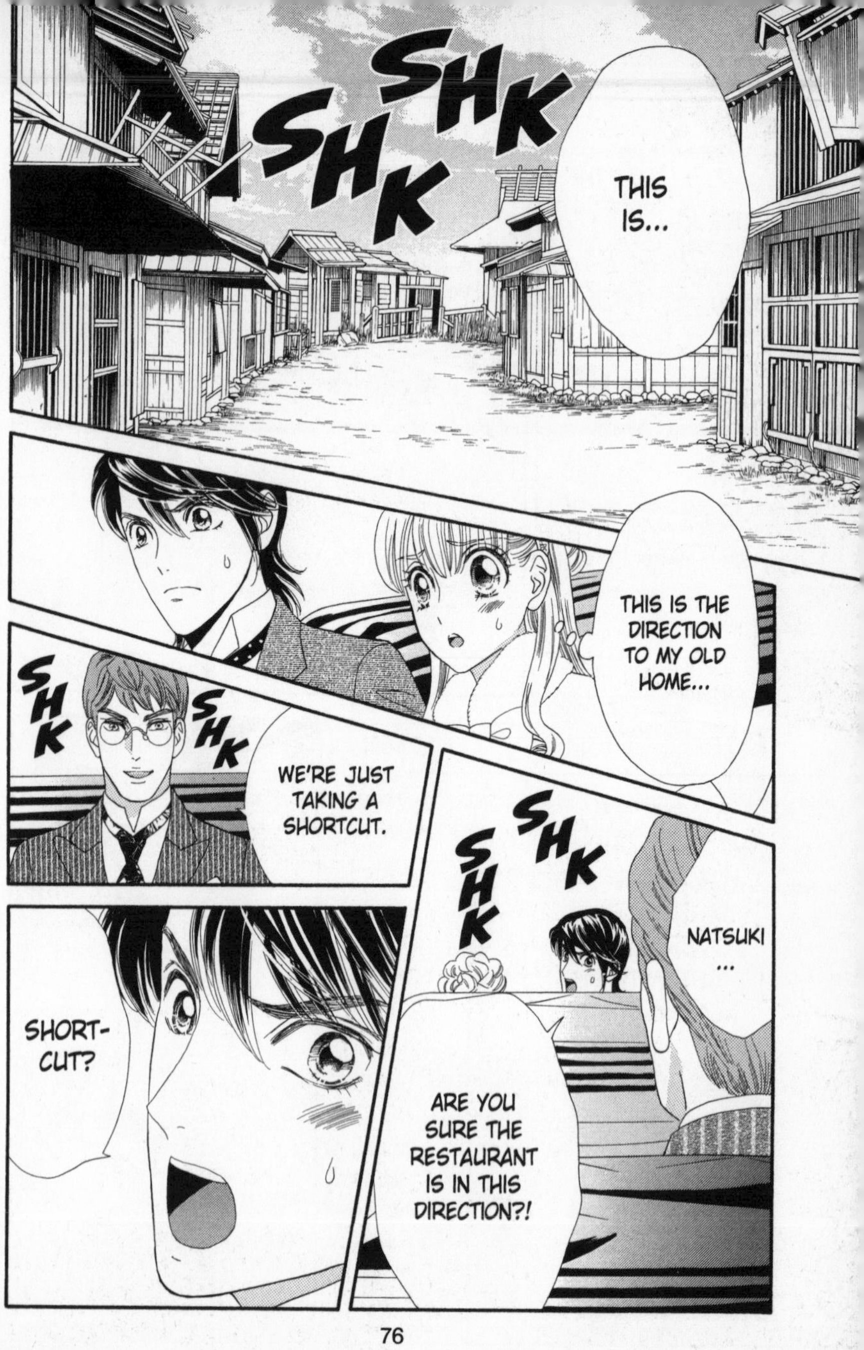
SHK SHK
SHK
THIS IS...
THIS IS THE DIRECTION TO MY OLD HOME...
SHK SHK
NATSUKI ...
ARE YOU SURE THE RESTAURANT IS IN THIS DIRECTION?!
SHK SHK
WE'RE JUST TAKING A SHORTCUT.
SHORT-CUT?

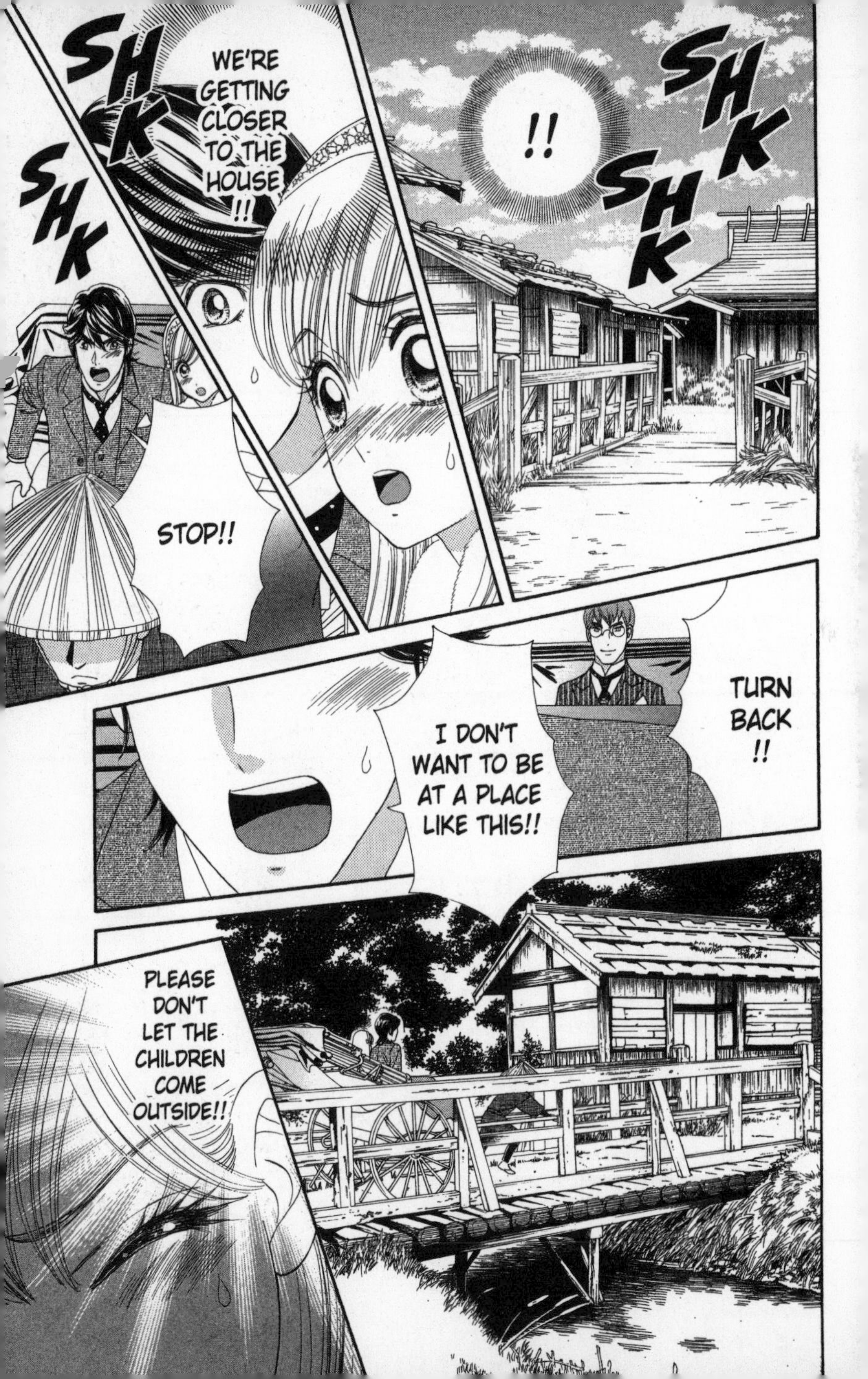
SHK
SHK
!!
SHK
WE'RE GETTING CLOSER TO THE HOUSE!!
SHK
STOP!!
TURN BACK!!
I DON'T WANT TO BE AT A PLACE LIKE THIS!!
PLEASE DON'T LET THE CHILDREN COME OUTSIDE!!

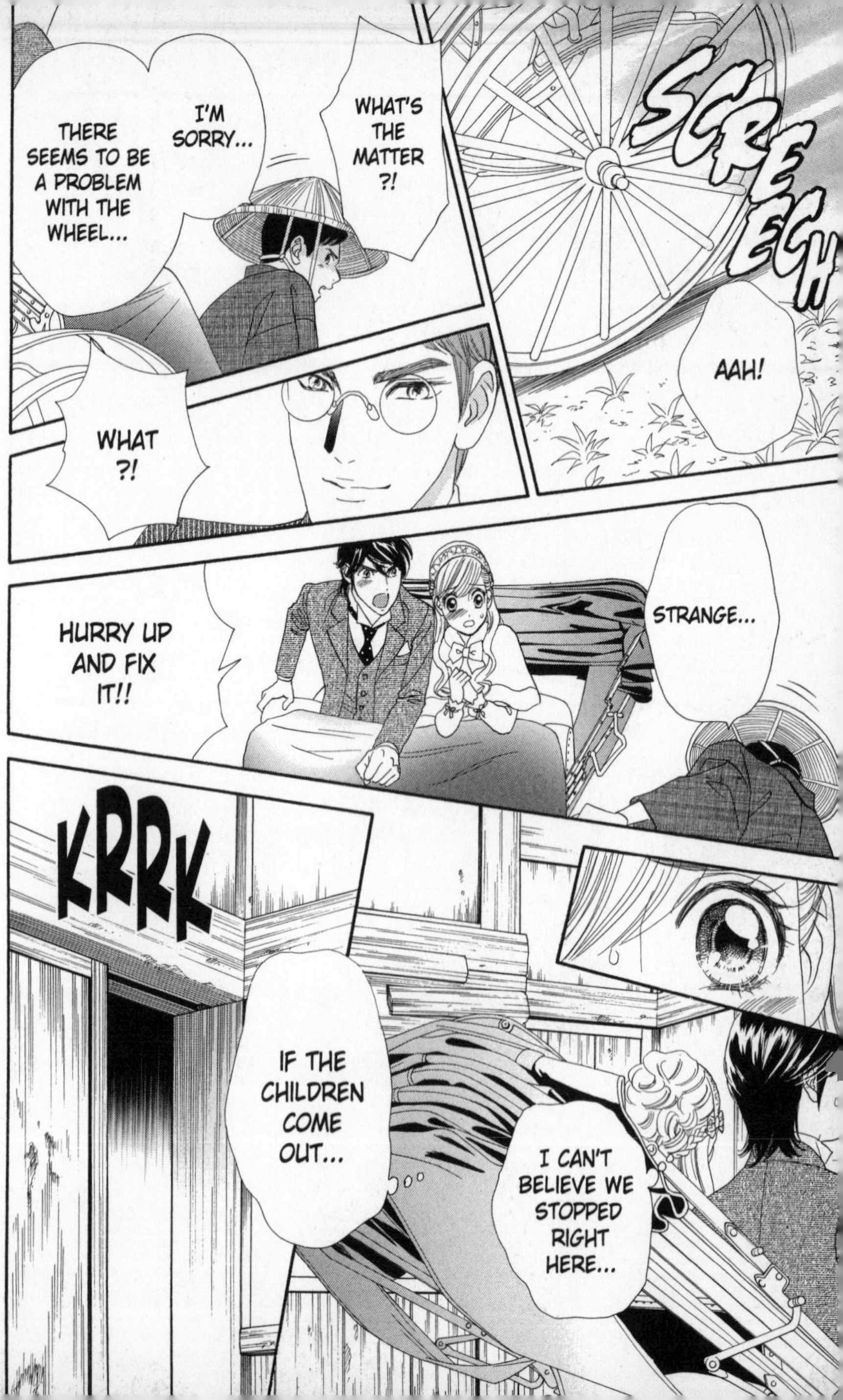
SCREECH
AAH!
WHAT'S THE MATTER?!
I'M SORRY...
THERE SEEMS TO BE A PROBLEM WITH THE WHEEL...
WHAT?!
STRANGE...
HURRY UP AND FIX IT!!
KRRK
IF THE CHILDREN COME OUT...
I CAN'T BELIEVE WE STOPPED RIGHT HERE...

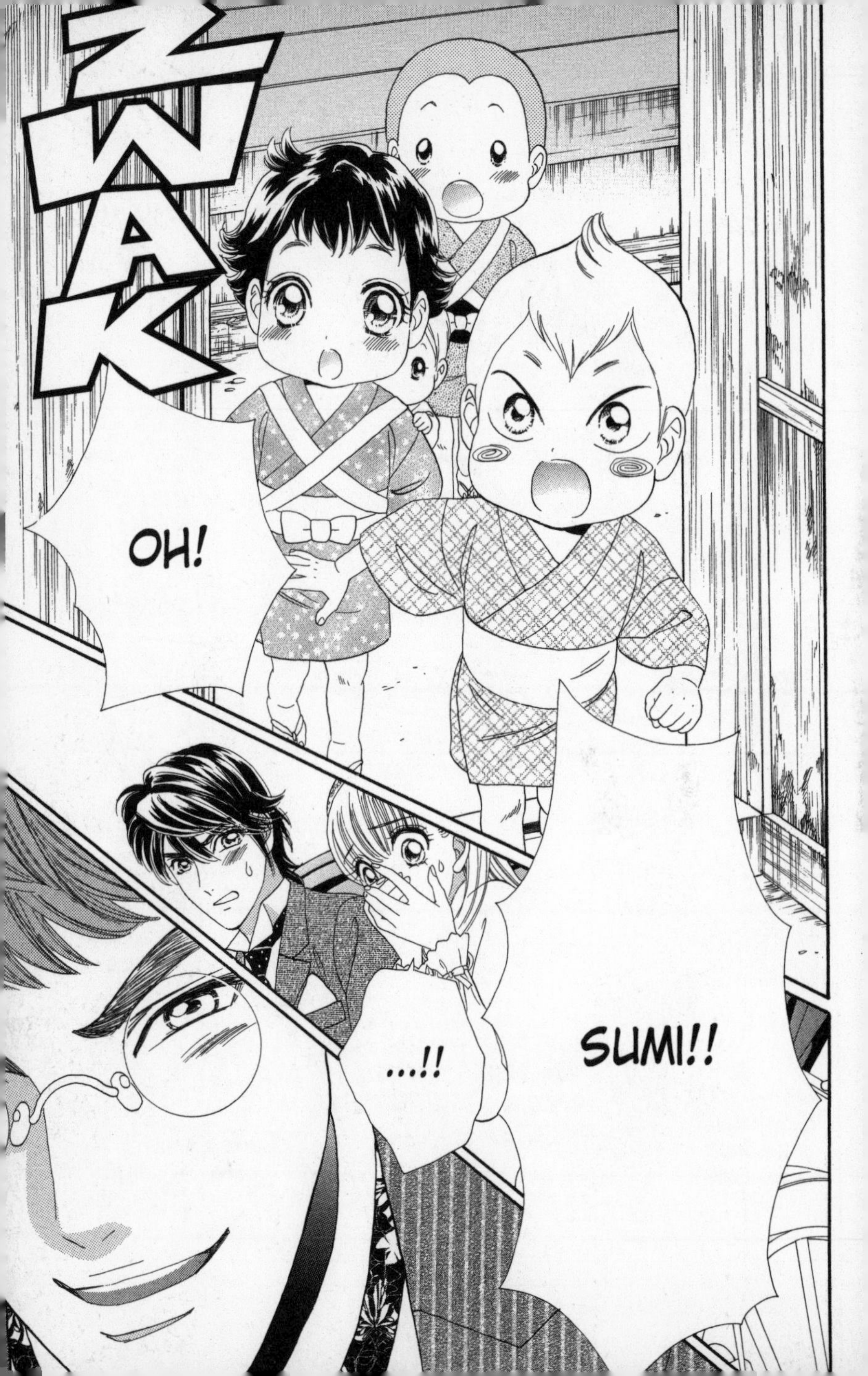
ZWAK
OH!
SUMI!!
...!!

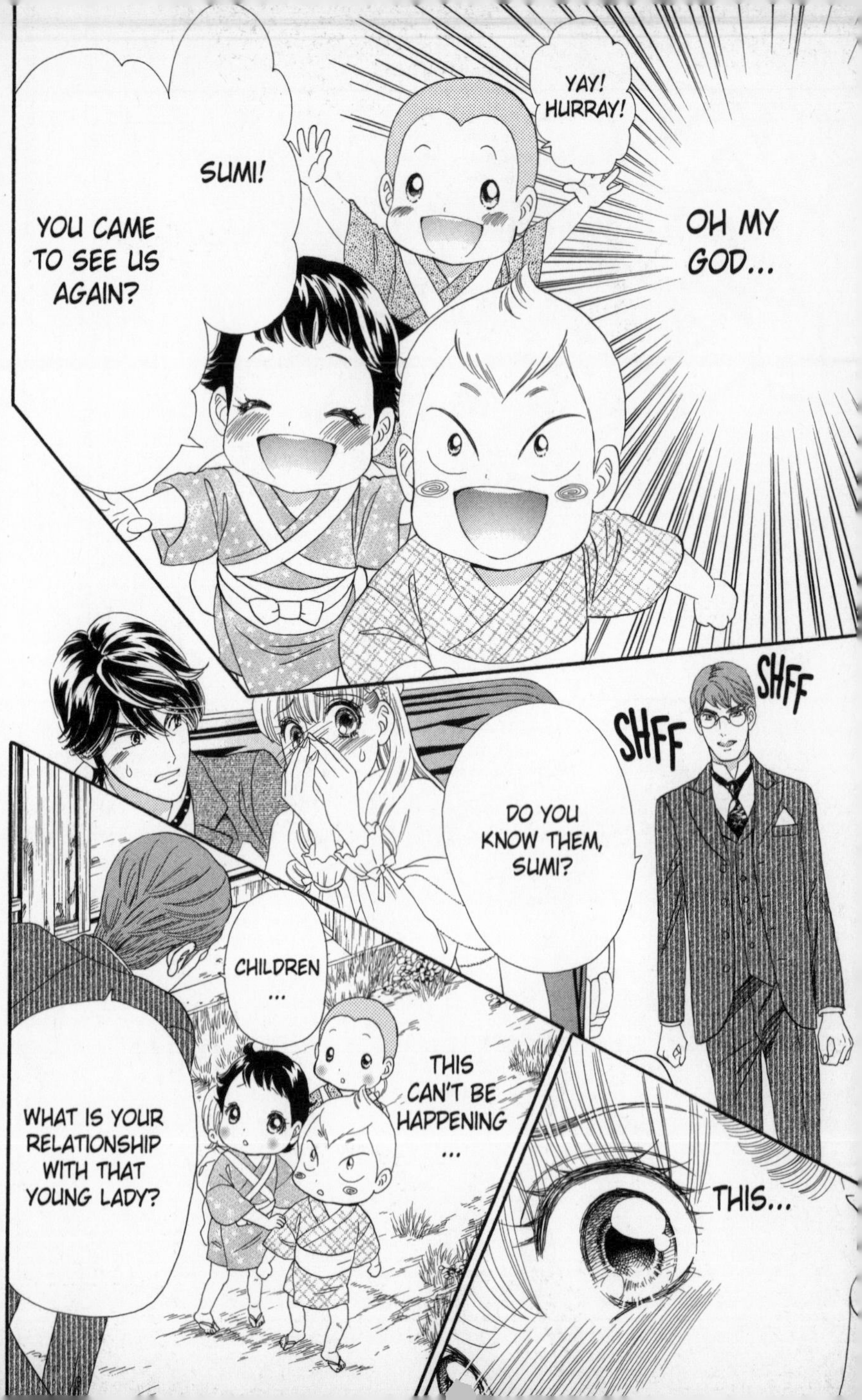

YAY! HURRAY!
OH MY GOD...
SUMI!
YOU CAME TO SEE US AGAIN?
SHFF
SHFF
DO YOU KNOW THEM, SUMI?
THIS...
CHILDREN ...
THIS CAN'T BE HAPPENING ...
WHAT IS YOUR RELATIONSHIP WITH THAT YOUNG LADY?

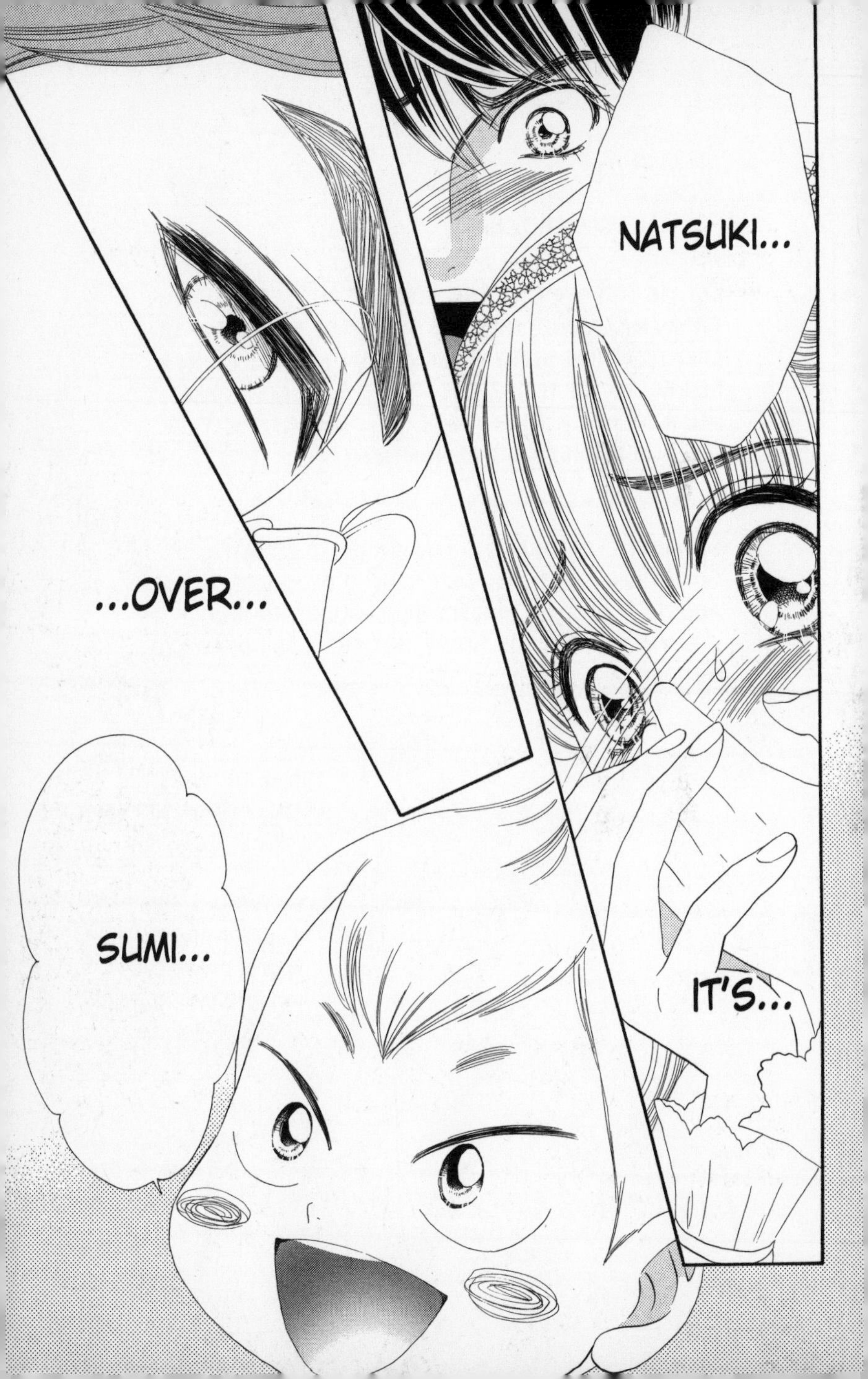
NATSUKI...
IT'S...
...OVER...
SUMI...

No. 3

RANDOM CHITCHAT!

Date . .

✿ LET ME GET BACK TO THE STORY ABOUT MY MANGA IN *RIBON* MAGAZINE. THIS WAS THE FIRST TIME I HAD TO CREATE A NEW STORY WHILE ALREADY WORKING ON A SERIES. TO TOP IT OFF, THE READERS OF *RIBON* ARE MUCH YOUNGER THAN THOSE OF *MARGARET*, SO THIS WAS A VERY DIFFICULT ASSIGNMENT.

✿ MY MOTTO FOR DRAWING MANGA IS "TO CREATE SOMETHING THAT CAN BE ENJOYED BY CHILDREN AND ADULTS ALIKE," SO I DIDN'T HAVE MUCH TROUBLE COMING UP WITH THE STORY, BUT THE WAY I DRAW DID BECOME A PROBLEM.

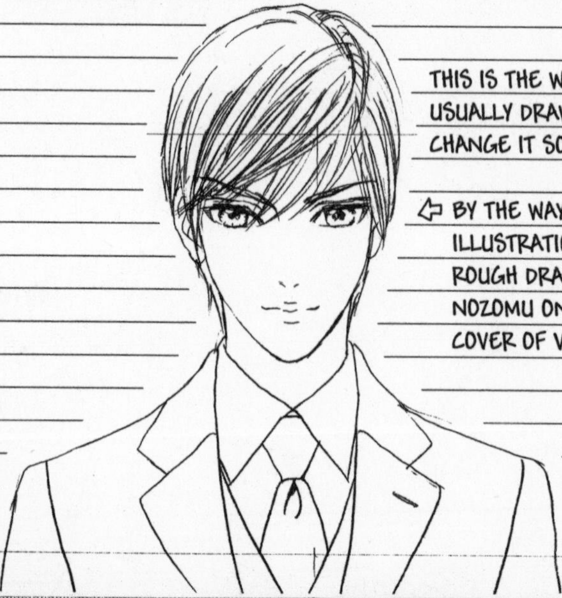

THIS IS THE WAY I USUALLY DRAW, SO I HAD TO CHANGE IT SOMEHOW... ♪

⇦ BY THE WAY, THIS ILLUSTRATION IS THE ROUGH DRAFT OF NOZOMU ON THE BACK COVER OF VOLUME 3.

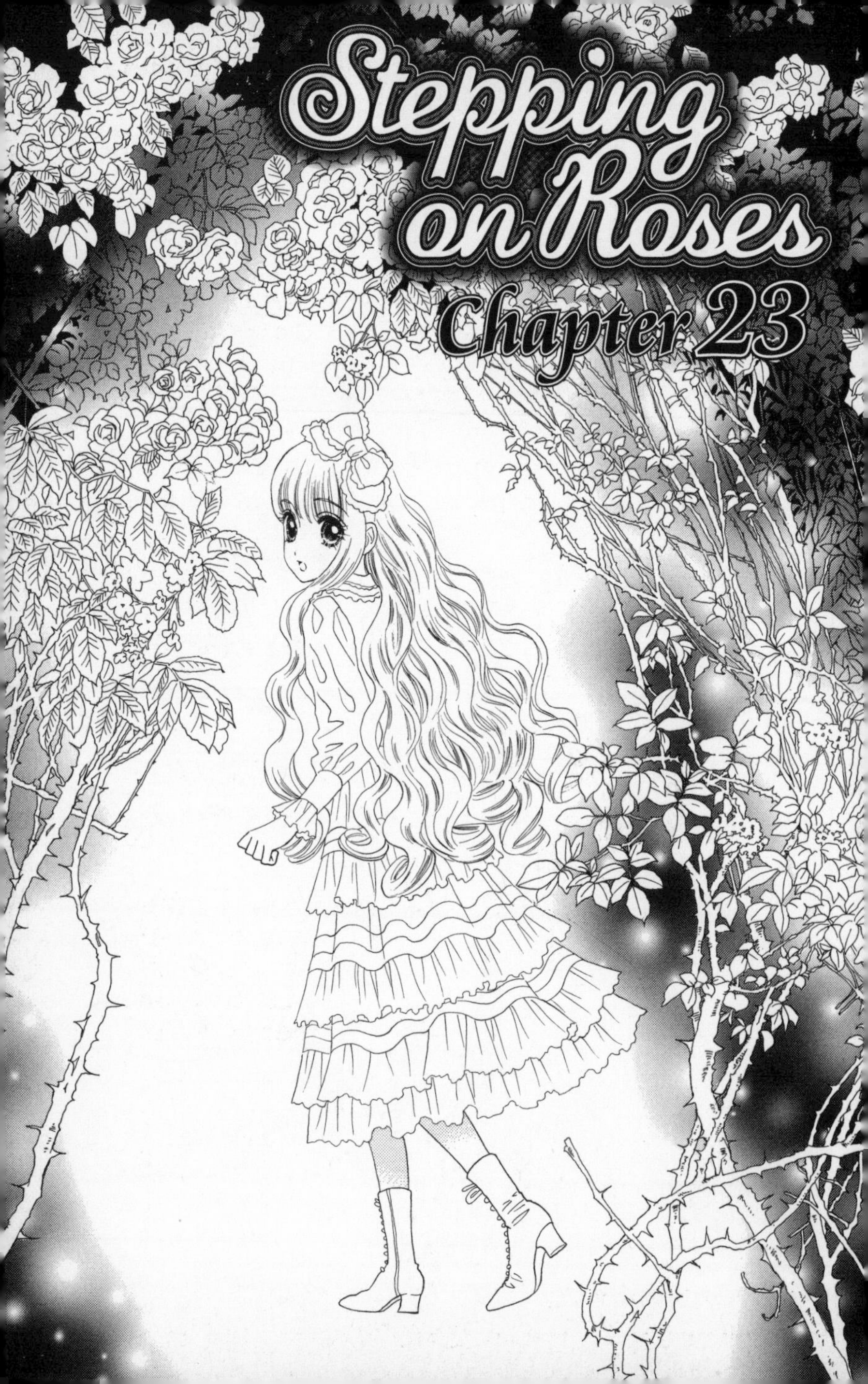
Stepping on Roses
Chapter 23

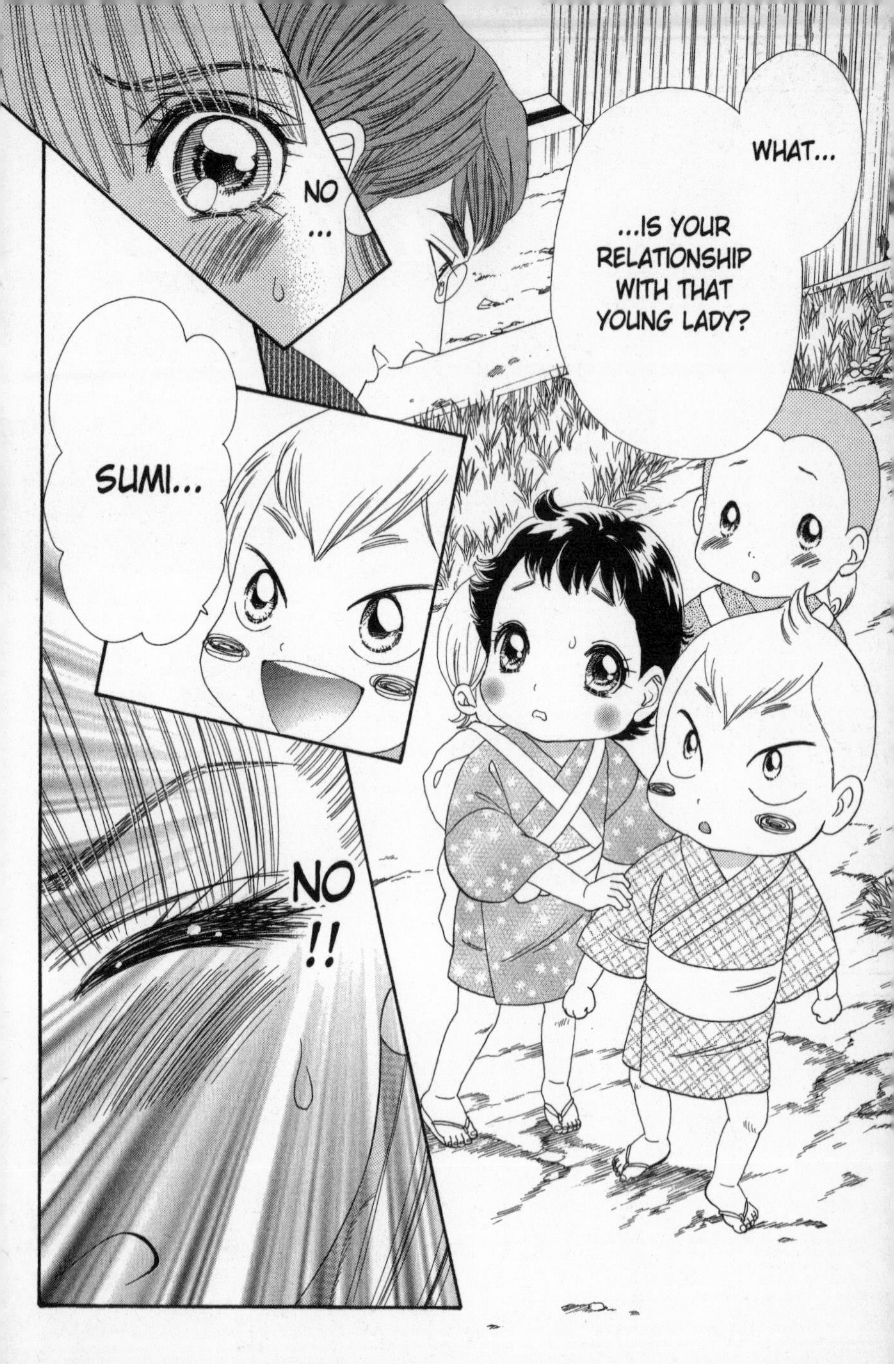
WHAT...
...IS YOUR RELATIONSHIP WITH THAT YOUNG LADY?
NO ...
SUMI...
NO !!

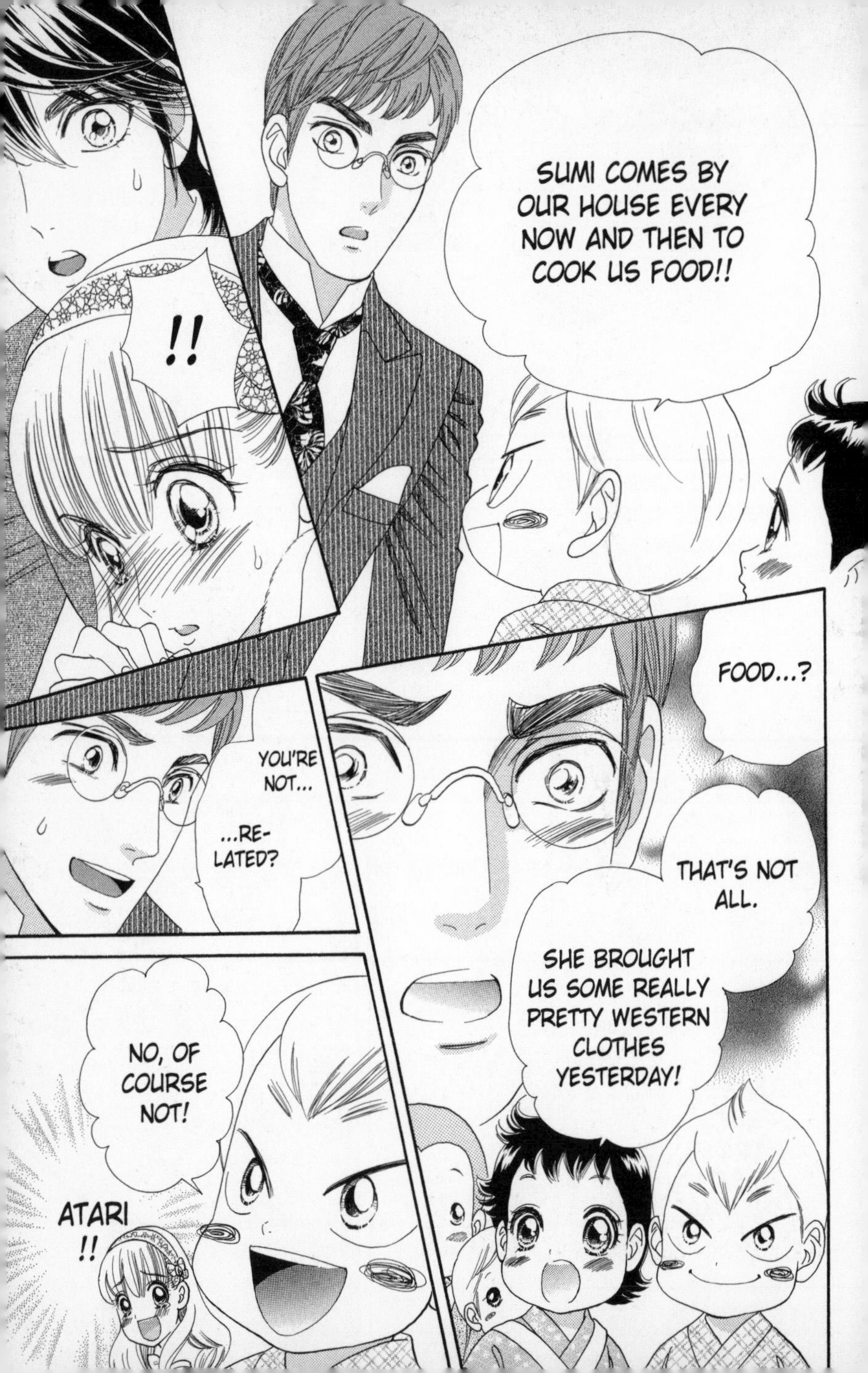
SUMI COMES BY OUR HOUSE EVERY NOW AND THEN TO COOK US FOOD!!
!!
FOOD...?
THAT'S NOT ALL.
SHE BROUGHT US SOME REALLY PRETTY WESTERN CLOTHES YESTERDAY!
YOU'RE NOT...
...RE-LATED?
NO, OF COURSE NOT!
ATARI !!

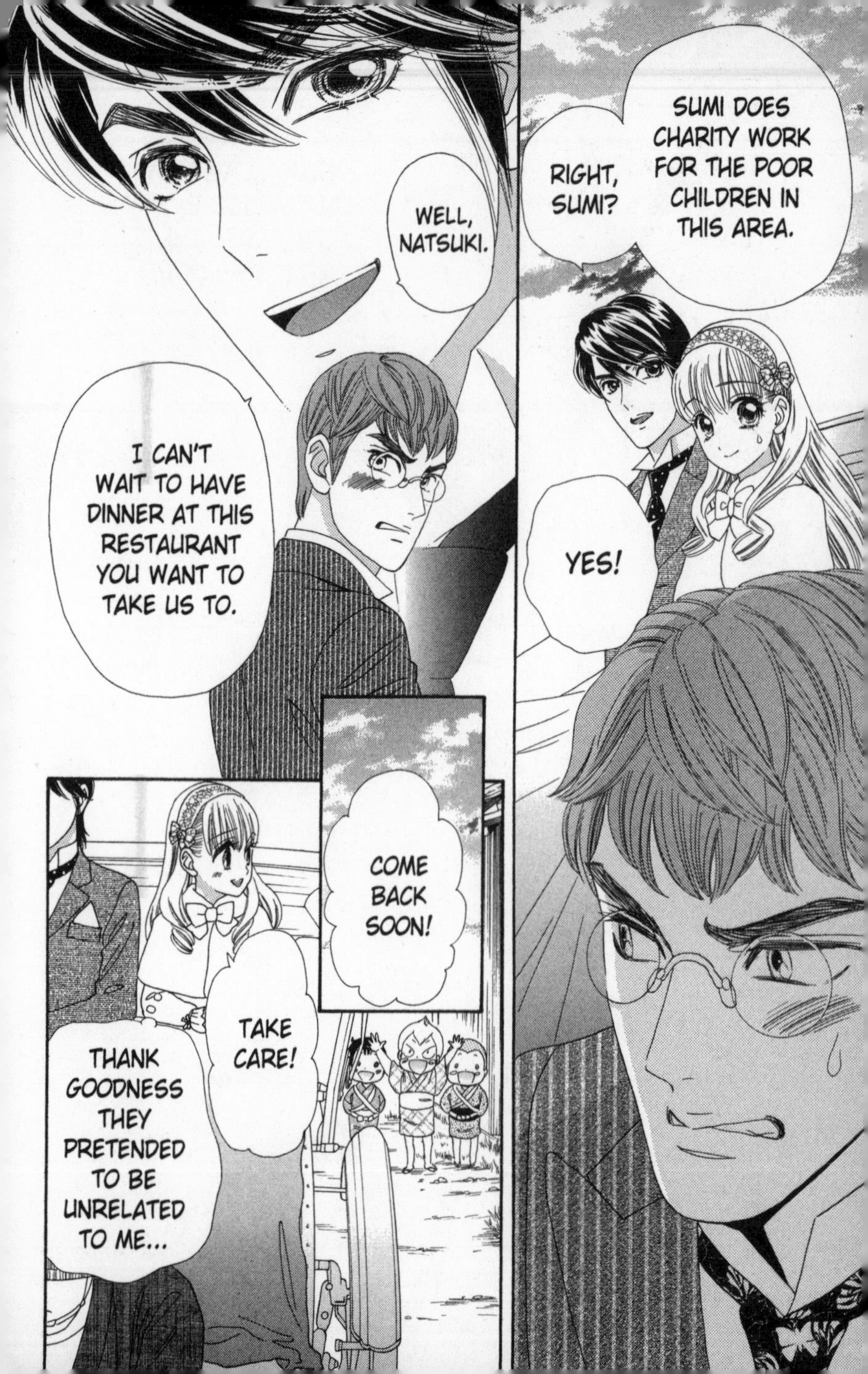

SUMI DOES CHARITY WORK FOR THE POOR CHILDREN IN THIS AREA.
RIGHT, SUMI?
YES!
WELL, NATSUKI.
I CAN'T WAIT TO HAVE DINNER AT THIS RESTAURANT YOU WANT TO TAKE US TO.
COME BACK SOON!
TAKE CARE!
THANK GOODNESS THEY PRETENDED TO BE UNRELATED TO ME...

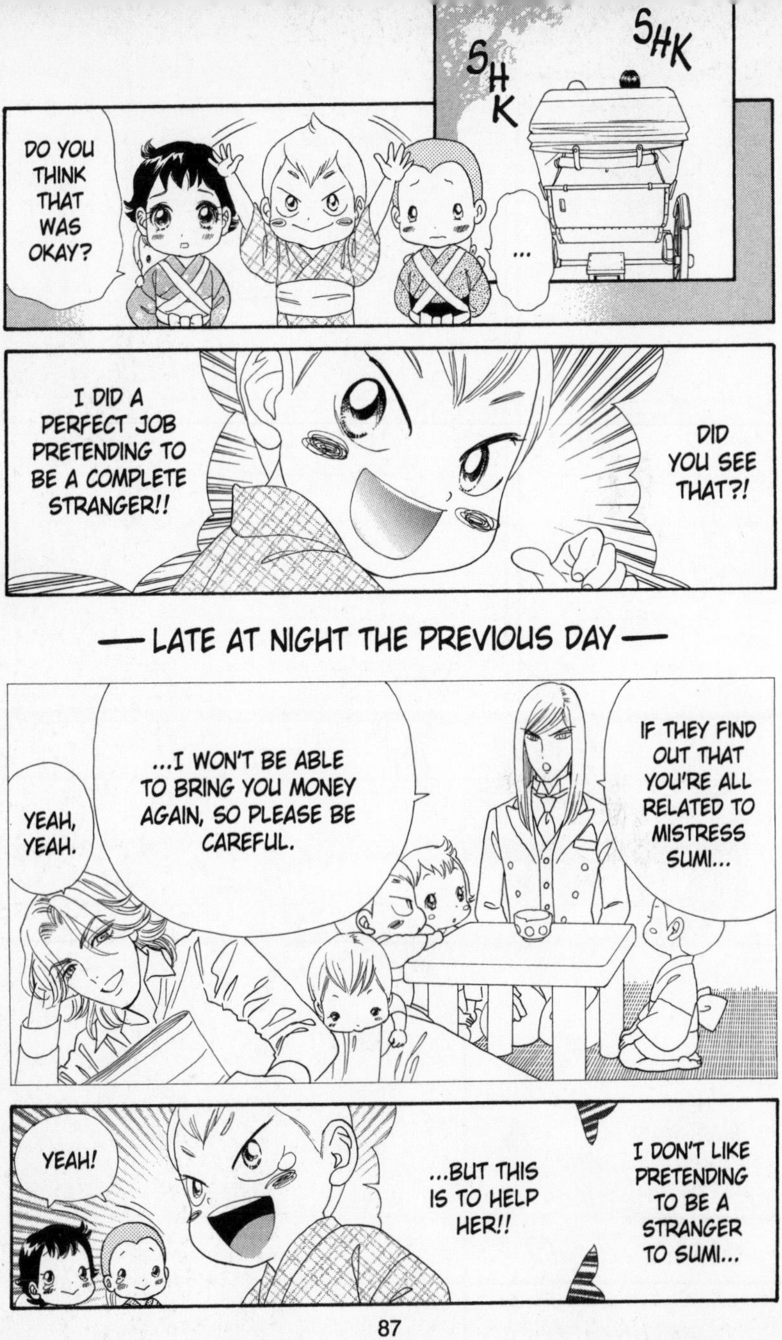
SHK
SHK
...
DO YOU THINK THAT WAS OKAY?
DID YOU SEE THAT?!
I DID A PERFECT JOB PRETENDING TO BE A COMPLETE STRANGER!!
—LATE AT NIGHT THE PREVIOUS DAY—
IF THEY FIND OUT THAT YOU'RE ALL RELATED TO MISTRESS SUMI...
...I WON'T BE ABLE TO BRING YOU MONEY AGAIN, SO PLEASE BE CAREFUL.
YEAH, YEAH.
I DON'T LIKE PRETENDING TO BE A STRANGER TO SUMI...
...BUT THIS IS TO HELP HER!!
YEAH!

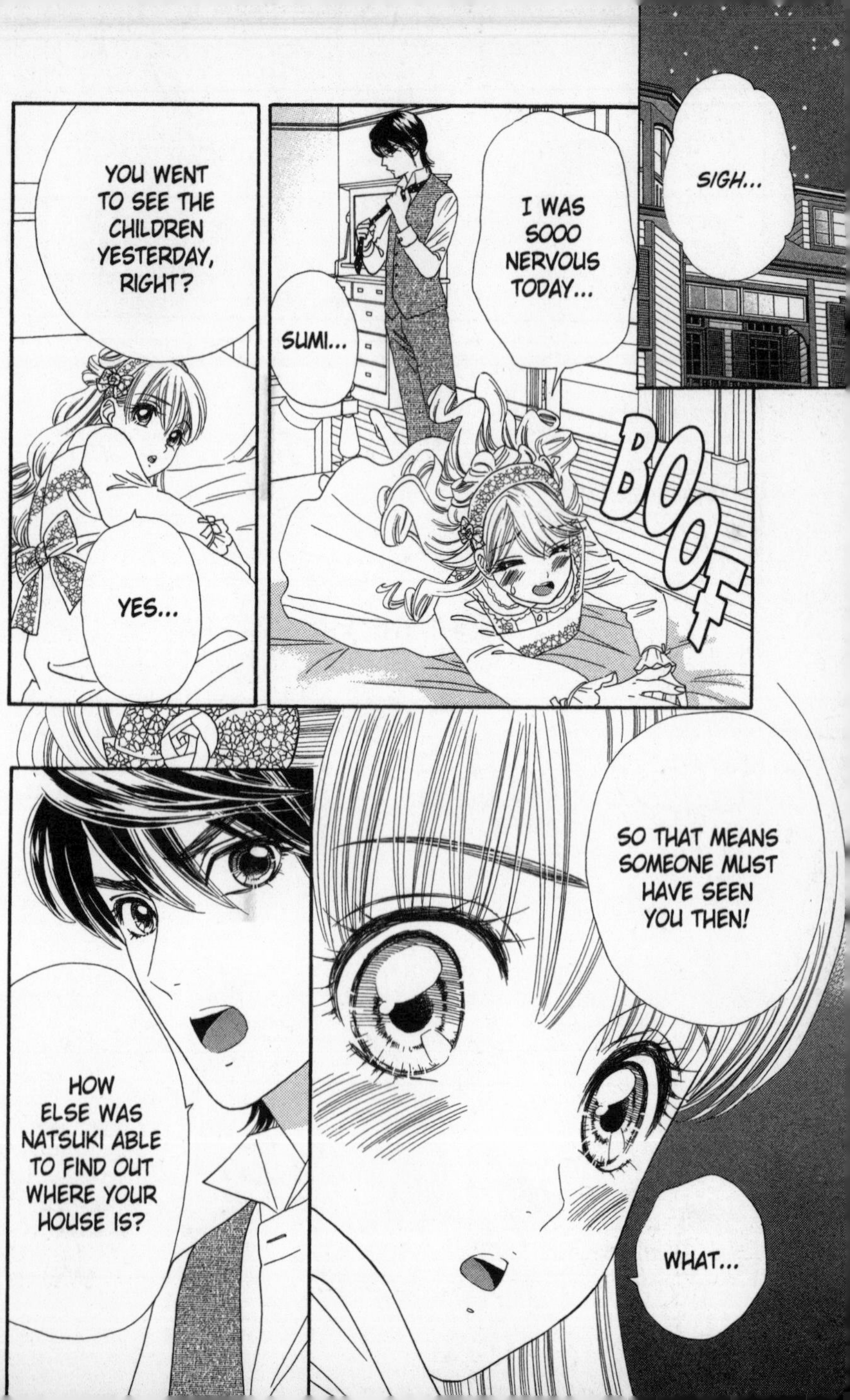
SIGH...
I WAS SOOO NERVOUS TODAY...
BOOF
SUMI...
YOU WENT TO SEE THE CHILDREN YESTERDAY, RIGHT?
YES...
SO THAT MEANS SOMEONE MUST HAVE SEEN YOU THEN!
WHAT...
HOW ELSE WAS NATSUKI ABLE TO FIND OUT WHERE YOUR HOUSE IS?

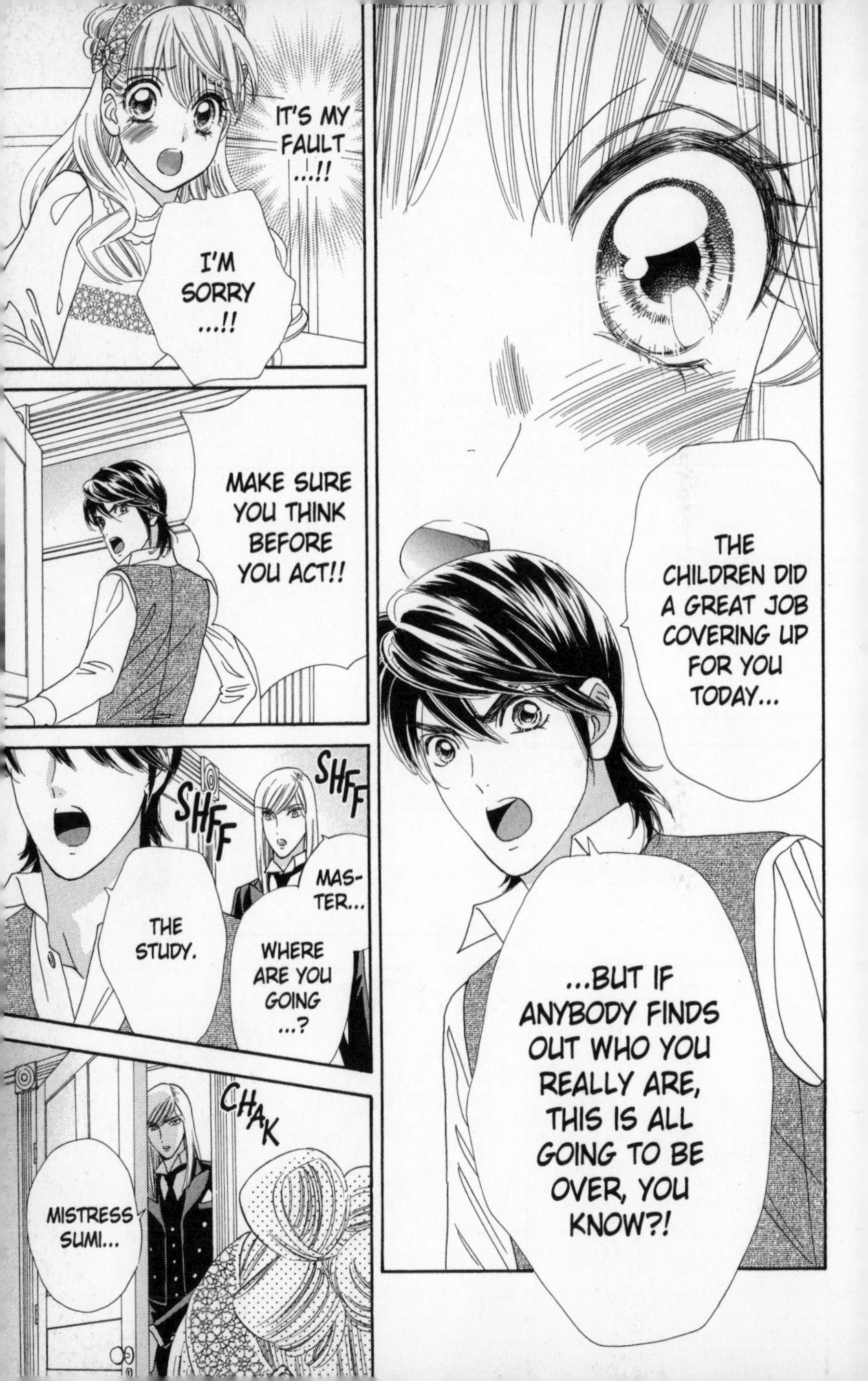
THE CHILDREN DID A GREAT JOB COVERING UP FOR YOU TODAY...
...BUT IF ANYBODY FINDS OUT WHO YOU REALLY ARE, THIS IS ALL GOING TO BE OVER, YOU KNOW?!
IT'S MY FAULT ...!!
I'M SORRY ...!!
MAKE SURE YOU THINK BEFORE YOU ACT!!
SHFF
SHFF
MAS-TER... WHERE ARE YOU GOING ...?
THE STUDY.
CHAK
MISTRESS SUMI...

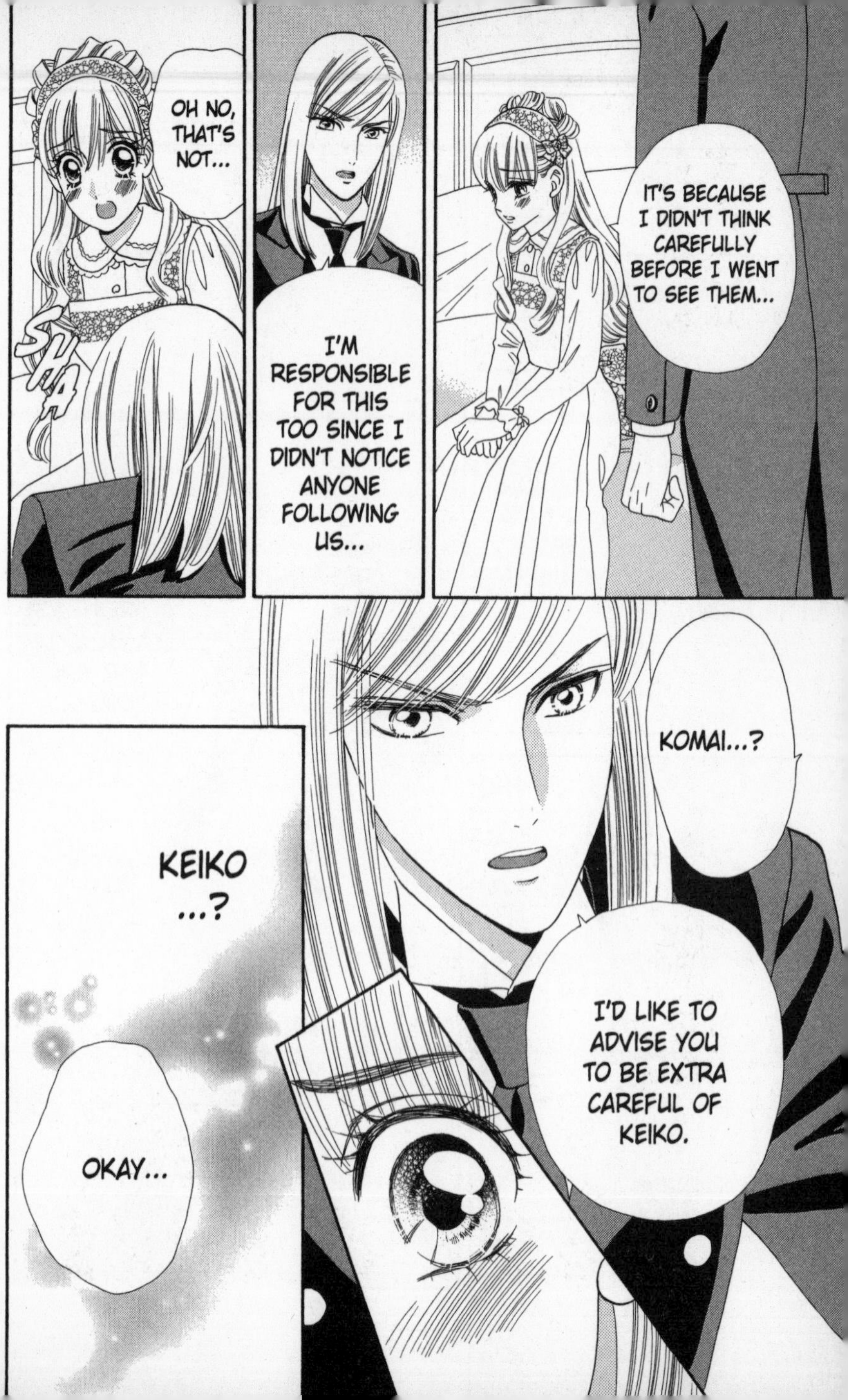
IT'S BECAUSE I DIDN'T THINK CAREFULLY BEFORE I WENT TO SEE THEM...
I'M RESPONSIBLE FOR THIS TOO SINCE I DIDN'T NOTICE ANYONE FOLLOWING US...
OH NO, THAT'S NOT...
SHA
KOMAI...?
I'D LIKE TO ADVISE YOU TO BE EXTRA CAREFUL OF KEIKO.
KEIKO ...?
OKAY...

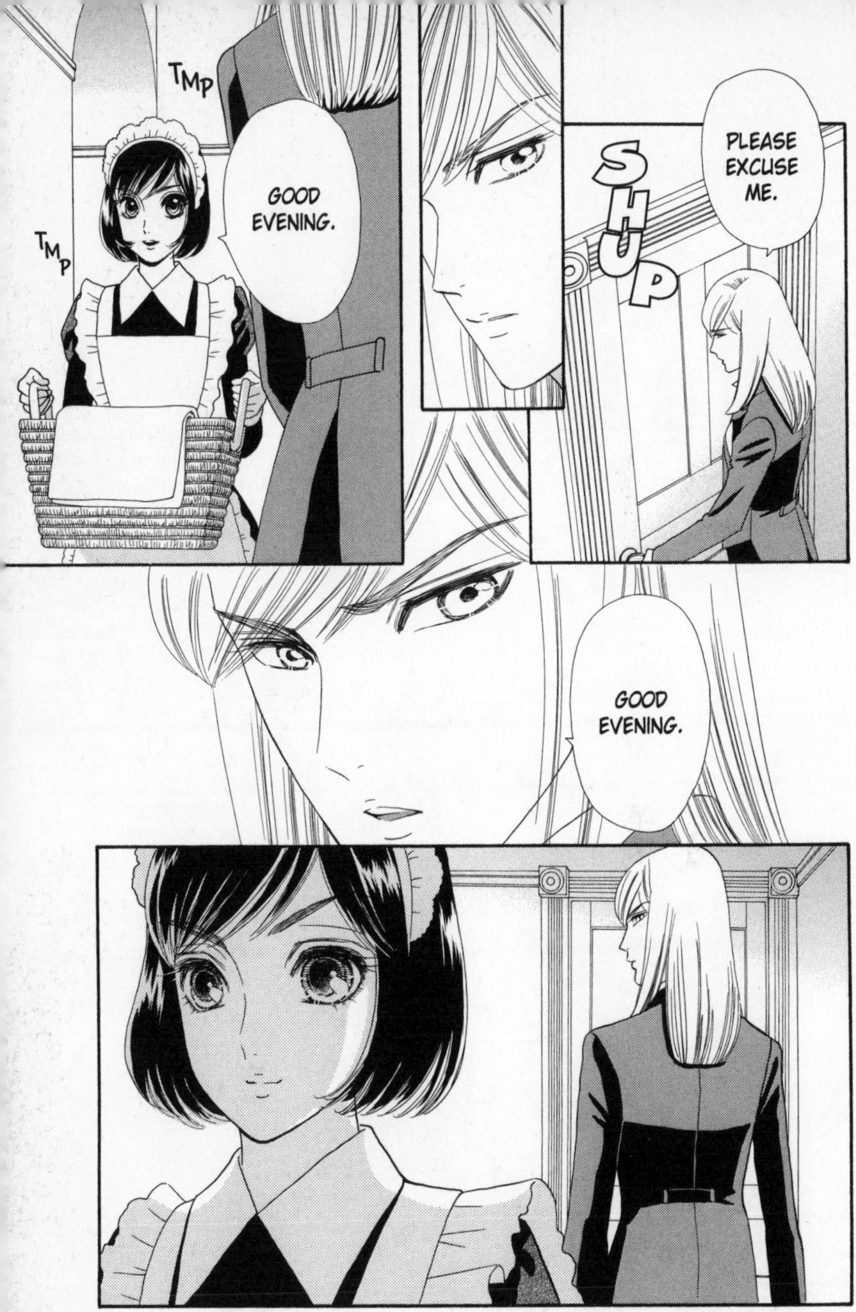
PLEASE EXCUSE ME.
SHUP
TMP
GOOD EVENING.
TMP
GOOD EVENING.

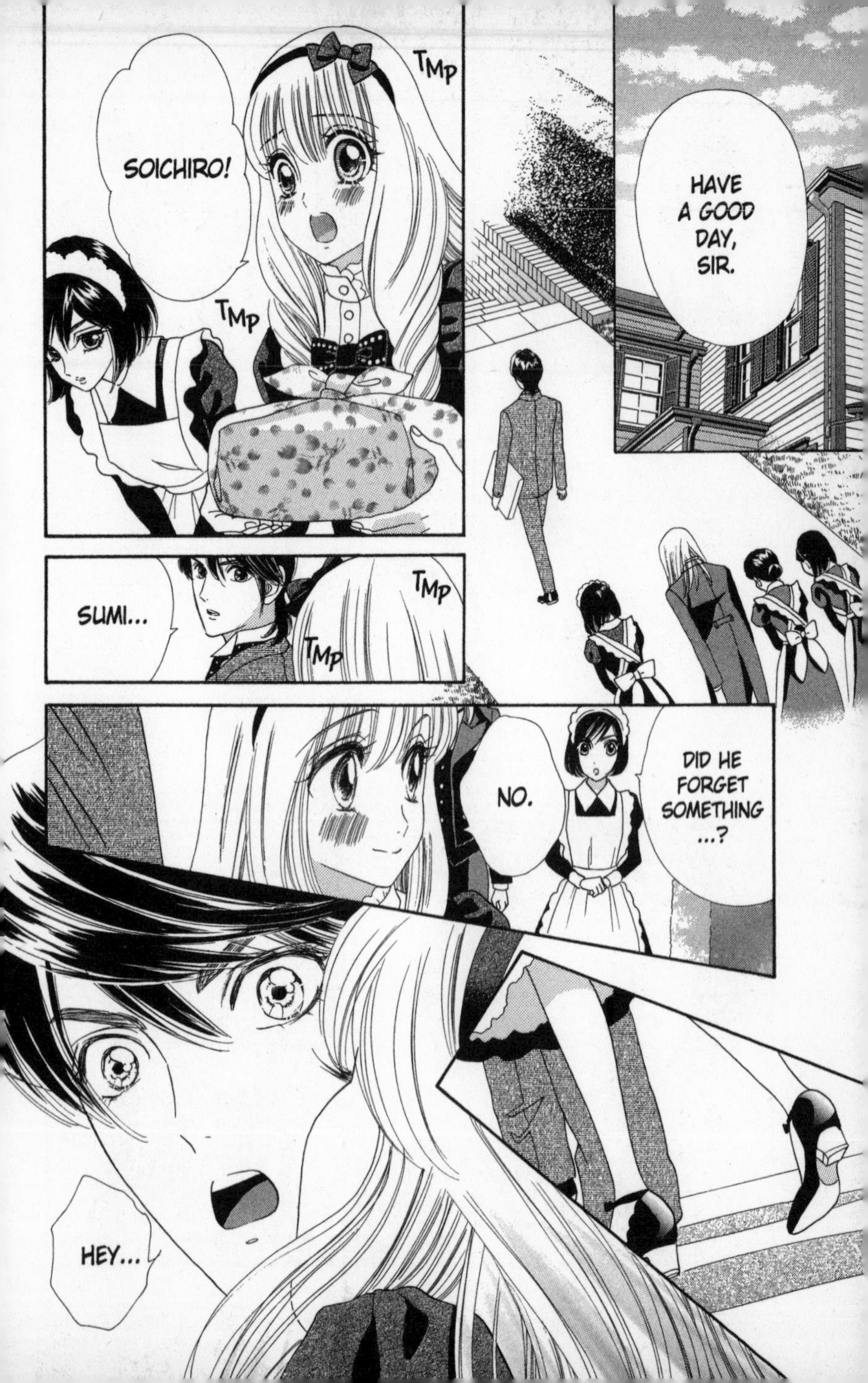
HAVE A GOOD DAY, SIR.
SOICHIRO!
TMP
TMP
SUMI...
TMP
TMP
DID HE FORGET SOMETHING ...?
NO.
HEY...

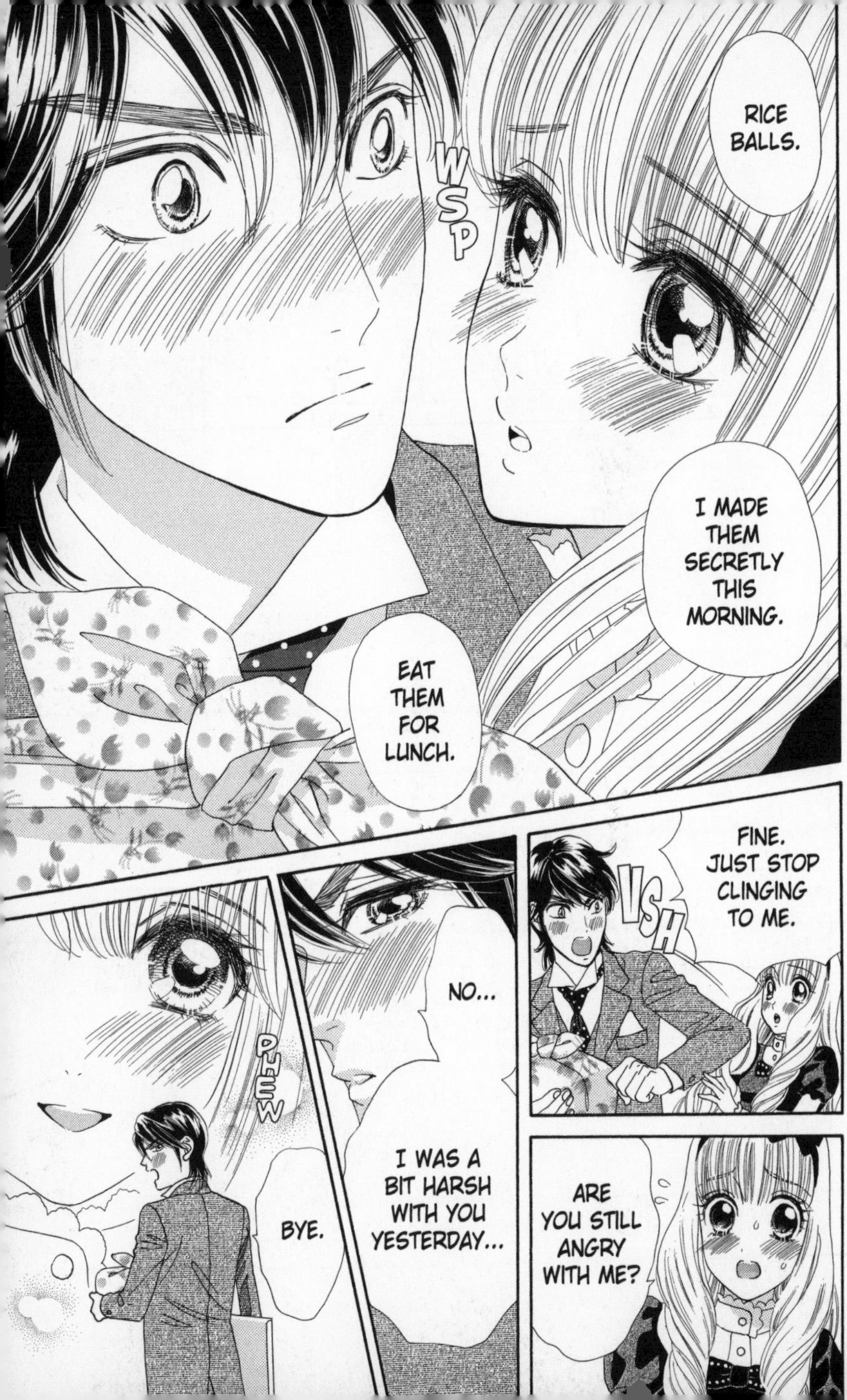
RICE BALLS.
WSP
I MADE THEM SECRETLY THIS MORNING.
EAT THEM FOR LUNCH.
FINE. JUST STOP CLINGING TO ME.
VSH
ARE YOU STILL ANGRY WITH ME?
NO...
I WAS A BIT HARSH WITH YOU YESTERDAY...
PHEW
BYE.

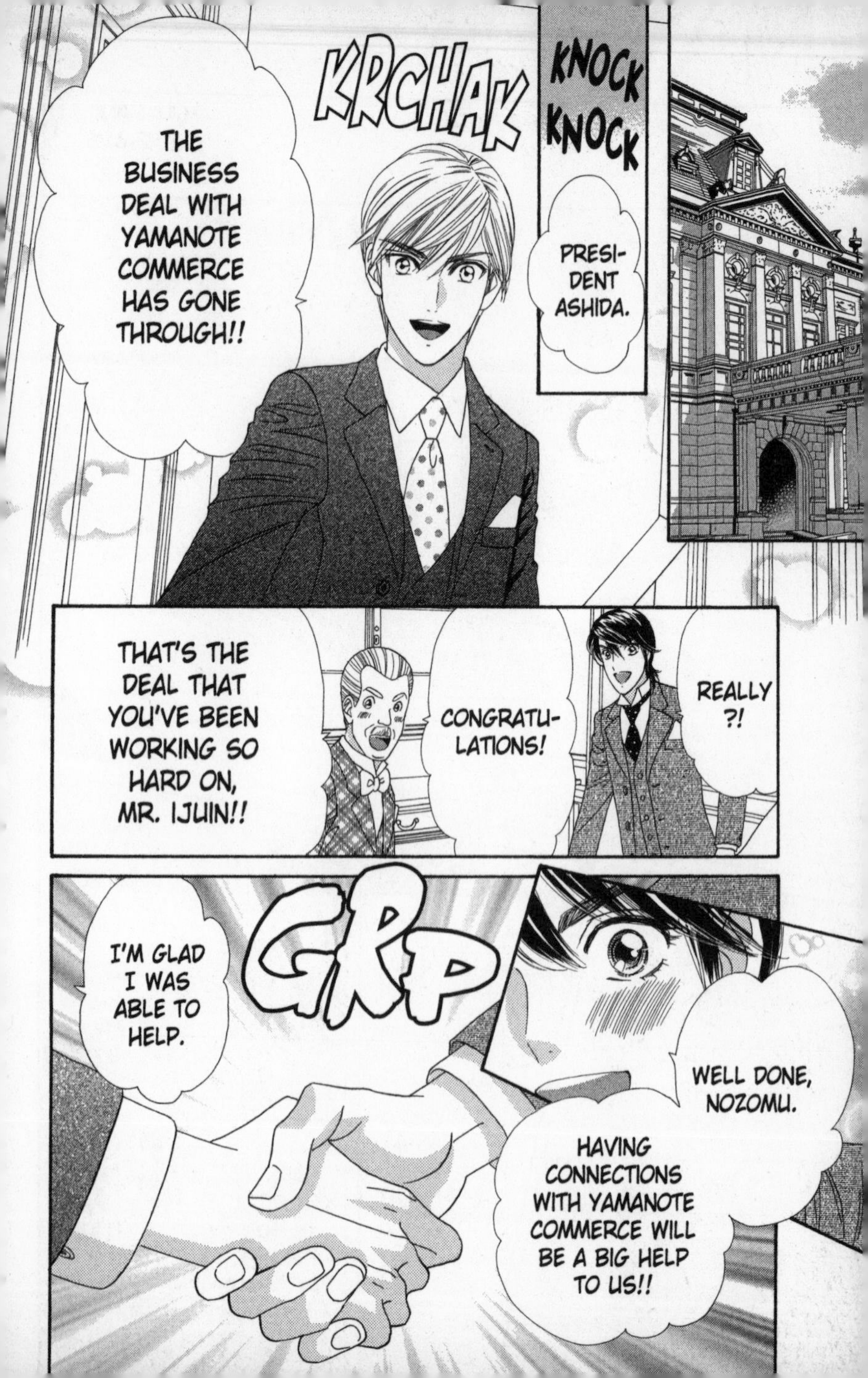
KNOCK KNOCK
PRESIDENT ASHIDA.
KRCHAK
THE BUSINESS DEAL WITH YAMANOTE COMMERCE HAS GONE THROUGH!!
REALLY?!
CONGRATULATIONS!
THAT'S THE DEAL THAT YOU'VE BEEN WORKING SO HARD ON, MR. IJUIN!!
GRP
WELL DONE, NOZOMU.
HAVING CONNECTIONS WITH YAMANOTE COMMERCE WILL BE A BIG HELP TO US!!
I'M GLAD I WAS ABLE TO HELP.

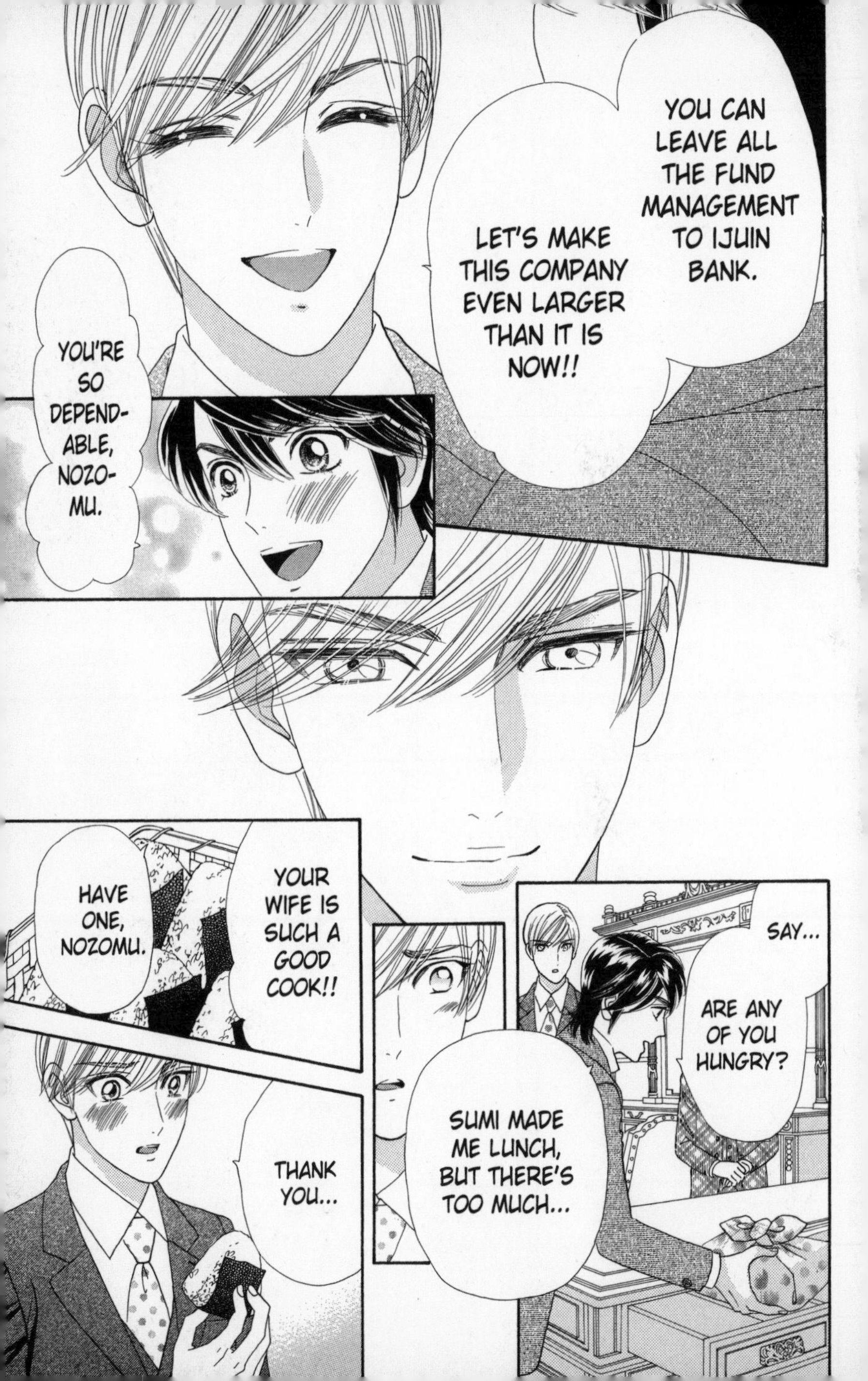
YOU CAN LEAVE ALL THE FUND MANAGEMENT TO IJUIN BANK.
LET'S MAKE THIS COMPANY EVEN LARGER THAN IT IS NOW!!
YOU'RE SO DEPEND-ABLE, NOZO-MU.
SAY...
ARE ANY OF YOU HUNGRY?
SUMI MADE ME LUNCH, BUT THERE'S TOO MUCH...
YOUR WIFE IS SUCH A GOOD COOK!!
HAVE ONE, NOZOMU.
THANK YOU...

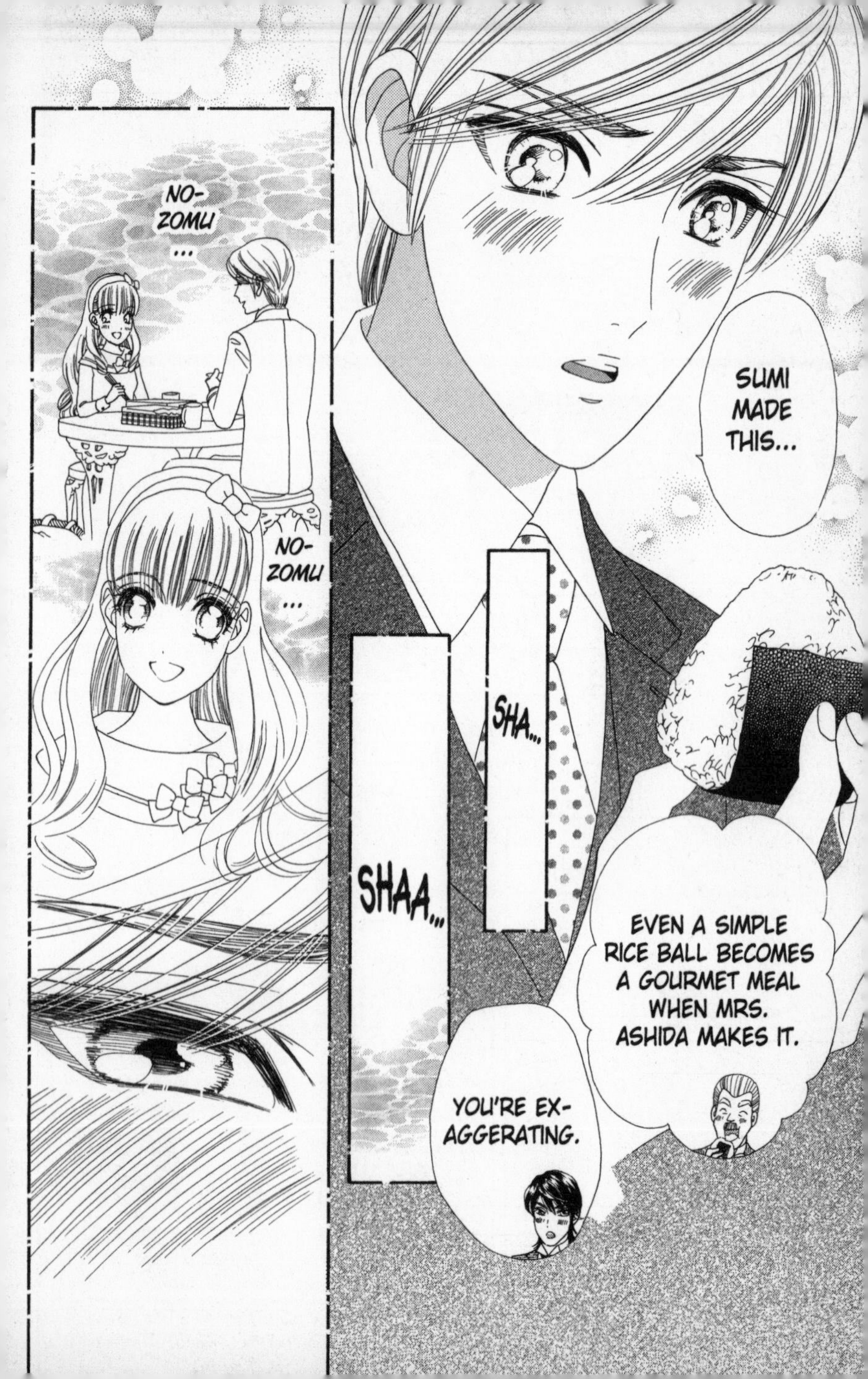
SUMI MADE THIS...
EVEN A SIMPLE RICE BALL BECOMES A GOURMET MEAL WHEN MRS. ASHIDA MAKES IT.
YOU'RE EX-AGGERATING.
SHA...
SHAA...
NO-ZOMU ...
NO-ZOMU ...

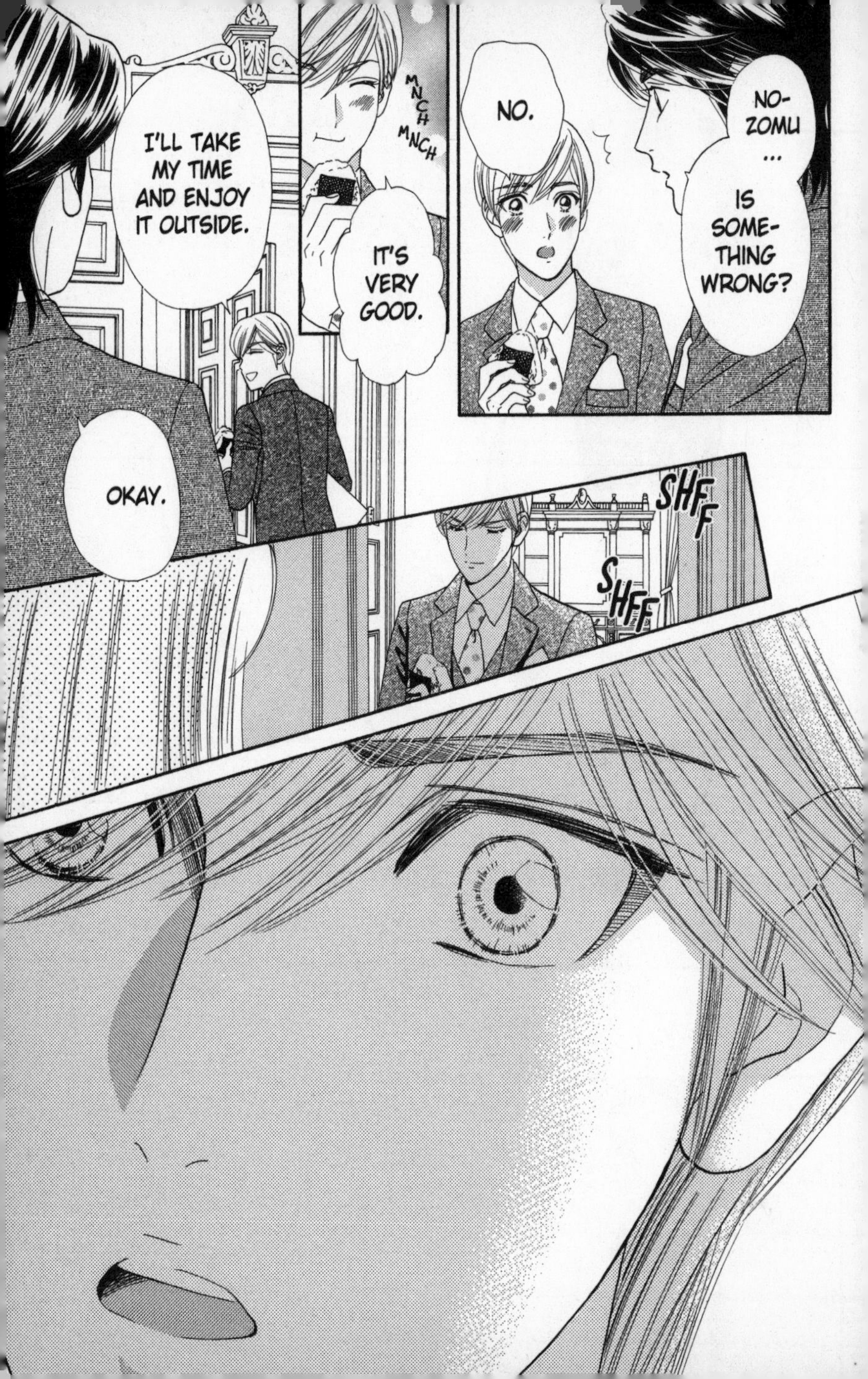
NO-ZOMU ... IS SOMETHING WRONG?
NO.
MNCH MNCH
IT'S VERY GOOD.
I'LL TAKE MY TIME AND ENJOY IT OUTSIDE.
OKAY.
SHFF
SHFF

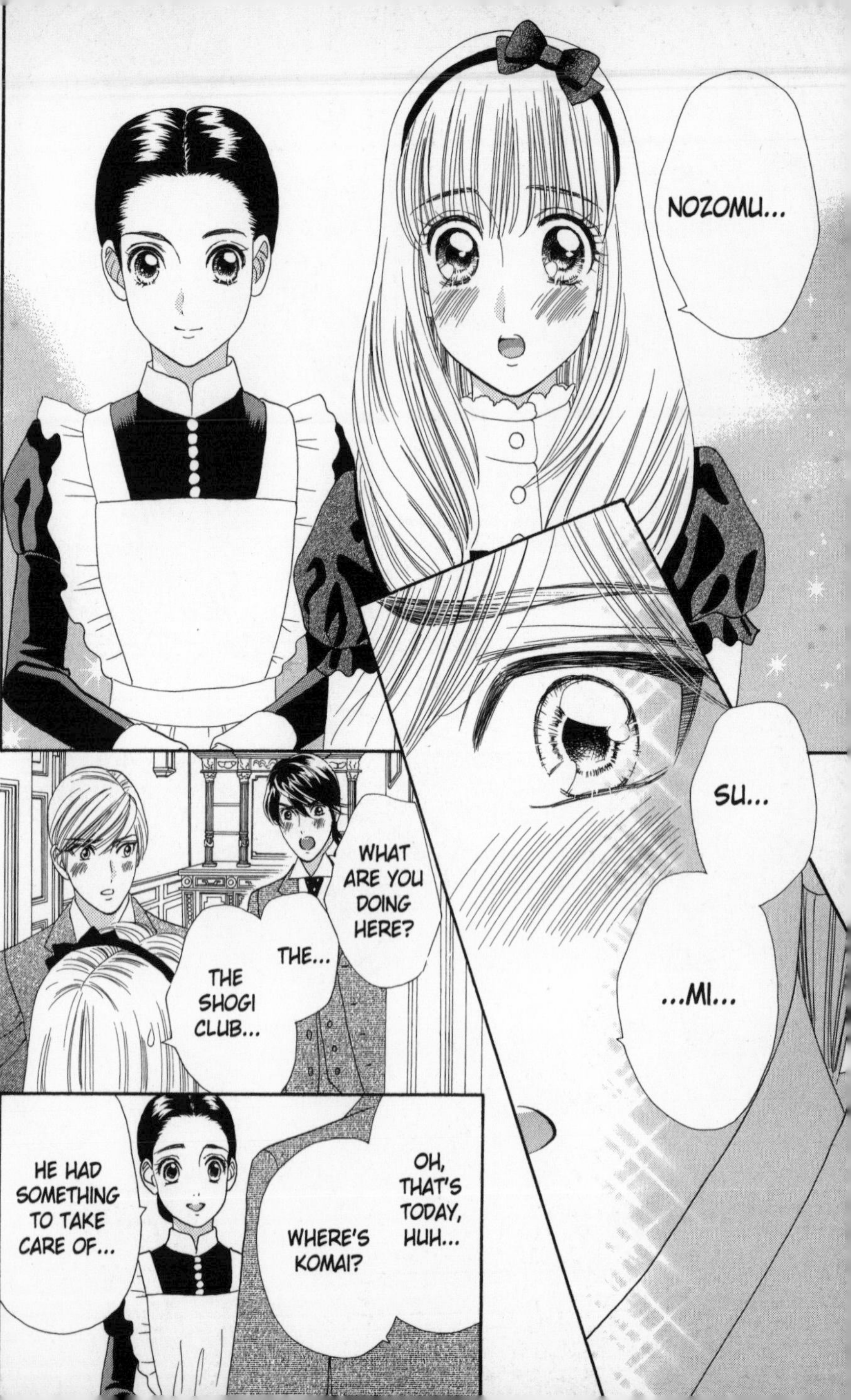
NOZOMU...
SU...
...MI...
WHAT ARE YOU DOING HERE?
THE...
THE SHOGI CLUB...
OH, THAT'S TODAY, HUH...
WHERE'S KOMAI?
HE HAD SOMETHING TO TAKE CARE OF...

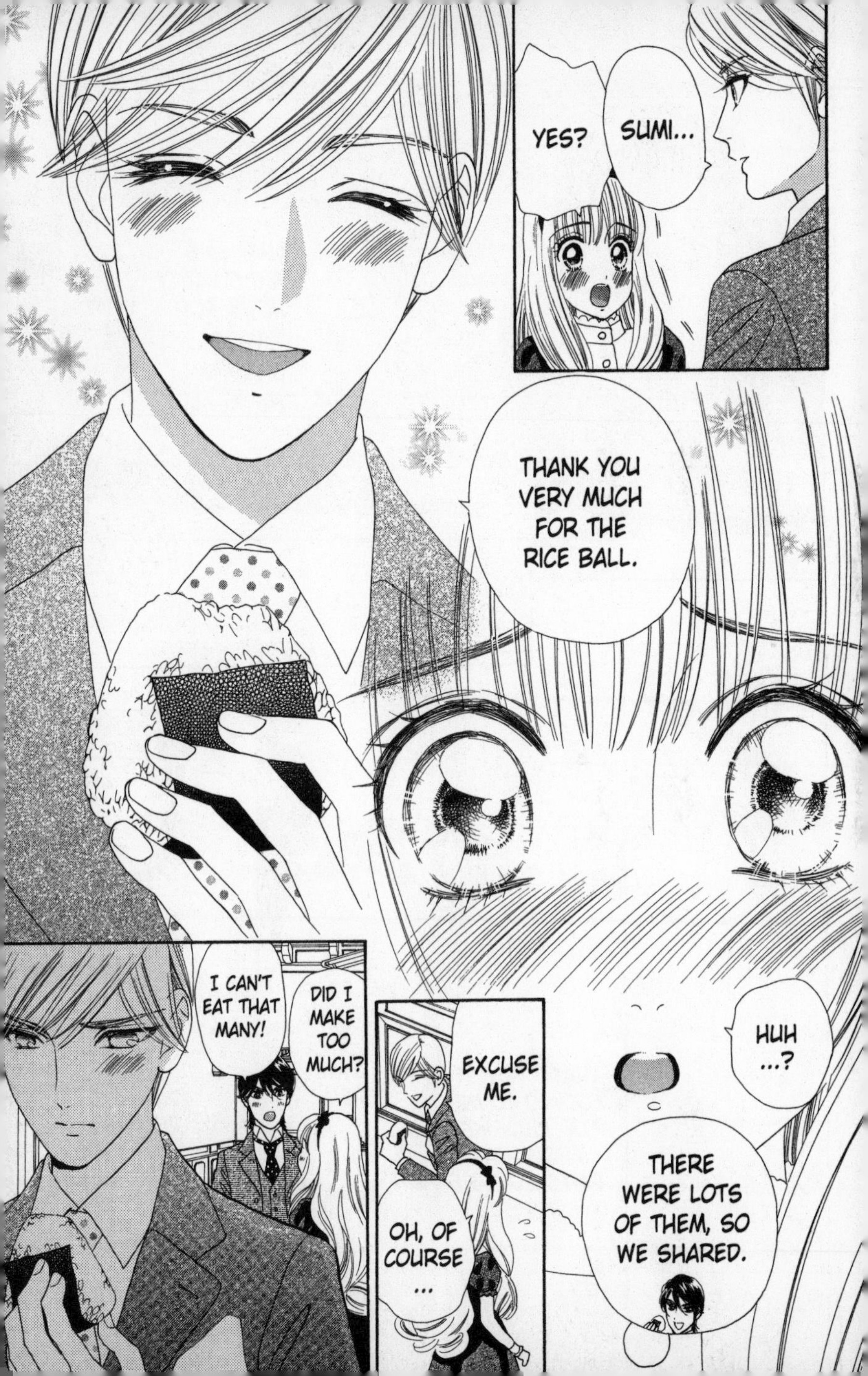
SUMI...
YES?
THANK YOU VERY MUCH FOR THE RICE BALL.
HUH ...?
THERE WERE LOTS OF THEM, SO WE SHARED.
EXCUSE ME.
OH, OF COURSE ...
DID I MAKE TOO MUCH?
I CAN'T EAT THAT MANY!

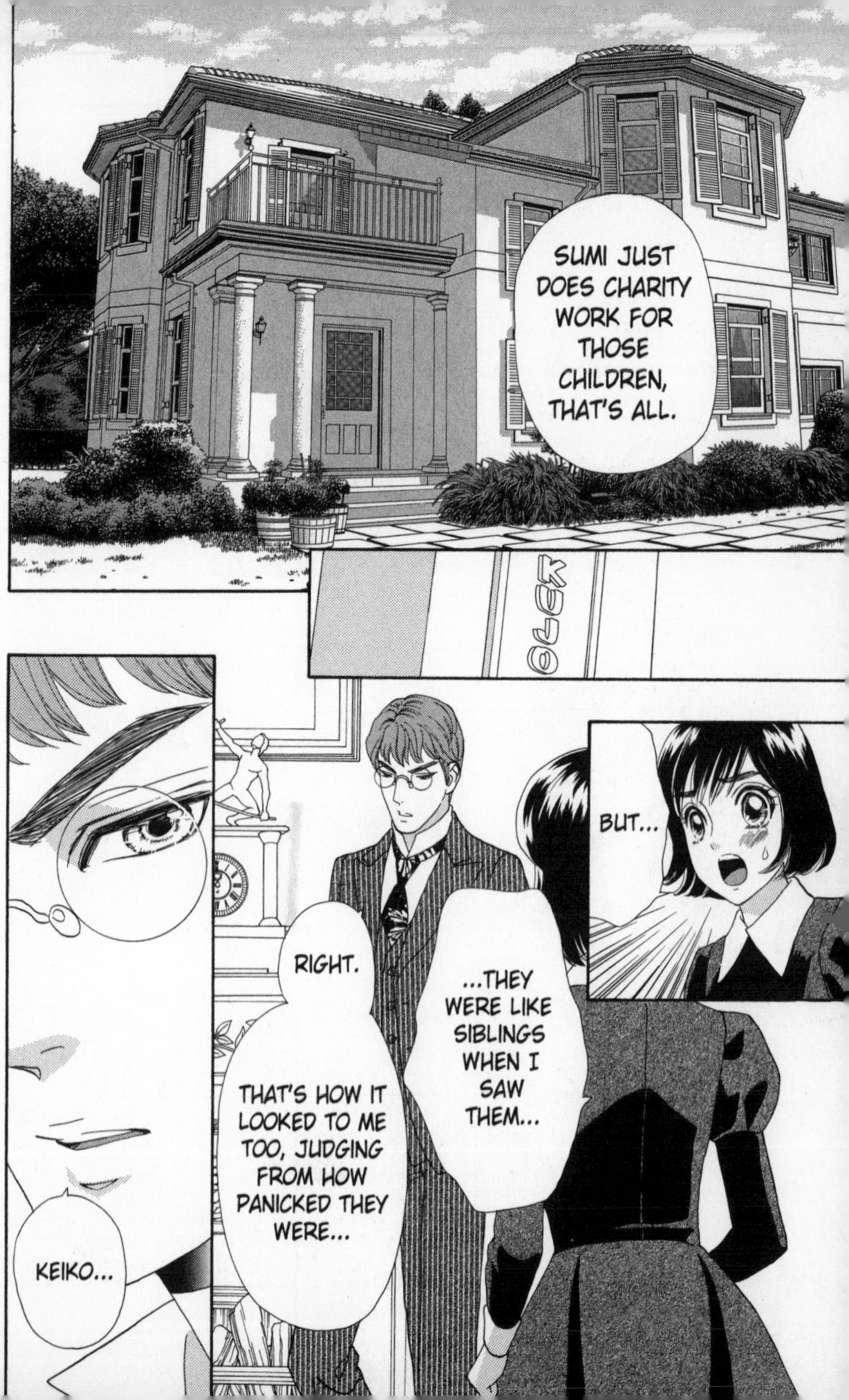
SUMI JUST DOES CHARITY WORK FOR THOSE CHILDREN, THAT'S ALL.
KUJO
BUT...
...THEY WERE LIKE SIBLINGS WHEN I SAW THEM...
RIGHT.
THAT'S HOW IT LOOKED TO ME TOO, JUDGING FROM HOW PANICKED THEY WERE...
KEIKO...

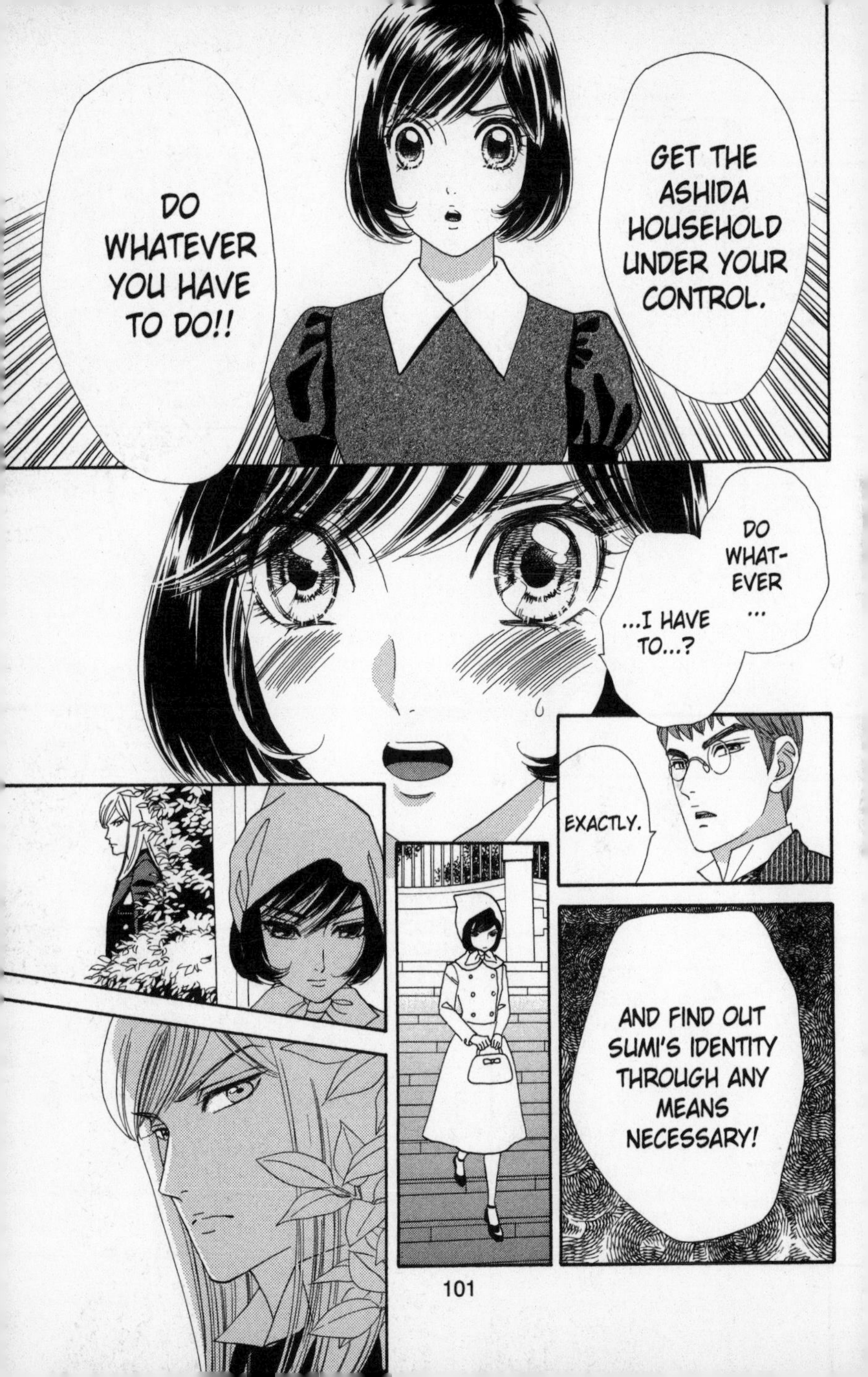
GET THE ASHIDA HOUSEHOLD UNDER YOUR CONTROL.
DO WHATEVER YOU HAVE TO DO!!
DO WHAT-EVER...
...I HAVE TO...?
EXACTLY.
AND FIND OUT SUMI'S IDENTITY THROUGH ANY MEANS NECESSARY!

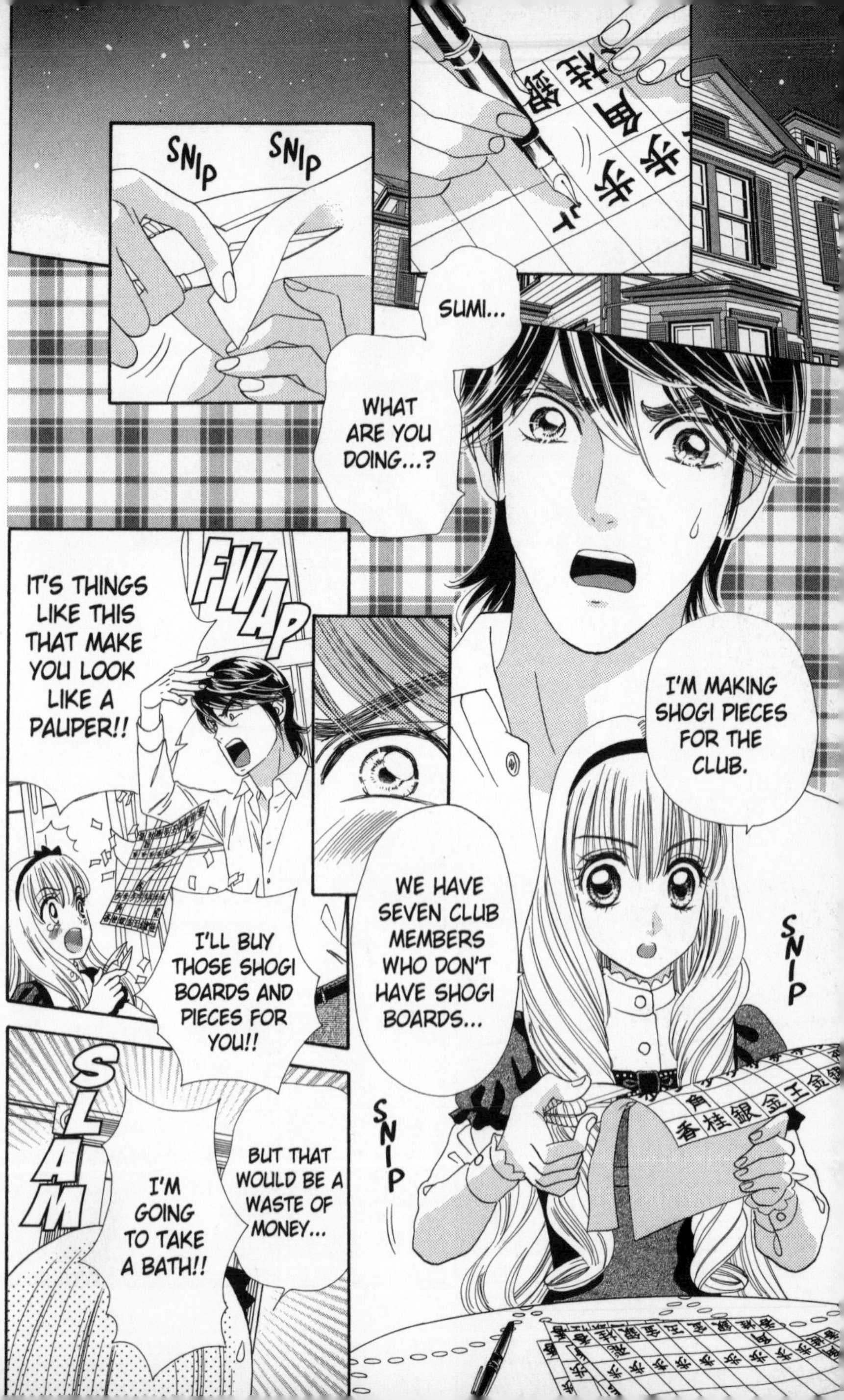
SNIP SNIP
SUMI...
WHAT ARE YOU DOING...?
I'M MAKING SHOGI PIECES FOR THE CLUB.
WE HAVE SEVEN CLUB MEMBERS WHO DON'T HAVE SHOGI BOARDS...
SNIP
SNIP
FWAP
IT'S THINGS LIKE THIS THAT MAKE YOU LOOK LIKE A PAUPER!!
I'LL BUY THOSE SHOGI BOARDS AND PIECES FOR YOU!!
BUT THAT WOULD BE A WASTE OF MONEY...
I'M GOING TO TAKE A BATH!!
SLAM

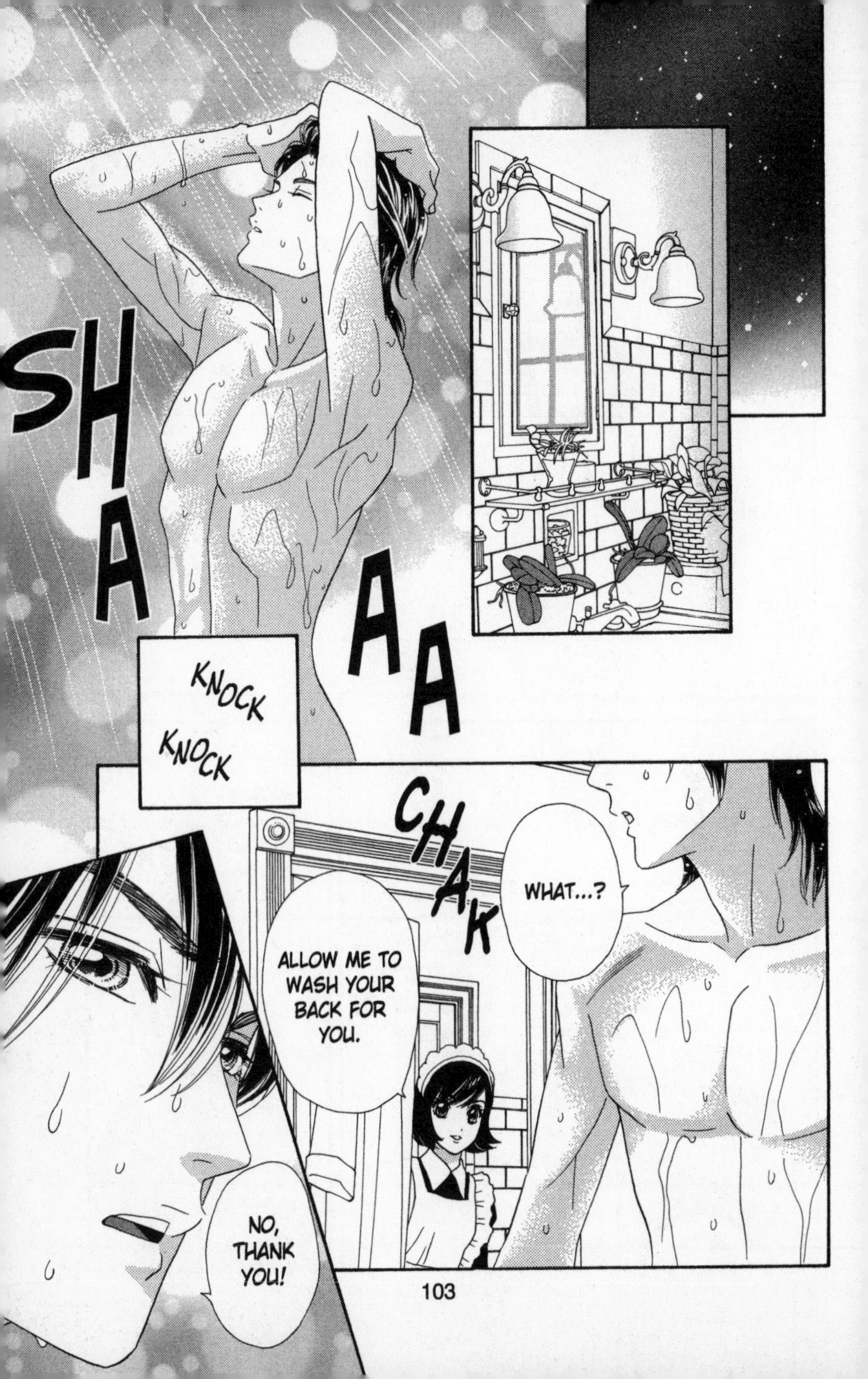
SHAAAA
KNOCK KNOCK
CHAK
WHAT...?
ALLOW ME TO WASH YOUR BACK FOR YOU.
NO, THANK YOU!

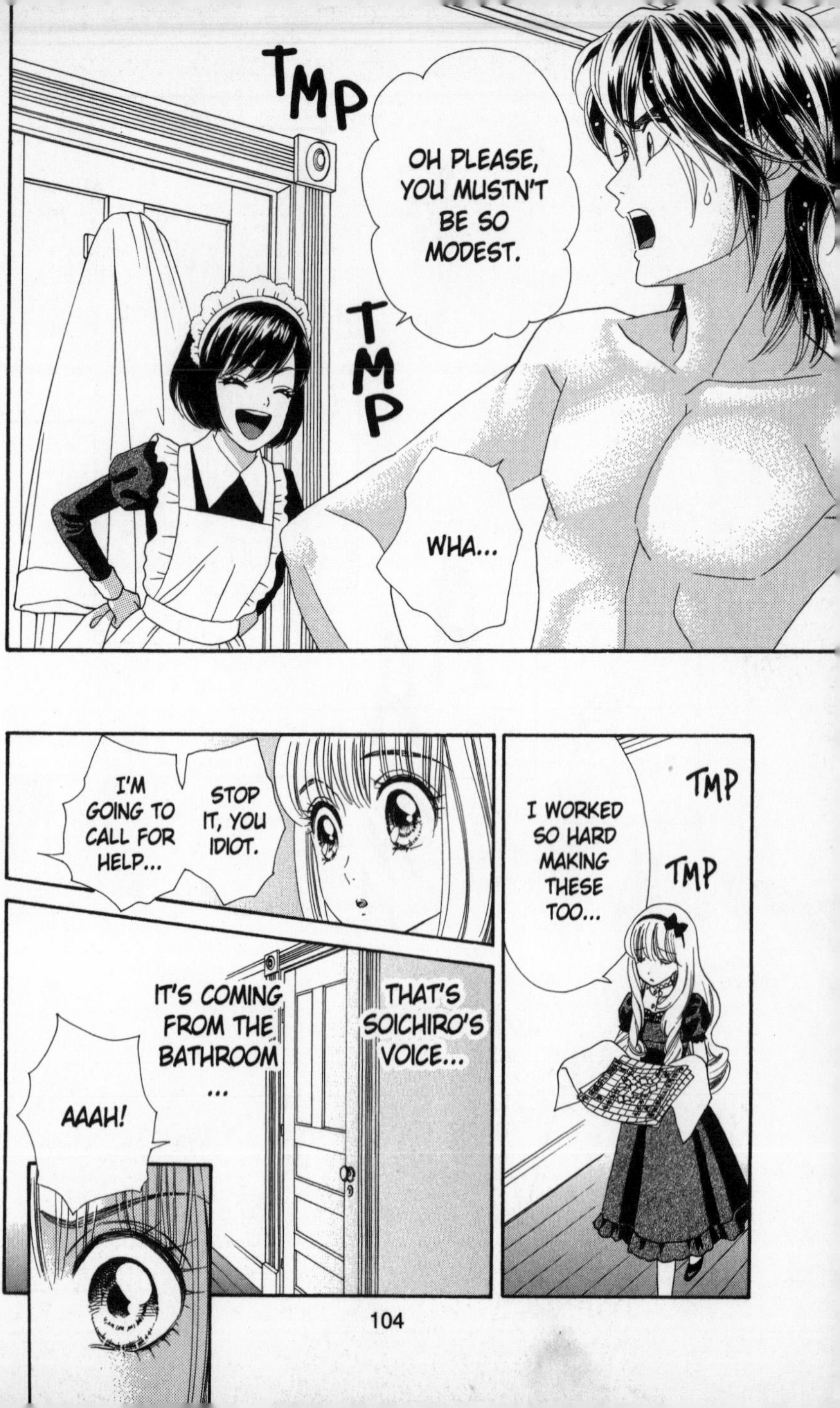
OH PLEASE, YOU MUSTN'T BE SO MODEST.
TMP
TMP
WHA...
TMP
TMP
I WORKED SO HARD MAKING THESE TOO...
STOP IT, YOU IDIOT.
I'M GOING TO CALL FOR HELP...
THAT'S SOICHIRO'S VOICE...
IT'S COMING FROM THE BATHROOM ...
AAAH!

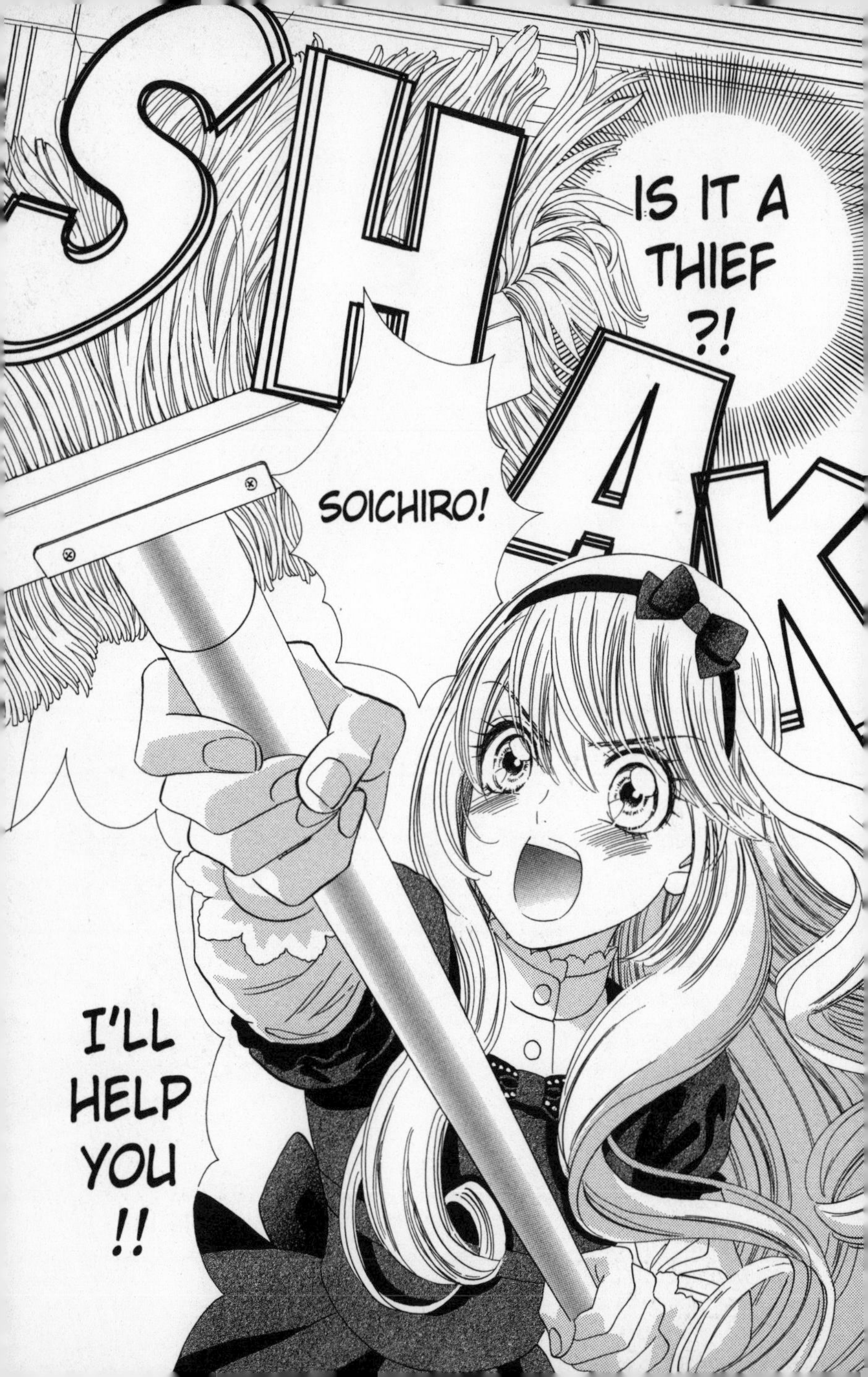
IS IT A THIEF ?!
SHAK
SOICHIRO!
I'LL HELP YOU !!

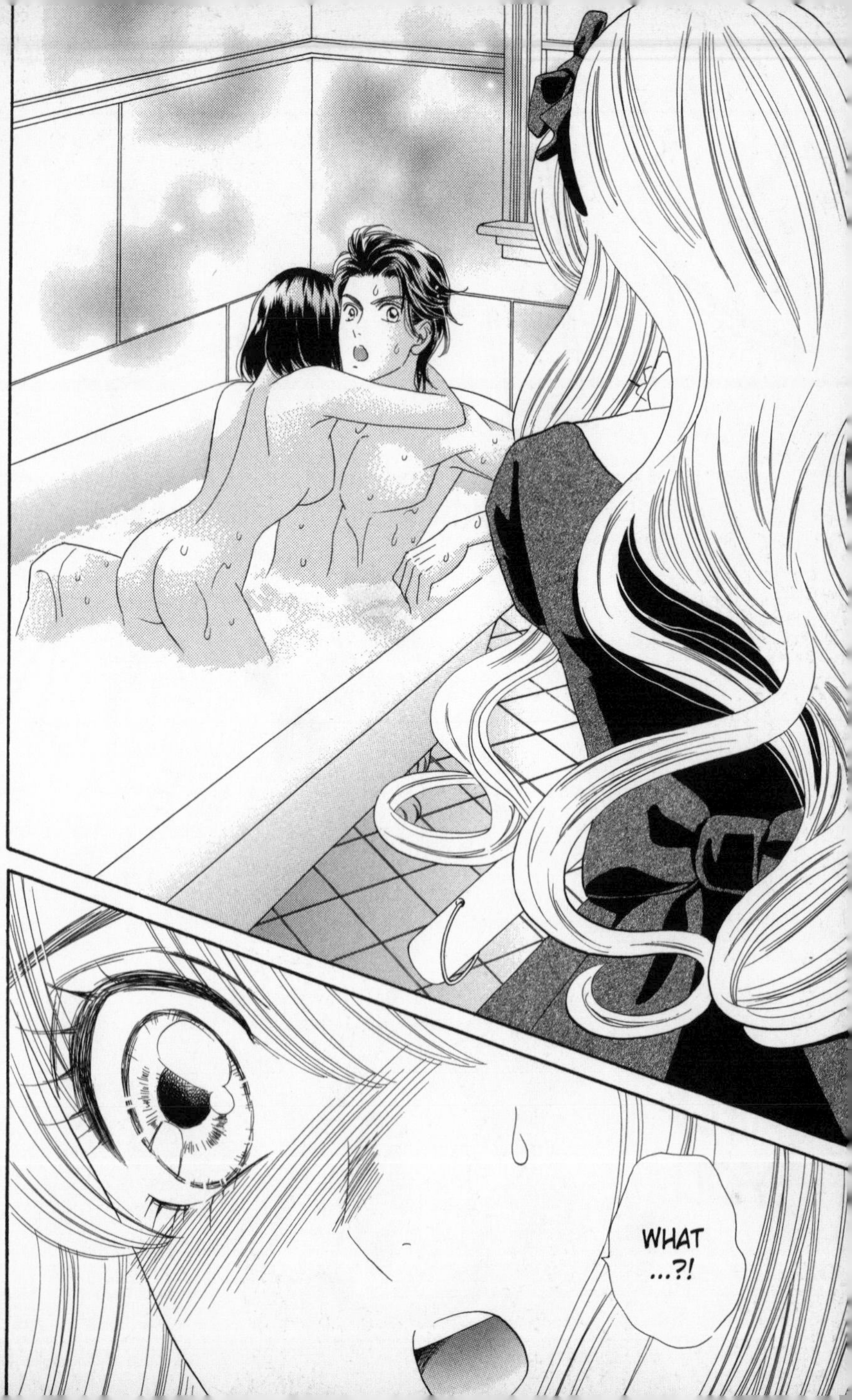
WHAT ...?!

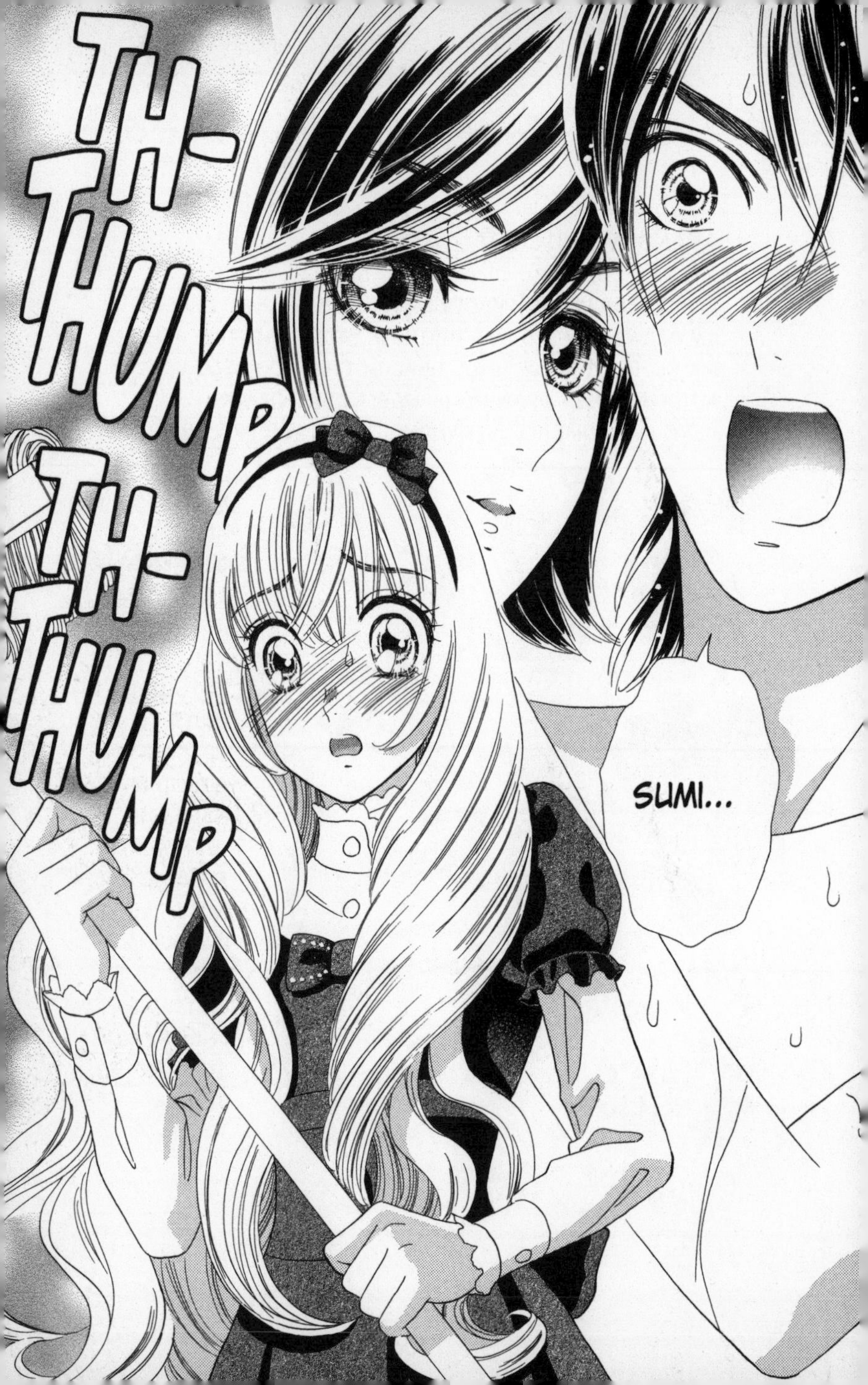
TH-THUMP TH-THUMP
SUMI...

No. 4

RANDOM CHITCHAT!

Date . .

✽ I NEEDED A LOT OF PRACTICE AND RESEARCH TO CHANGE MY DRAWING STYLE FOR JUST ONE STORY, BUT THIS HELPED ME REFINE THINGS SINCE I HAD GOTTEN TOO USED TO AUTOMATICALLY DRAWING MANGA A CERTAIN WAY.
HERE ARE SOME ILLUSTRATIONS I DREW FOR PRACTICE.

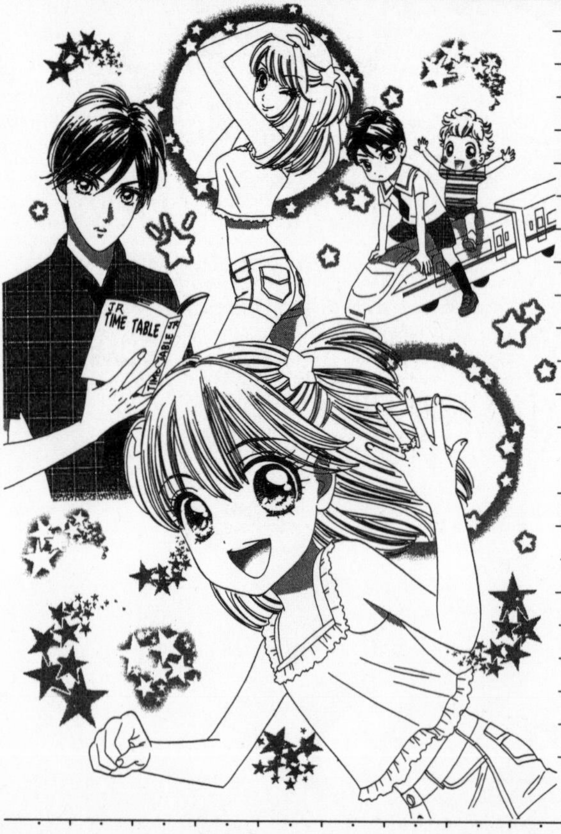
JR TIME TABLE

THESE DRAWINGS ARE A BIT DIFFERENT FROM THE ACTUAL MANGA.

TO TELL YOU THE TRUTH, I'M STILL WORKING ON BOTH THE *RIBON* PIECE AND *STEPPING ON ROSES* AT THE SAME TIME, SO I'M HAVING A TOUGH TIME SWITCHING FROM ONE DRAWING STYLE TO THE OTHER.

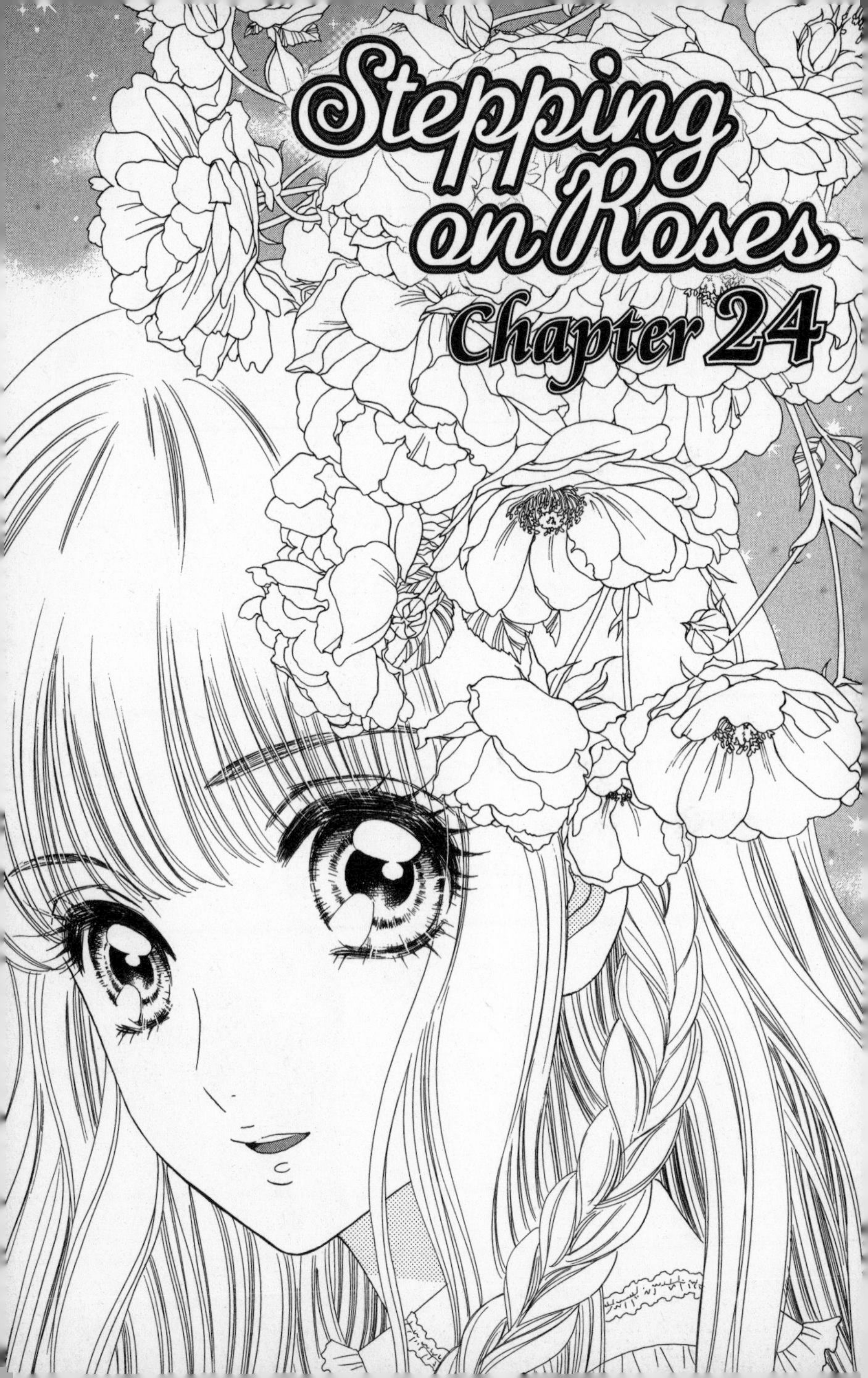
Stepping on Roses
Chapter 24

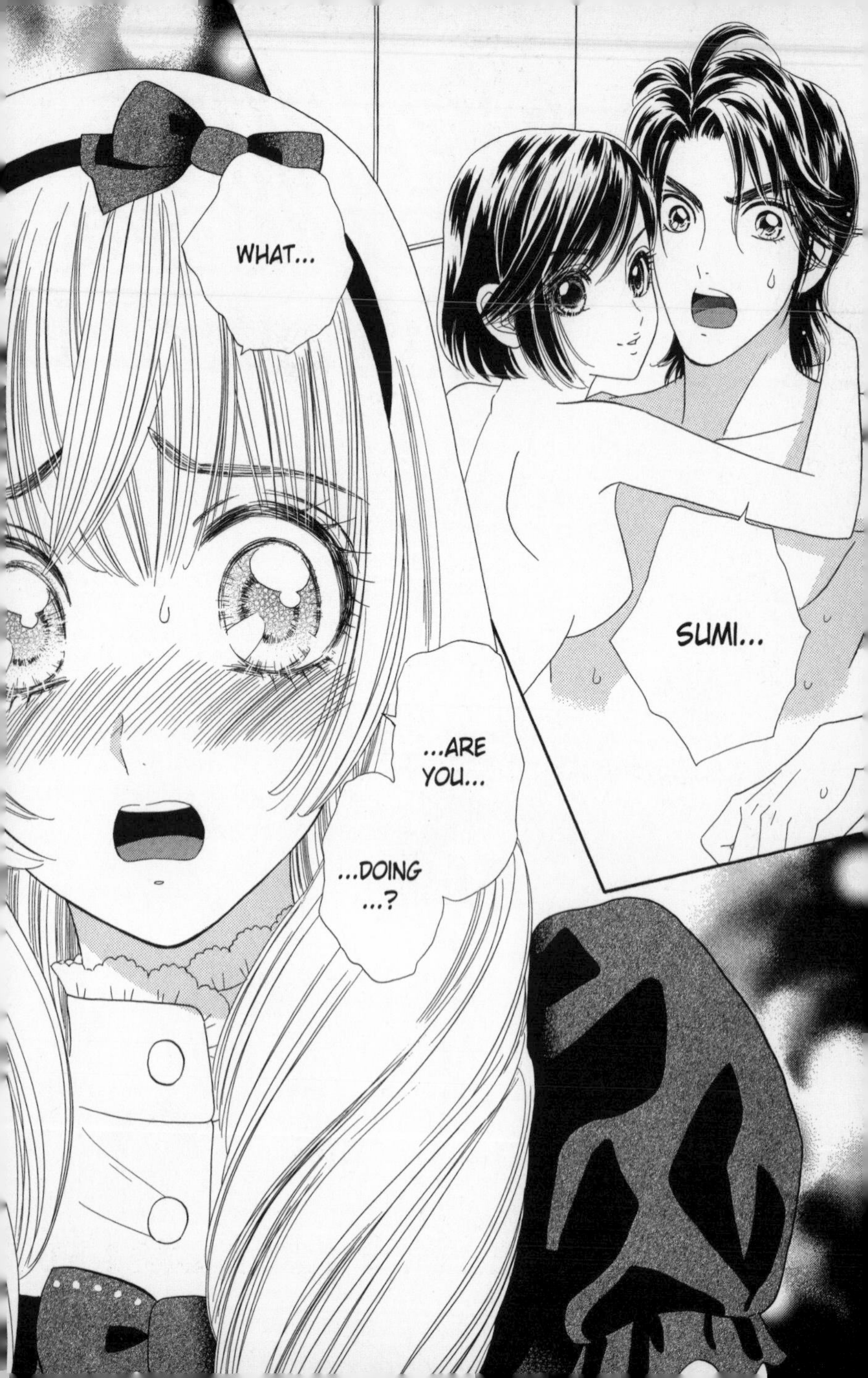
SUMI...
WHAT...
...ARE YOU...
...DOING ...?

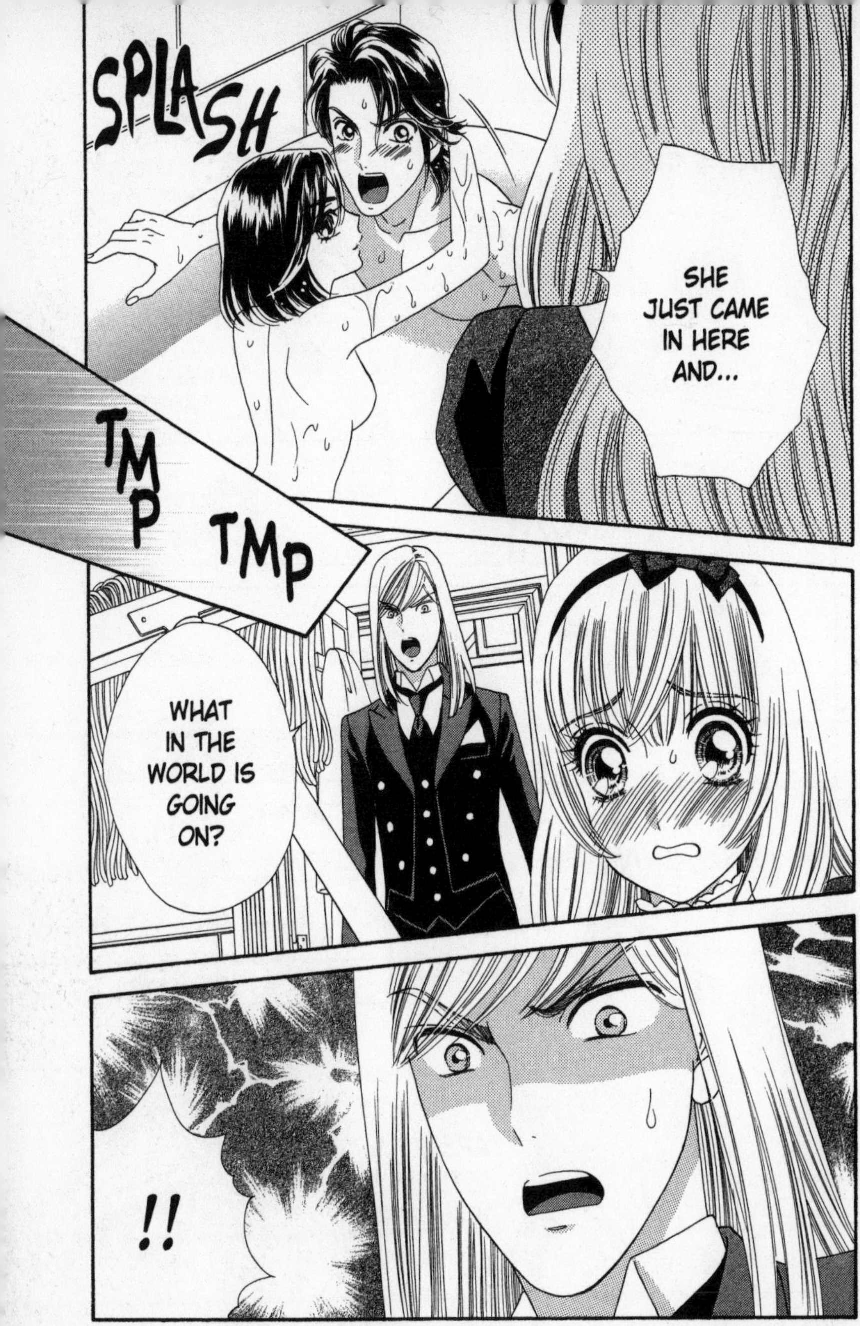
SHE JUST CAME IN HERE AND...
SPLASH
TMP TMP
WHAT IN THE WORLD IS GOING ON?
!!

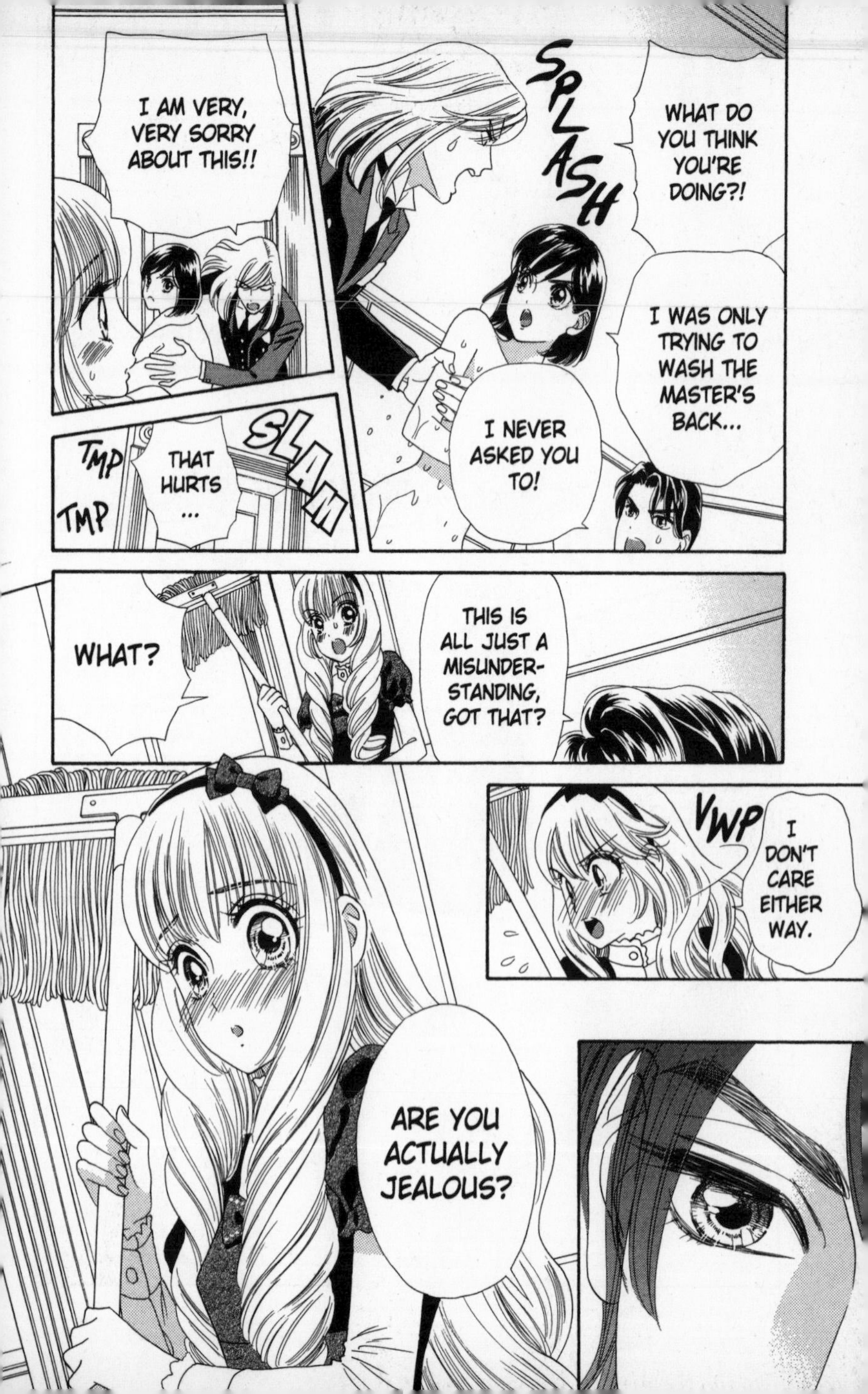
WHAT DO YOU THINK YOU'RE DOING?!
SPLASH
I WAS ONLY TRYING TO WASH THE MASTER'S BACK...
I NEVER ASKED YOU TO!
I AM VERY, VERY SORRY ABOUT THIS!!
SLAM
THAT HURTS ...
TMP
TMP
THIS IS ALL JUST A MISUNDER-STANDING, GOT THAT?
WHAT?
I DON'T CARE EITHER WAY.
VWP
ARE YOU ACTUALLY JEALOUS?

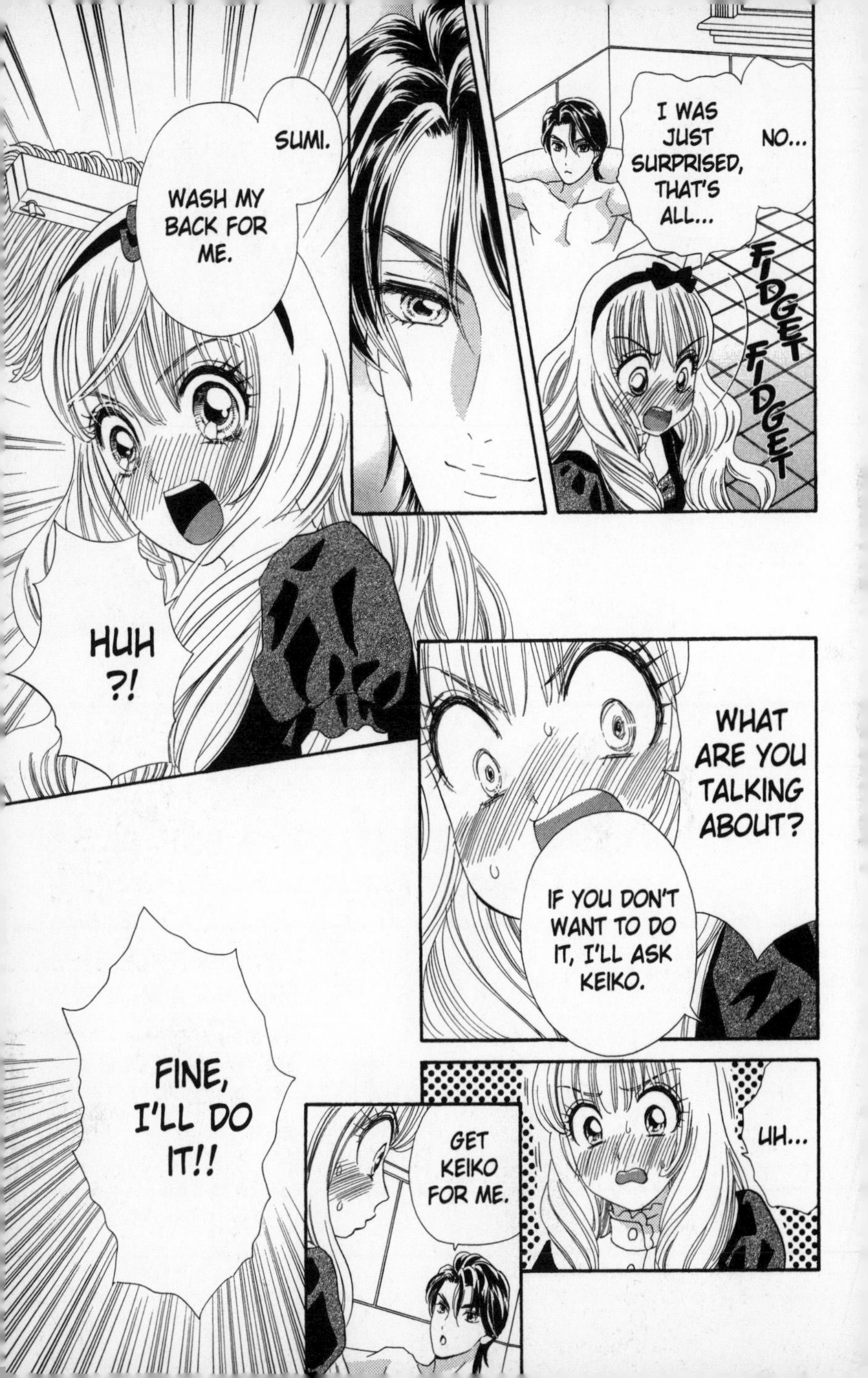
NO...
I WAS JUST SURPRISED, THAT'S ALL...
FIDGET FIDGET
SUMI.
WASH MY BACK FOR ME.
HUH?!
WHAT ARE YOU TALKING ABOUT?
IF YOU DON'T WANT TO DO IT, I'LL ASK KEIKO.
UH...
GET KEIKO FOR ME.
FINE, I'LL DO IT!!

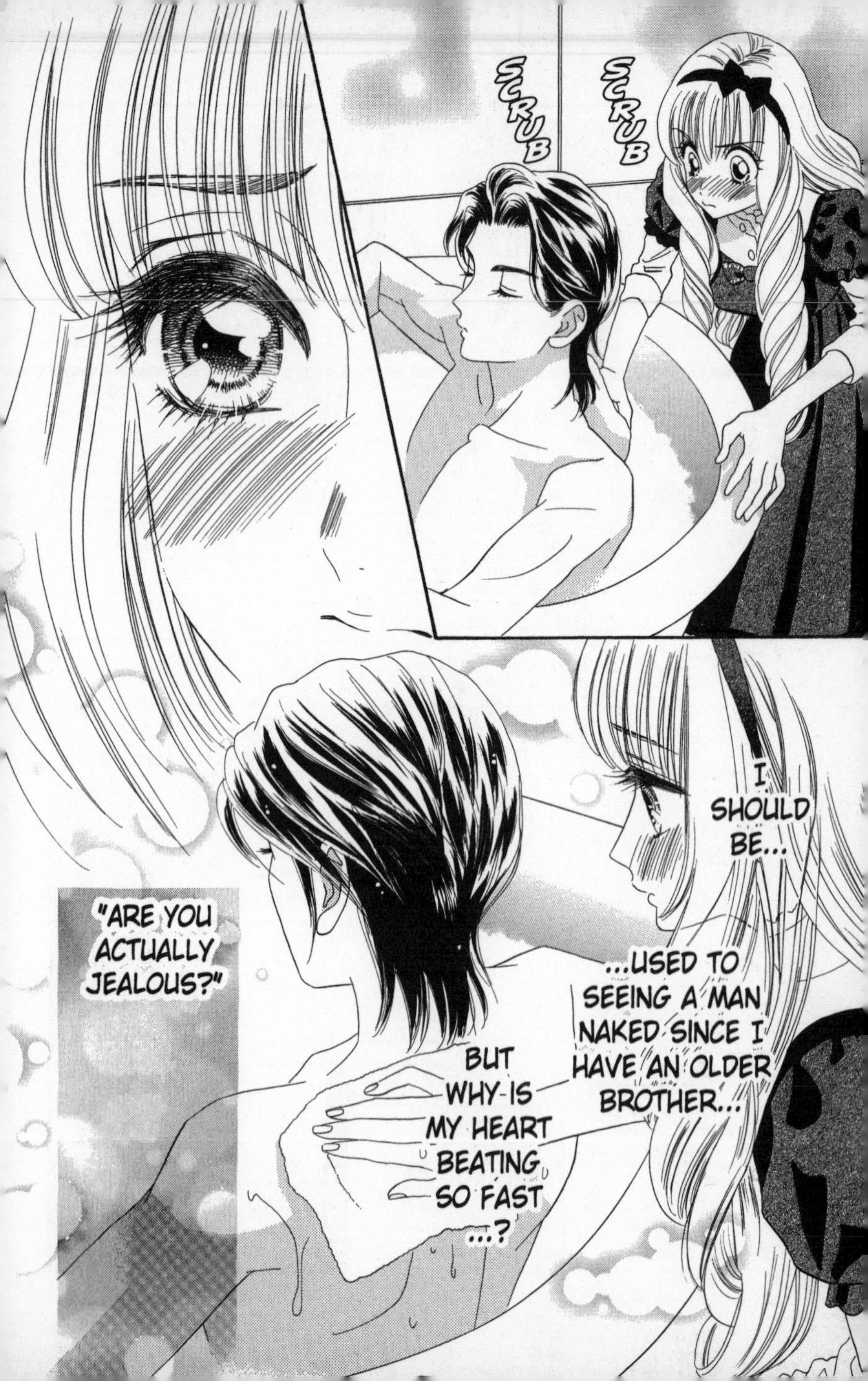
SCRUB
SCRUB
I SHOULD BE...
...USED TO SEEING A MAN NAKED SINCE I HAVE AN OLDER BROTHER...
BUT WHY IS MY HEART BEATING SO FAST ...?
"ARE YOU ACTUALLY JEALOUS?"

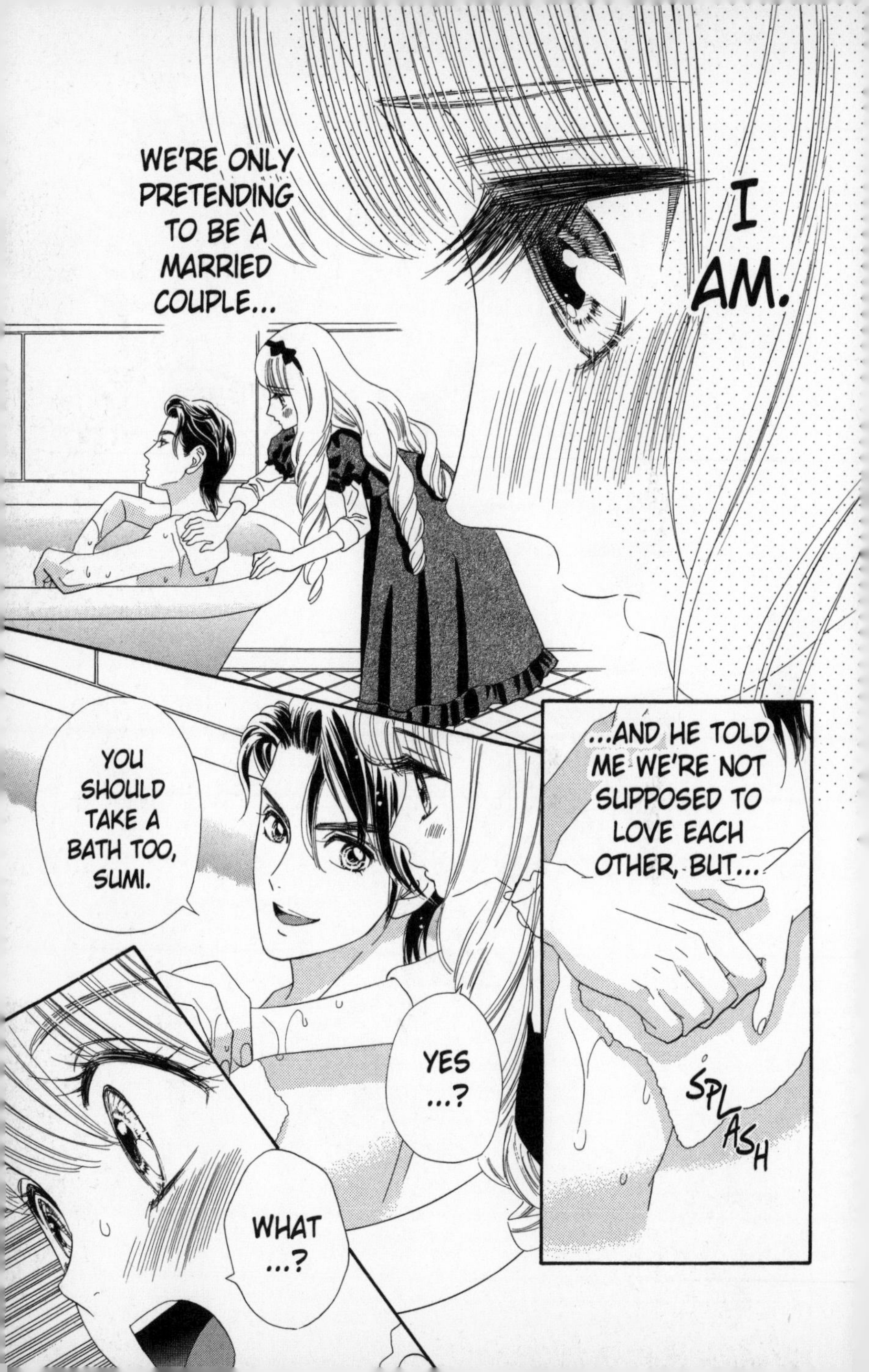
I AM.
WE'RE ONLY PRETENDING TO BE A MARRIED COUPLE...
...AND HE TOLD ME WE'RE NOT SUPPOSED TO LOVE EACH OTHER, BUT...
SPLASH
YOU SHOULD TAKE A BATH TOO, SUMI.
YES ...?
WHAT ...?

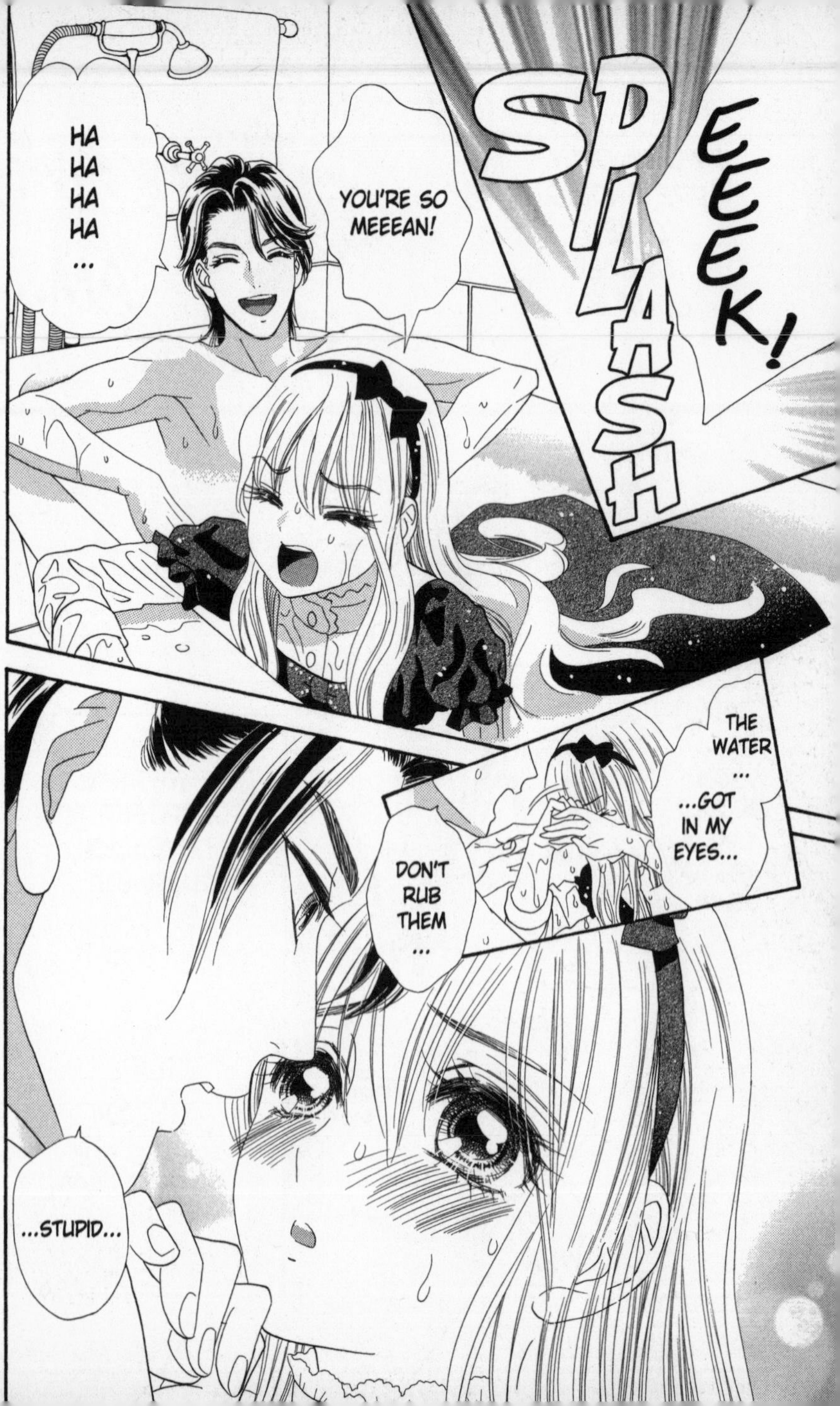
SPLASH
EEEK!
YOU'RE SO MEEEAN!
HA HA HA HA ...
THE WATER ... ...GOT IN MY EYES...
DON'T RUB THEM ...
...STUPID...

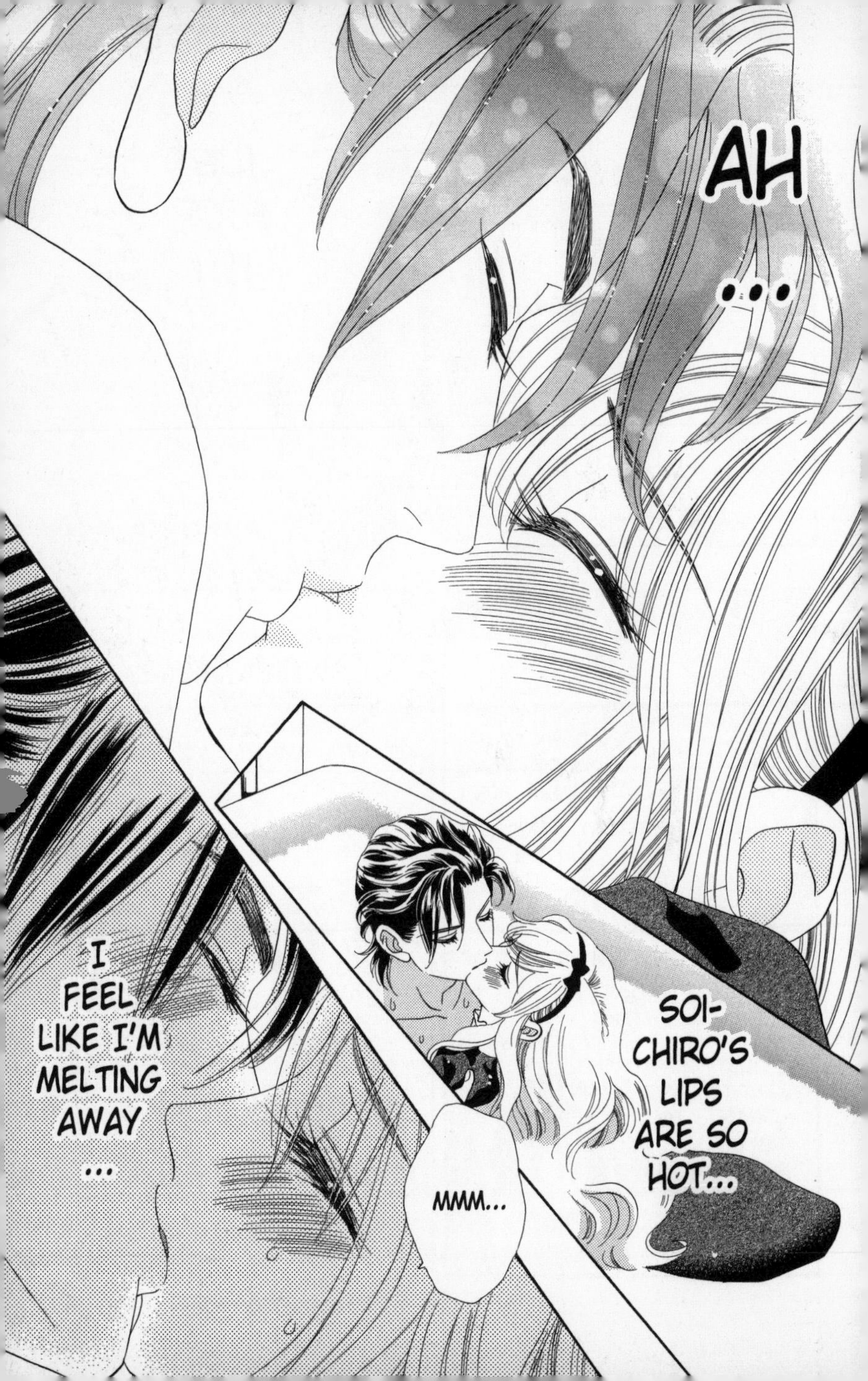
AH ...
SOI-CHIRO'S LIPS ARE SO HOT...
MMM...
I FEEL LIKE I'M MELTING AWAY ...

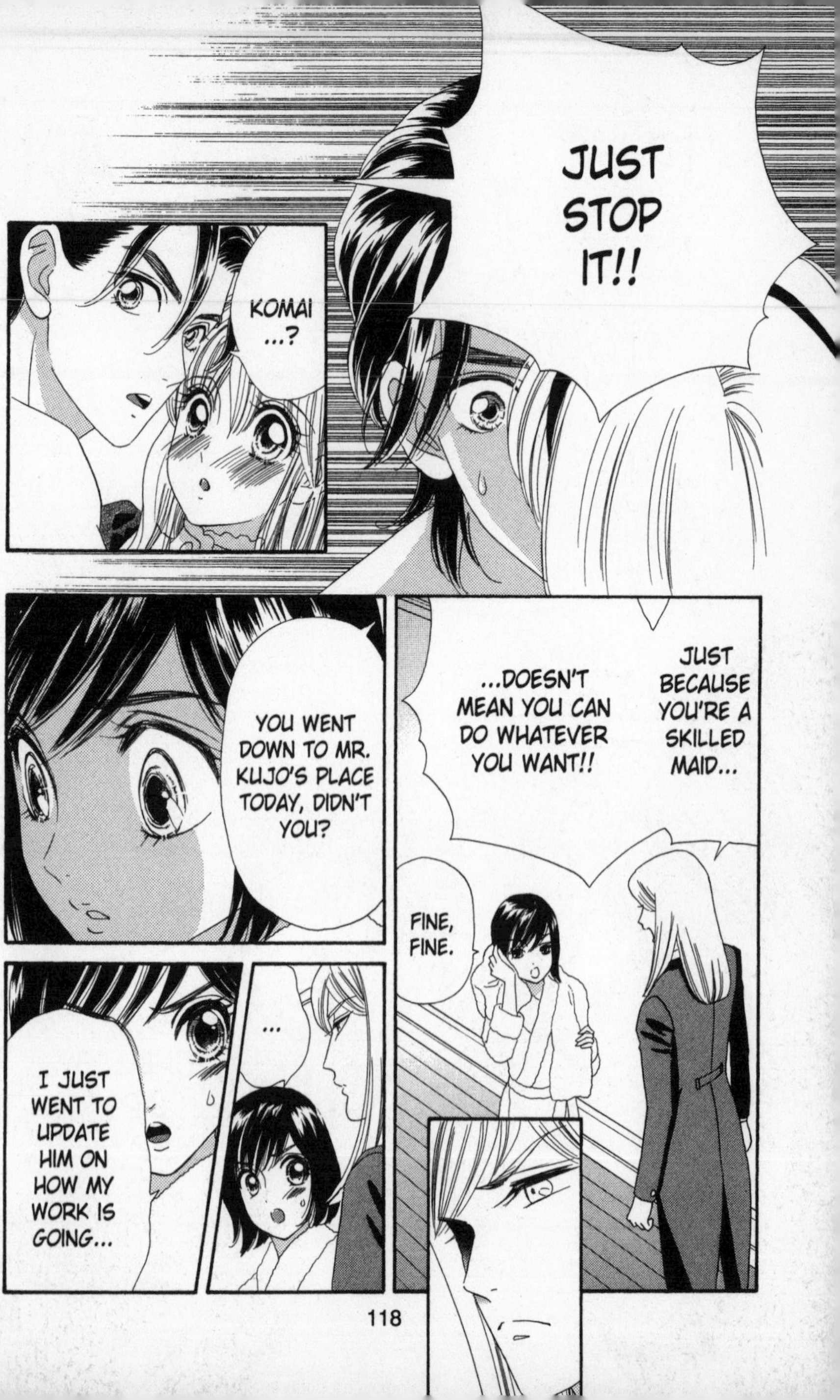
JUST STOP IT!!
KOMAI ...?
JUST BECAUSE YOU'RE A SKILLED MAID...
...DOESN'T MEAN YOU CAN DO WHATEVER YOU WANT!!
FINE, FINE.
YOU WENT DOWN TO MR. KUJO'S PLACE TODAY, DIDN'T YOU?
...
I JUST WENT TO UPDATE HIM ON HOW MY WORK IS GOING...

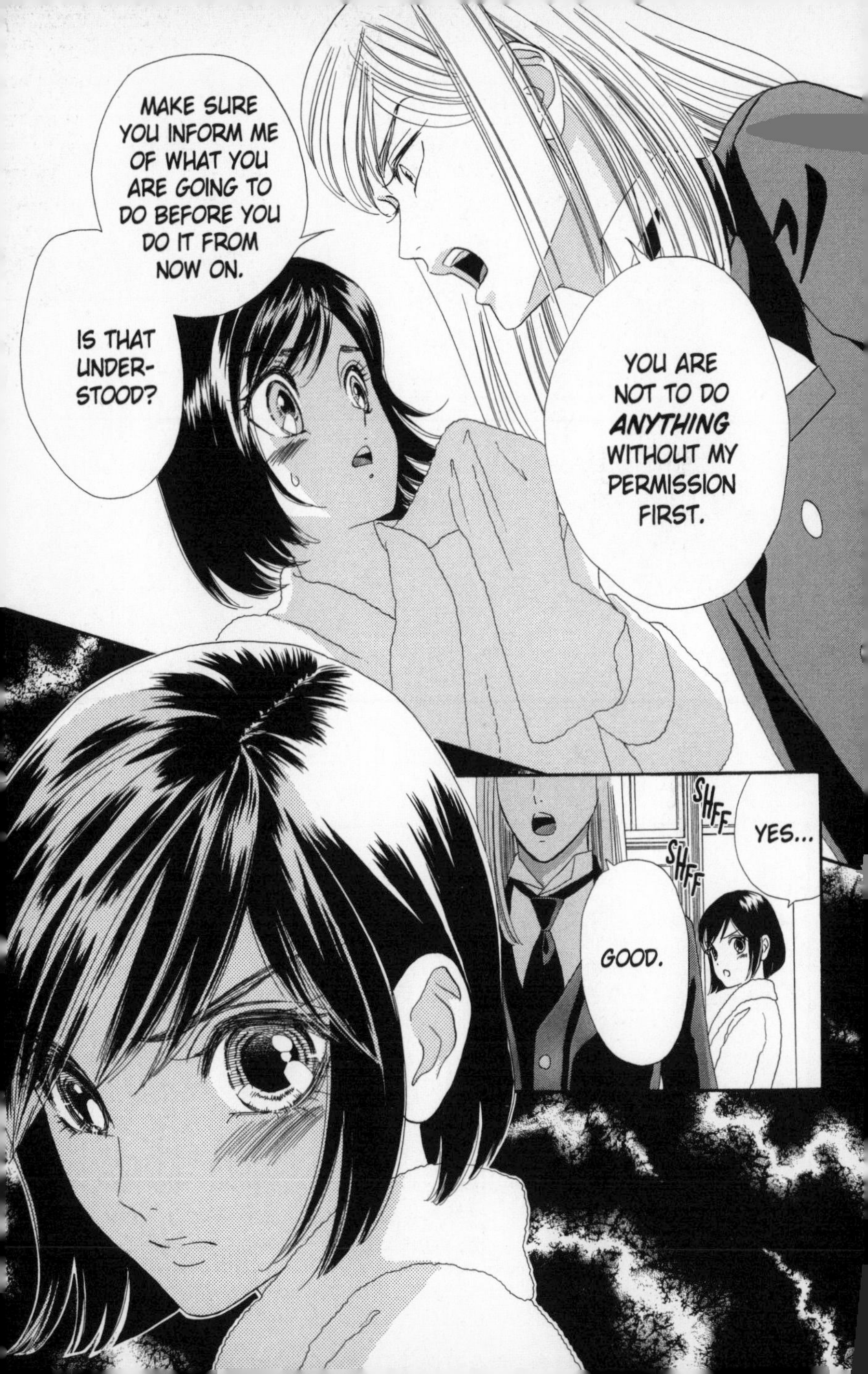
YOU ARE NOT TO DO *ANYTHING* WITHOUT MY PERMISSION FIRST.
MAKE SURE YOU INFORM ME OF WHAT YOU ARE GOING TO DO BEFORE YOU DO IT FROM NOW ON.
IS THAT UNDER-STOOD?
SHFF
SHFF
YES...
GOOD.

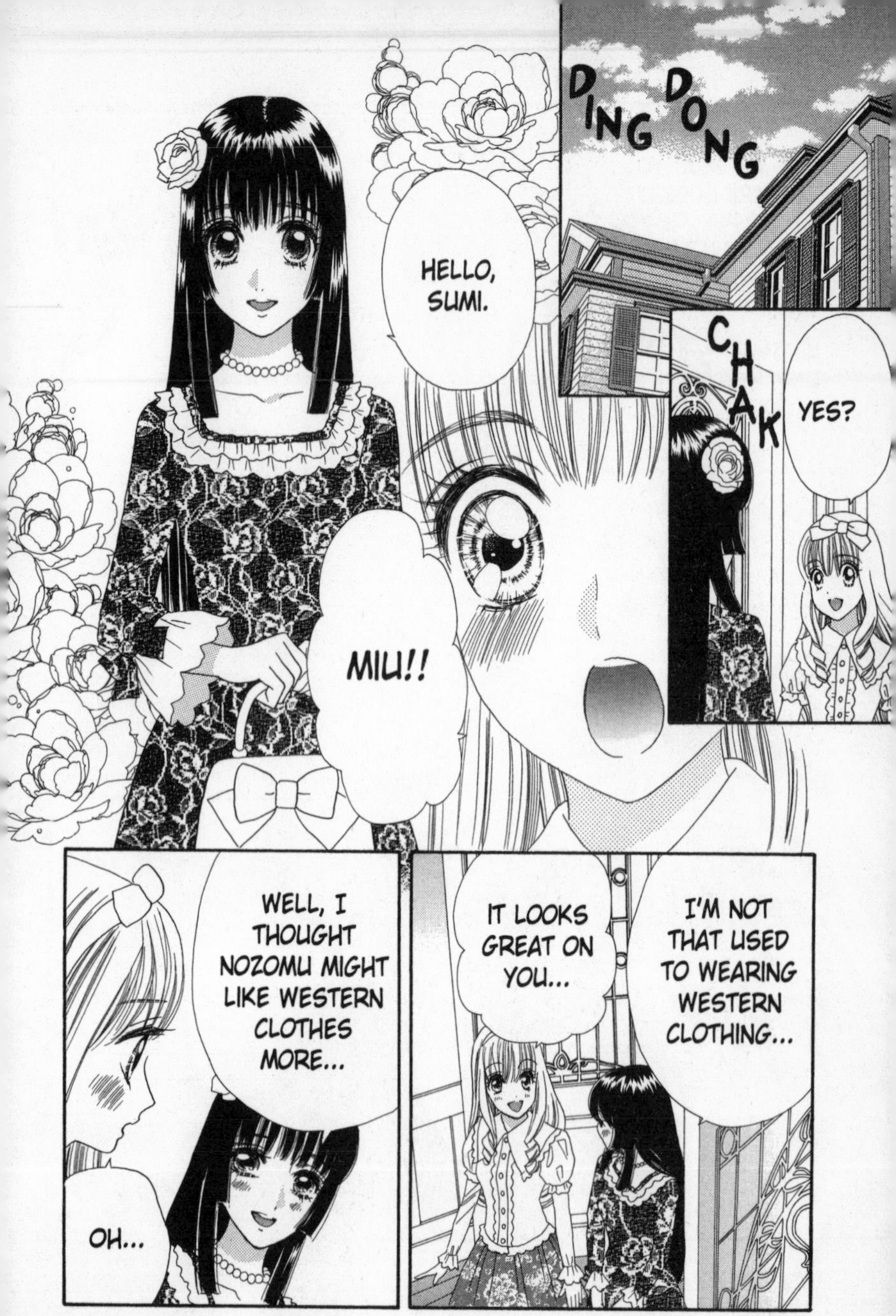
DING DONG
CHAK
YES?
HELLO, SUMI.
MIU!!
I'M NOT THAT USED TO WEARING WESTERN CLOTHING...
IT LOOKS GREAT ON YOU...
WELL, I THOUGHT NOZOMU MIGHT LIKE WESTERN CLOTHES MORE...
OH...

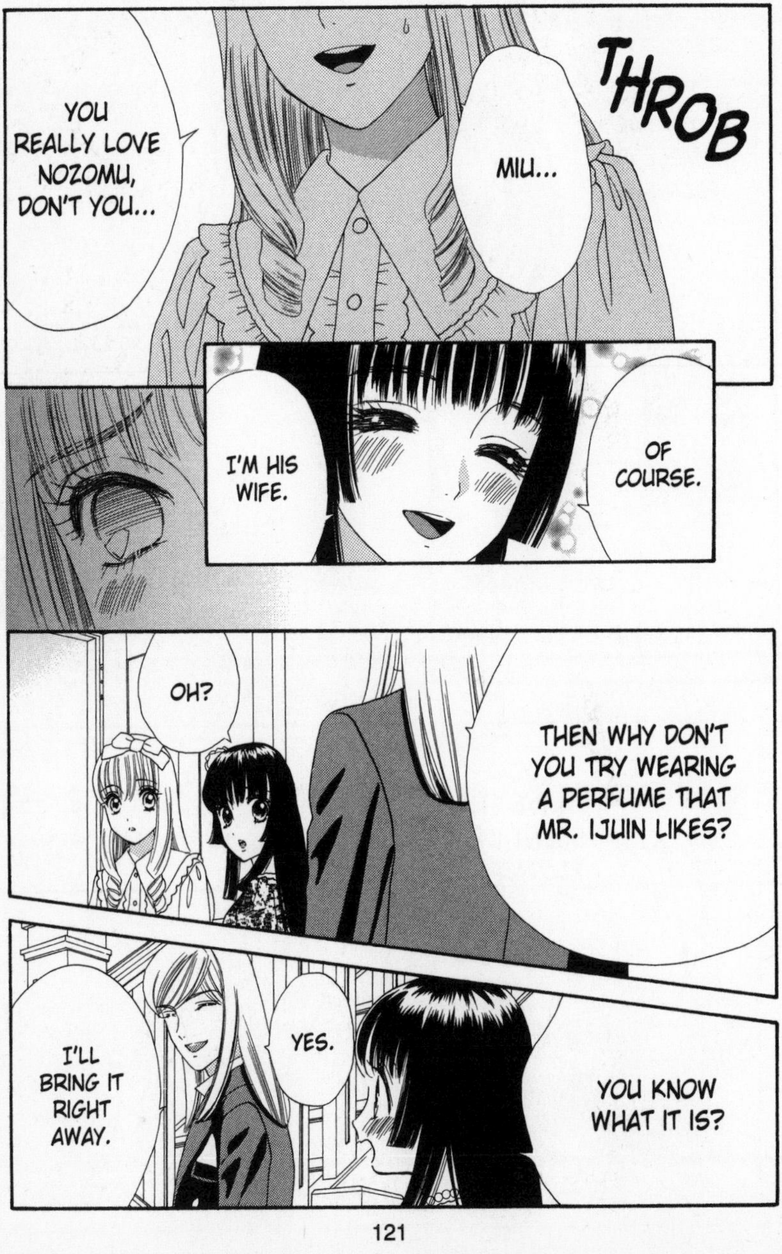
THROB
MIU...
YOU REALLY LOVE NOZOMU, DON'T YOU...
OF COURSE.
I'M HIS WIFE.
THEN WHY DON'T YOU TRY WEARING A PERFUME THAT MR. IJUIN LIKES?
OH?
YOU KNOW WHAT IT IS?
YES.
I'LL BRING IT RIGHT AWAY.

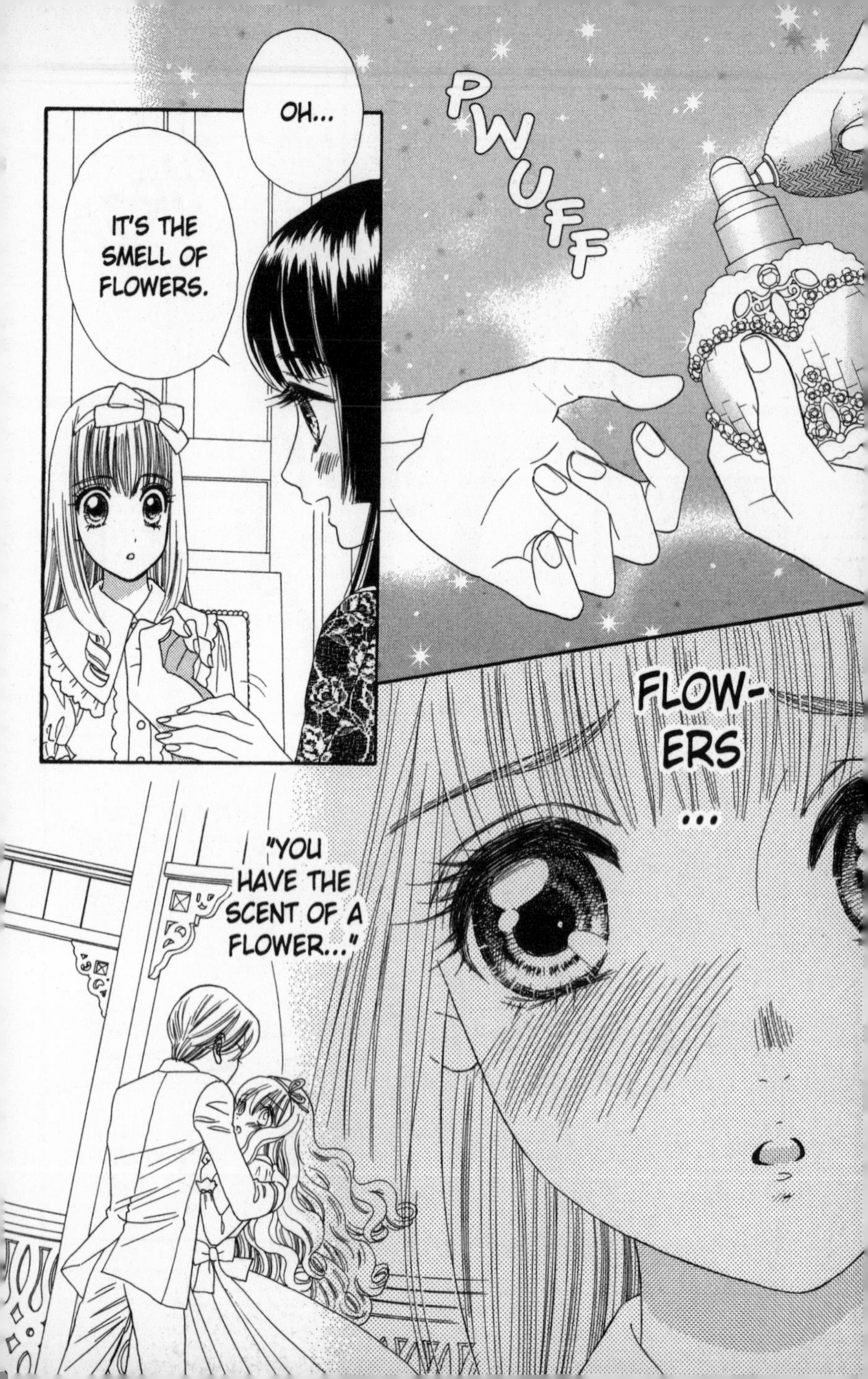
PWUFF
OH...
IT'S THE SMELL OF FLOWERS.
FLOW-ERS...
"YOU HAVE THE SCENT OF A FLOWER..."

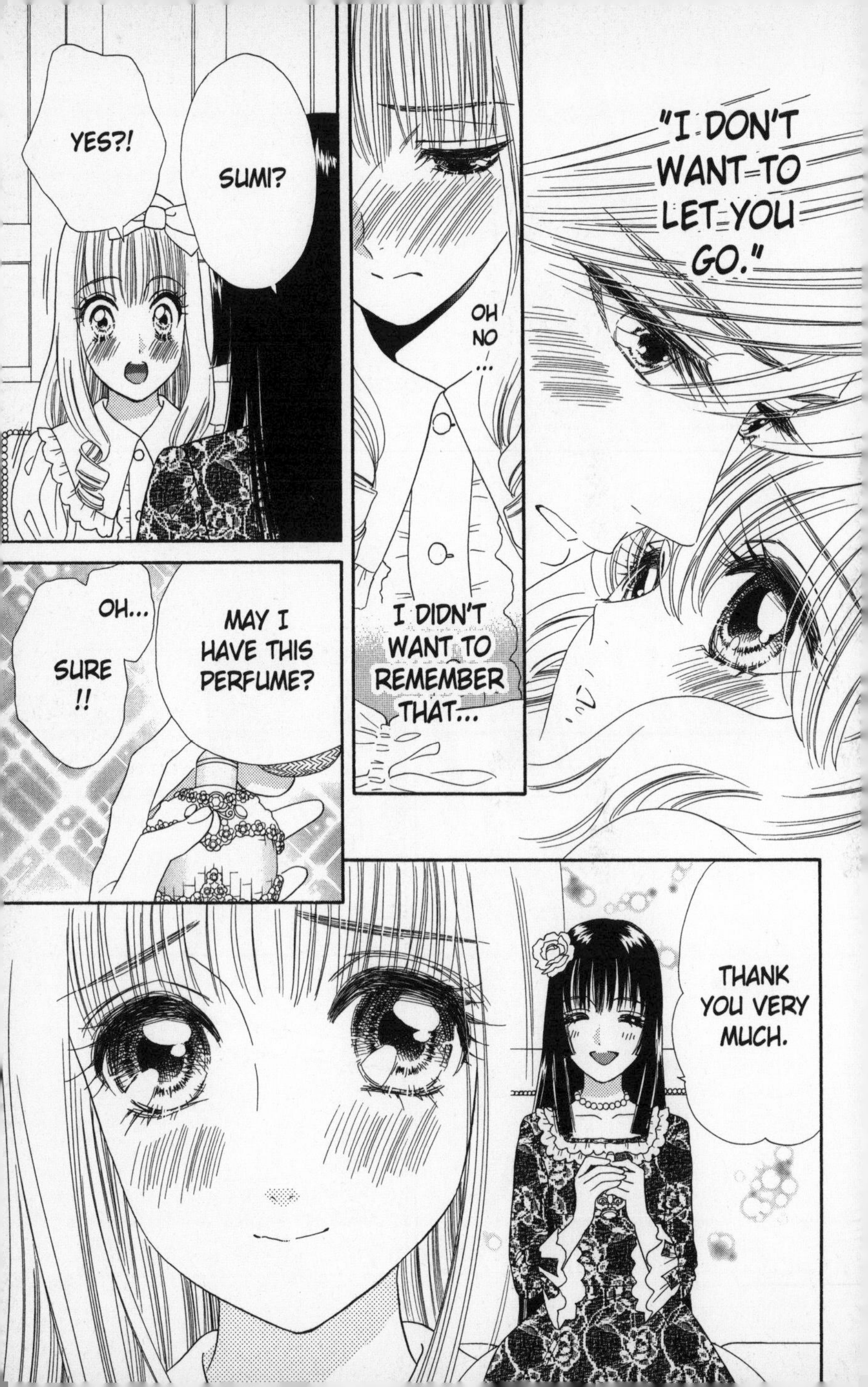
"I DON'T WANT TO LET YOU GO."
OH NO ...
I DIDN'T WANT TO REMEMBER THAT...
SUMI?
YES?!
MAY I HAVE THIS PERFUME?
OH... SURE !!
THANK YOU VERY MUCH.

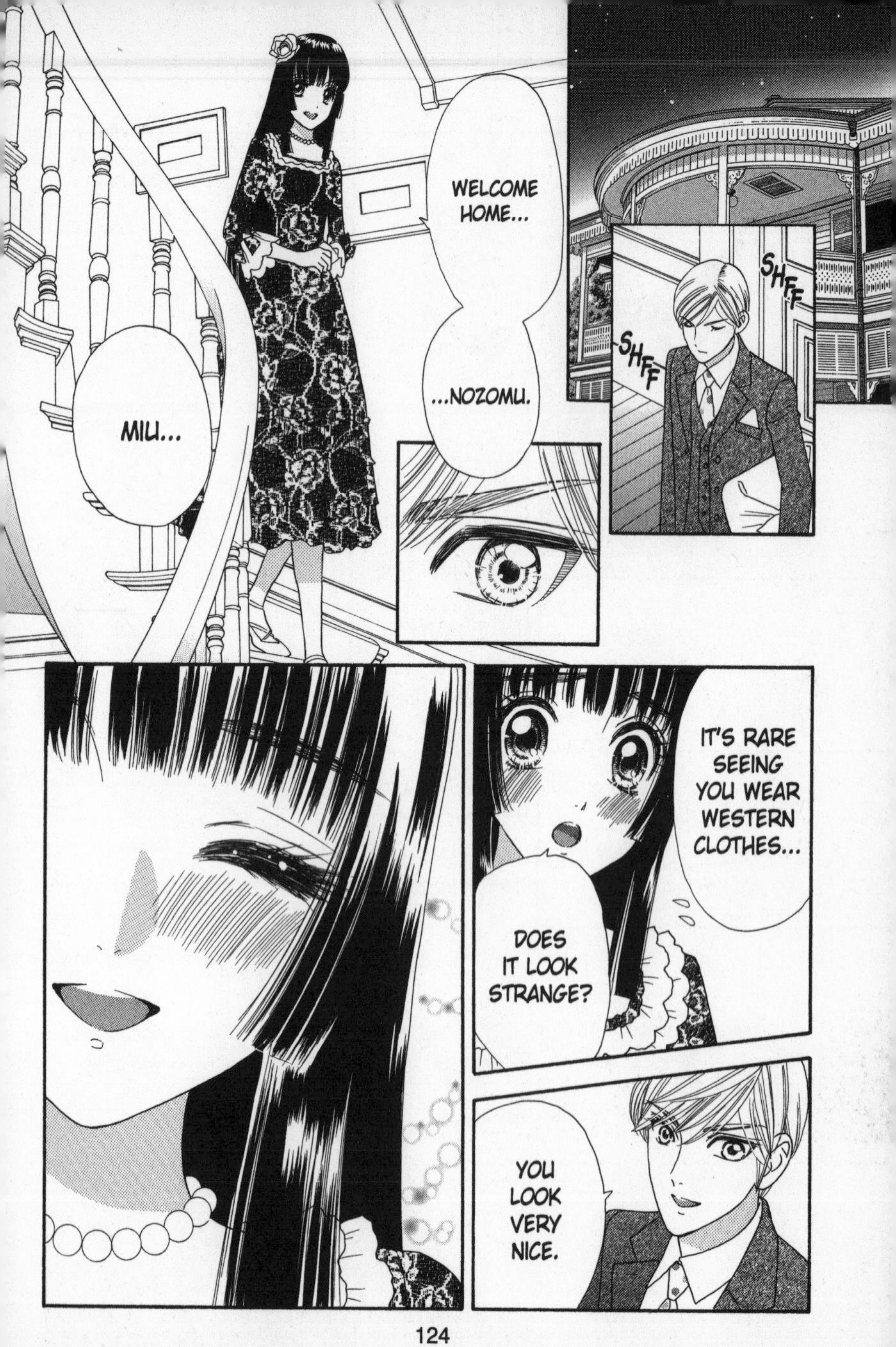
SHFF
SHFF
WELCOME HOME...
...NOZOMU.
MIU...
IT'S RARE SEEING YOU WEAR WESTERN CLOTHES...
DOES IT LOOK STRANGE?
YOU LOOK VERY NICE.

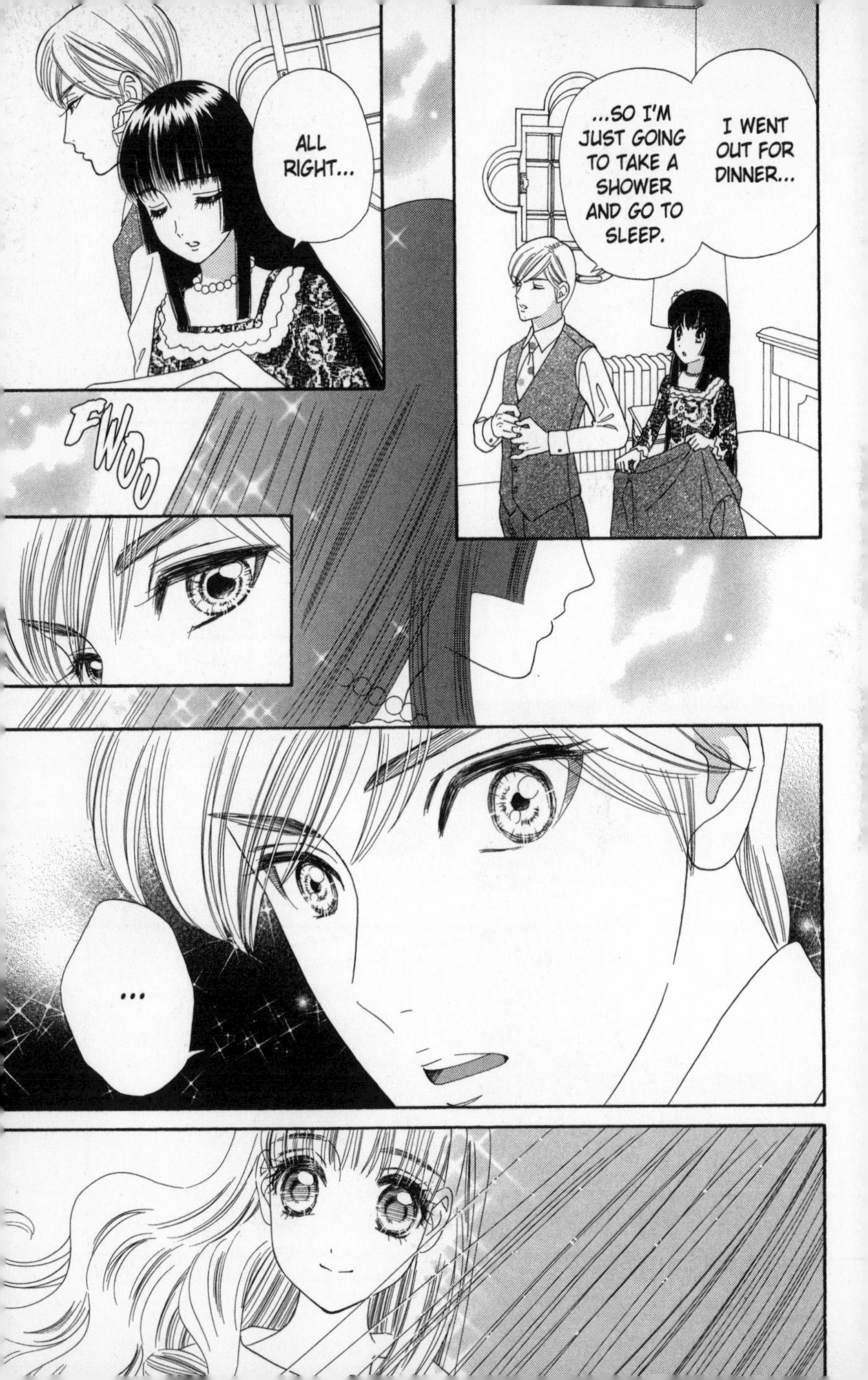
I WENT OUT FOR DINNER...
...SO I'M JUST GOING TO TAKE A SHOWER AND GO TO SLEEP.
ALL RIGHT...
FWOO
...

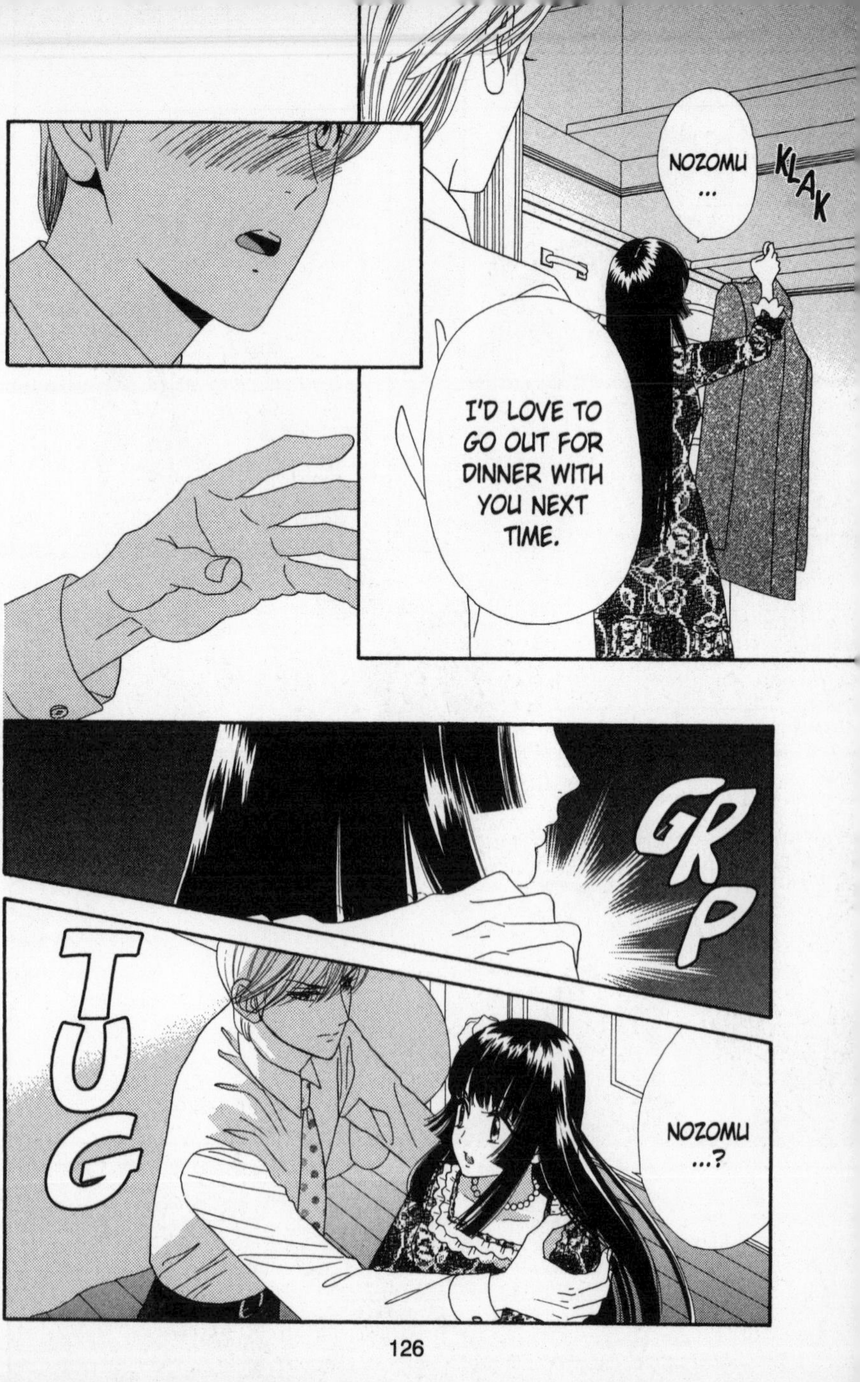
NOZOMU ...
KLAK
I'D LOVE TO GO OUT FOR DINNER WITH YOU NEXT TIME.
GRP
NOZOMU ...?
TUG

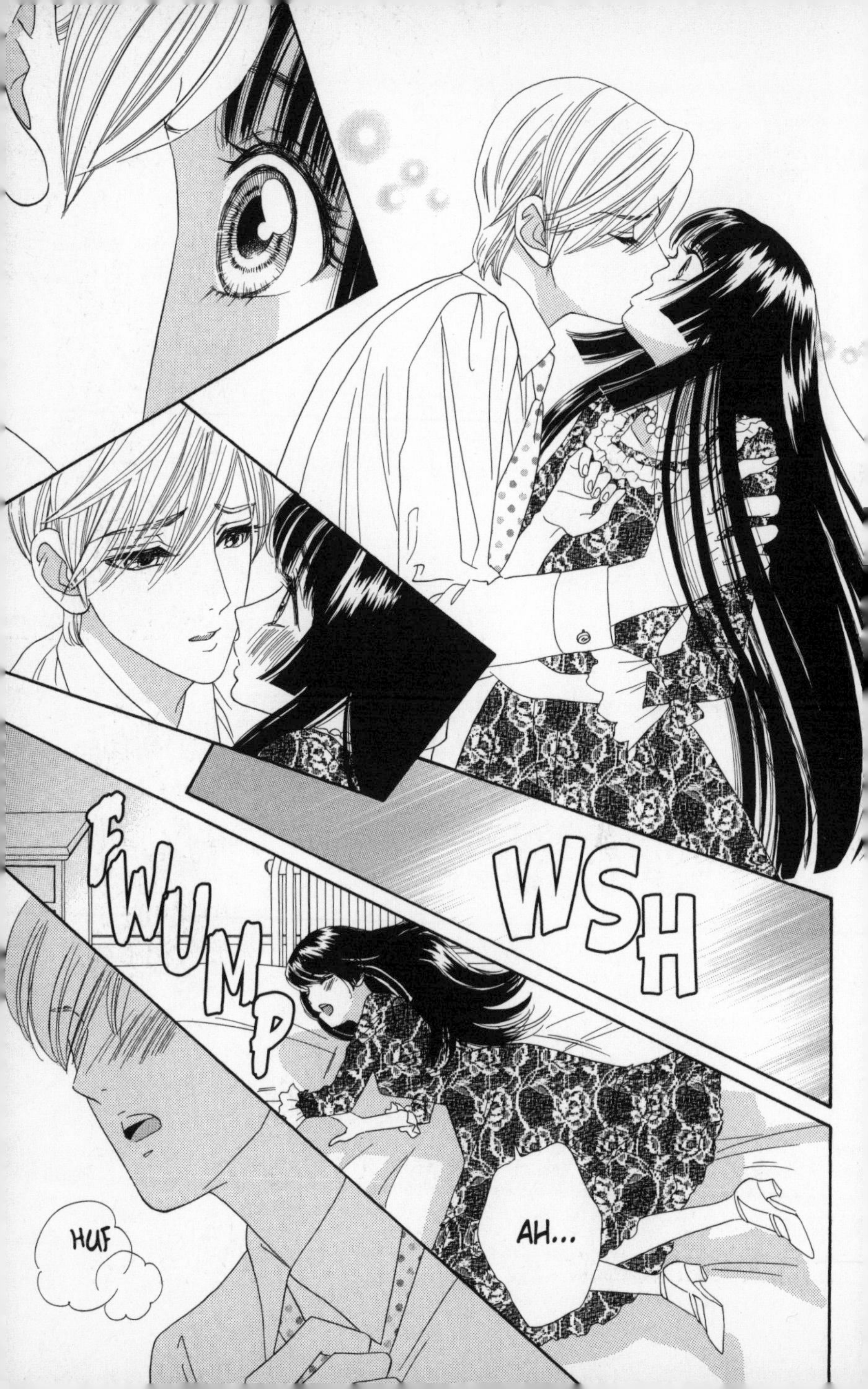
WSH
FWUMP
AH...
HUF

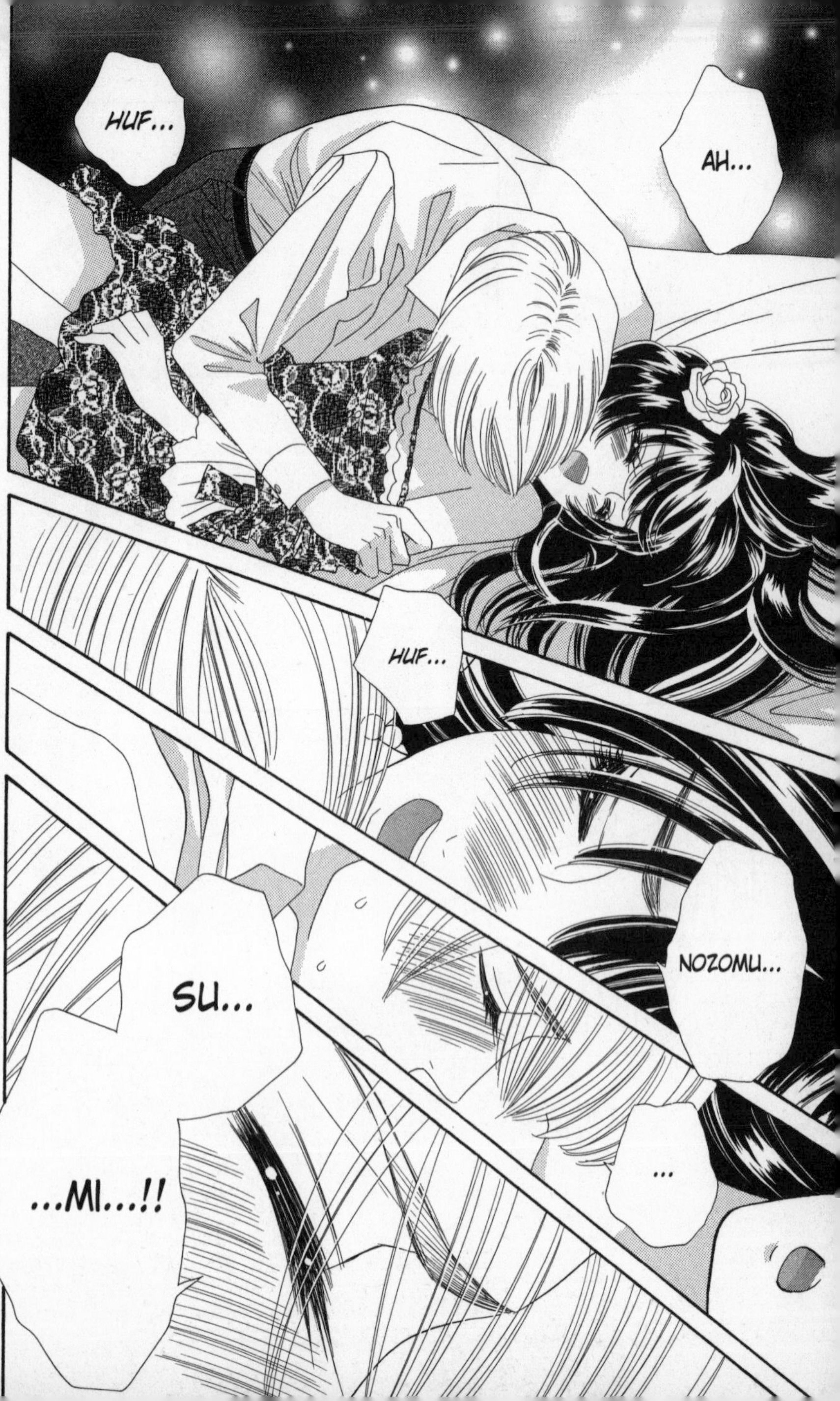
AH...
HUF...
HUF...
NOZOMU...
SU...
...
...MI...!!

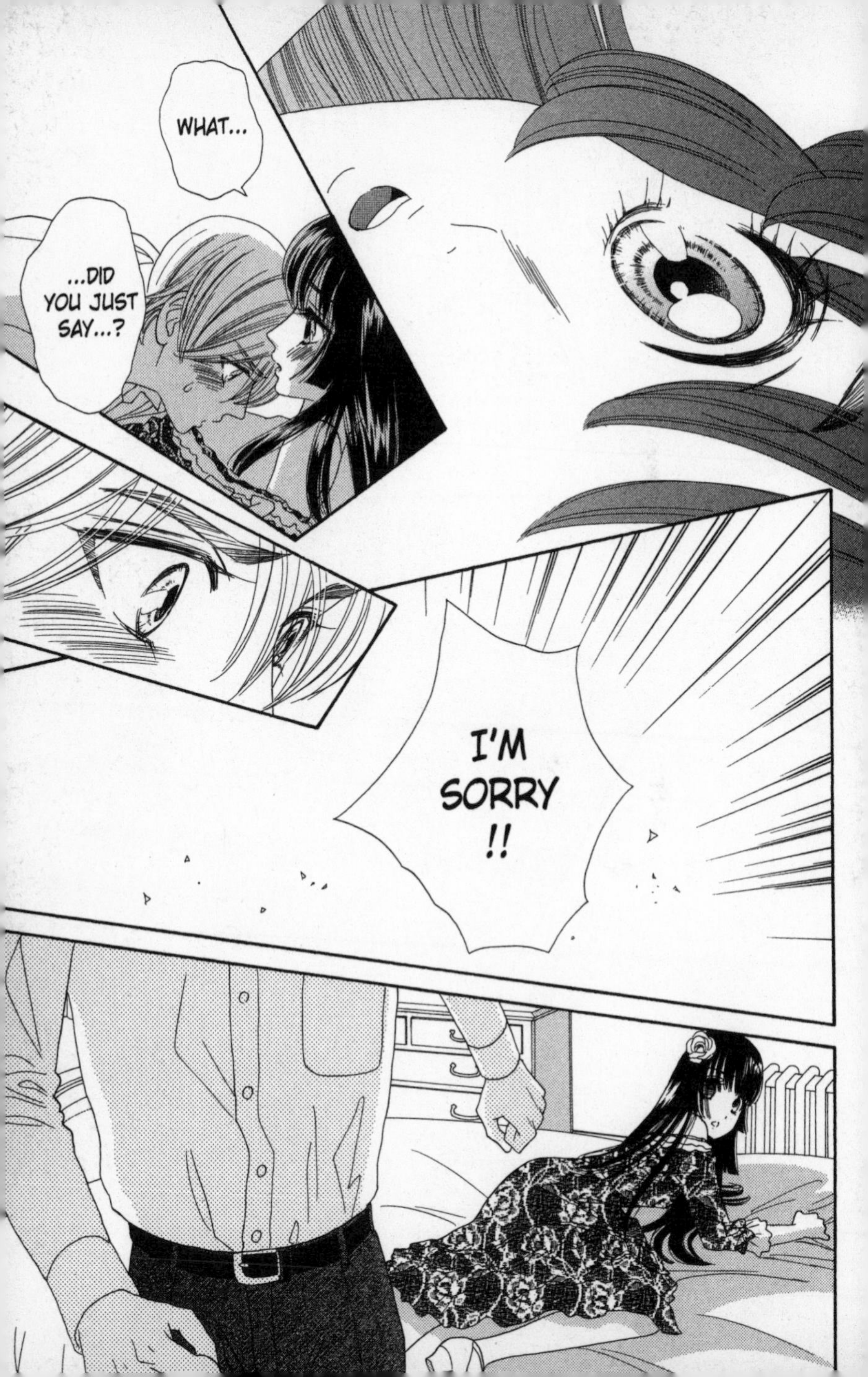
WHAT...
...DID YOU JUST SAY...?
I'M SORRY !!

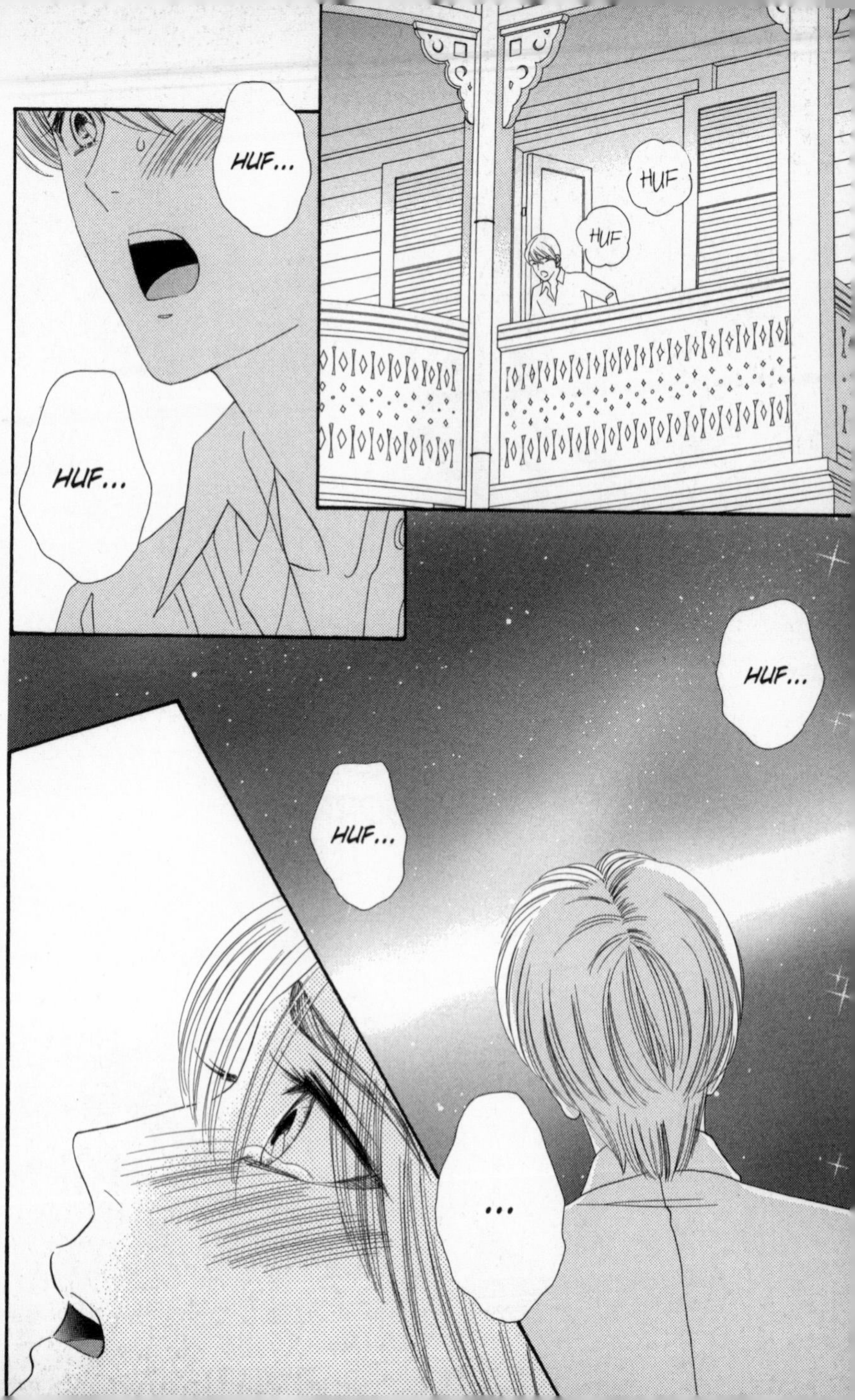
HUF
HUF
HUF...
HUF...
HUF...
HUF...
...

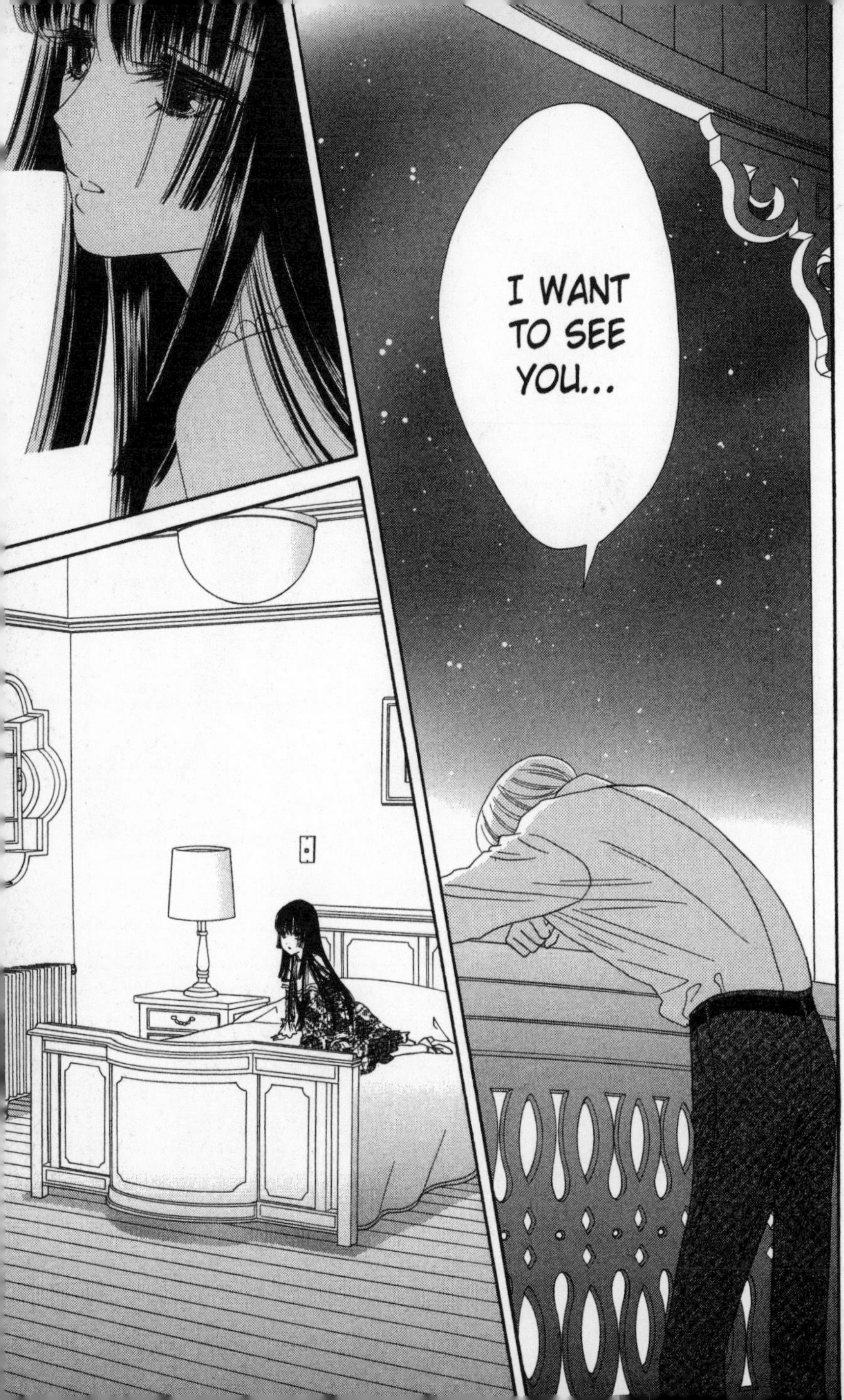
I WANT TO SEE YOU...

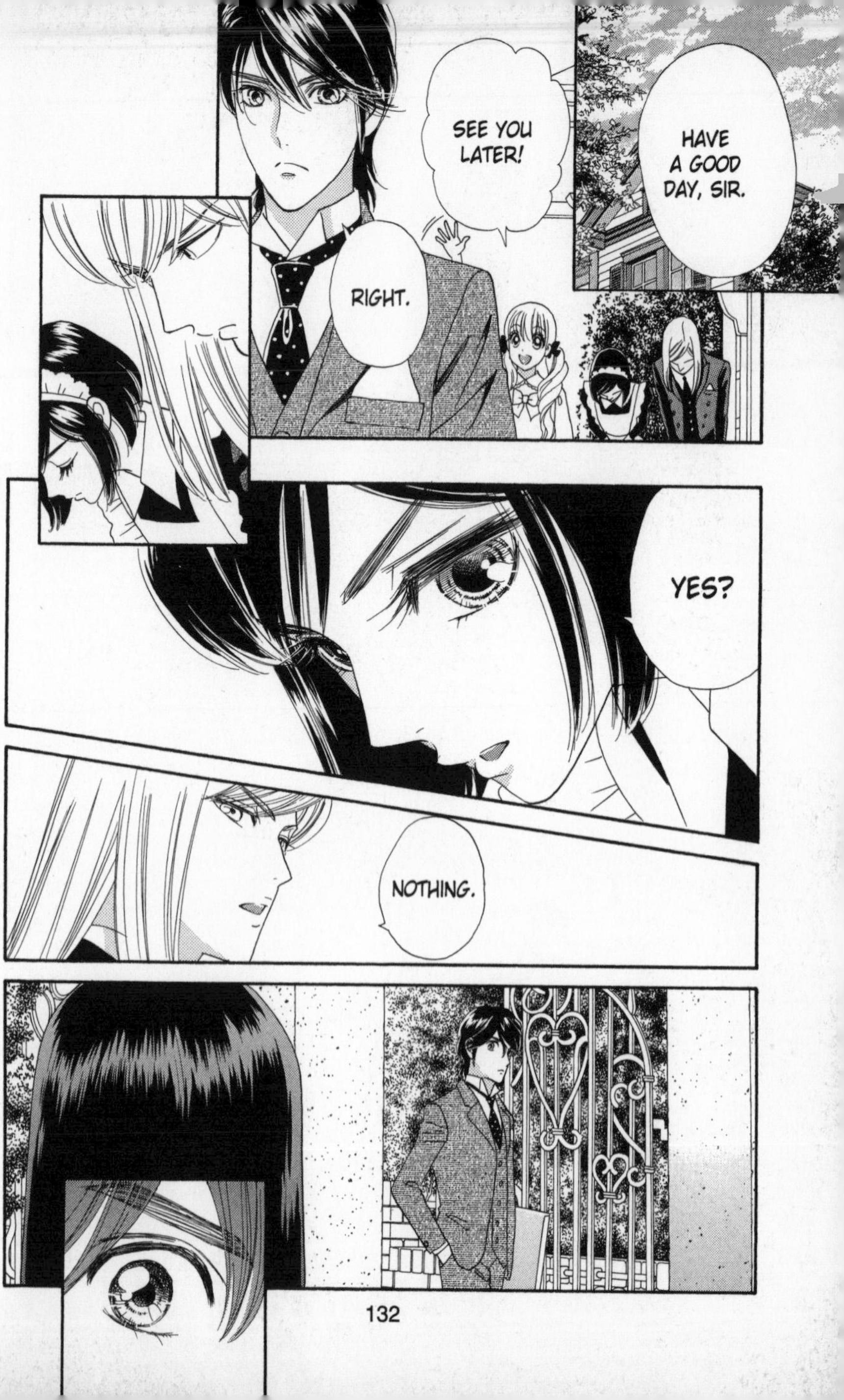
HAVE A GOOD DAY, SIR.
SEE YOU LATER!
RIGHT.
YES?
NOTHING.

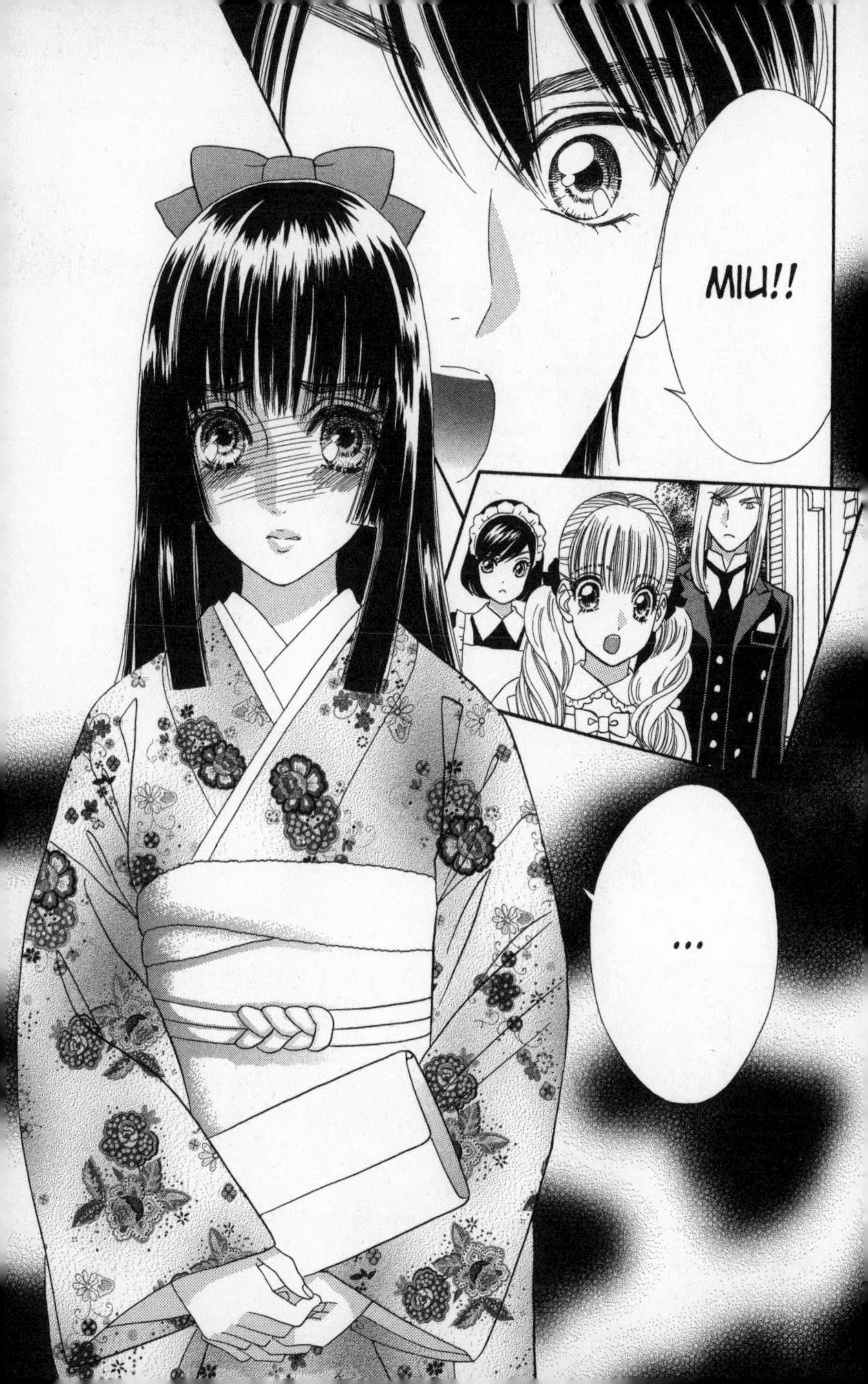
MIU!!
...

No. 5

RANDOM CHITCHAT!

Date

❀ THE FIRST HALF, WHICH IS 32 PAGES LONG, IS IN THE MAY EDITION OF *RIBON* MAGAZINE—IT CAME OUT ON APRIL 3. THE SECOND HALF, WHICH IS 31 PAGES LONG, IS IN THE JUNE EDITION. THAT CAME OUT ON MAY 2. THE TITLE OF THE MANGA IS *SUPER EXPRESS ☆ HIYO*. IF YOU'RE ABLE TO GET THE MAGAZINES, I'D LOVE IT IF YOU CHECKED OUT THIS STORY. ♪

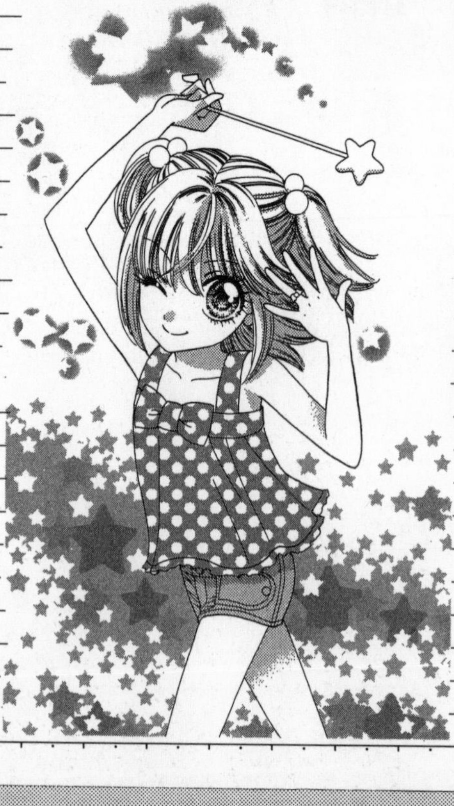

❀ IT'S BASICALLY ABOUT A 5TH GRADE STUDENT CALLED HIYO WHO'S IN A HURRY TO BECOME A GROWN-UP.

NOTE: THE STORY'S NOT SUPER DRAMATIC, BUT I THINK I'VE DRAWN IT IN A WAY THAT ADULTS CAN ENJOY IT TOO.

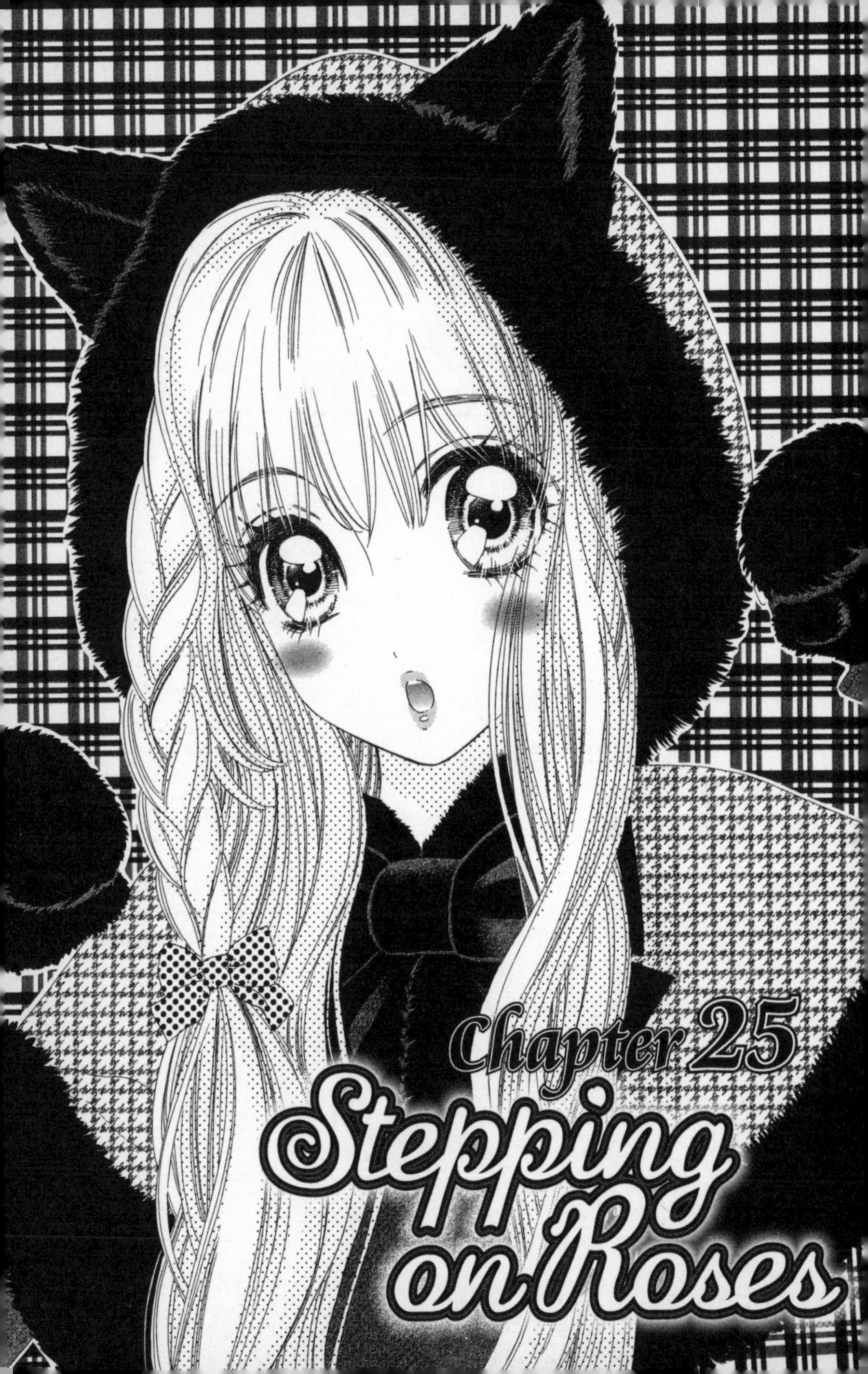
Chapter 25
Stepping on Roses

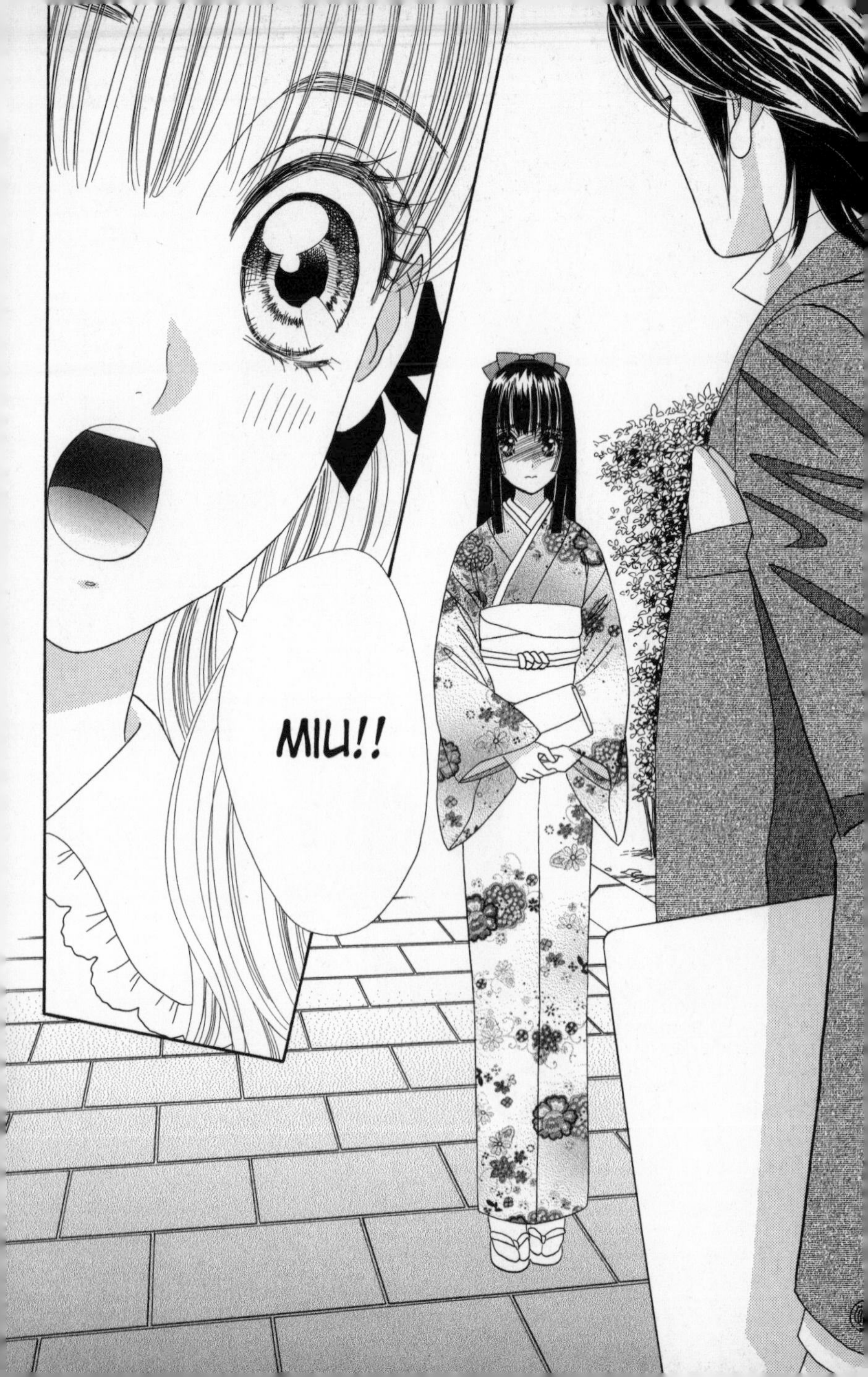
MIU!!

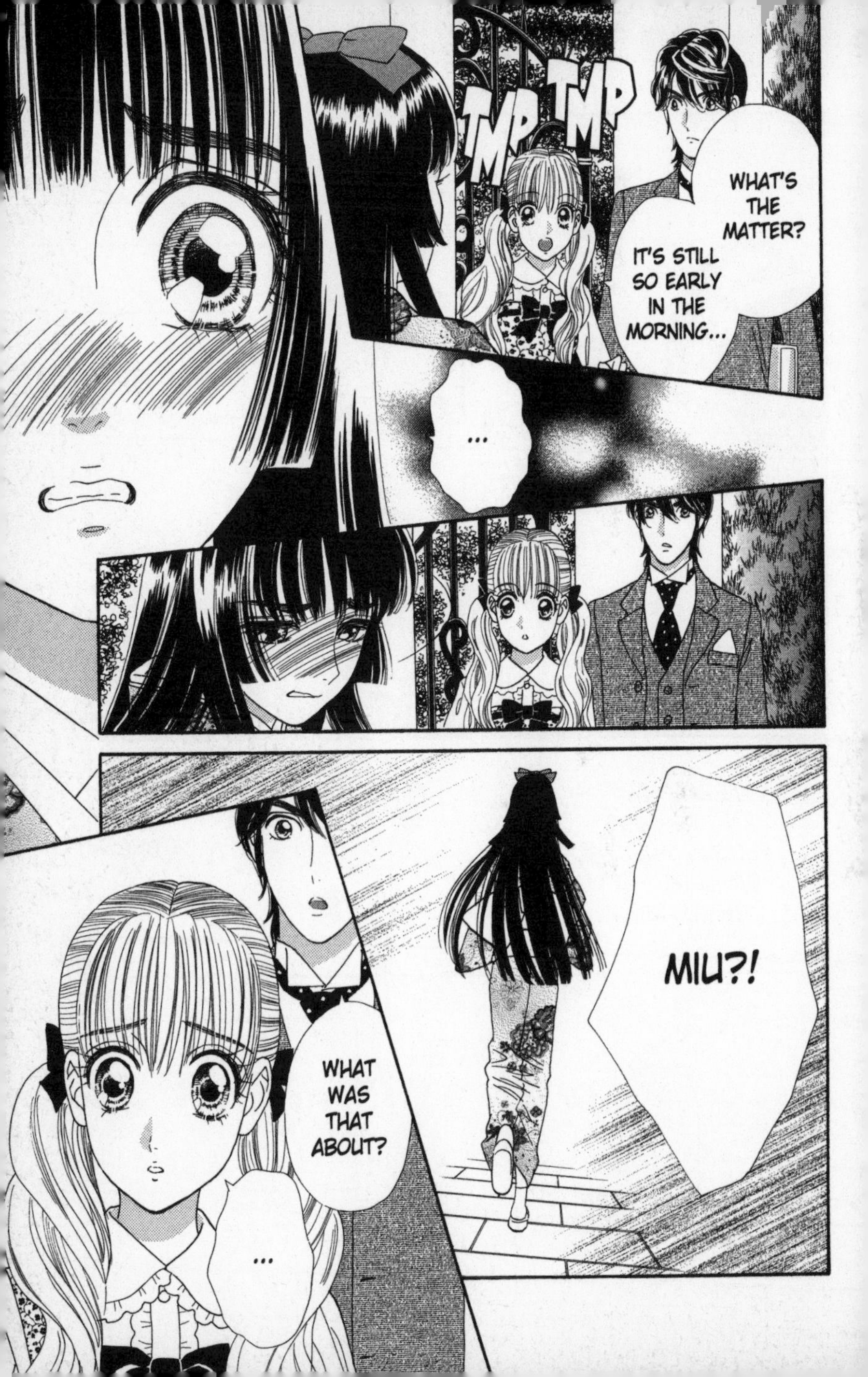
TMP TMP
WHAT'S THE MATTER?
IT'S STILL SO EARLY IN THE MORNING...
...
MIU?!
WHAT WAS THAT ABOUT?
...

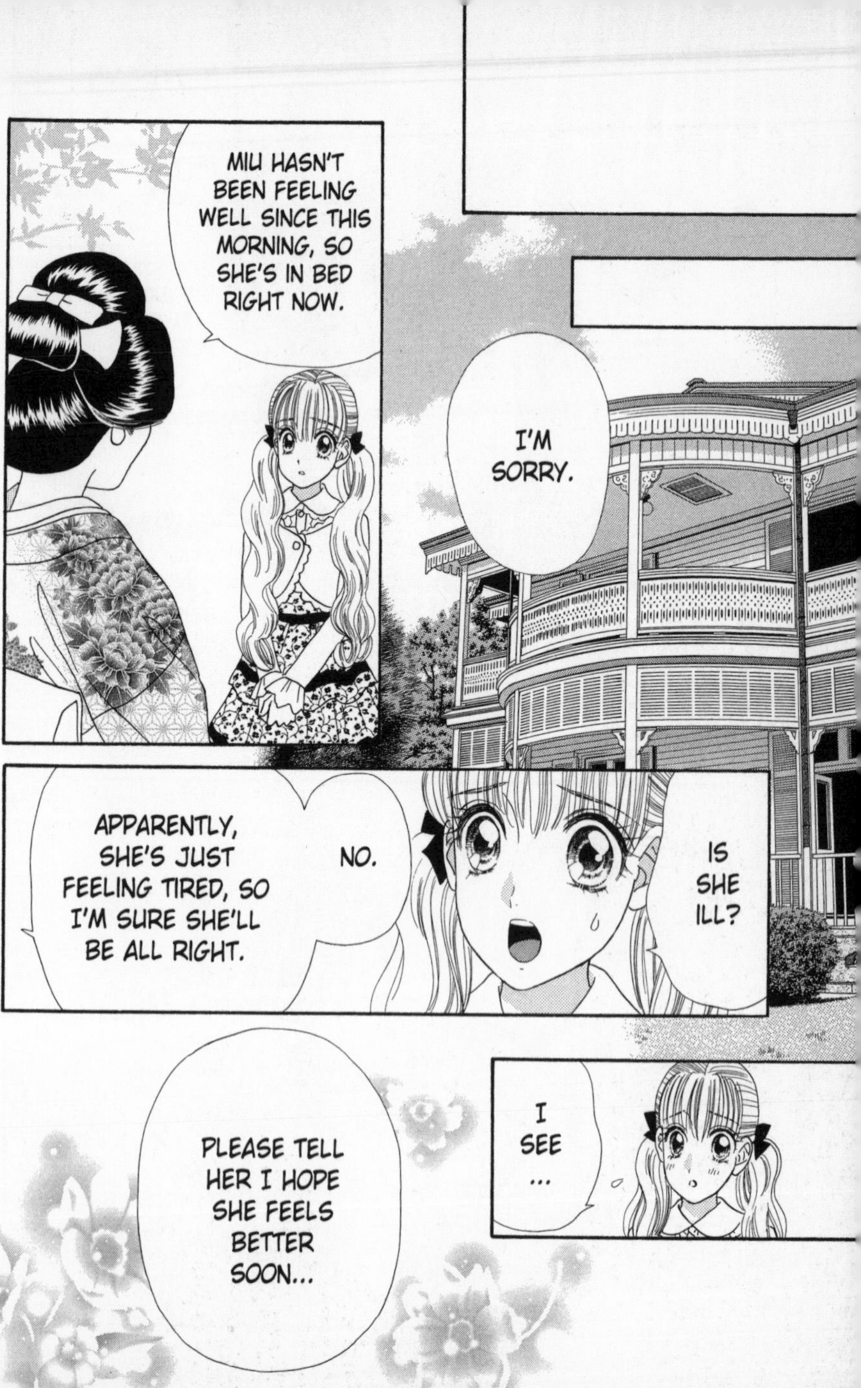
I'M SORRY.
MIU HASN'T BEEN FEELING WELL SINCE THIS MORNING, SO SHE'S IN BED RIGHT NOW.
IS SHE ILL?
NO.
APPARENTLY, SHE'S JUST FEELING TIRED, SO I'M SURE SHE'LL BE ALL RIGHT.
I SEE ...
PLEASE TELL HER I HOPE SHE FEELS BETTER SOON...

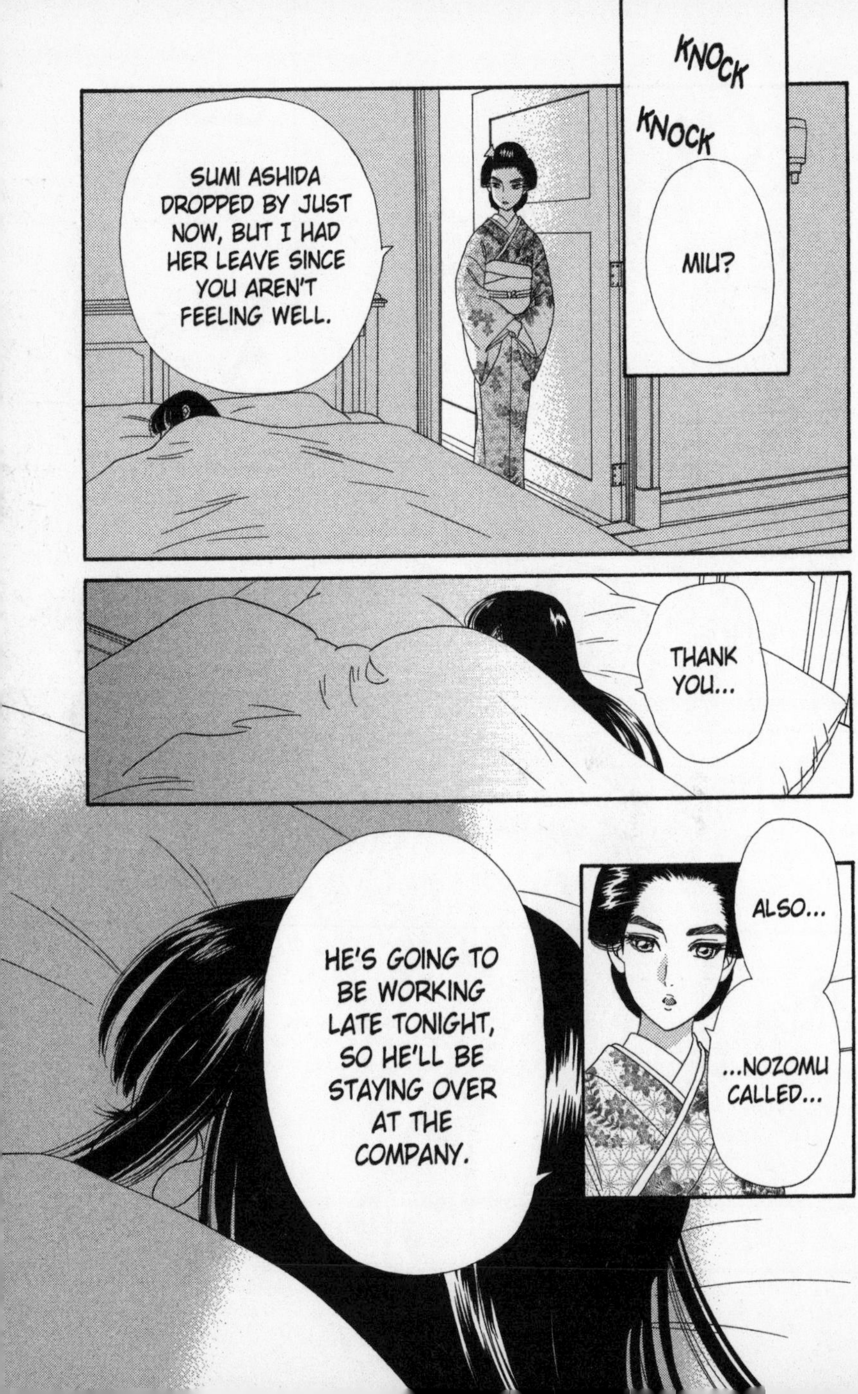
KNOCK
KNOCK
MIU?
SUMI ASHIDA DROPPED BY JUST NOW, BUT I HAD HER LEAVE SINCE YOU AREN'T FEELING WELL.
THANK YOU...
ALSO...
...NOZOMU CALLED...
HE'S GOING TO BE WORKING LATE TONIGHT, SO HE'LL BE STAYING OVER AT THE COMPANY.

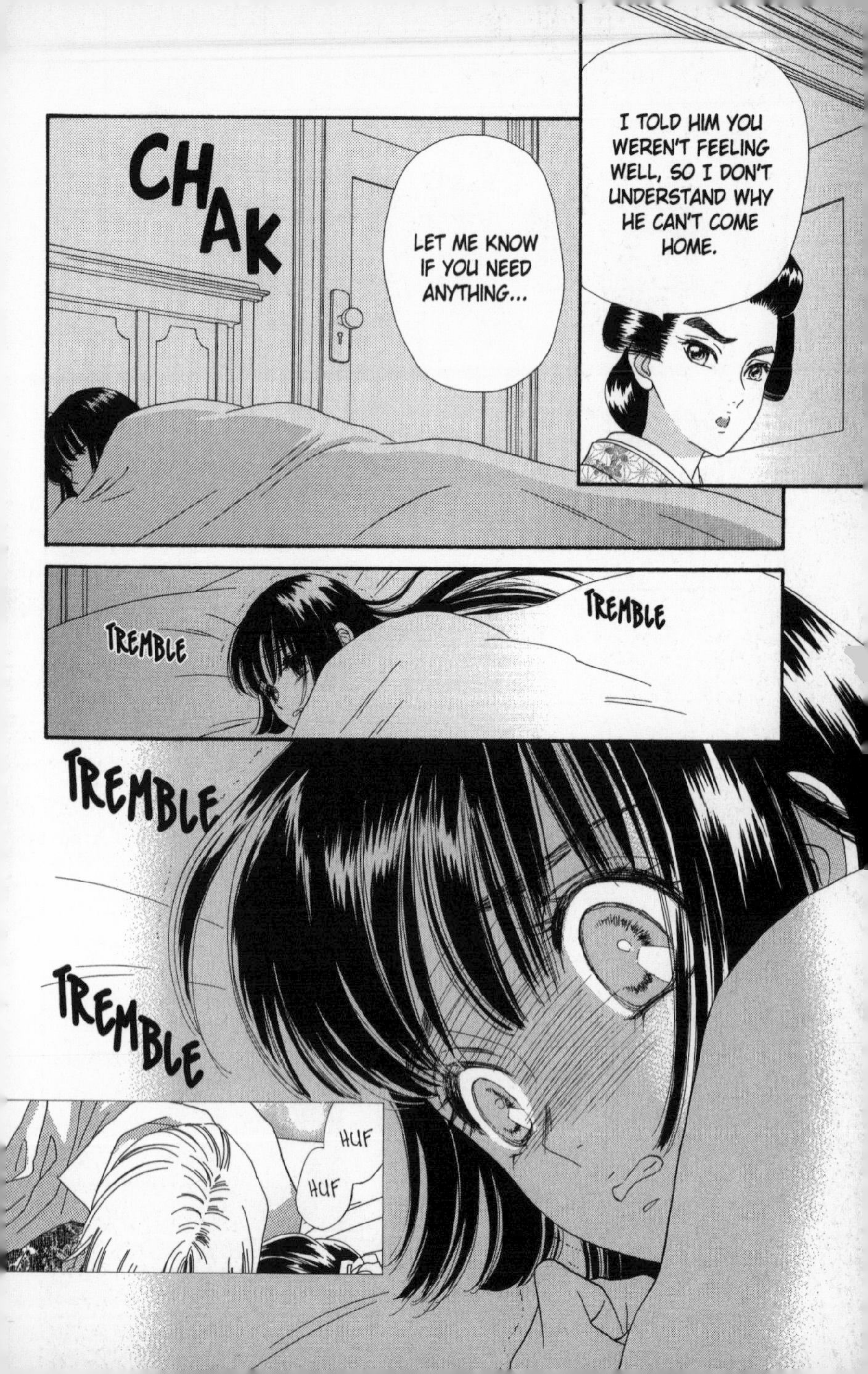
I TOLD HIM YOU WEREN'T FEELING WELL, SO I DON'T UNDERSTAND WHY HE CAN'T COME HOME.
CHAK
LET ME KNOW IF YOU NEED ANYTHING...
TREMBLE
TREMBLE
TREMBLE
TREMBLE
HUF
HUF

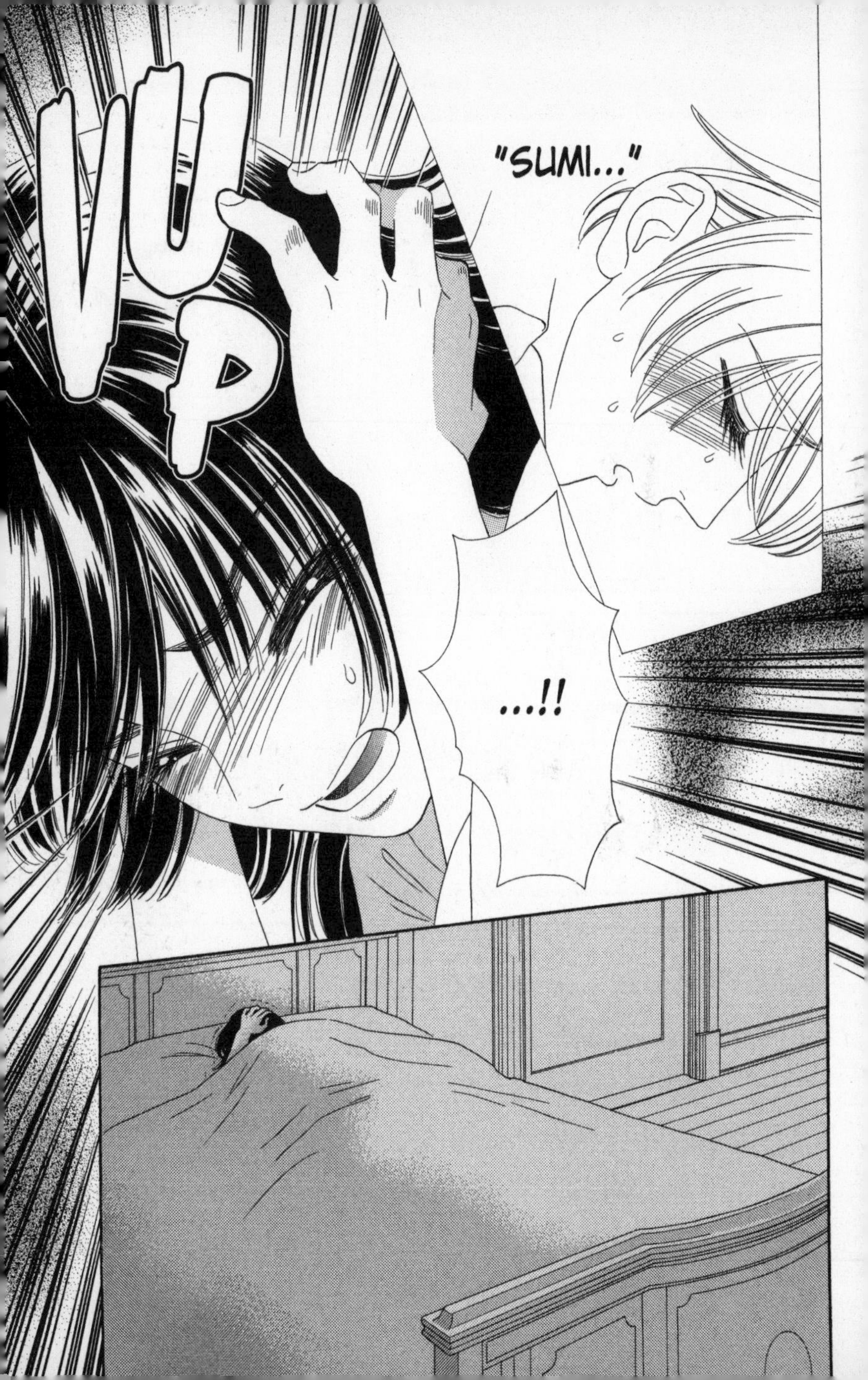
"SUMI..."
...!!
VUP

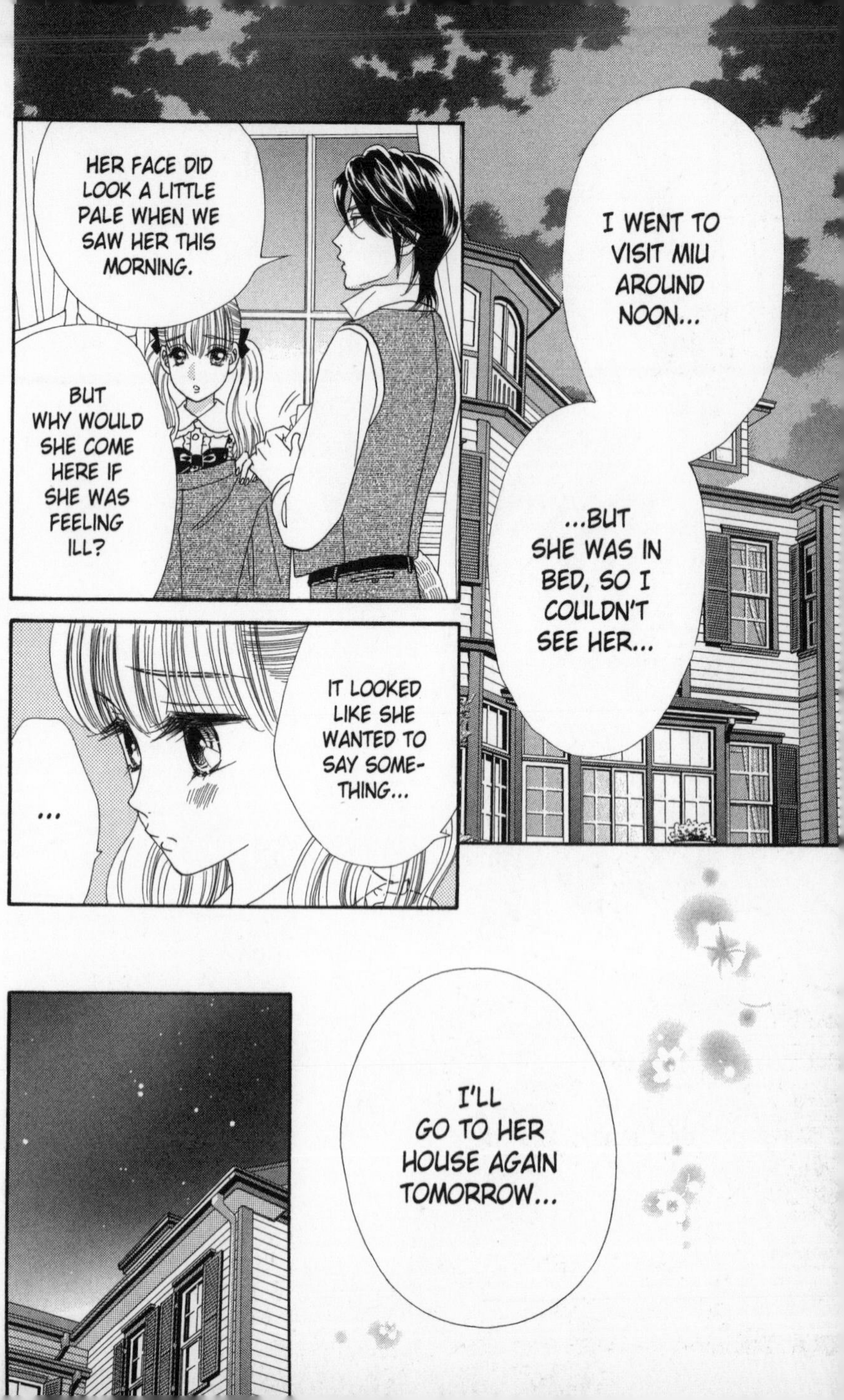
I WENT TO VISIT MIU AROUND NOON...
...BUT SHE WAS IN BED, SO I COULDN'T SEE HER...
HER FACE DID LOOK A LITTLE PALE WHEN WE SAW HER THIS MORNING.
BUT WHY WOULD SHE COME HERE IF SHE WAS FEELING ILL?
IT LOOKED LIKE SHE WANTED TO SAY SOME-THING...
...
I'LL GO TO HER HOUSE AGAIN TOMORROW...

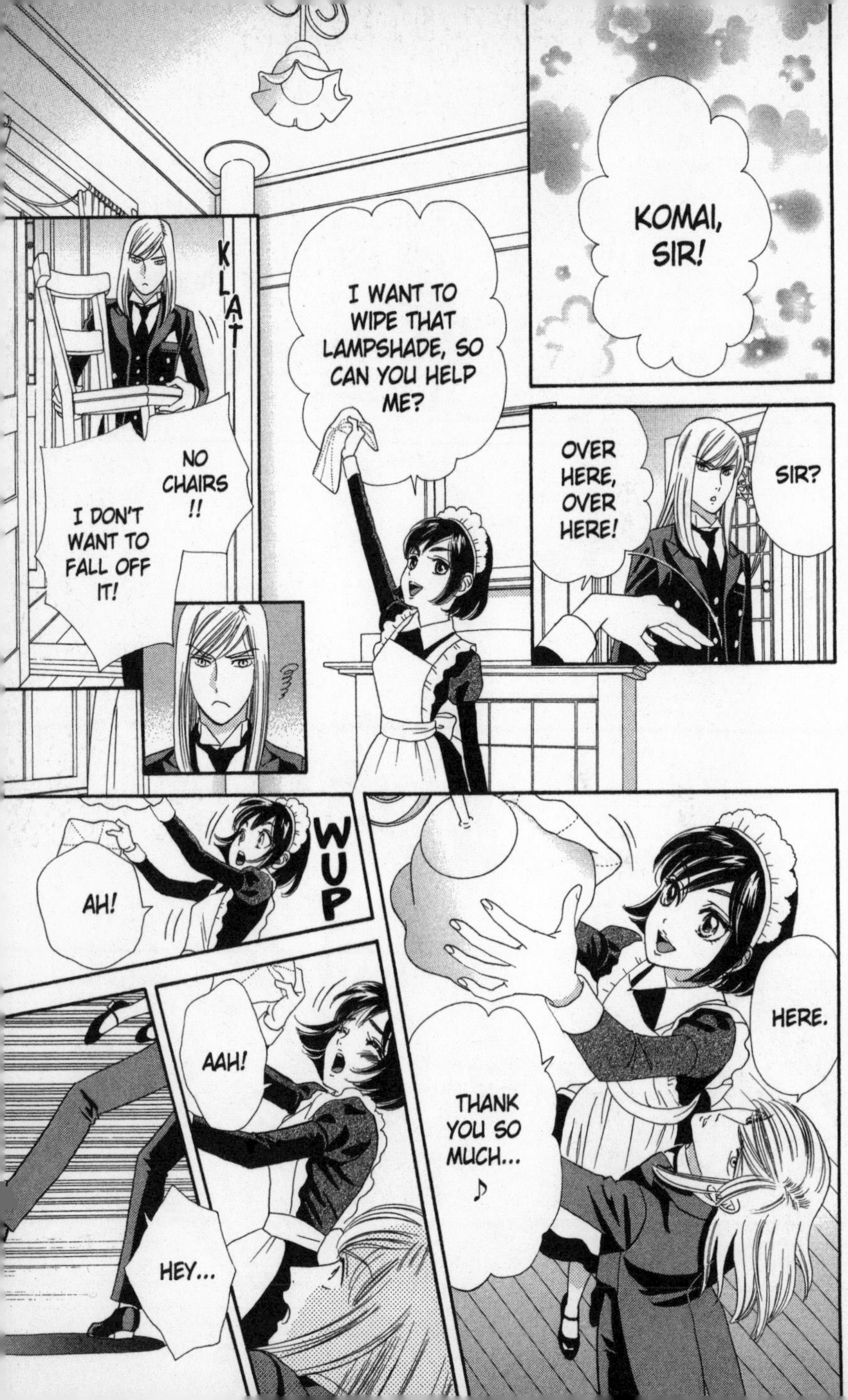

KOMAI, SIR!
SIR?
OVER HERE, OVER HERE!
I WANT TO WIPE THAT LAMPSHADE, SO CAN YOU HELP ME?
KLAT
NO CHAIRS !!
I DON'T WANT TO FALL OFF IT!
HERE.
THANK YOU SO MUCH... ♪
WUP
AH!
AAH!
HEY...

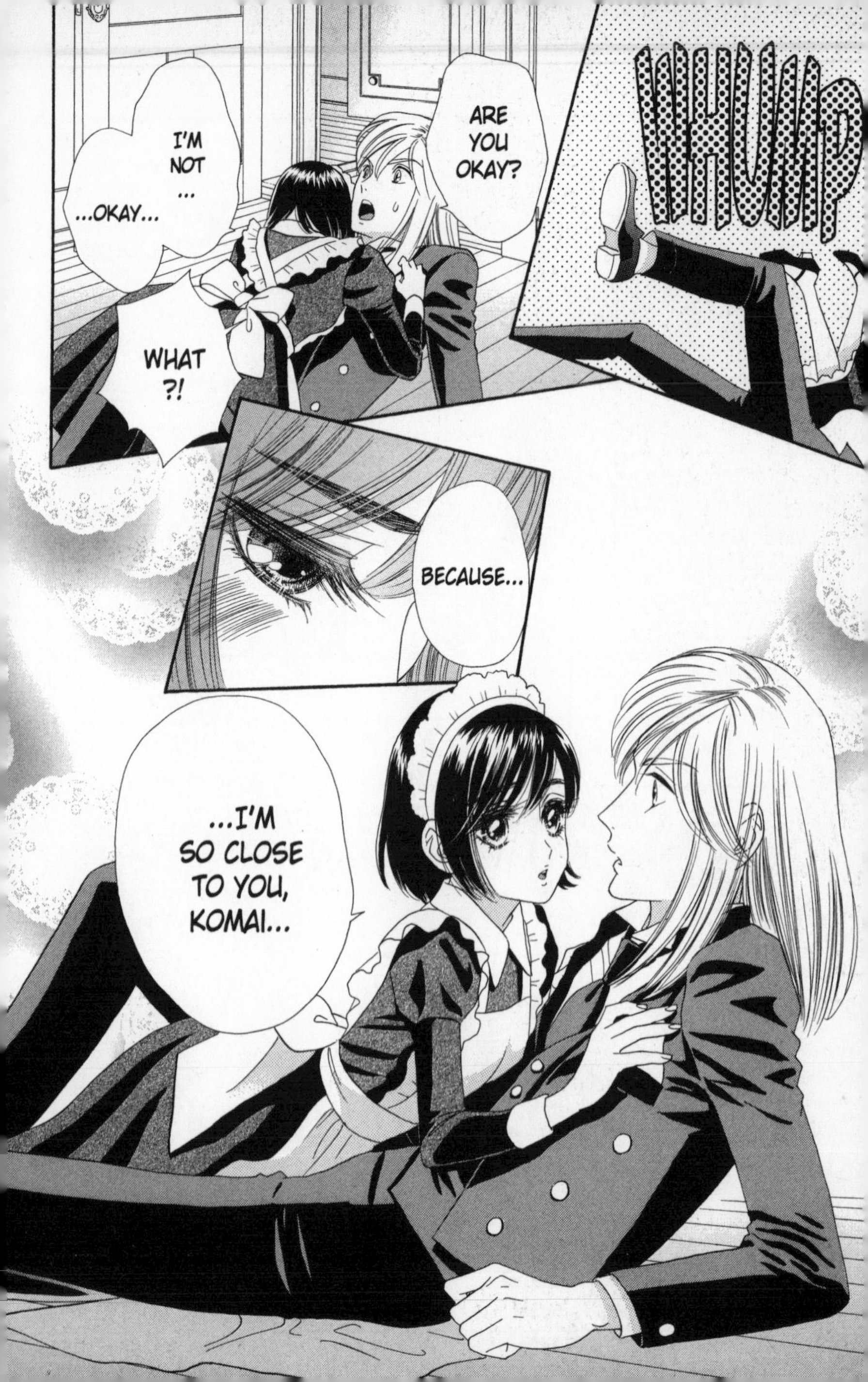
WHUMP
ARE YOU OKAY?
I'M NOT ...
...OKAY...
WHAT ?!
BECAUSE...
...I'M SO CLOSE TO YOU, KOMAI...

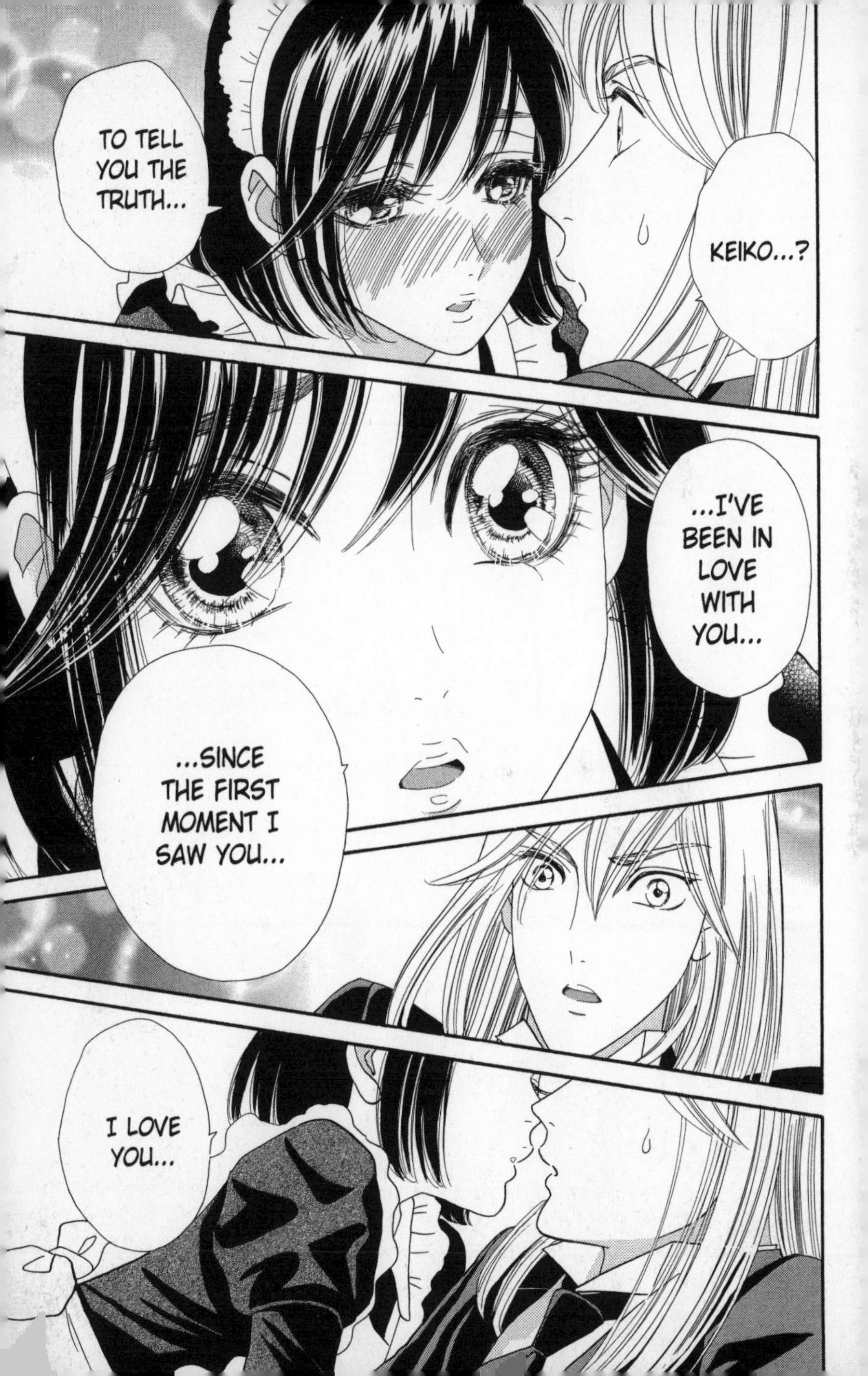
KEIKO...?
TO TELL YOU THE TRUTH...
...I'VE BEEN IN LOVE WITH YOU...
...SINCE THE FIRST MOMENT I SAW YOU...
I LOVE YOU...

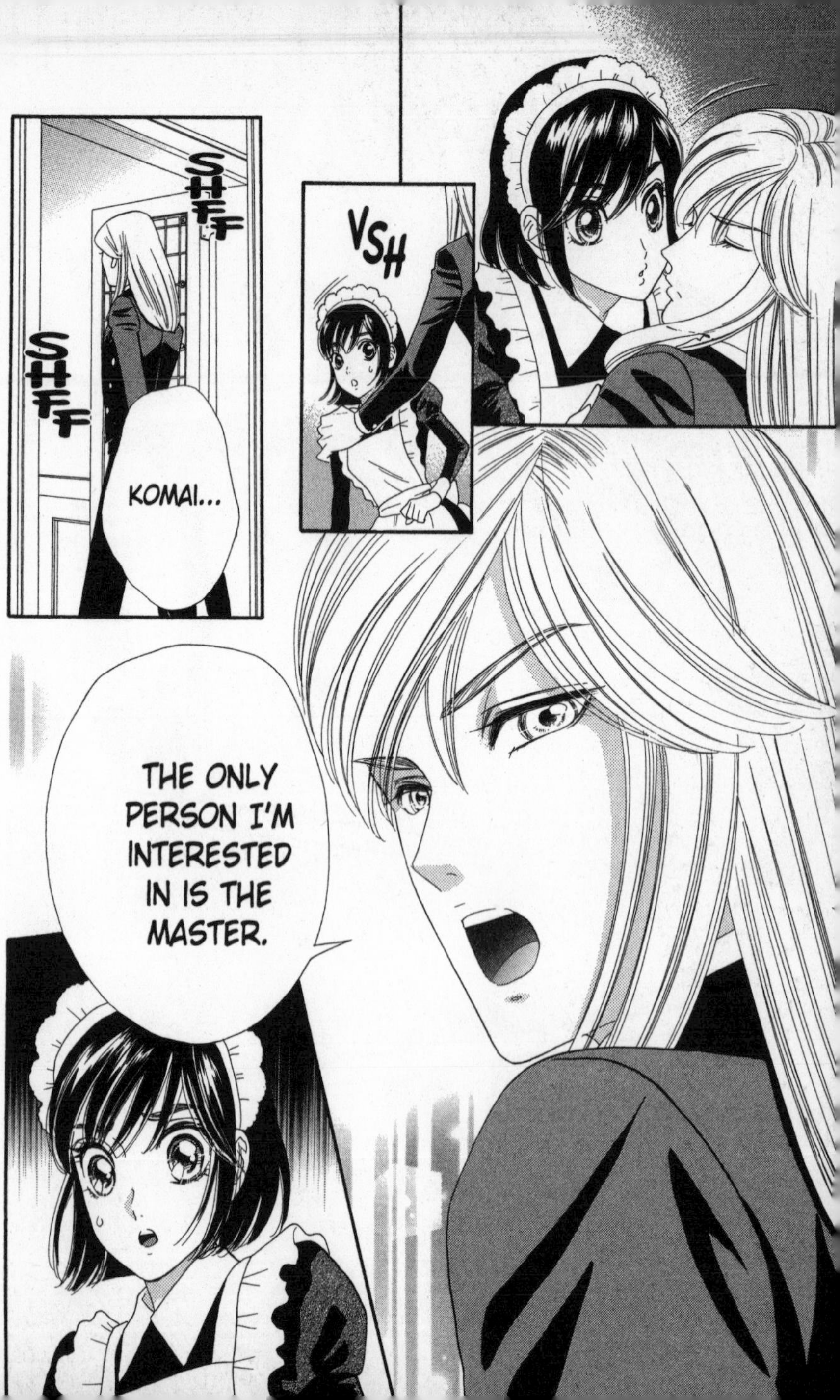
VSH
SHFF
SHFF
KOMAI...
THE ONLY PERSON I'M INTERESTED IN IS THE MASTER.

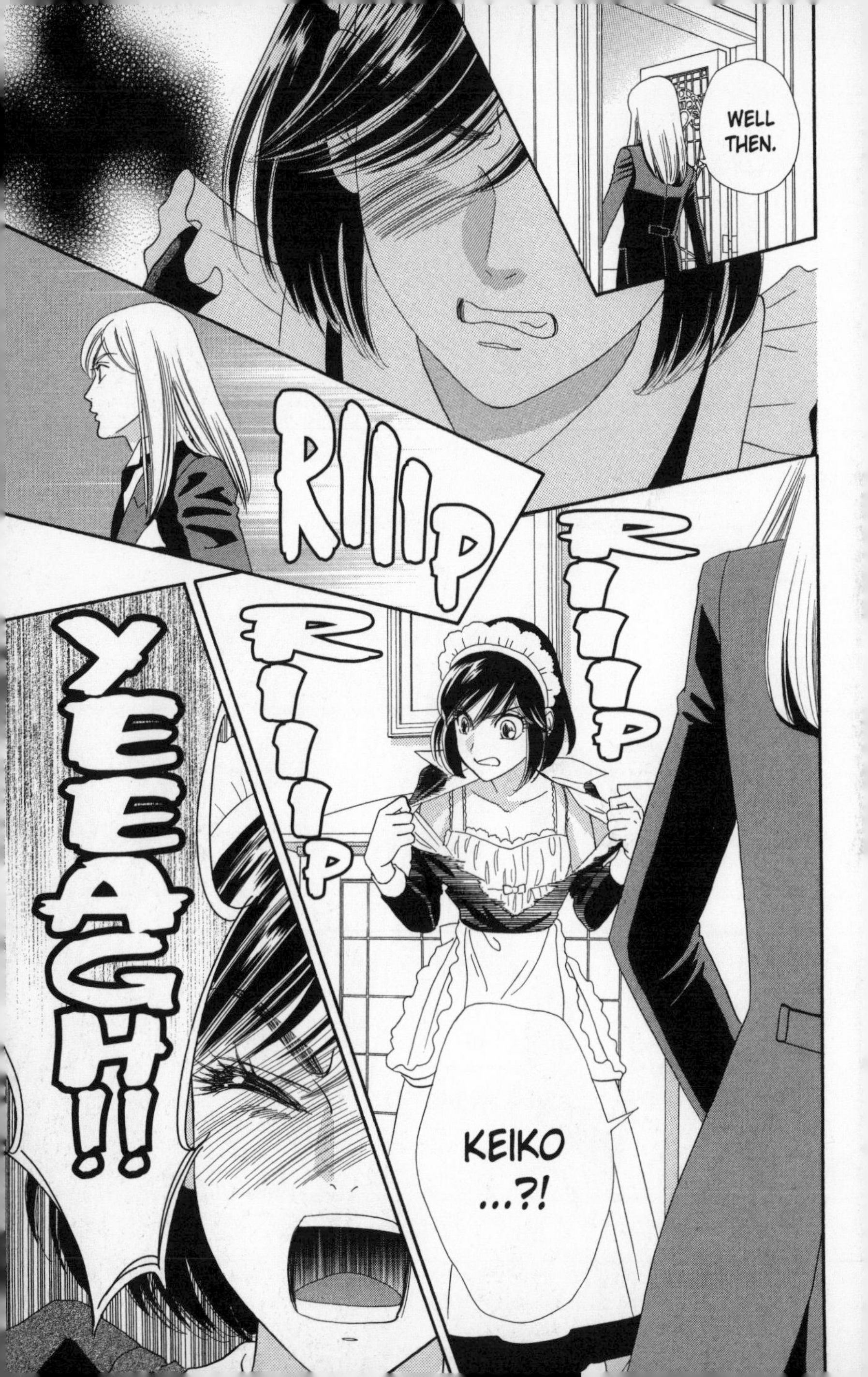
WELL THEN.
RIIIP
RIIIP
RIIIP
KEIKO ...?!
YEAGH!!

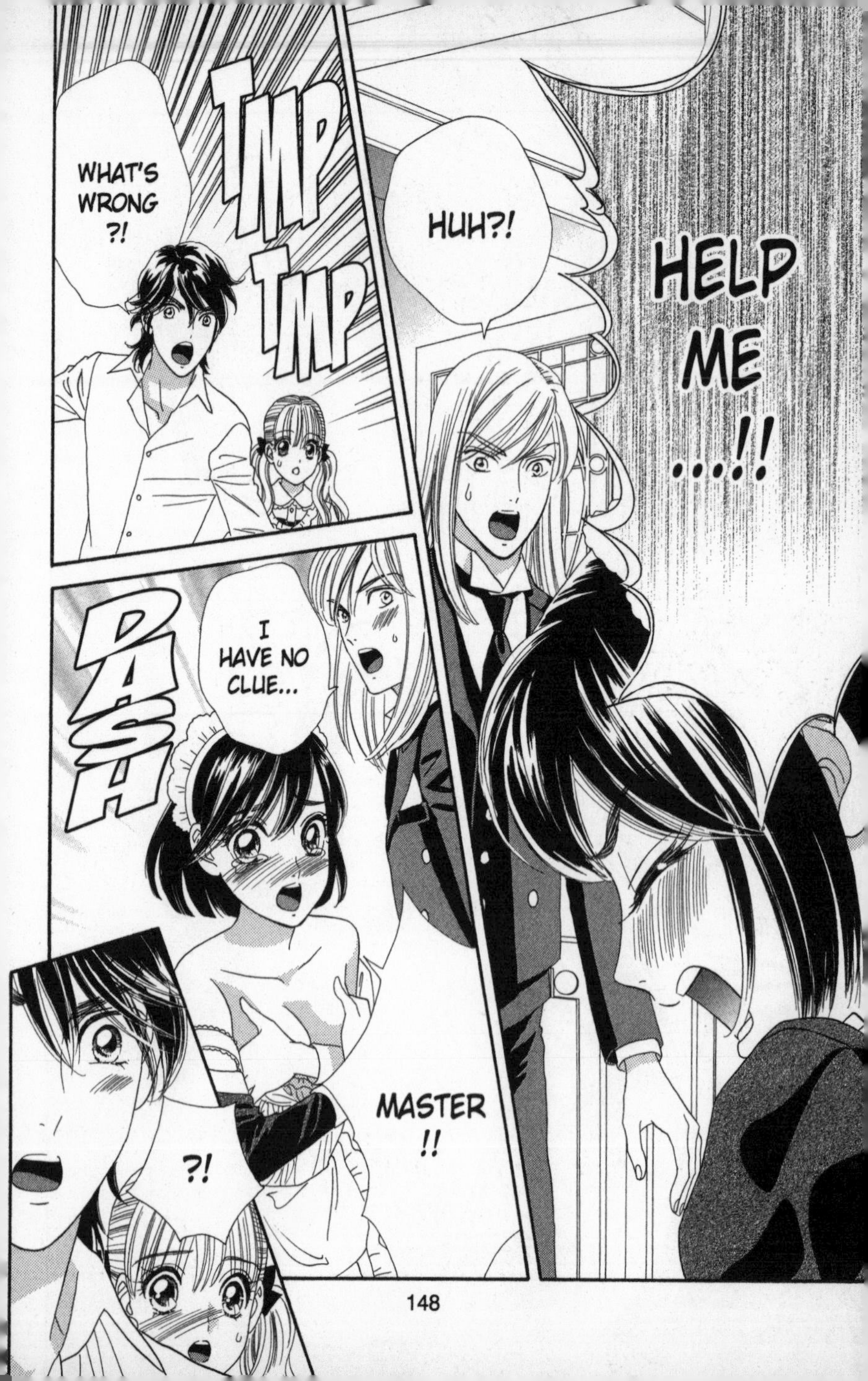
HELP ME ...!!
HUH?!
TMP TMP
WHAT'S WRONG ?!
DASA
I HAVE NO CLUE...
MASTER !!
?!

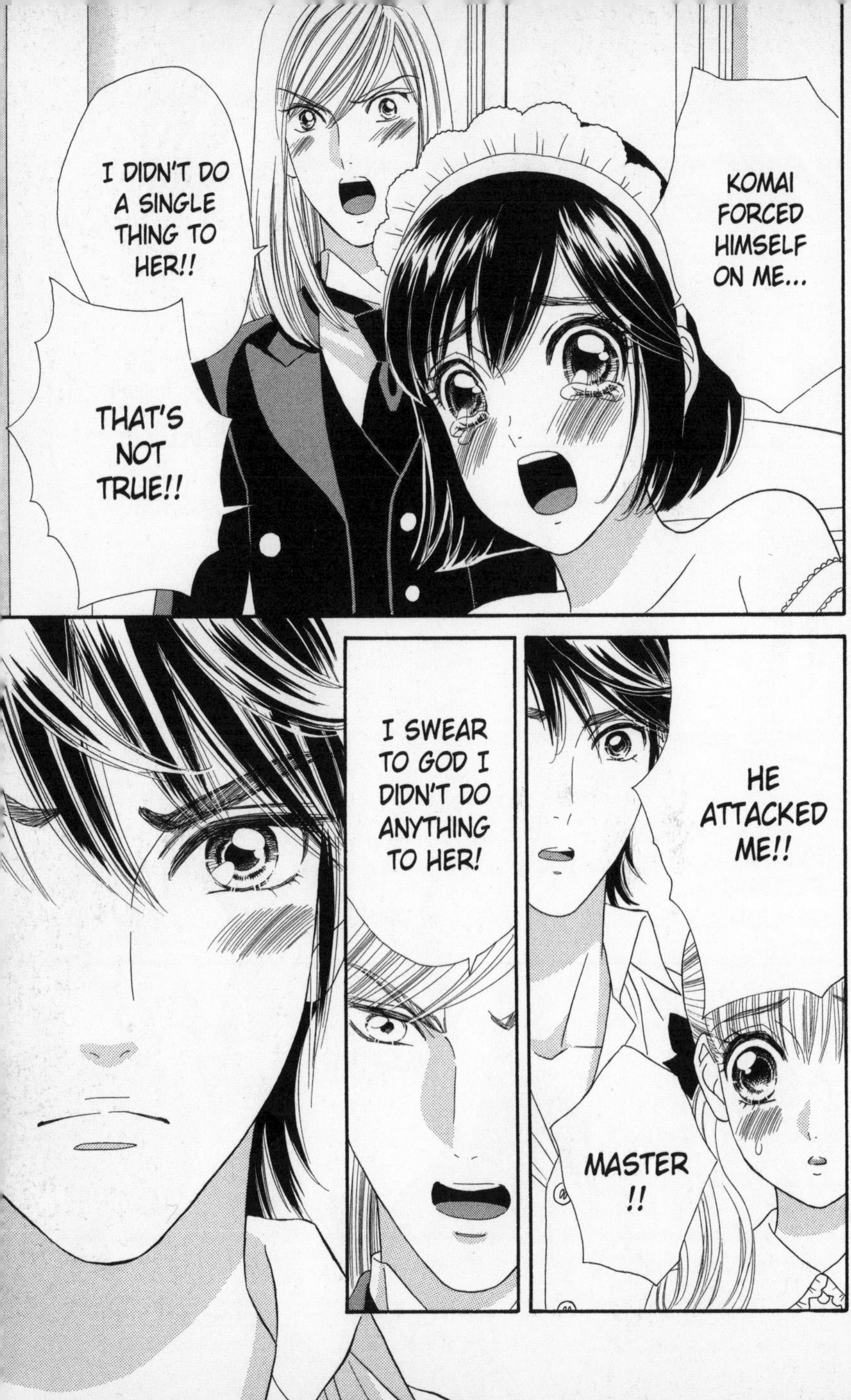
KOMAI FORCED HIMSELF ON ME...
I DIDN'T DO A SINGLE THING TO HER!!
THAT'S NOT TRUE!!
HE ATTACKED ME!!
MASTER !!
I SWEAR TO GOD I DIDN'T DO ANYTHING TO HER!

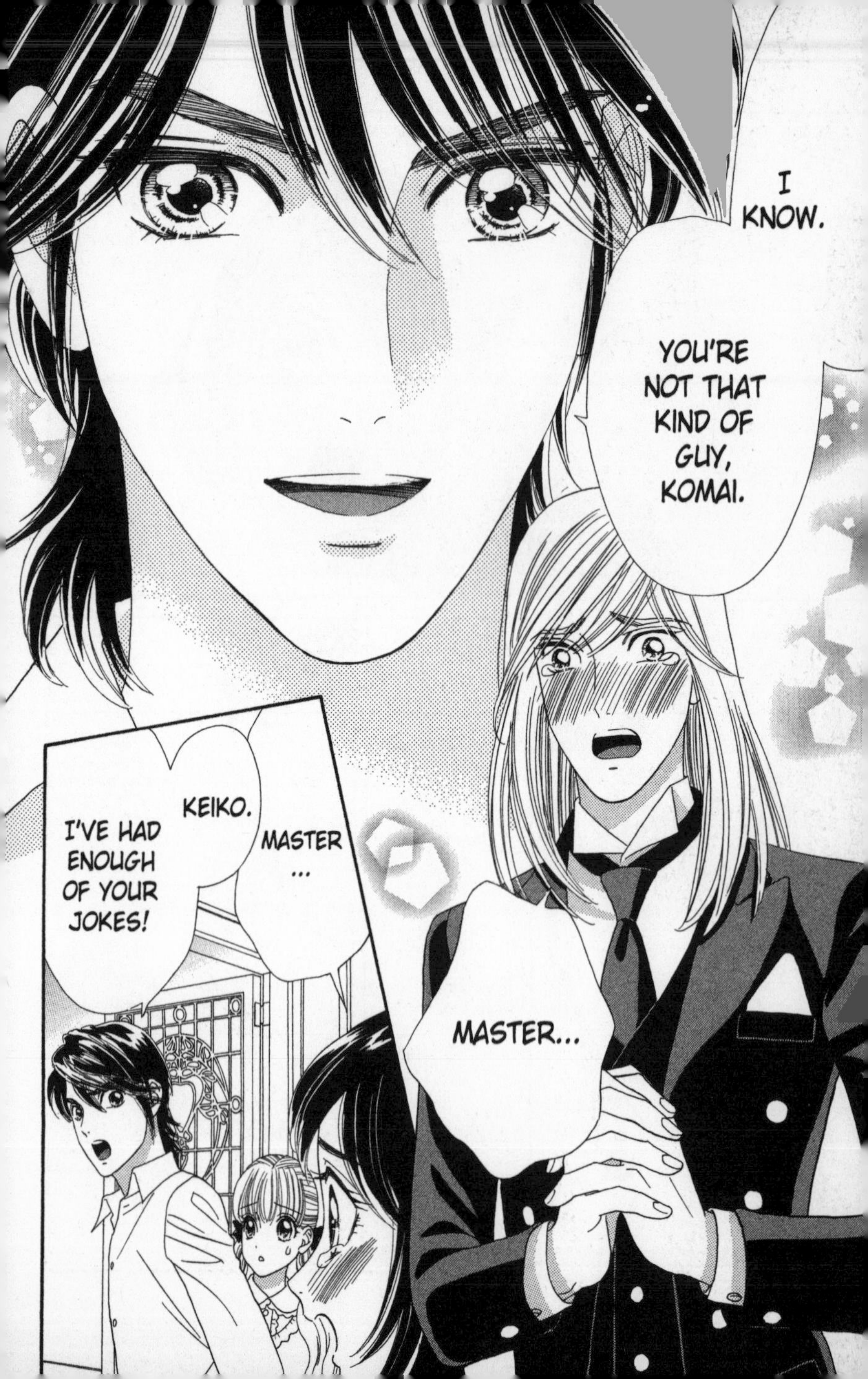
I KNOW.
YOU'RE NOT THAT KIND OF GUY, KOMAI.
MASTER...
MASTER ...
KEIKO.
I'VE HAD ENOUGH OF YOUR JOKES!

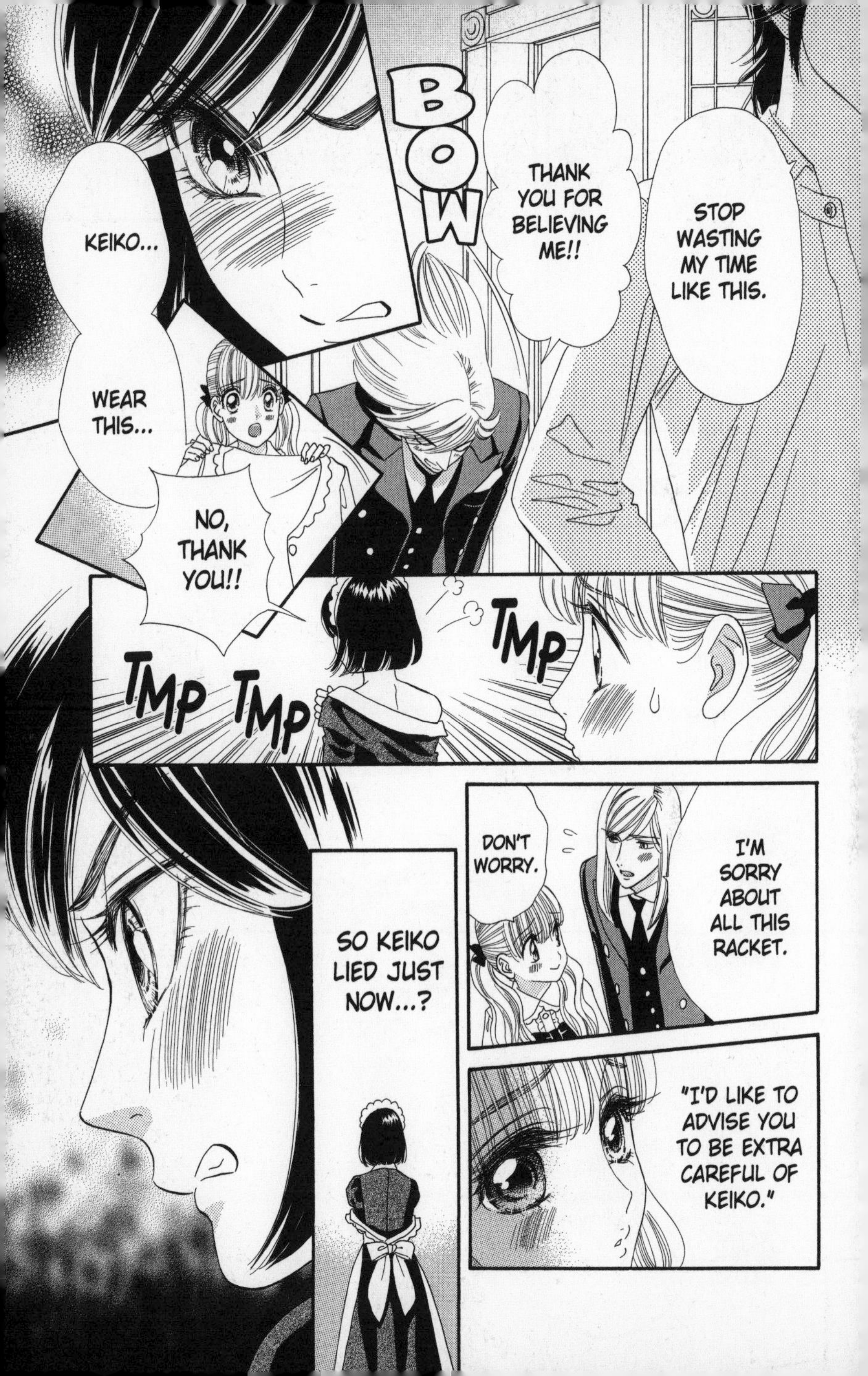
STOP WASTING MY TIME LIKE THIS.
THANK YOU FOR BELIEVING ME!!
BOW
KEIKO...
WEAR THIS...
NO, THANK YOU!!
TMP
TMP TMP
I'M SORRY ABOUT ALL THIS RACKET.
DON'T WORRY.
"I'D LIKE TO ADVISE YOU TO BE EXTRA CAREFUL OF KEIKO."
SO KEIKO LIED JUST NOW...?

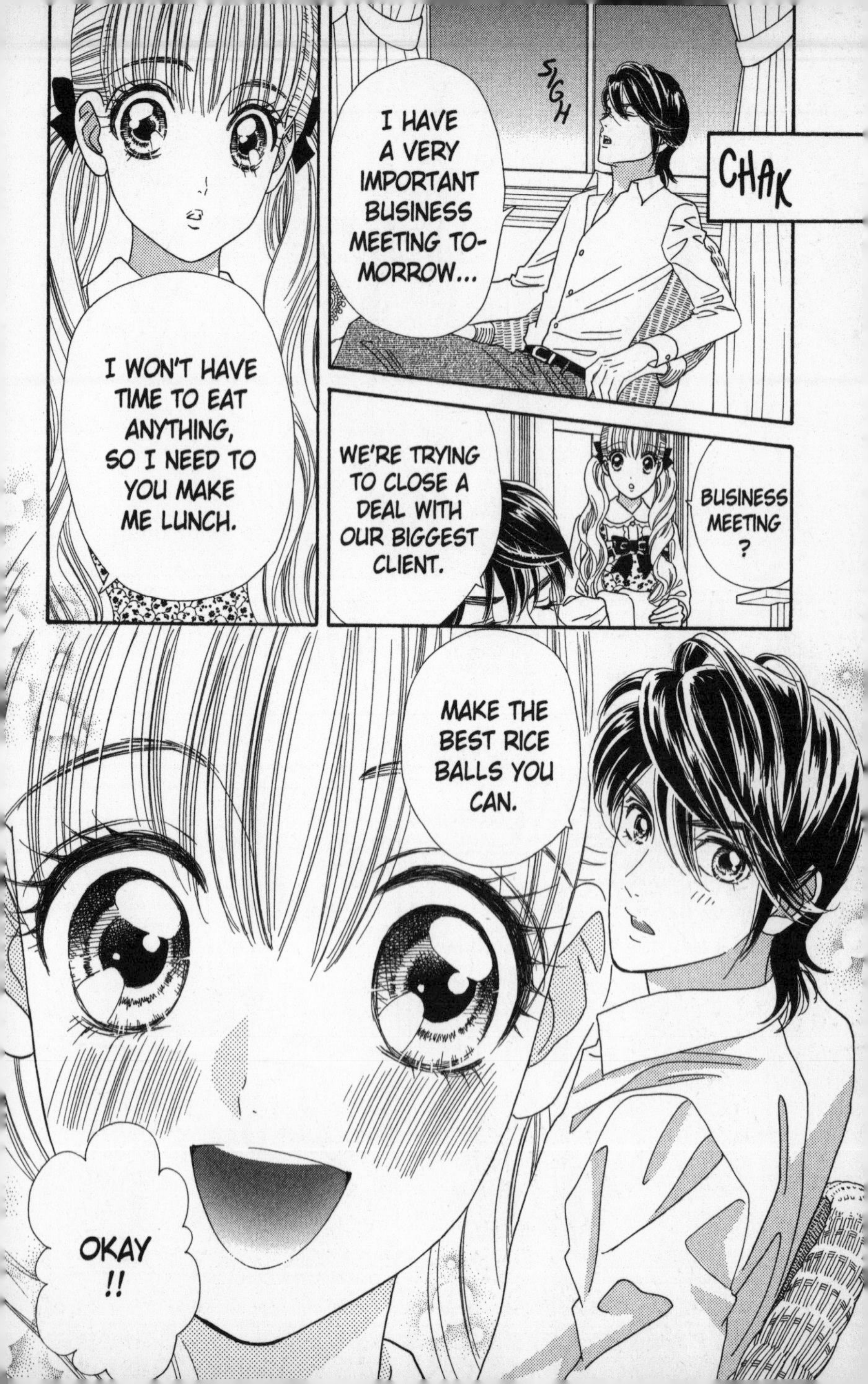
CHAK
SIGH
I HAVE A VERY IMPORTANT BUSINESS MEETING TO-MORROW...
BUSINESS MEETING ?
WE'RE TRYING TO CLOSE A DEAL WITH OUR BIGGEST CLIENT.
I WON'T HAVE TIME TO EAT ANYTHING, SO I NEED TO YOU MAKE ME LUNCH.
MAKE THE BEST RICE BALLS YOU CAN.
OKAY !!

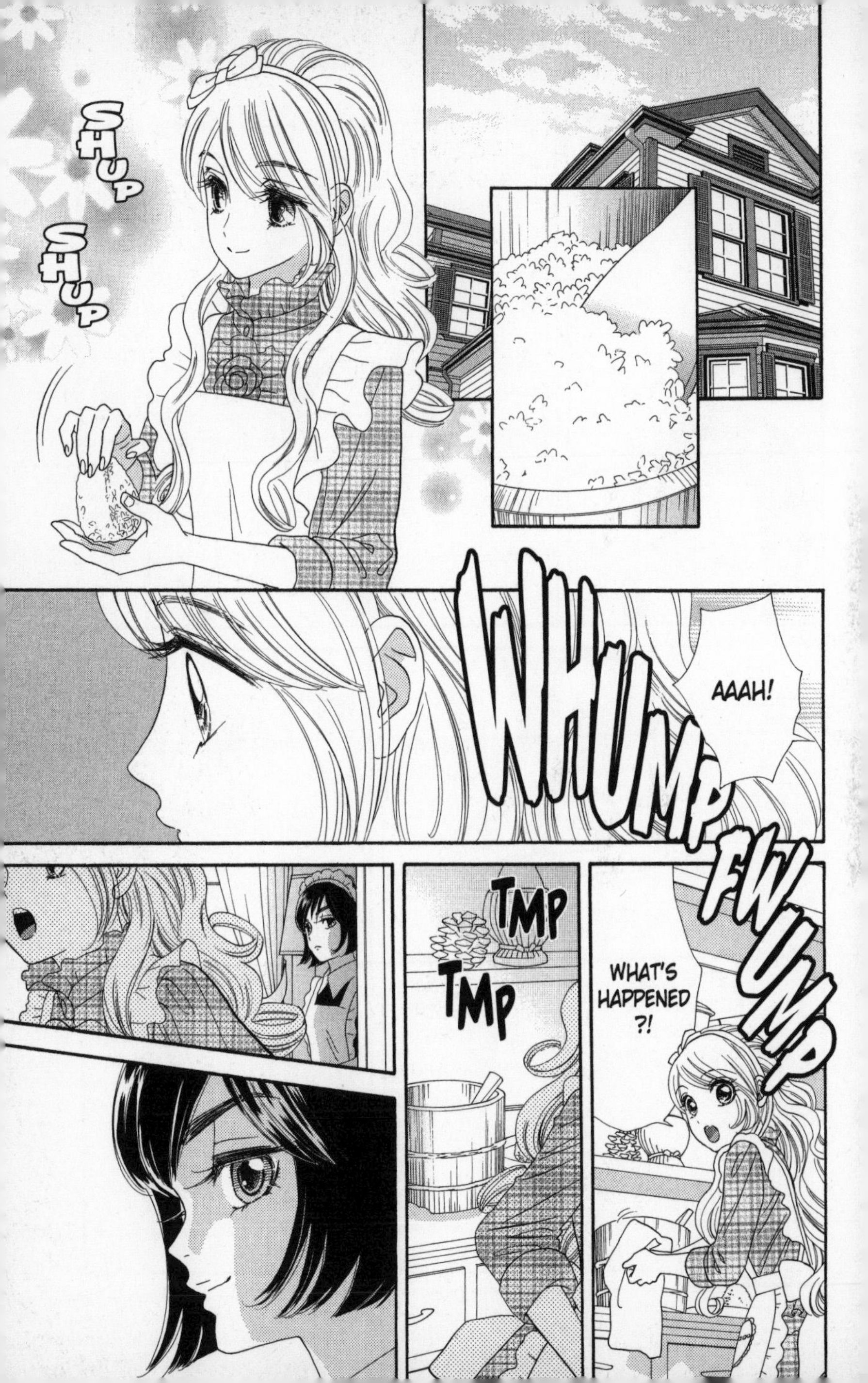
SHUP SHUP
SHUP SHUP
AAAH!
WHUMP
FWUMP
WHAT'S HAPPENED ?!
TMP
TMP

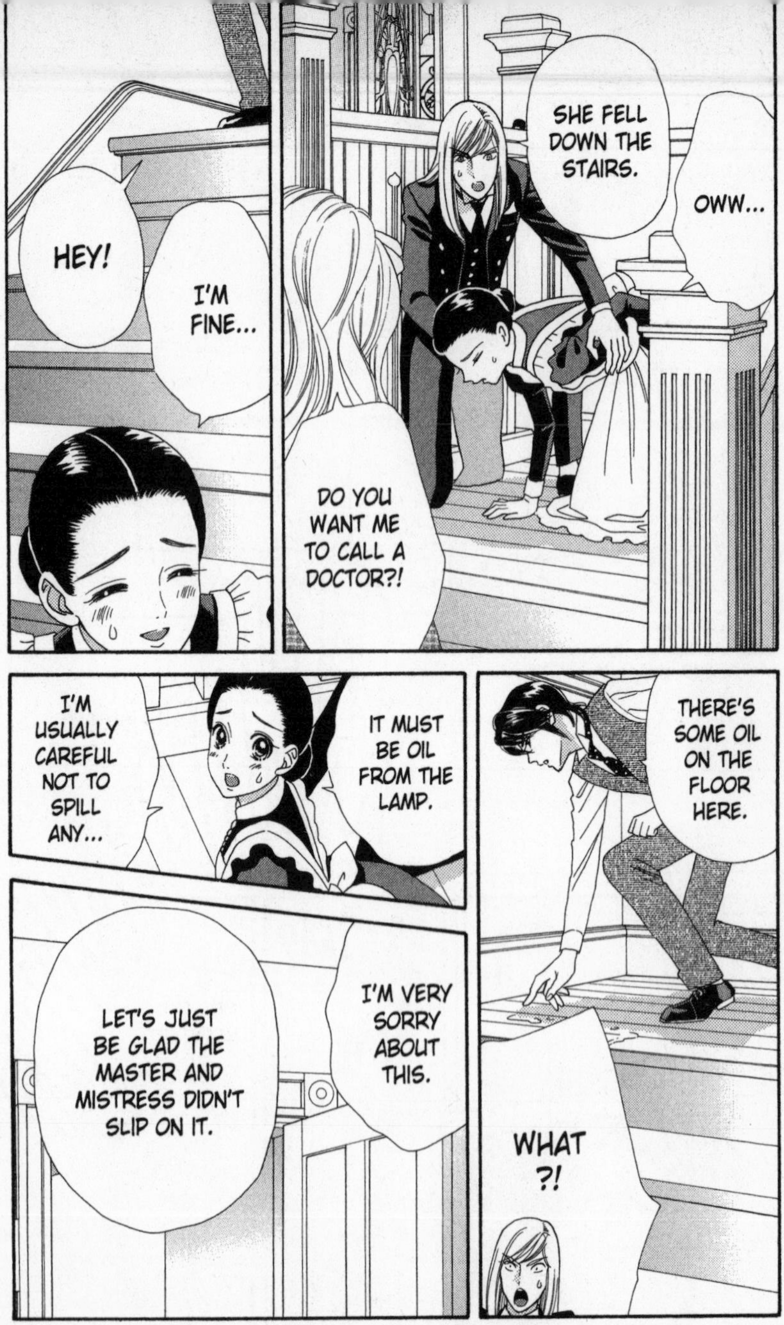
OWW...
SHE FELL DOWN THE STAIRS.
DO YOU WANT ME TO CALL A DOCTOR?!
I'M FINE...
HEY!
THERE'S SOME OIL ON THE FLOOR HERE.
WHAT ?!
IT MUST BE OIL FROM THE LAMP.
I'M USUALLY CAREFUL NOT TO SPILL ANY...
I'M VERY SORRY ABOUT THIS.
LET'S JUST BE GLAD THE MASTER AND MISTRESS DIDN'T SLIP ON IT.

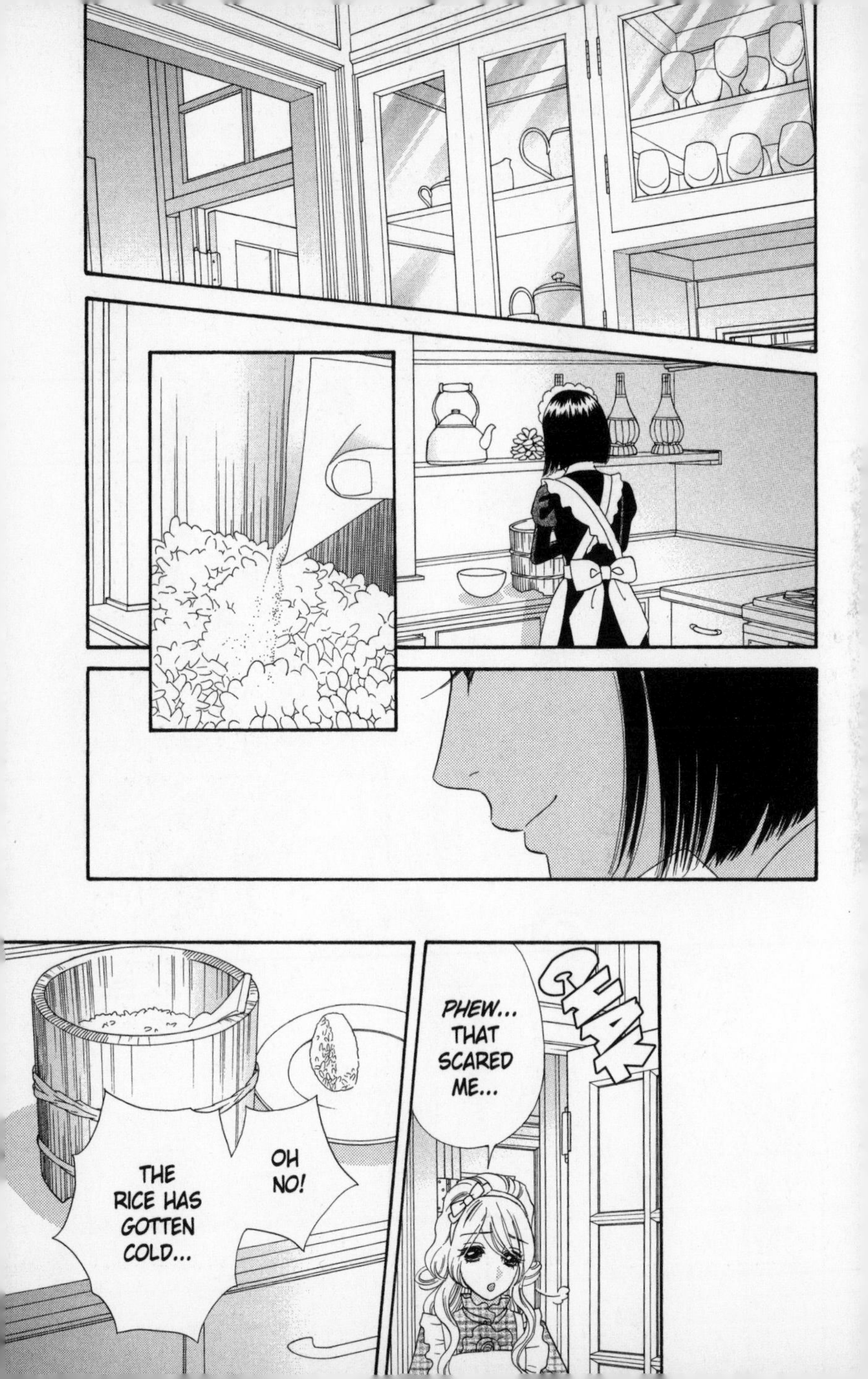
CHAK
PHEW... THAT SCARED ME...
OH NO!
THE RICE HAS GOTTEN COLD...

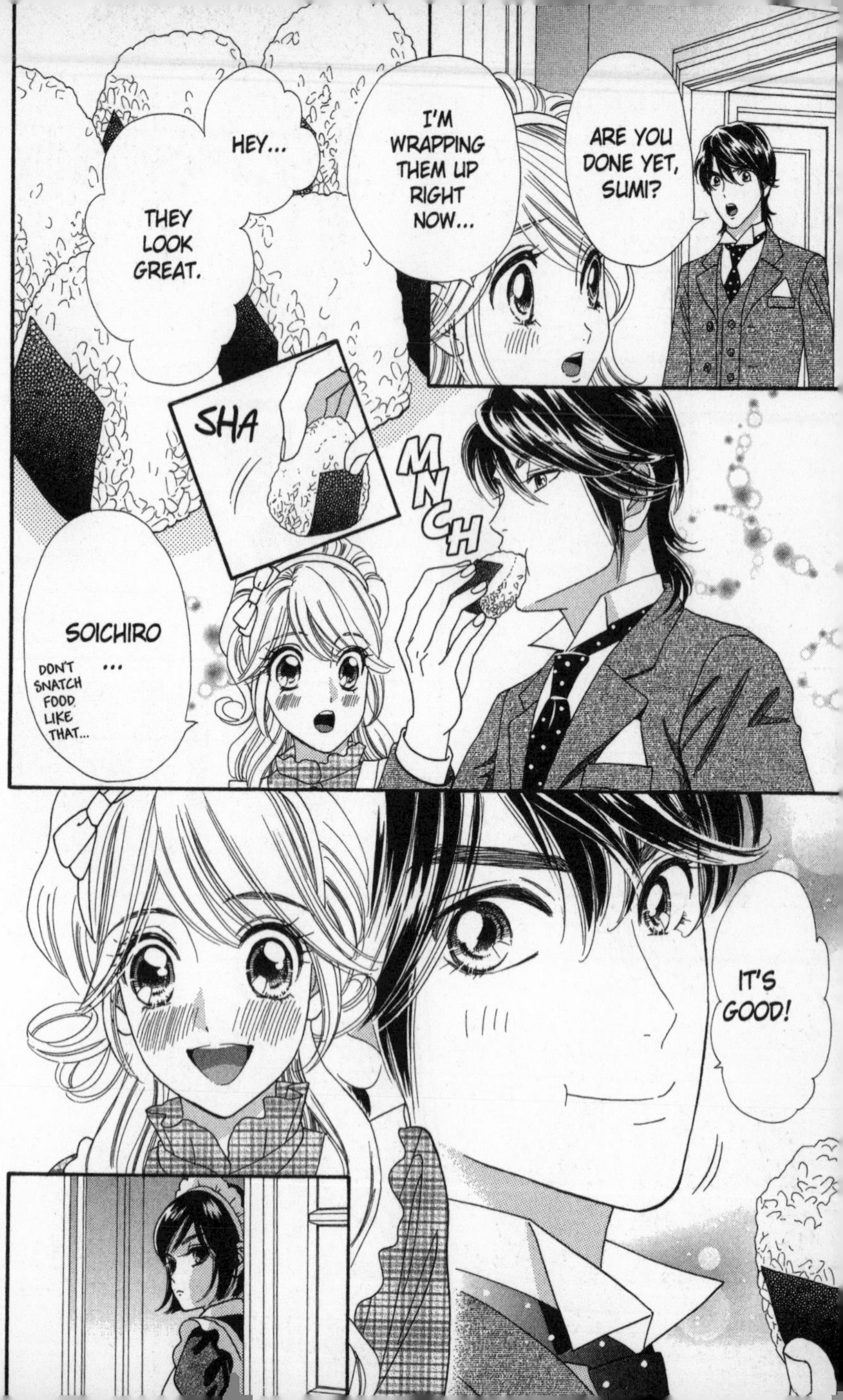
ARE YOU DONE YET, SUMI?
I'M WRAPPING THEM UP RIGHT NOW...
HEY...
THEY LOOK GREAT.
SHA
MNCH
SOICHIRO ...
DON'T SNATCH FOOD LIKE THAT...
IT'S GOOD!

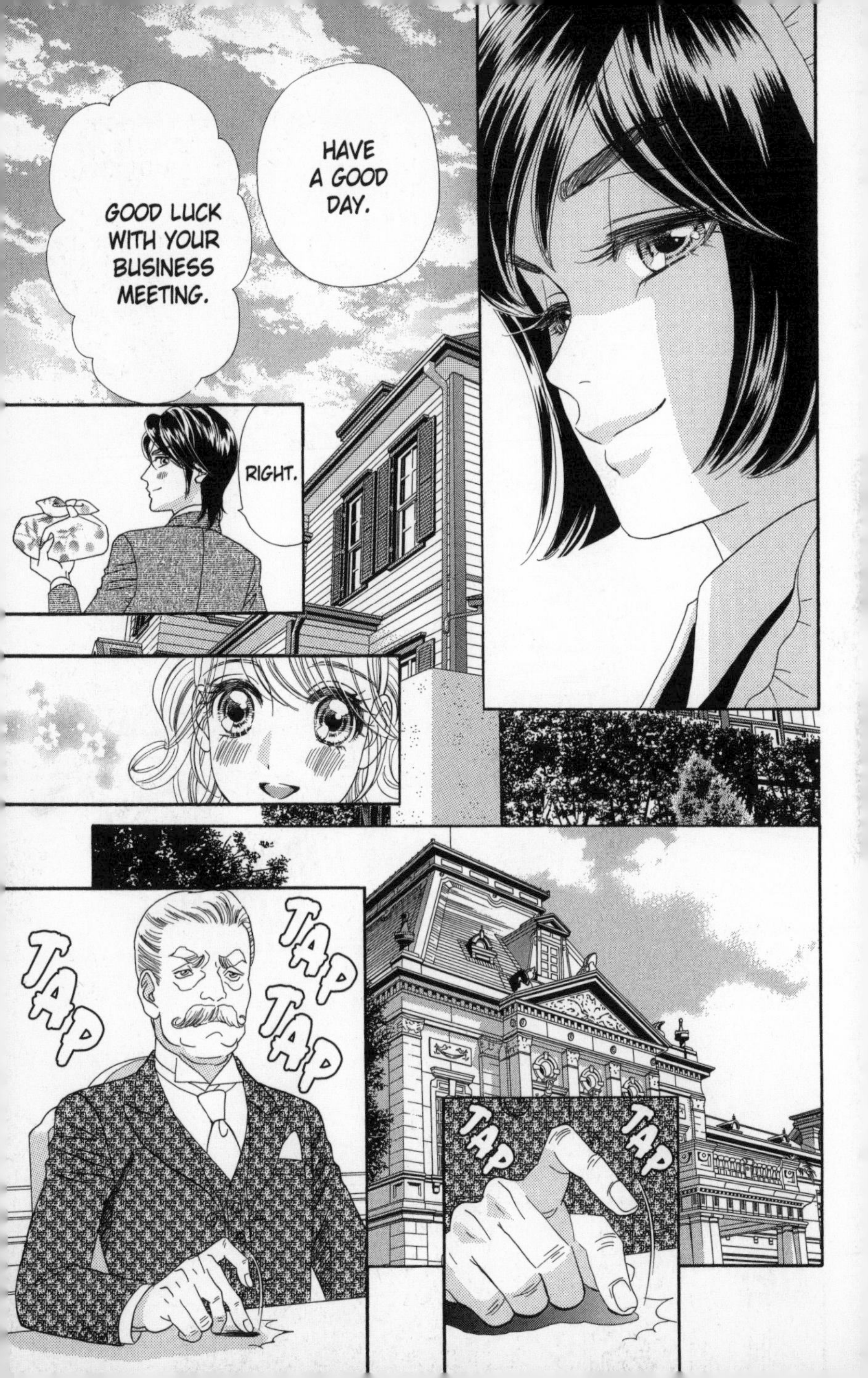
HAVE A GOOD DAY.
GOOD LUCK WITH YOUR BUSINESS MEETING.
RIGHT.
TAP
TAP
TAP TAP
TAP

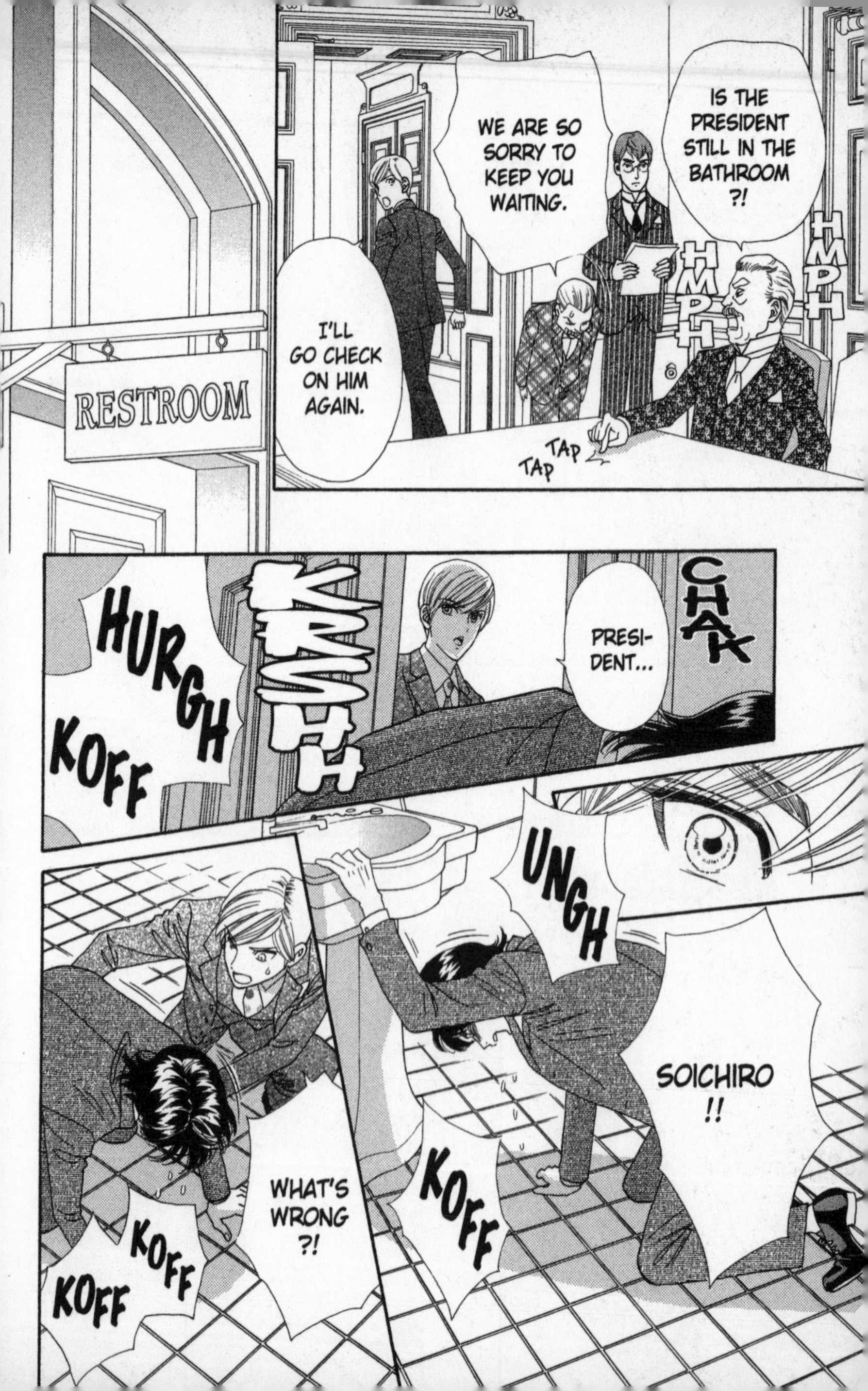
IS THE PRESIDENT STILL IN THE BATHROOM ?!
HMPH
HMPH
WE ARE SO SORRY TO KEEP YOU WAITING.
I'LL GO CHECK ON HIM AGAIN.
TAP TAP
RESTROOM
CHAK
PRESI-DENT...
KRSHH
HURGH
KOFF
UNGH
SOICHIRO !!
KOFF
WHAT'S WRONG ?!
KOFF
KOFF

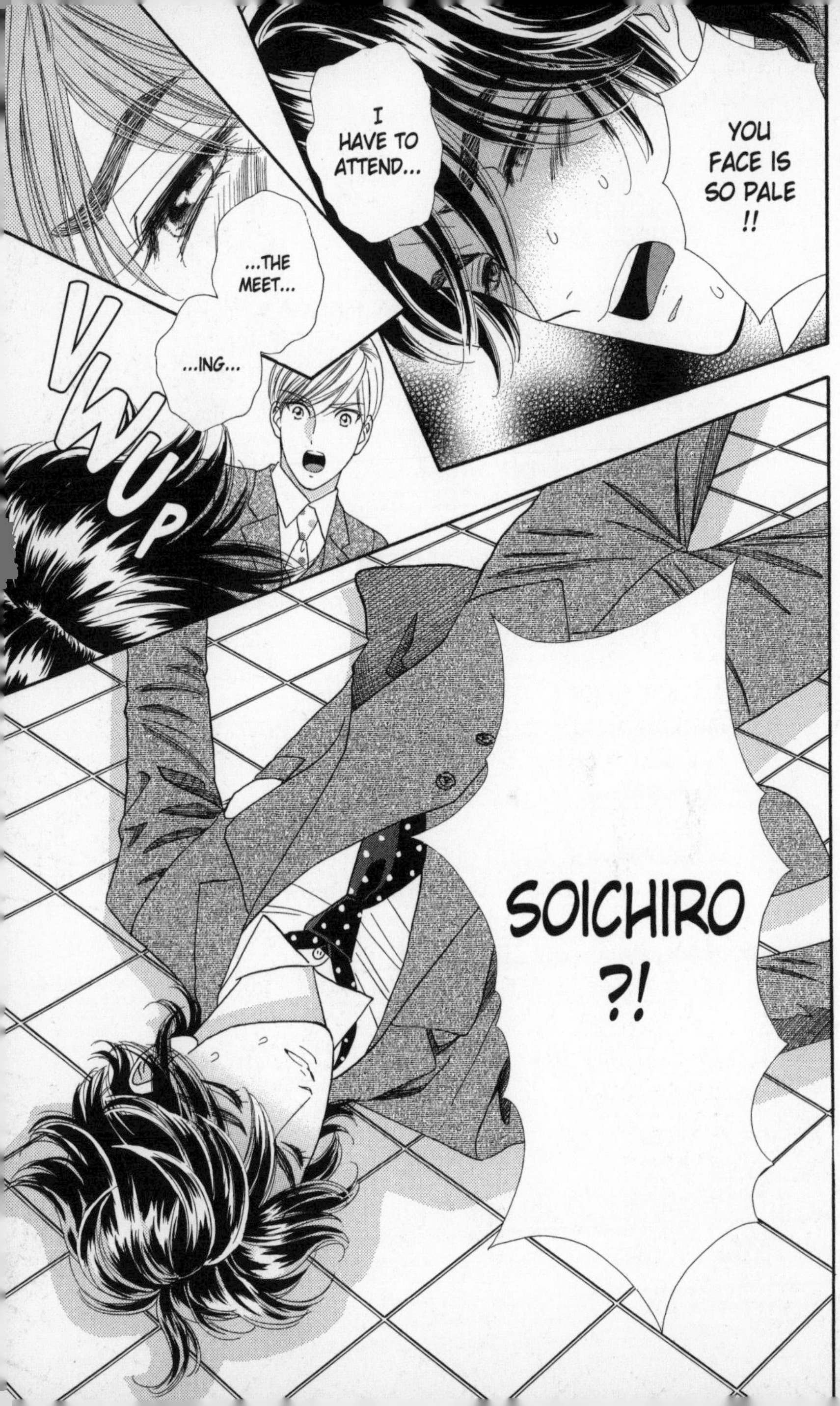
YOU FACE IS SO PALE !!
I HAVE TO ATTEND...
...THE MEET...
...ING...
VWUP
SOICHIRO ?!

No. 6

RANDOM CHITCHAT!

Date .   .

✳ I THOUGHT THIS WAS MY FIRST MANGA WITH AN
ELEMENTARY SCHOOL STUDENT AS THE MAIN
CHARACTER, BUT THEN I REMEMBERED I DID A
50-PAGE ONE-SHOT IN ISSUE 21 OF *MARGARET*
BACK IN 2001 CALLED *CHUPA!*
IT'S A MODERN-DAY STORY THAT I'D CREATED
RIGHT BEFORE I STARTED THE *TAIL OF THE MOON*
SERIES (WHICH IS A NINJA STORY). THE STYLE OF
THAT MANGA DIDN'T REALLY FIT WITH A NINJA
STORY, HOWEVER, SO IT WAS NEVER INCLUDED
WITH THOSE GRAPHIC NOVELS.

I'M NOT SURE IF IT'LL FIT WITH THIS
MELODRAMATIC STORY EITHER, BUT I HOPE YOU
ALL GET A CHANCE TO READ THAT ONE-SHOT
SOMEDAY.

I'LL CONTINUE TO DO MY BEST ON *STEPPING ON
ROSES*, SO PLEASE CONTINUE TO SUPPORT ME.

✳ IF YOU HAVE ANY COMMENTS, PLEASE
SEND THEM TO THE FOLLOWING ADDRESS:
RINKO UEDA
C/O STEPPING ON ROSES EDITOR
VIZ MEDIA
P.O. BOX 77010
SAN FRANCISCO, CA 94107

SEE YOU ALL IN VOLUME 5! ♥   Rinko 😊 Ueda ♡

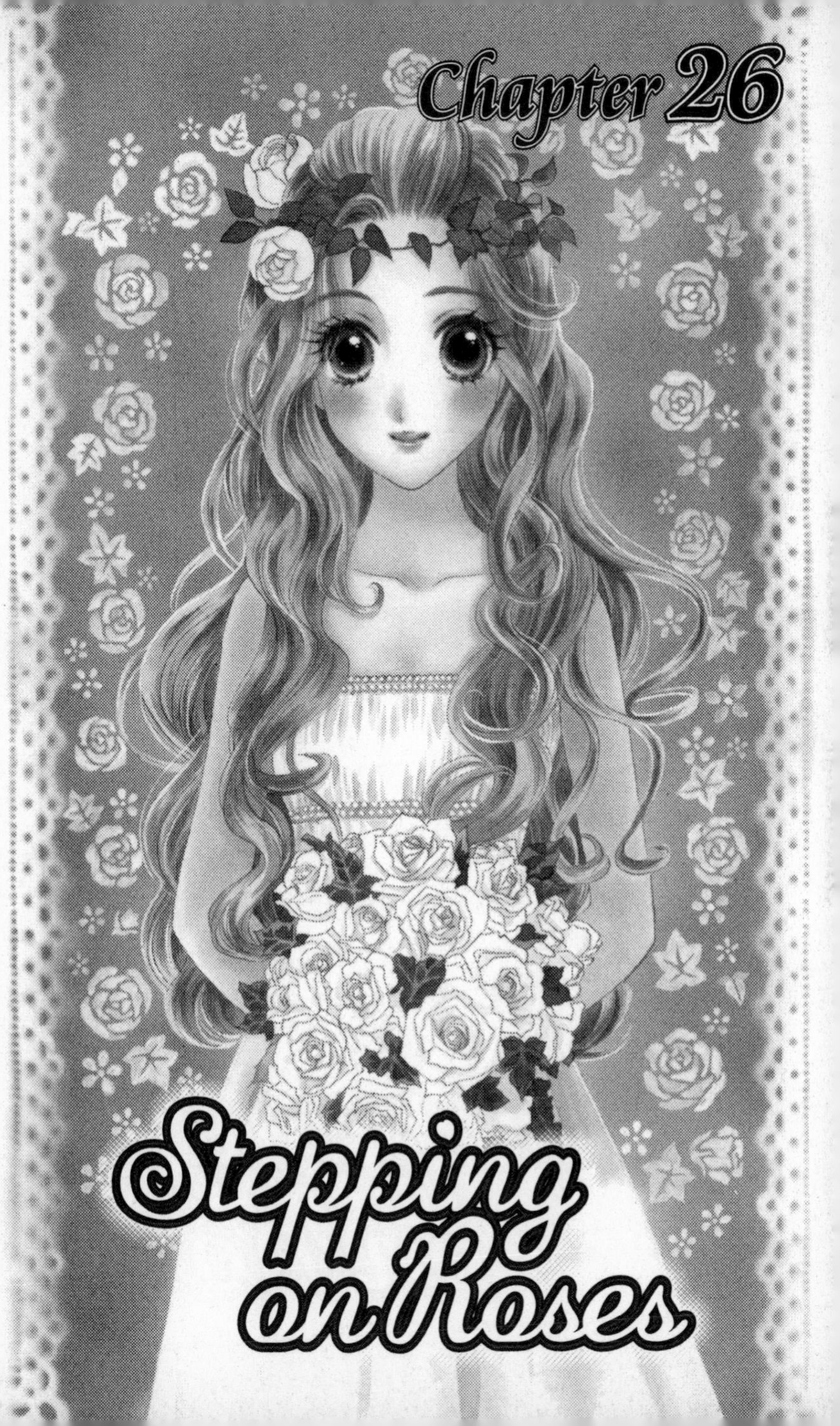
Chapter 26
Stepping on Roses

Stepping on Roses

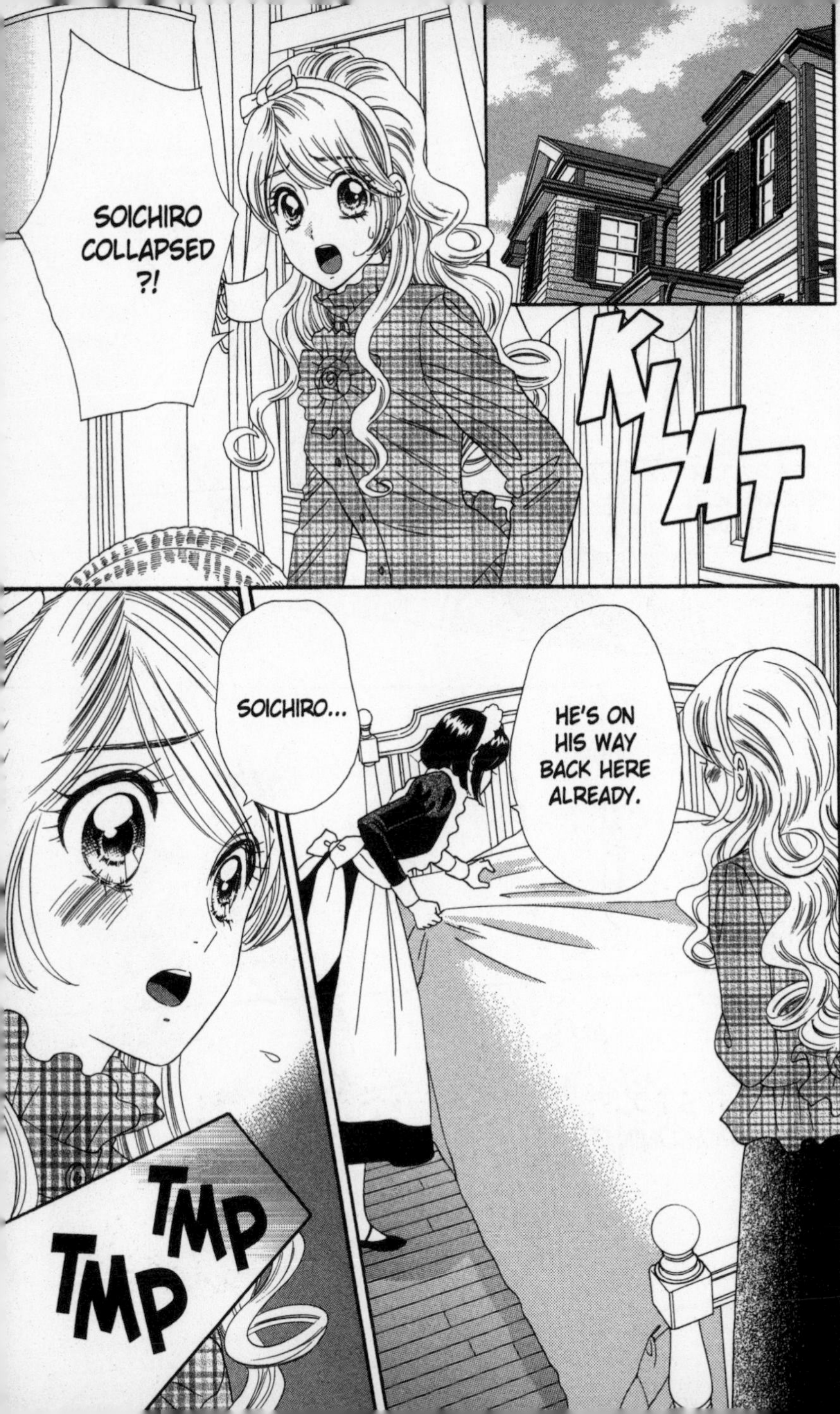
KLAT
SOICHIRO COLLAPSED ?!
HE'S ON HIS WAY BACK HERE ALREADY.
SOICHIRO...
TMP TMP

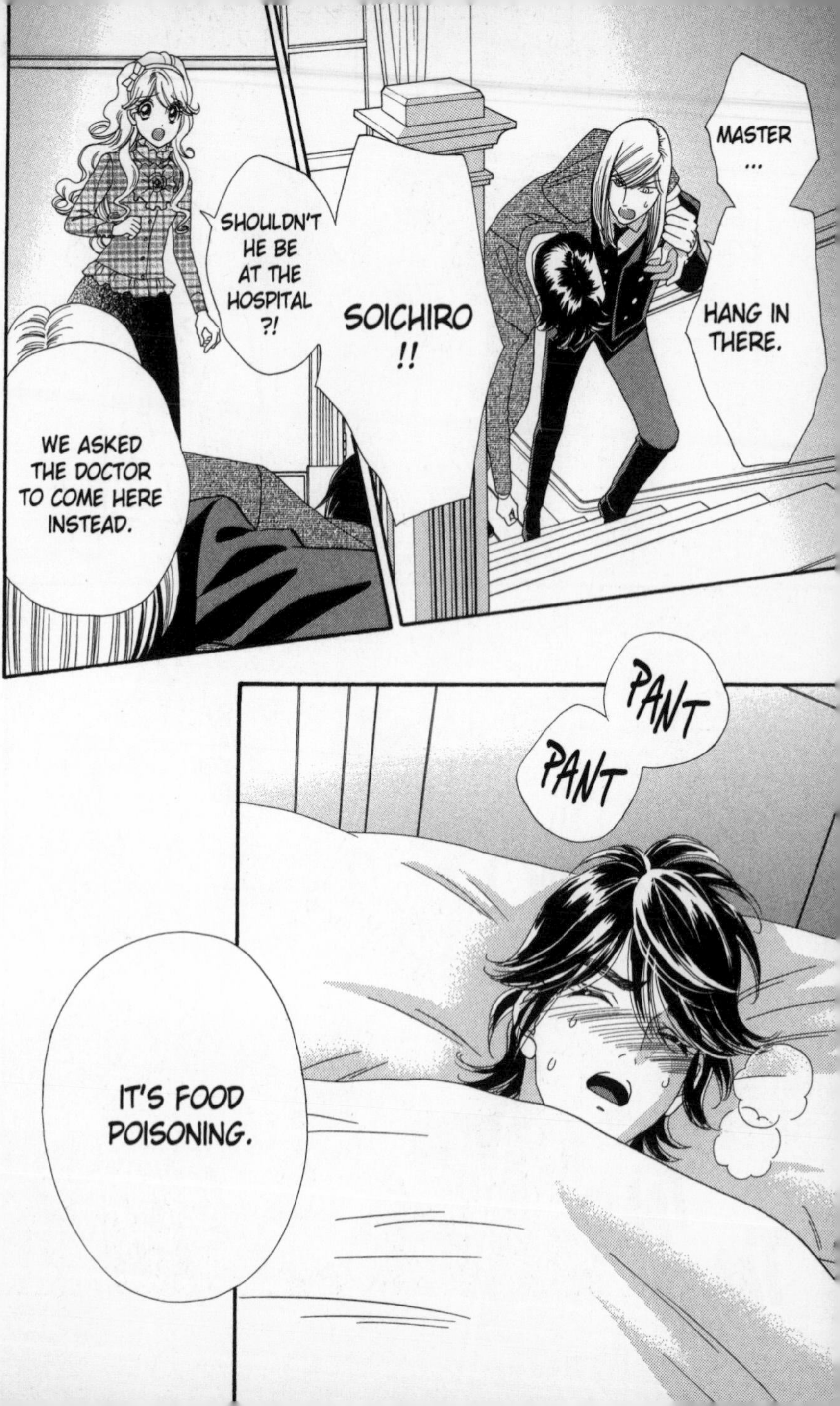
MASTER ...
HANG IN THERE.
SOICHIRO !!
SHOULDN'T HE BE AT THE HOSPITAL ?!
WE ASKED THE DOCTOR TO COME HERE INSTEAD.
PANT
PANT
IT'S FOOD POISONING.

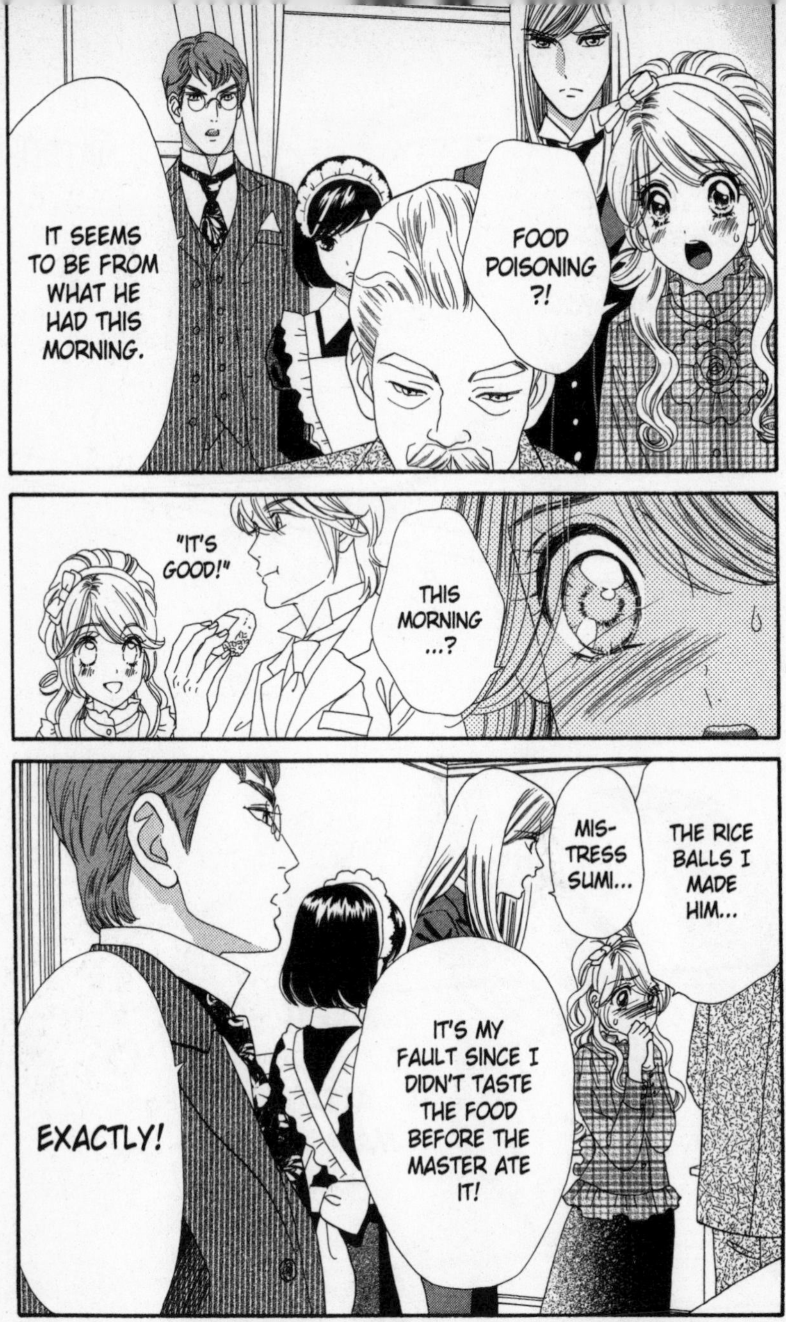
FOOD POISONING ?!
IT SEEMS TO BE FROM WHAT HE HAD THIS MORNING.
THIS MORNING ...?
"IT'S GOOD!"
THE RICE BALLS I MADE HIM...
MIS-TRESS SUMI...
IT'S MY FAULT SINCE I DIDN'T TASTE THE FOOD BEFORE THE MASTER ATE IT!
EXACTLY!

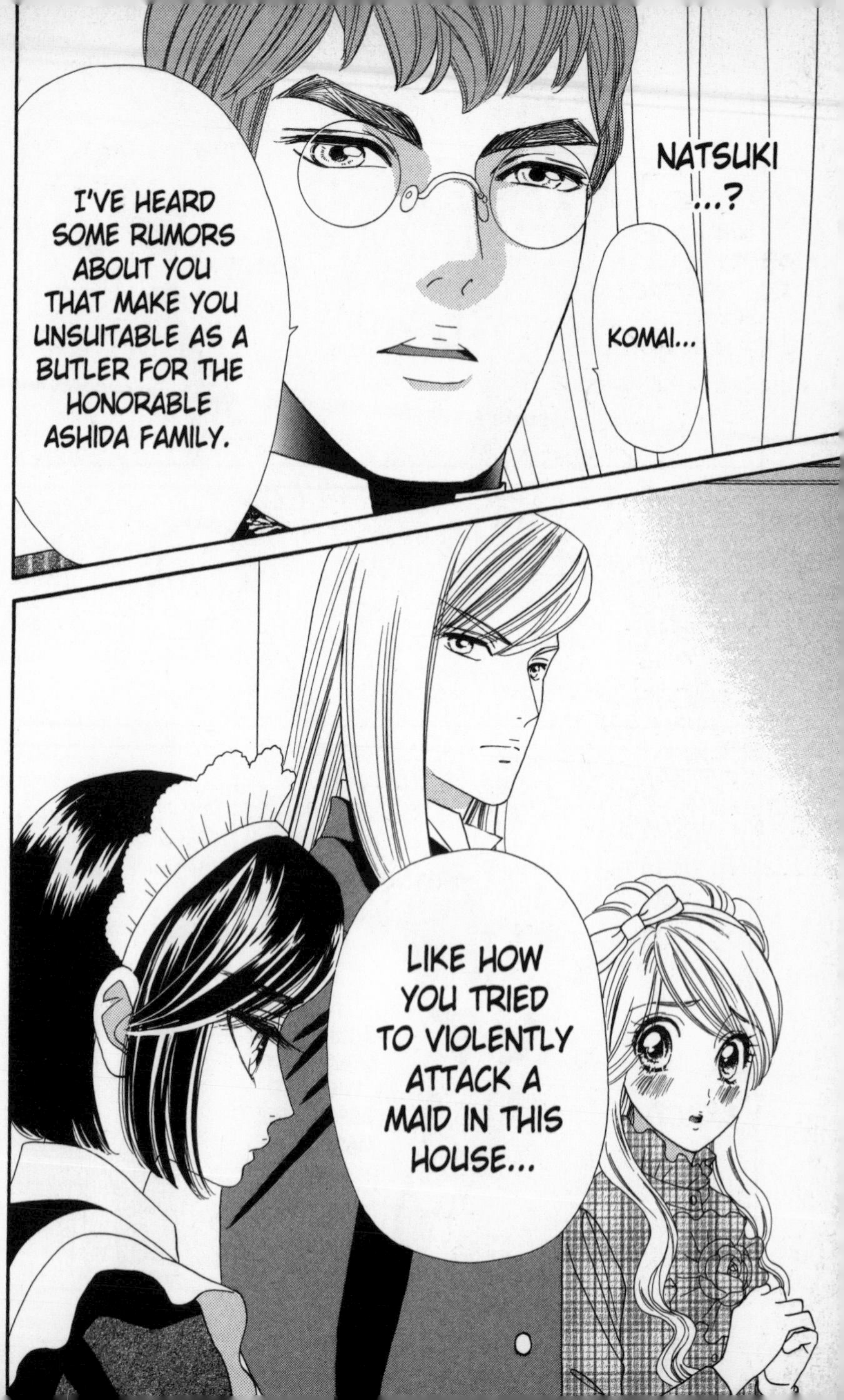
NATSUKI ...?
KOMAI...
I'VE HEARD SOME RUMORS ABOUT YOU THAT MAKE YOU UNSUITABLE AS A BUTLER FOR THE HONORABLE ASHIDA FAMILY.
LIKE HOW YOU TRIED TO VIOLENTLY ATTACK A MAID IN THIS HOUSE...

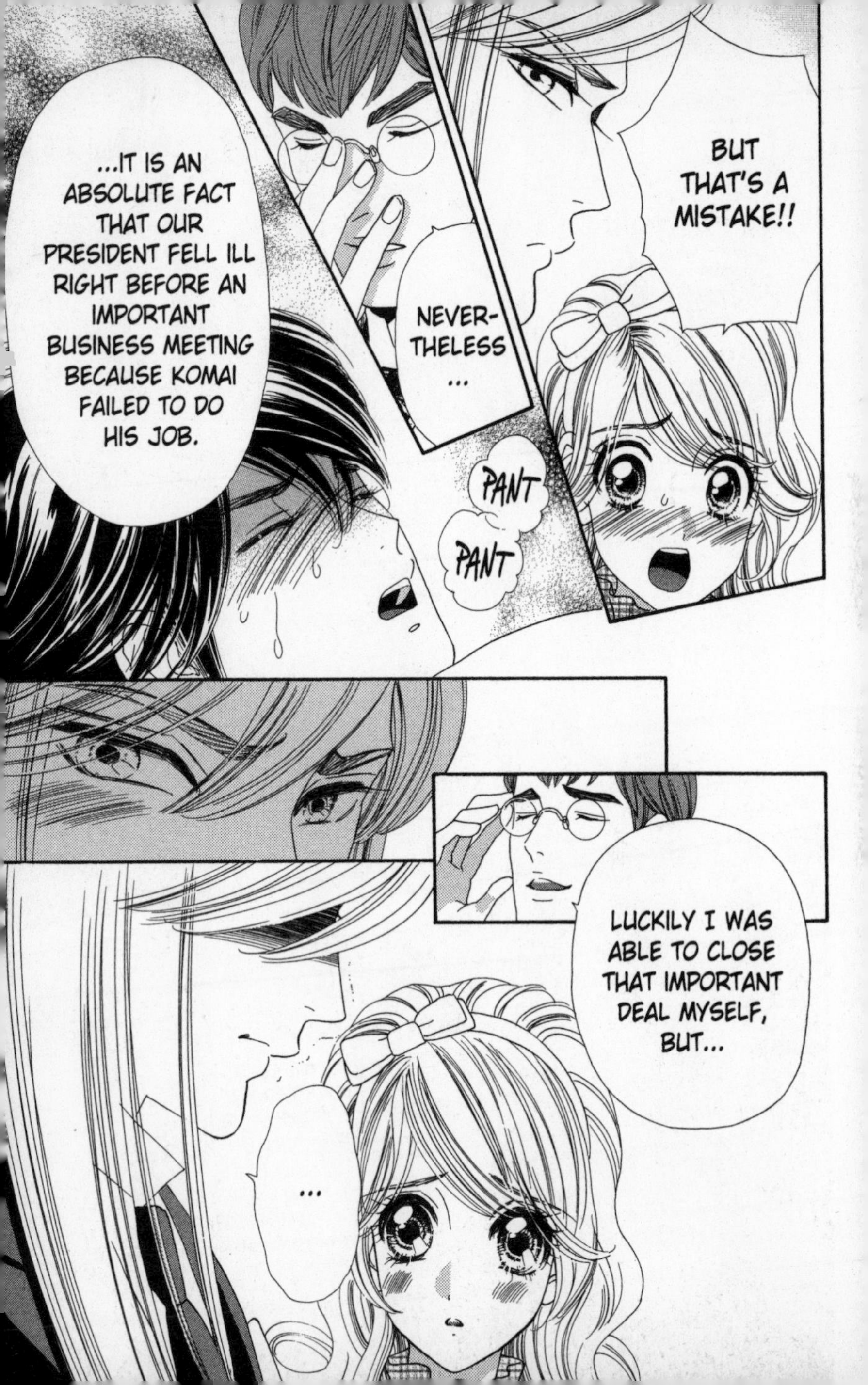
BUT THAT'S A MISTAKE!!
NEVER-THELESS ...
...IT IS AN ABSOLUTE FACT THAT OUR PRESIDENT FELL ILL RIGHT BEFORE AN IMPORTANT BUSINESS MEETING BECAUSE KOMAI FAILED TO DO HIS JOB.
PANT
PANT
LUCKILY I WAS ABLE TO CLOSE THAT IMPORTANT DEAL MYSELF, BUT...
...

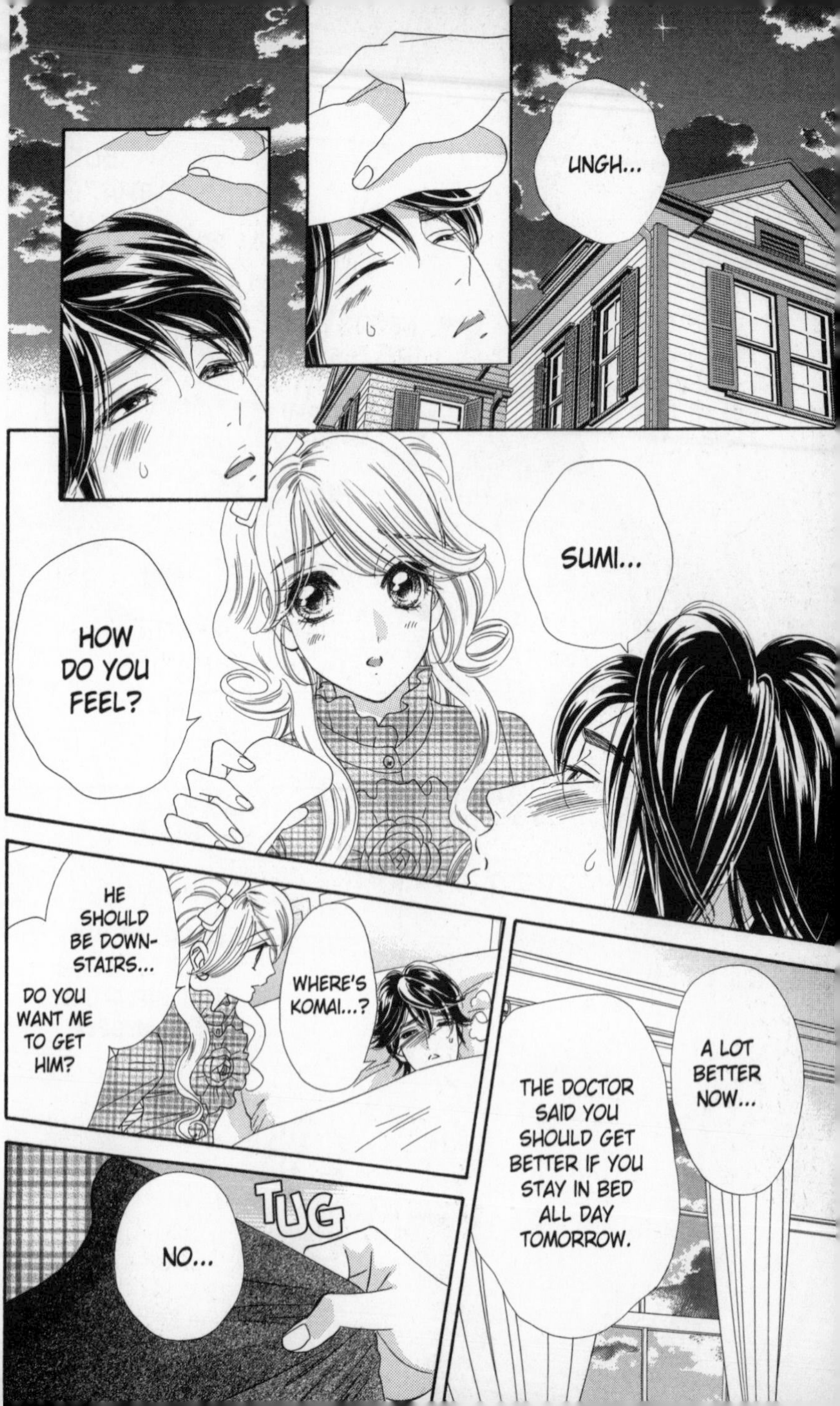
UNGH...
SUMI...
HOW DO YOU FEEL?
A LOT BETTER NOW...
THE DOCTOR SAID YOU SHOULD GET BETTER IF YOU STAY IN BED ALL DAY TOMORROW.
WHERE'S KOMAI...?
HE SHOULD BE DOWN-STAIRS...
DO YOU WANT ME TO GET HIM?
TUG
NO...

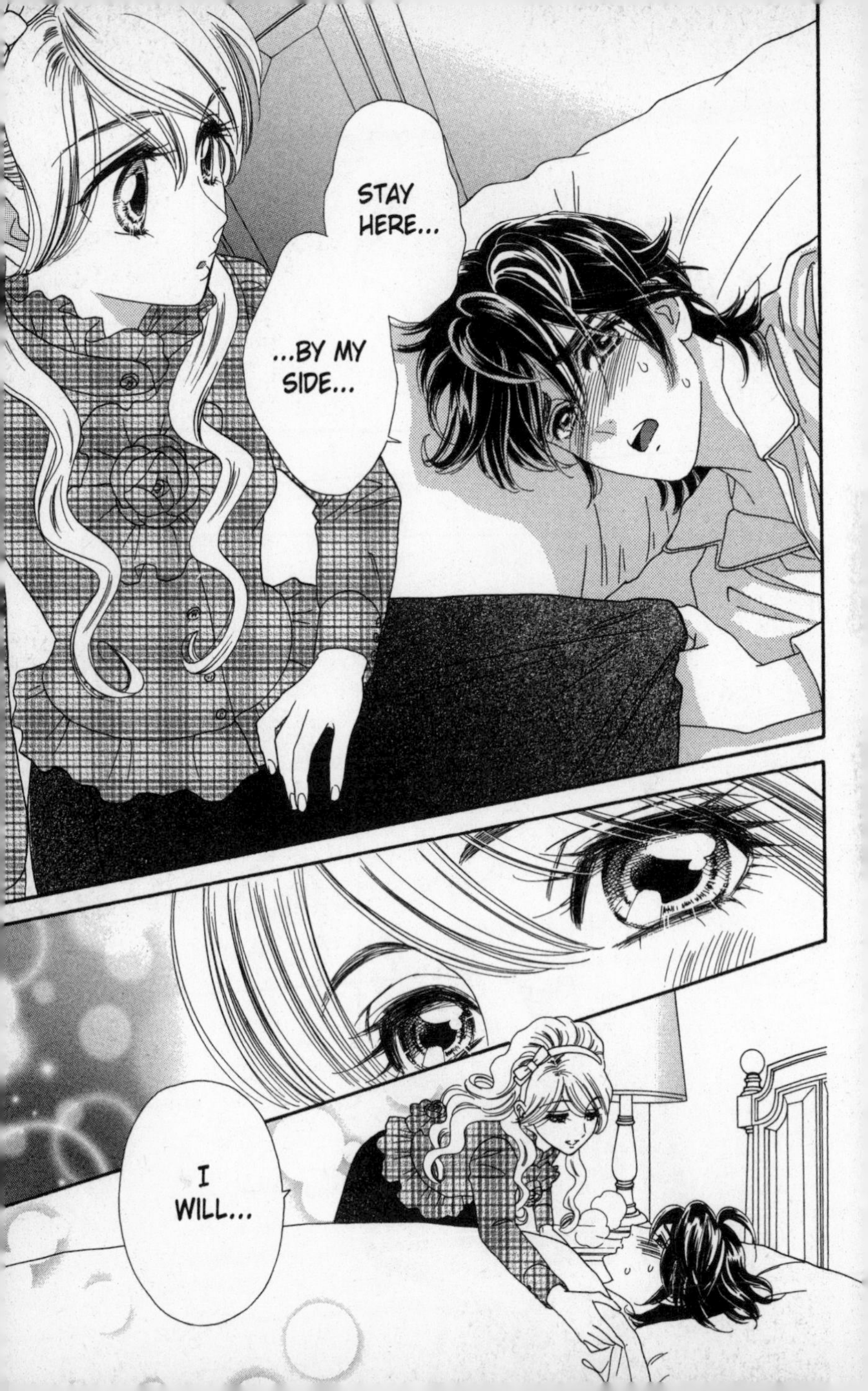
STAY HERE...
...BY MY SIDE...
I WILL...

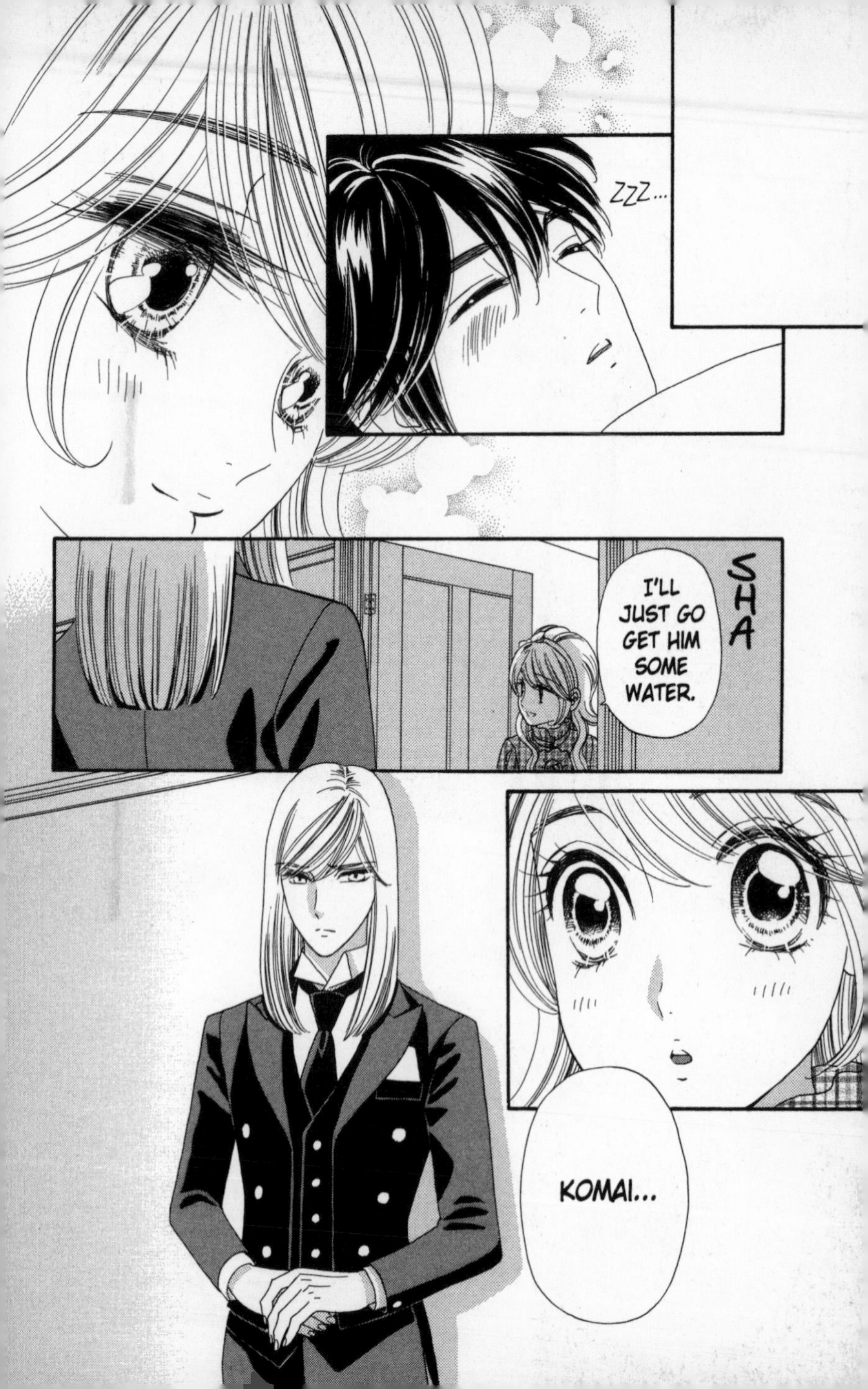
ZZZ...
SHA
I'LL JUST GO GET HIM SOME WATER.
KOMAI...

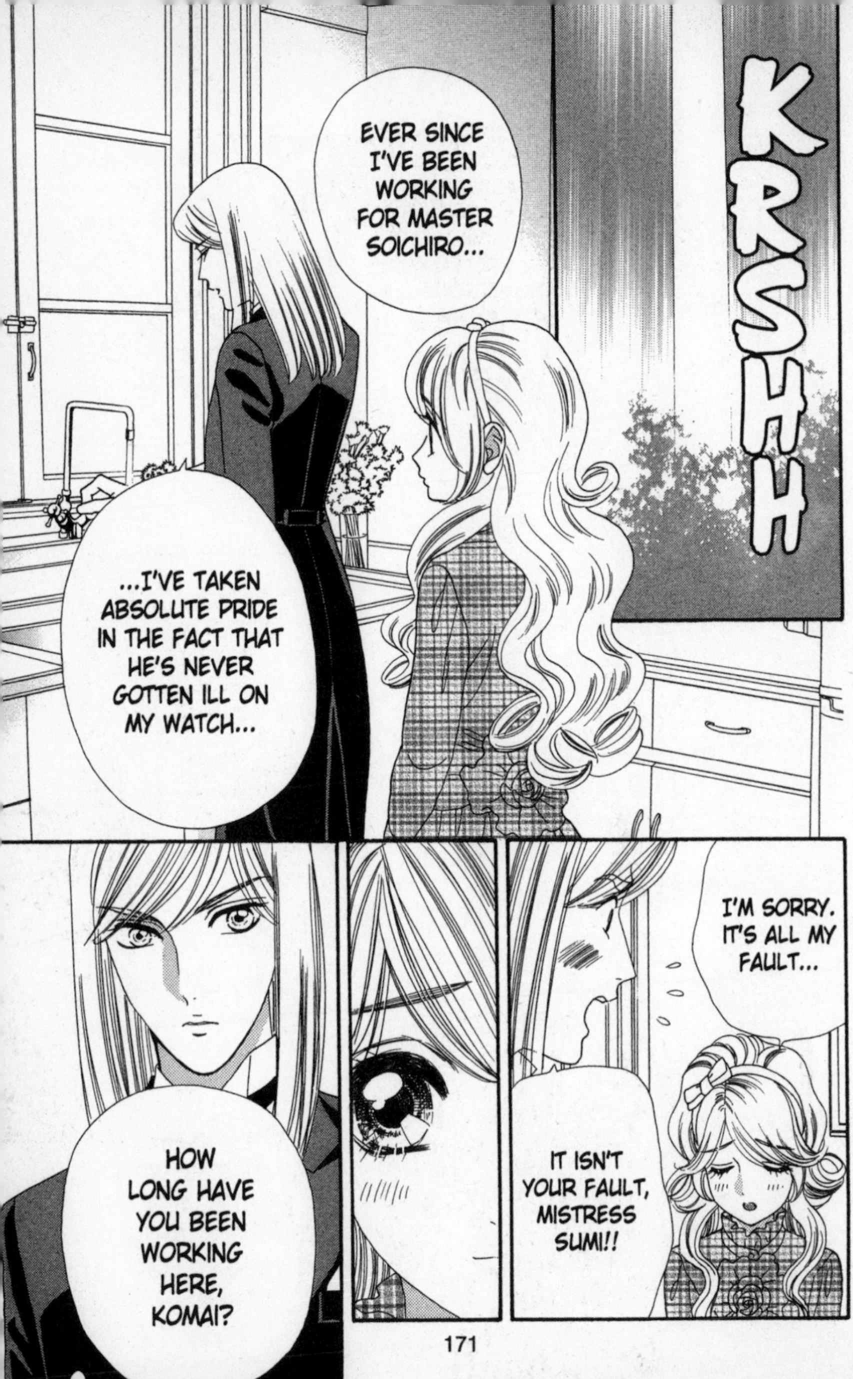
KRSHHH
EVER SINCE I'VE BEEN WORKING FOR MASTER SOICHIRO...
...I'VE TAKEN ABSOLUTE PRIDE IN THE FACT THAT HE'S NEVER GOTTEN ILL ON MY WATCH...
I'M SORRY. IT'S ALL MY FAULT...
IT ISN'T YOUR FAULT, MISTRESS SUMI!!
HOW LONG HAVE YOU BEEN WORKING HERE, KOMAI?

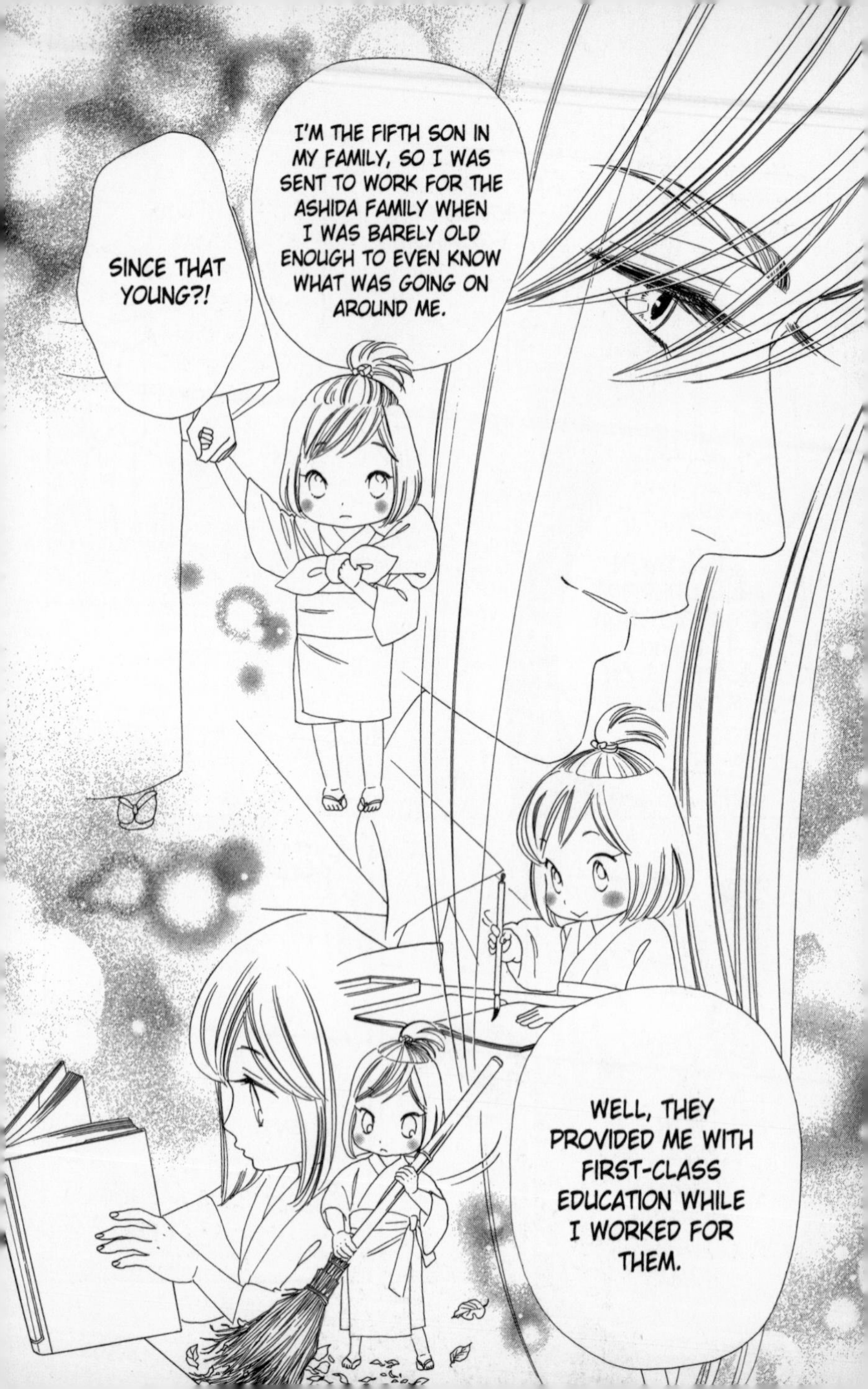
I'M THE FIFTH SON IN MY FAMILY, SO I WAS SENT TO WORK FOR THE ASHIDA FAMILY WHEN I WAS BARELY OLD ENOUGH TO EVEN KNOW WHAT WAS GOING ON AROUND ME.
SINCE THAT YOUNG?!
WELL, THEY PROVIDED ME WITH FIRST-CLASS EDUCATION WHILE I WORKED FOR THEM.

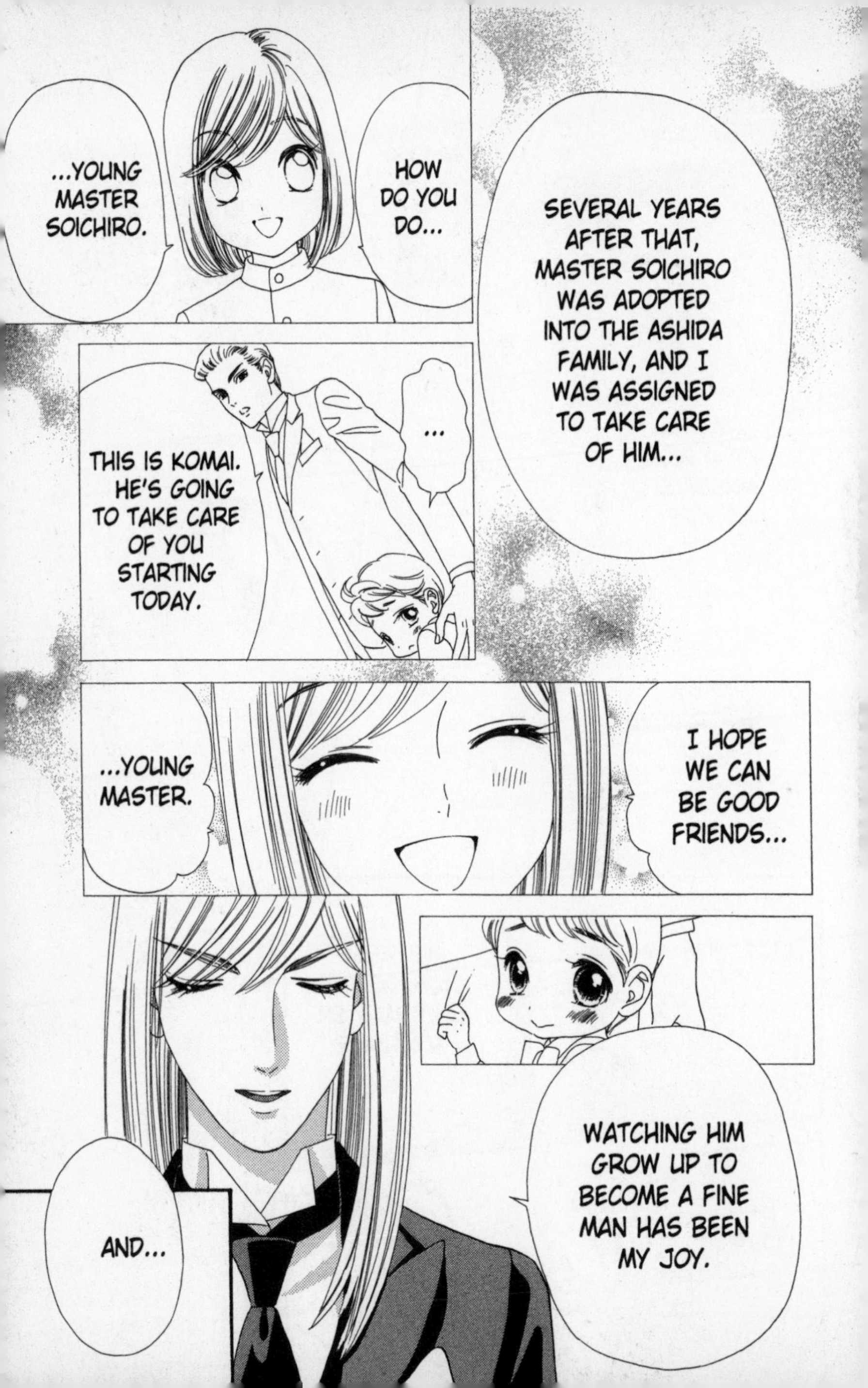
SEVERAL YEARS AFTER THAT, MASTER SOICHIRO WAS ADOPTED INTO THE ASHIDA FAMILY, AND I WAS ASSIGNED TO TAKE CARE OF HIM...
HOW DO YOU DO...
...YOUNG MASTER SOICHIRO.
...
THIS IS KOMAI. HE'S GOING TO TAKE CARE OF YOU STARTING TODAY.
I HOPE WE CAN BE GOOD FRIENDS...
...YOUNG MASTER.
WATCHING HIM GROW UP TO BECOME A FINE MAN HAS BEEN MY JOY.
AND...

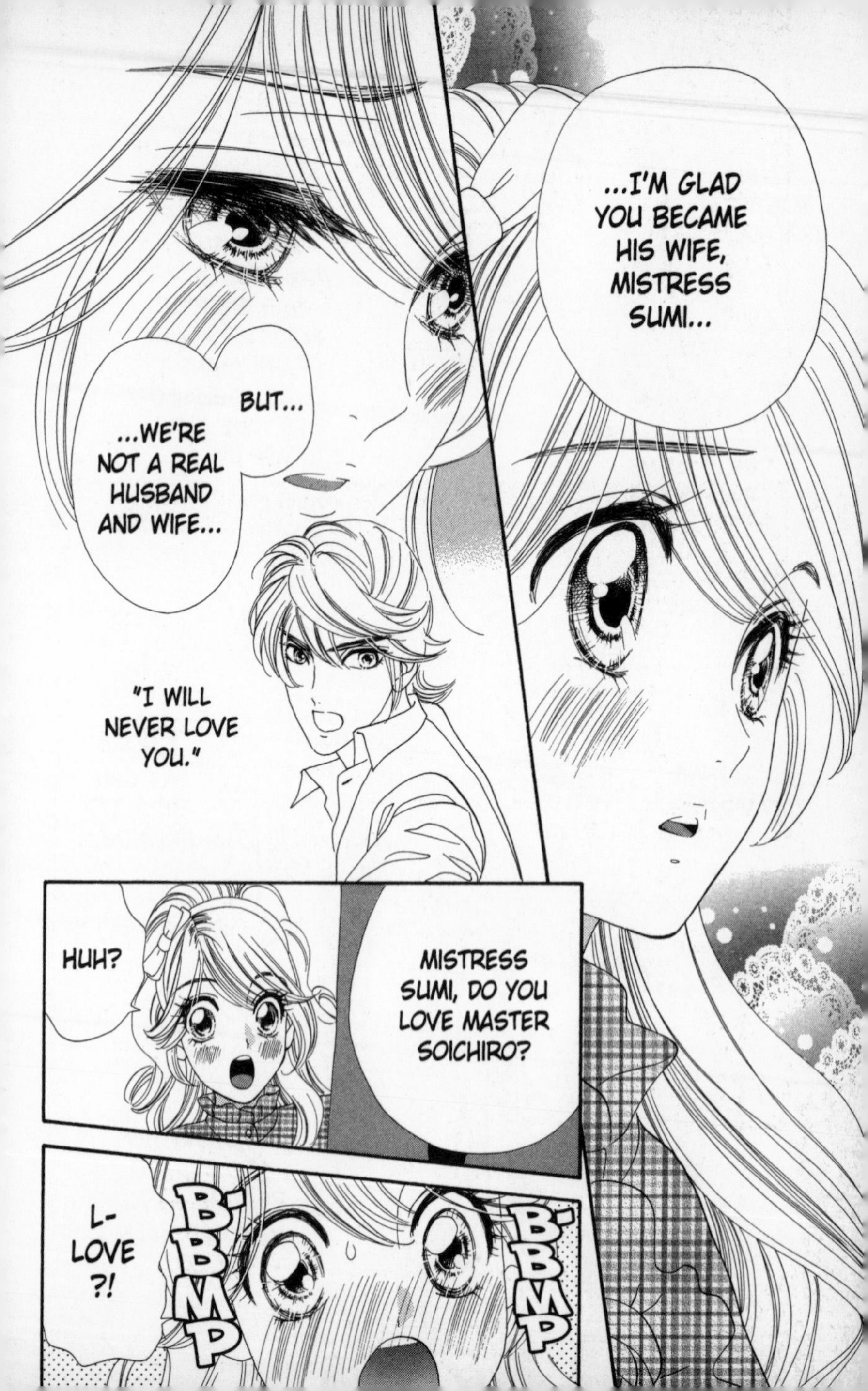
...I'M GLAD YOU BECAME HIS WIFE, MISTRESS SUMI...
BUT...
...WE'RE NOT A REAL HUSBAND AND WIFE...
"I WILL NEVER LOVE YOU."
MISTRESS SUMI, DO YOU LOVE MASTER SOICHIRO?
HUH?
B-BMP
B-BMP
L-LOVE?!

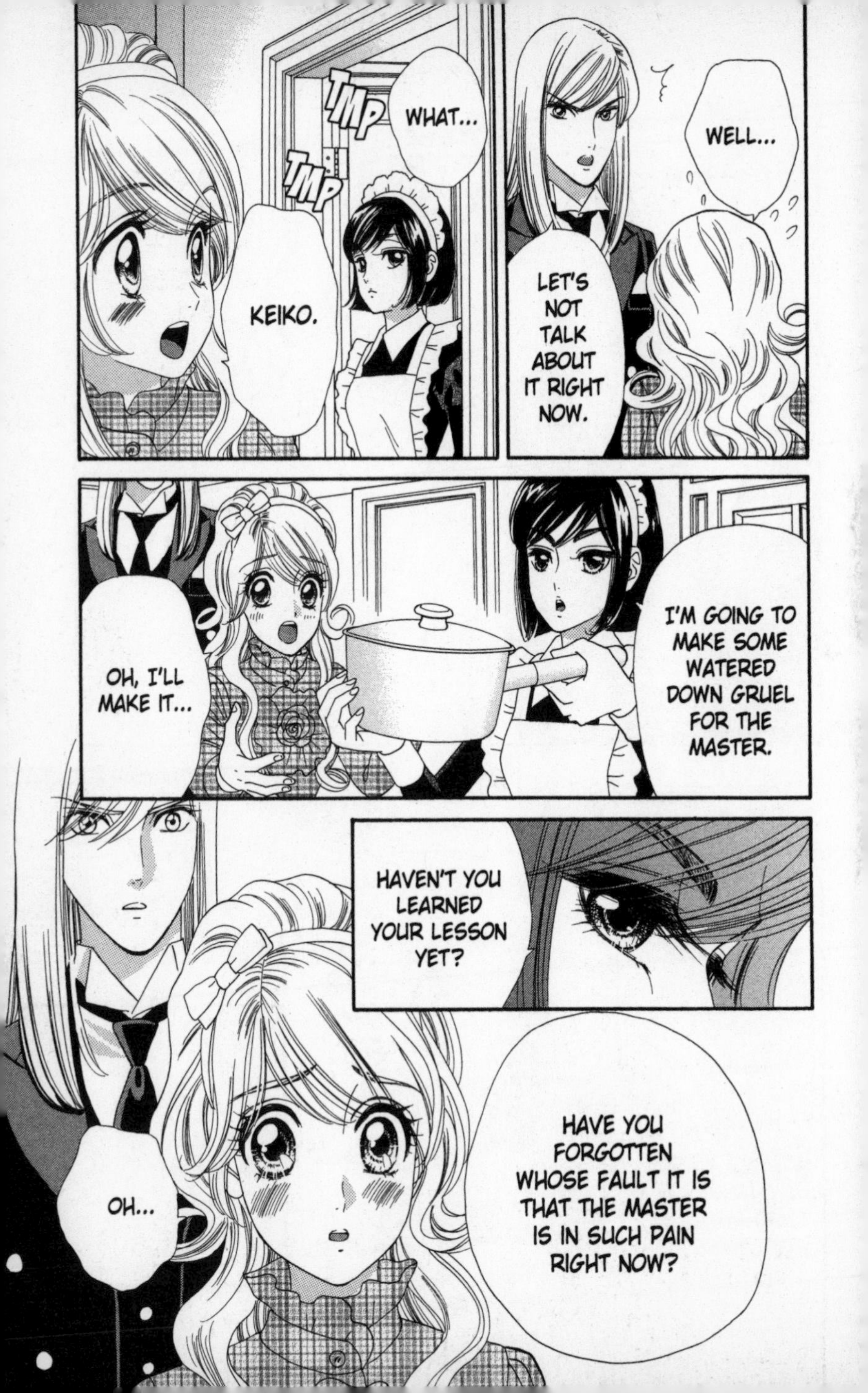
WELL...
LET'S NOT TALK ABOUT IT RIGHT NOW.
WHAT...
TMP
TMP
KEIKO.
I'M GOING TO MAKE SOME WATERED DOWN GRUEL FOR THE MASTER.
OH, I'LL MAKE IT...
HAVEN'T YOU LEARNED YOUR LESSON YET?
HAVE YOU FORGOTTEN WHOSE FAULT IT IS THAT THE MASTER IS IN SUCH PAIN RIGHT NOW?
OH...

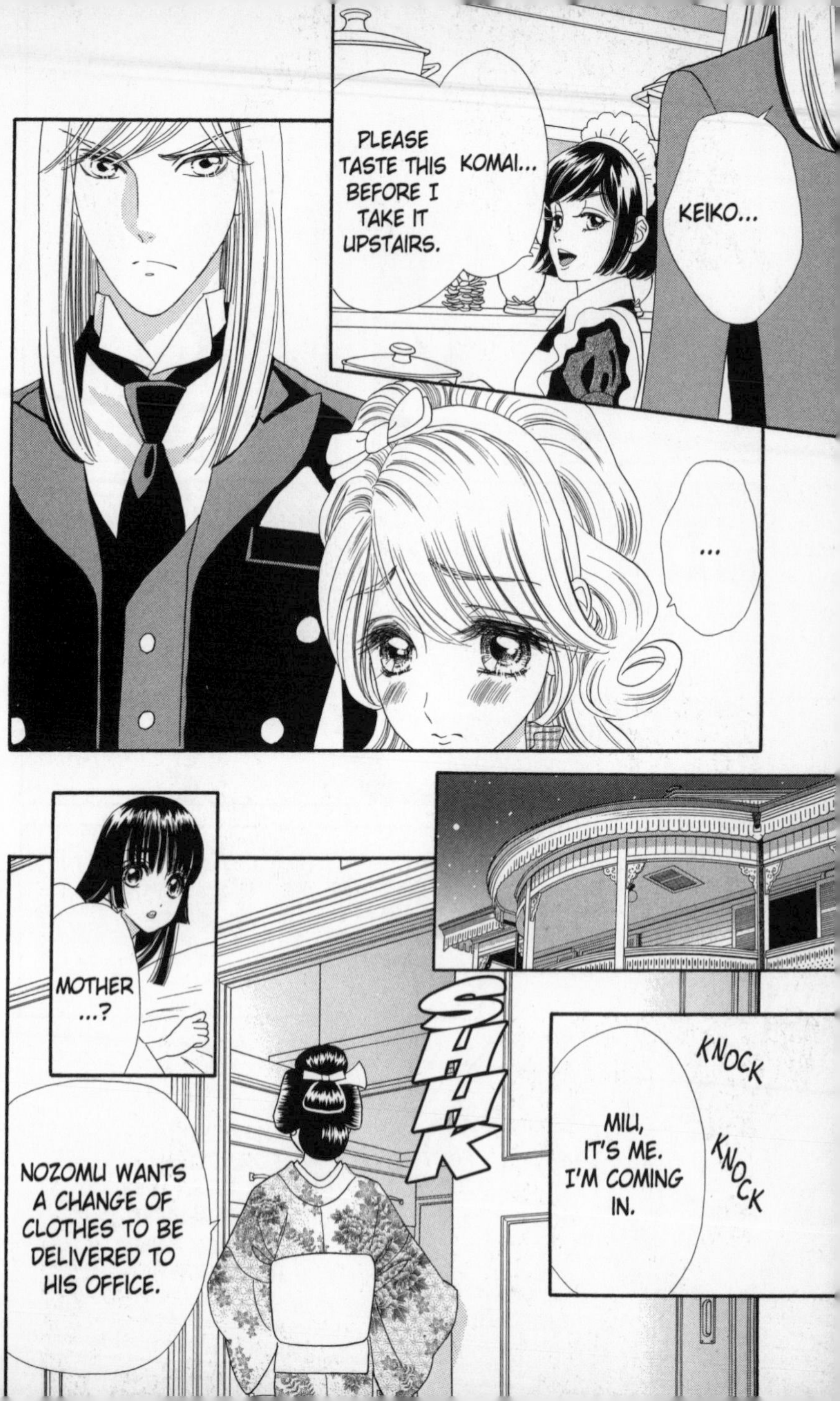
KEIKO...
KOMAI...
PLEASE TASTE THIS BEFORE I TAKE IT UPSTAIRS.
...
KNOCK KNOCK
MIU, IT'S ME. I'M COMING IN.
SHHK
MOTHER ...?
NOZOMU WANTS A CHANGE OF CLOTHES TO BE DELIVERED TO HIS OFFICE.

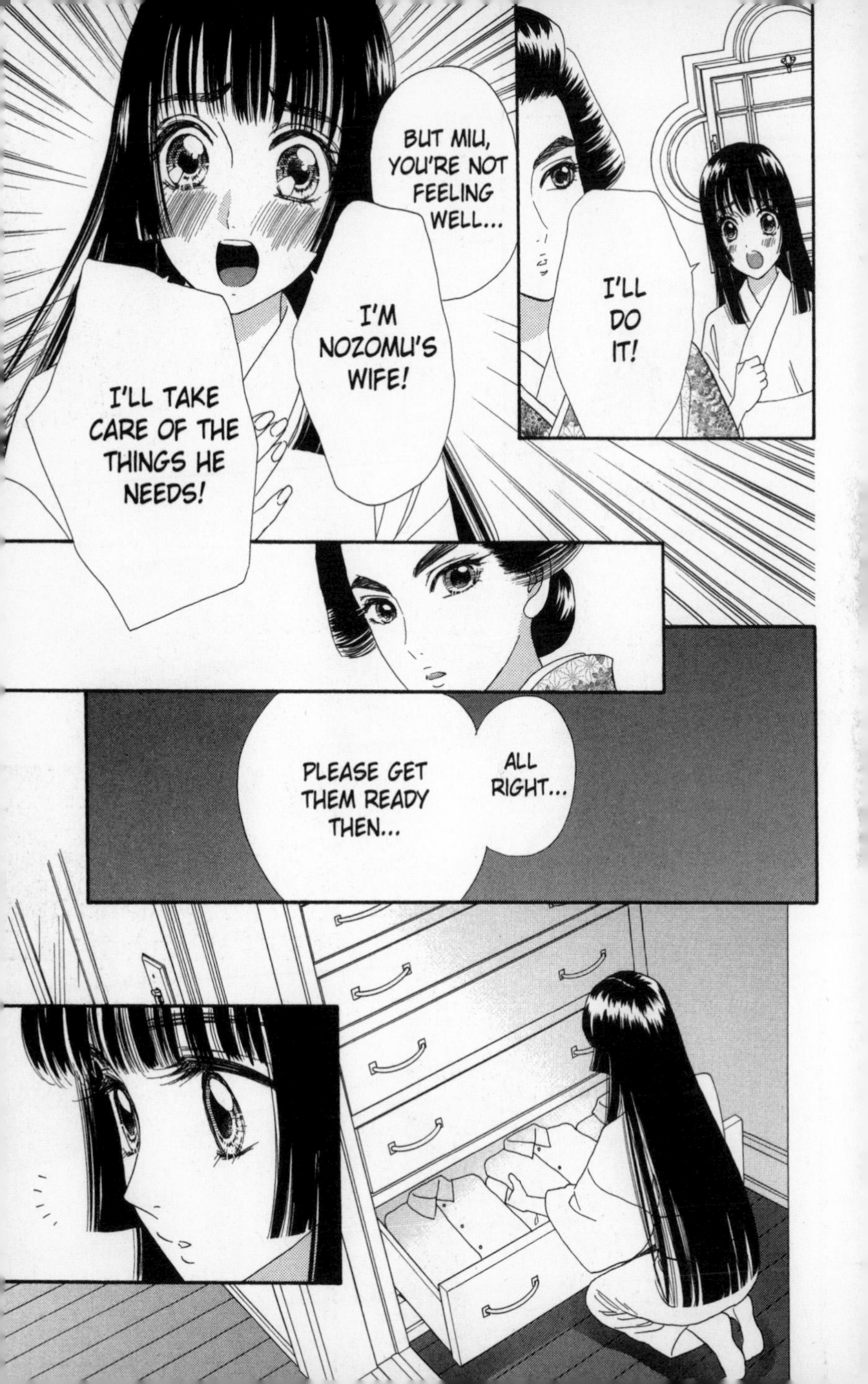
I'LL DO IT!
BUT MIU, YOU'RE NOT FEELING WELL...
I'M NOZOMU'S WIFE!
I'LL TAKE CARE OF THE THINGS HE NEEDS!
ALL RIGHT...
PLEASE GET THEM READY THEN...

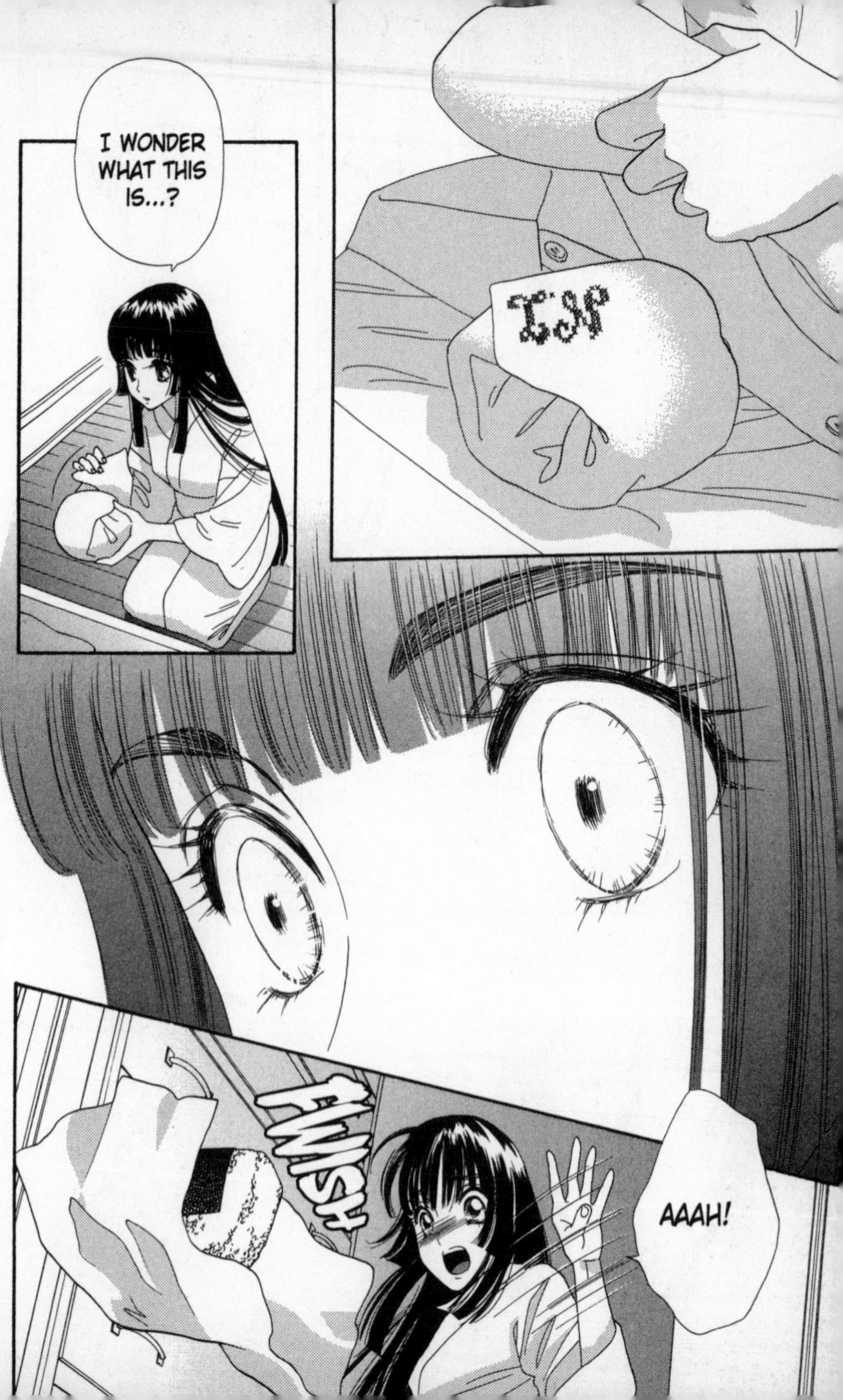
I WONDER WHAT THIS IS...?
AAAH!
FWISH

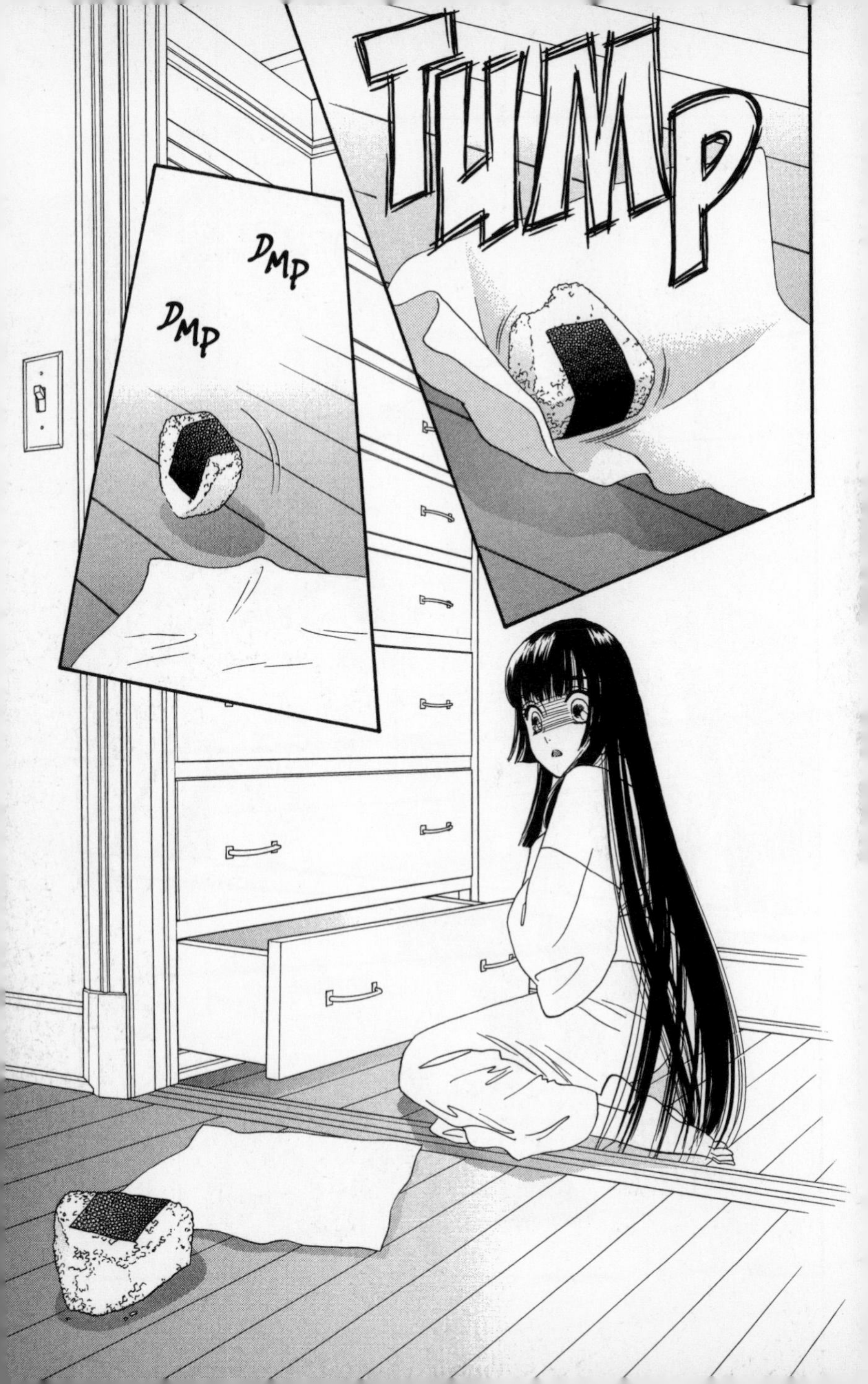
THUMP
DMP
DMP

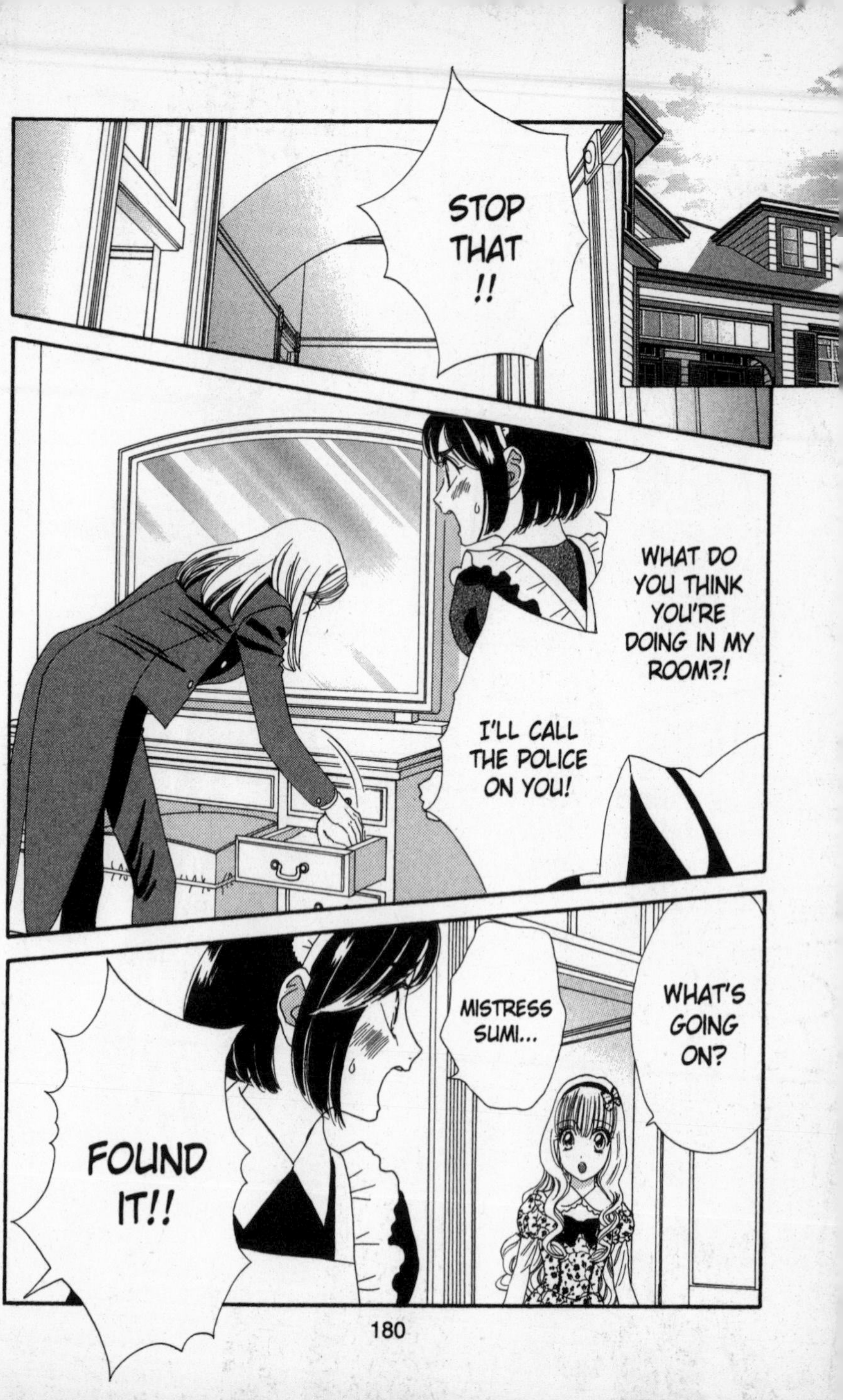
STOP THAT !!
WHAT DO YOU THINK YOU'RE DOING IN MY ROOM?!
I'LL CALL THE POLICE ON YOU!
WHAT'S GOING ON?
MISTRESS SUMI...
FOUND IT!!

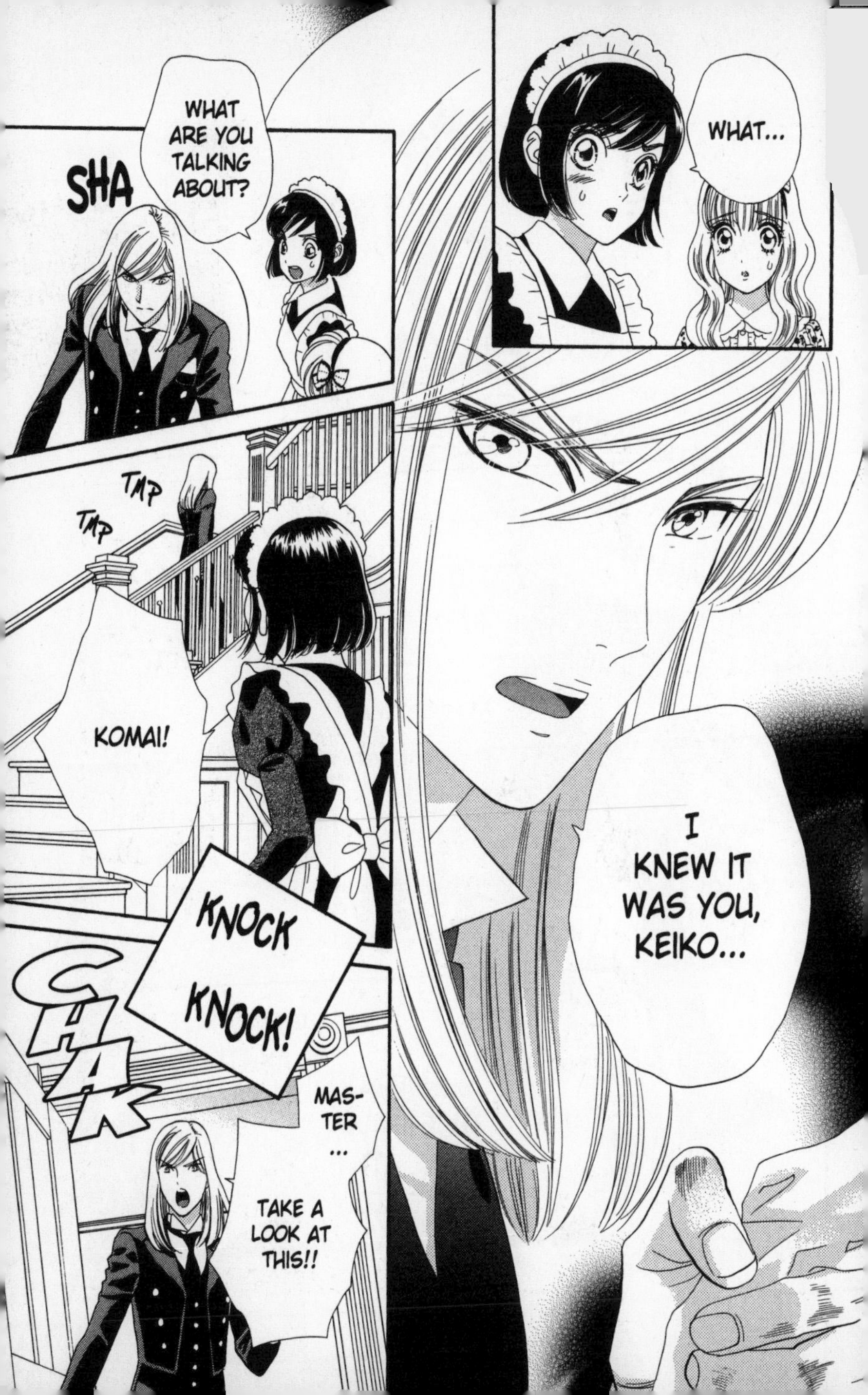
WHAT...
I KNEW IT WAS YOU, KEIKO...
WHAT ARE YOU TALKING ABOUT?
SHA
TMP
TMP
KOMAI!
KNOCK KNOCK!
CHAK
MASTER...
TAKE A LOOK AT THIS!!

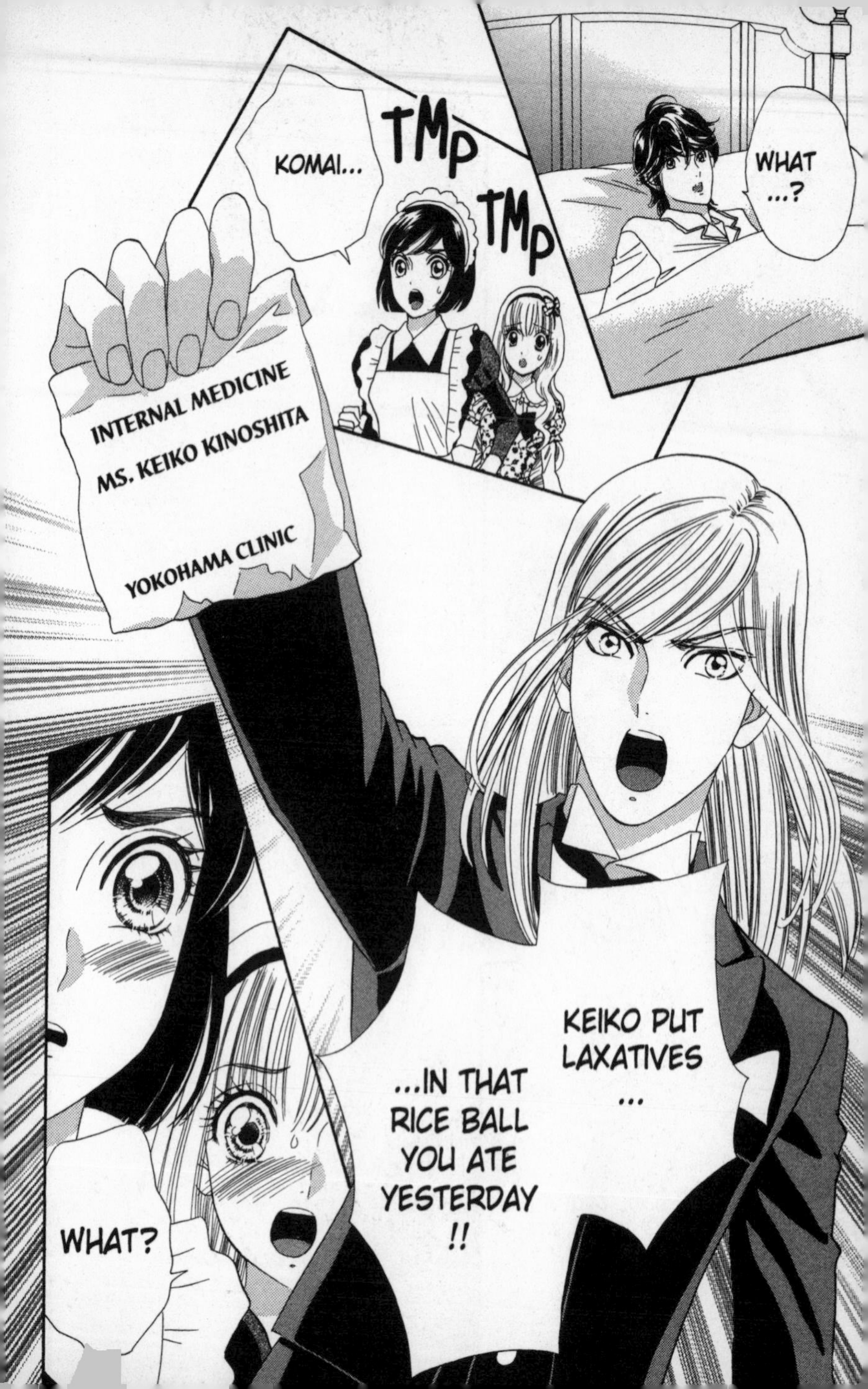

WHAT ...?
KOMAI...
TMP
TMP
INTERNAL MEDICINE
MS. KEIKO KINOSHITA
YOKOHAMA CLINIC
KEIKO PUT LAXATIVES ...
...IN THAT RICE BALL YOU ATE YESTERDAY !!
WHAT?

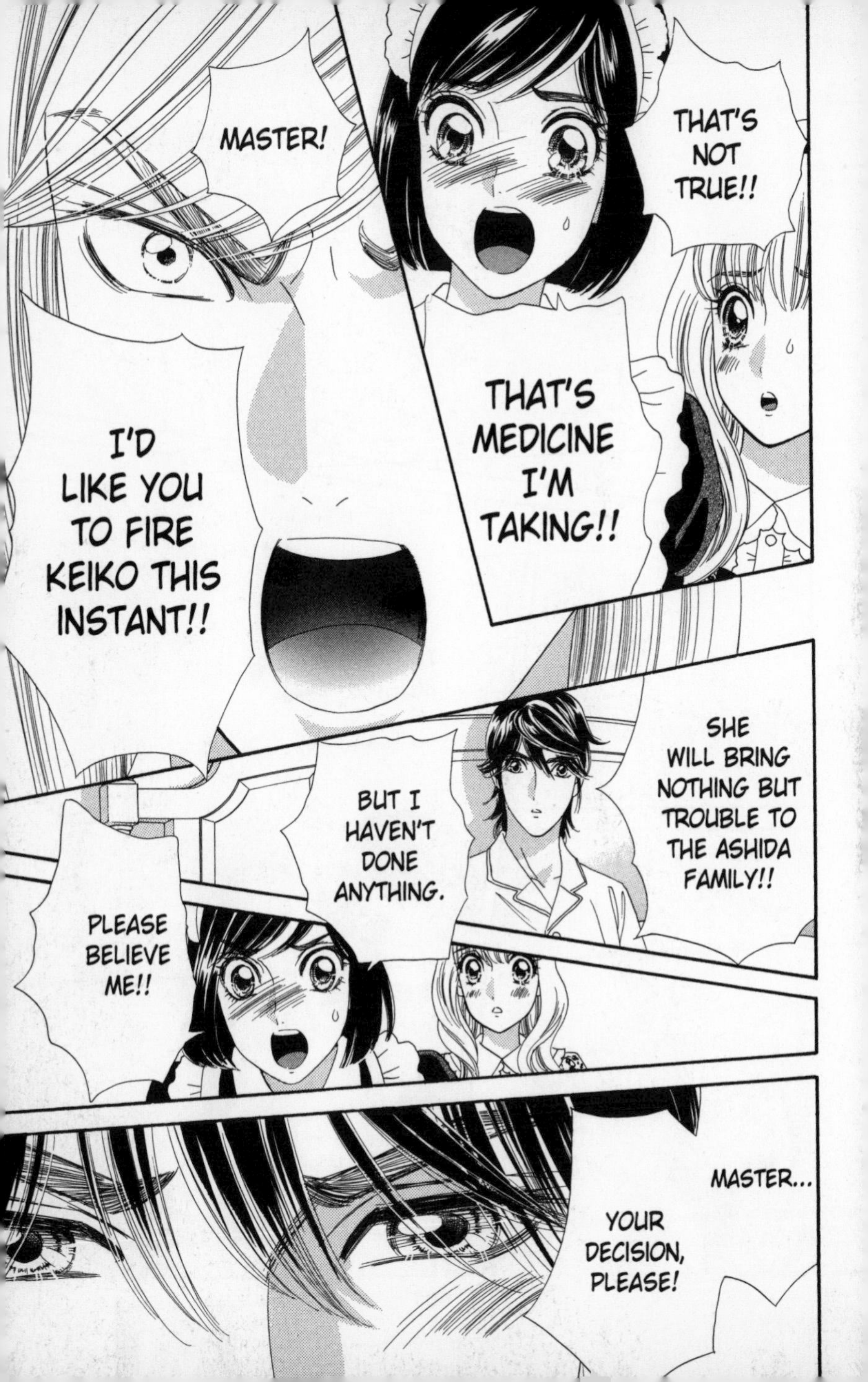
THAT'S NOT TRUE!!
THAT'S MEDICINE I'M TAKING!!
MASTER!
I'D LIKE YOU TO FIRE KEIKO THIS INSTANT!!
SHE WILL BRING NOTHING BUT TROUBLE TO THE ASHIDA FAMILY!!
BUT I HAVEN'T DONE ANYTHING.
PLEASE BELIEVE ME!!
MASTER...
YOUR DECISION, PLEASE!

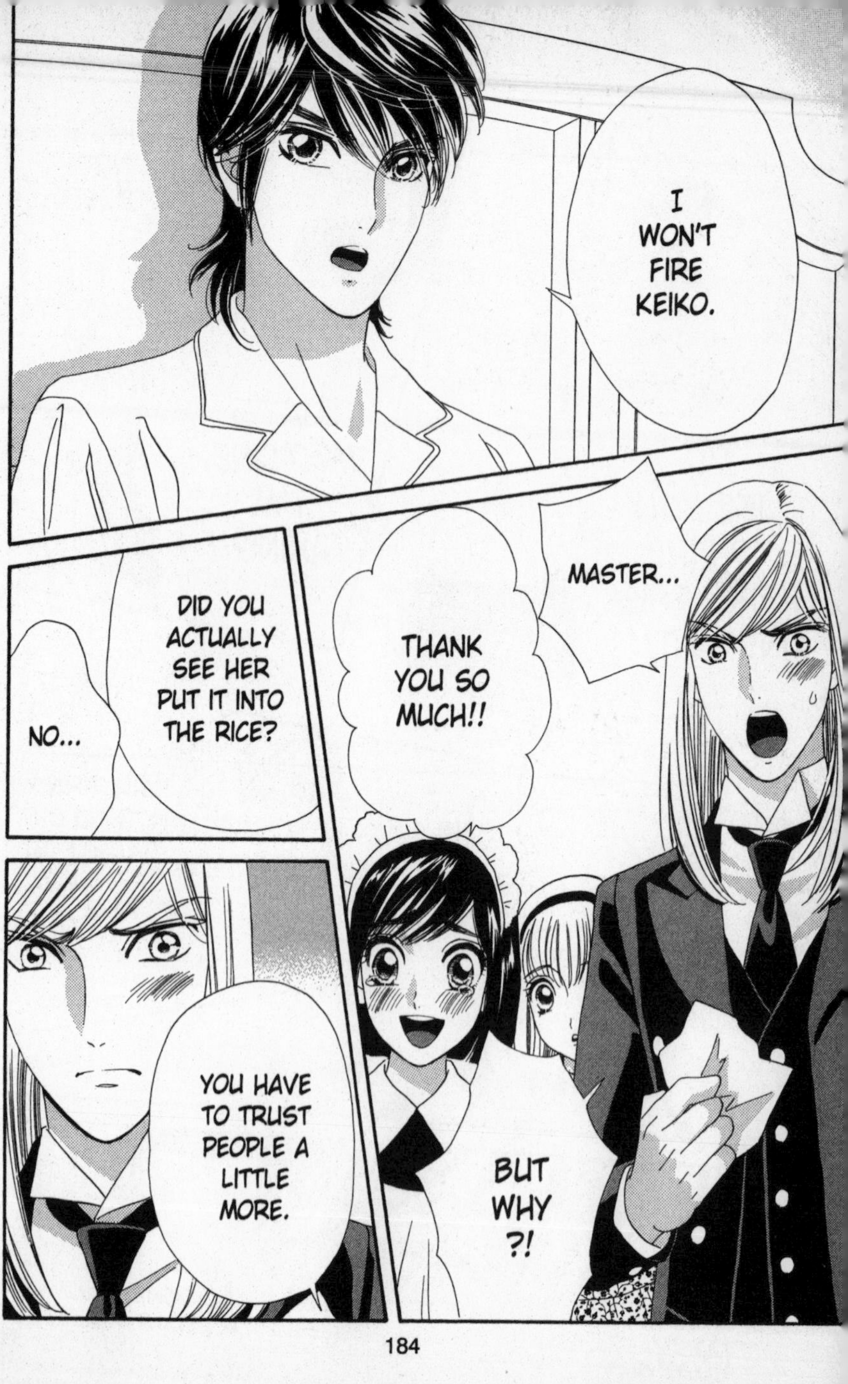
I WON'T FIRE KEIKO.
MASTER...
THANK YOU SO MUCH!!
BUT WHY ?!
DID YOU ACTUALLY SEE HER PUT IT INTO THE RICE?
NO...
YOU HAVE TO TRUST PEOPLE A LITTLE MORE.

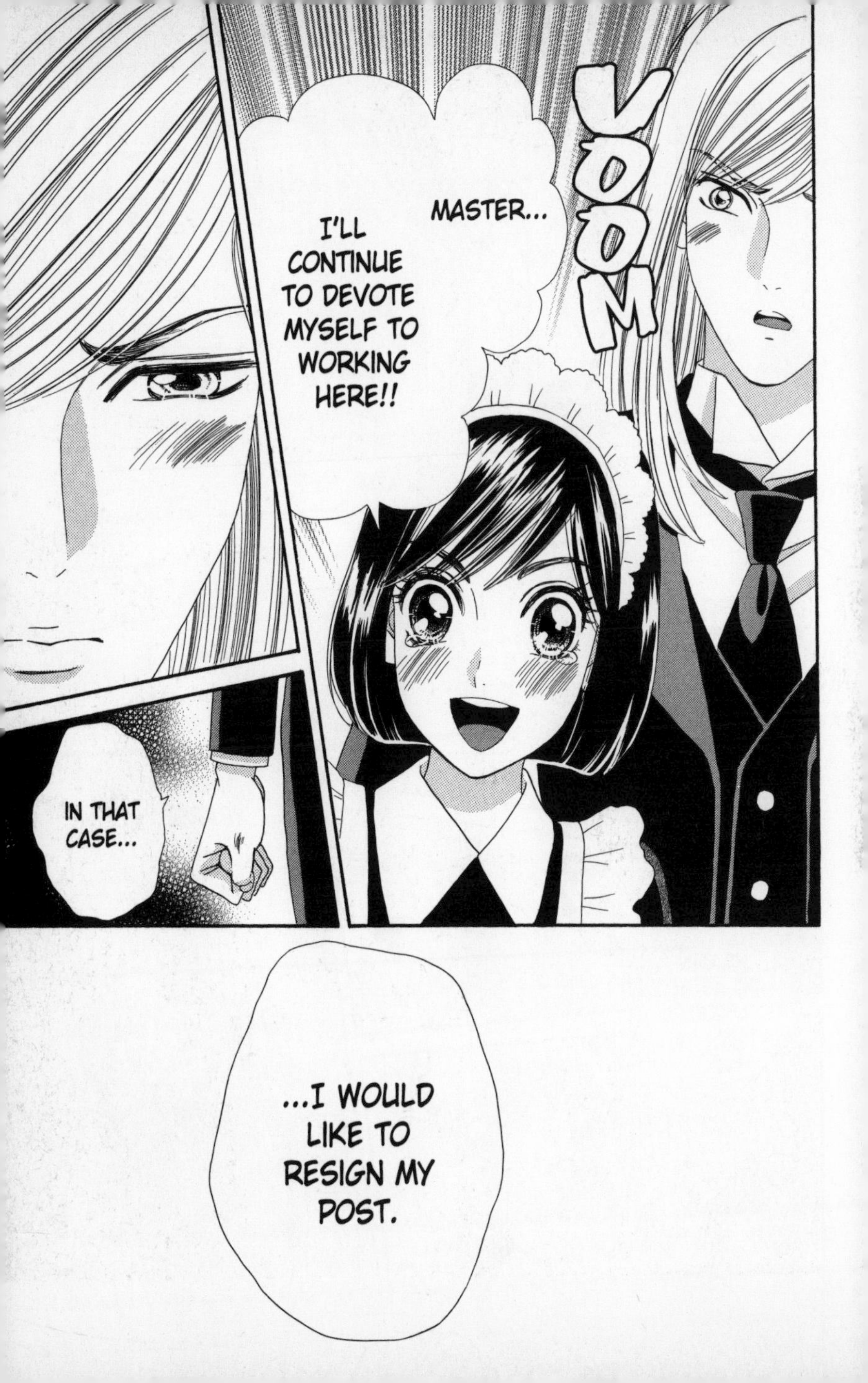
VOOM
MASTER...
I'LL CONTINUE TO DEVOTE MYSELF TO WORKING HERE!!
IN THAT CASE...
...I WOULD LIKE TO RESIGN MY POST.

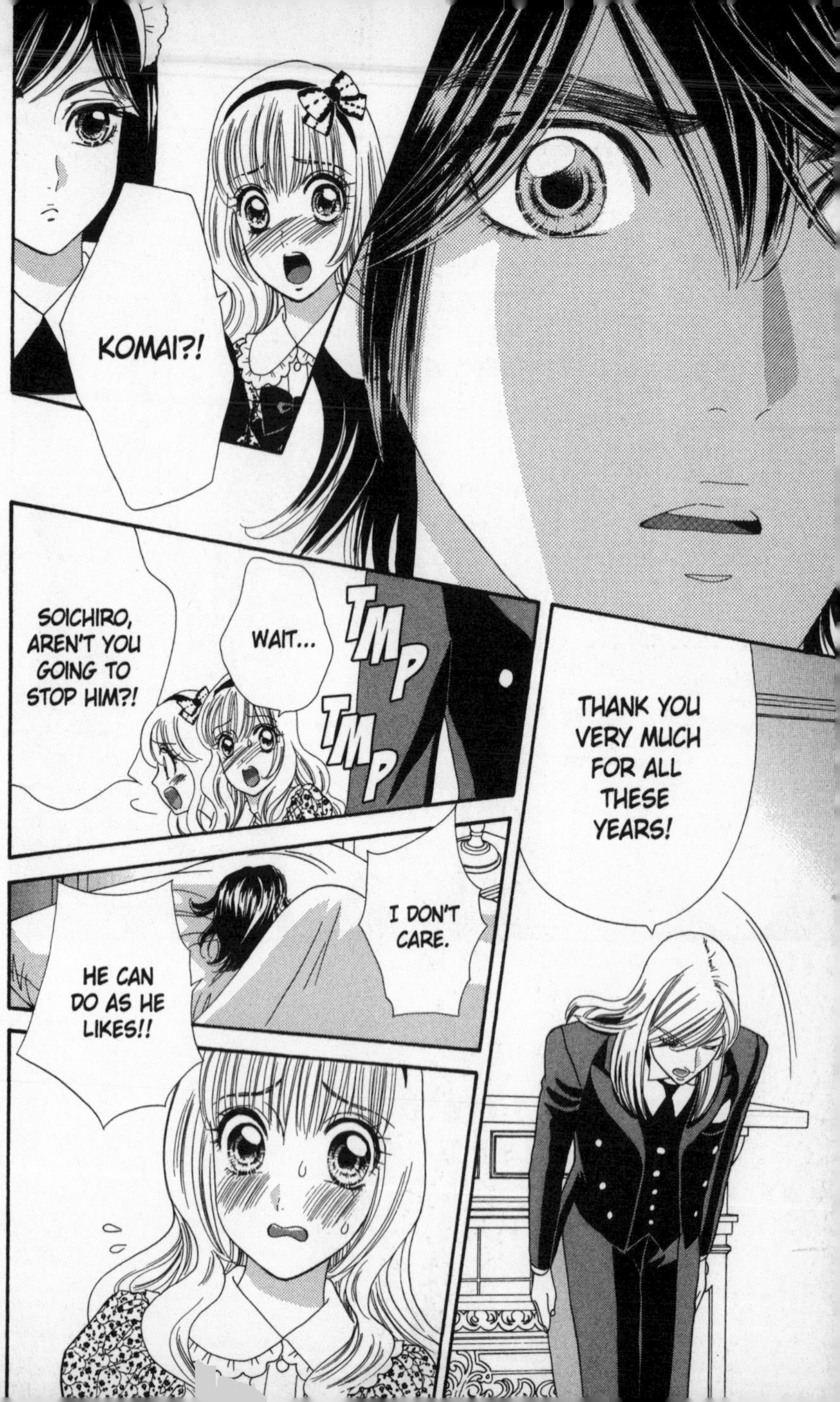
KOMAI?!
THANK YOU VERY MUCH FOR ALL THESE YEARS!
TMP TMP
WAIT...
SOICHIRO, AREN'T YOU GOING TO STOP HIM?!
I DON'T CARE.
HE CAN DO AS HE LIKES!!

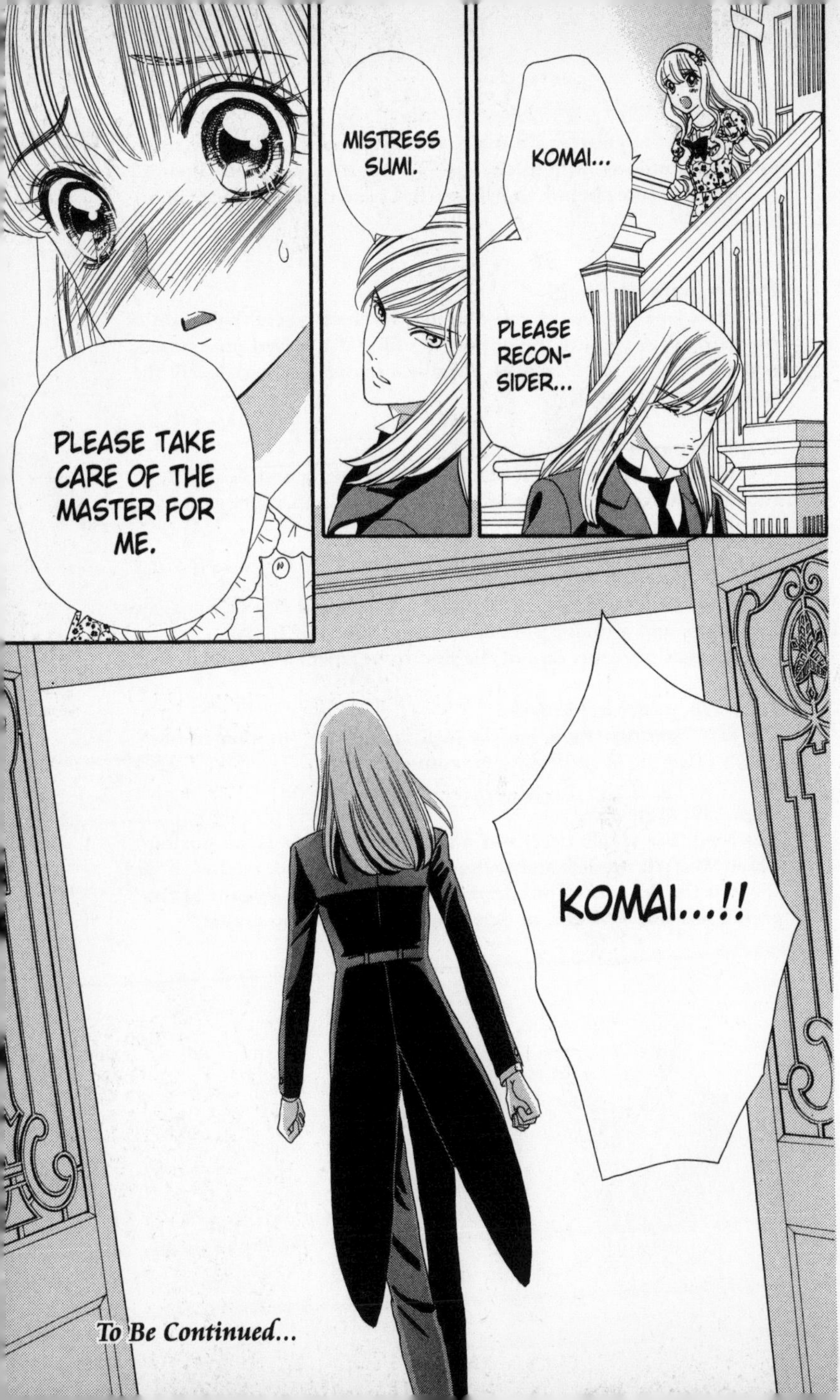
KOMAI...
PLEASE RECONSIDER...
MISTRESS SUMI.
PLEASE TAKE CARE OF THE MASTER FOR ME.
KOMAI...!!
To Be Continued...

Glossary

The setting of *Stepping on Roses* plays an important part in the story, as it showcases a unique time of change and transformation in Japan. Check out the notes below to help enrich your reading experience.

Page 6, panel 4: Shogi
Shogi is a Japanese board game similar to chess where the object of the game is to capture the opponent's king. It's played on a board, and each player has 20 pieces. Sumi is a master at shogi, a skill she revealed in volume 3.

Page 31, panel 4: Kinpira
A traditional Japanese dish that involves sautéing and simmering root vegetables such as burdock, carrots and lotus roots with a slightly sweet flavoring.

Page 41, panel 1: Yokohama
Sumi and Miu both live in Yokohama, the capital city of Kanagawa Prefecture and a major port city located south of Tokyo. Yokohama's port was one of the first to be opened to foreign trade.

Page 176, panel 6: Mother
Miu says "mother" here, but the kanji used is for "mother-in-law" (義母) since she is addressing Nozomu's mother.

Page 189: Meiji Era
The Meiji Era (1868–1912) was a time of reform in Japan during which Western models and technology were studied, borrowed and adapted for the sake of modernization. One of the slogans of this period was *bunmei kaika*, or "civilization and enlightenment."

This series is set in the Meiji Era, but since the main part of the story is filled with Western clothes and buildings, I tend to forget that it's actually a period drama. Obviously, Sumi's home isn't what you see in the present day, but I feel very happy and relaxed whenever I draw scenes near that rickety hut.

-Rinko Ueda

Rinko Ueda is from Nara Prefecture. She enjoys listening to the radio, drama CDs and Rakugo comedy performances. Her works include *Ryo*, a series based on the legend of Gojo Bridge; *Home*, a story about love crossing national boundaries; and *Tail of the Moon (Tsuki no Shippo)*, a romantic ninja comedy.

STEPPING ON ROSES
Vol. 4
Shojo Beat Edition

STORY AND ART BY
RINKO UEDA

Translation & Adaptation/Tetsuichiro Miyaki
Touch-up Art & Lettering/Mark McMurray
Design/Yukiko Whitley
Editor/Amy Yu

Printed in the U.S.A.

Published by VIZ Media, LLC
P.O. Box 77010
San Francisco, CA 94107

10 9 8 7 6 5 4 3 2 1
First printing, January 2011

www.viz.com
www.shojobeat.com

RATED T+ FOR OLDER TEEN

PARENTAL ADVISORY
STEPPING ON ROSES is rated T+ for Older Teen and is recommended for ages 16 and up. This volume contains brief nudity and sexual themes.
ratings.viz.com